# WAYWARD DAUGHTER

# WAYWARD DAUGHTER

## SARAH CHURCHILL AND HER WORLD

MIRANDA BROOKE

AMBERLEY

*To the kids who lived at Glena*

First published 2021

Amberley Publishing
The Hill, Stroud
Gloucestershire, GL5 4EP

www.amberley-books.com



British Library Cataloguing in Publication Data.
A catalogue record for this book is available from the British Library.

ISBN 978 1 3981 0740 3 (hardback)
ISBN 978 1 3981 0741 0 (ebook)

Typeset in 10pt on 12pt Sabon.
Typesetting by SJmagic DESIGN SERVICES, India.
Printed in Great Britain.

# Contents

# Illustrations

18. Vic and Sarah in *Idiot's Delight* (© Churchill Archives Centre)
19. Countess Triangi by Lisl Weil from Die Bühne 1932: No.325 p.21 and Triangi Photo Fayer from Die Bühne 1932: No.326 p.32 (ANNO/Austrian National Library)
20. Nazi propaganda: 'Churchill's noble kinsfolk' from Österreichischer Beobachter, 2 November 1939 p.11 (ANNO/Austrian National Library)
21. Churchill in 1940 (© Beeldbank WO2-NIOD)
22. Sarah, Vic and Phyllis at London Zoo 1940 (© Churchill Archives Centre)
23. Phyllis Flax née Luckett with Lady Soames 1990s (Flax Family)
24. Sarah Churchill with Wg Cdr Hodsoll (Author's Collection)
25. Concert for the Polish Relief Fund (© Churchill Archives Centre)
26. Vic and General Wade Hayes (© Churchill Archives Centre)
27. Sarah and Vic in *We Were Dancing* (© Churchill Archives Centre)
28. Sarah and Vic in *He Found a Star* (© Churchill Archives Centre)
29. Vic in *Get a Load of This* (© Collection: Paul van Yperen)
30. American Society's luncheon 1941 (Photo: © Churchill Archives Centre)
31. Churchill inspecting bomb damage (© Contributor: Fremantle/Alamy Stock Photo)
32. Winant in Co. Durham 1942 (© Telegraph Media Group Limited)
33. Maurine Mulliner (© Wisconsin Historical Society IM104662)
34. Halloween Party 1942 (© Wood Family and Medmenham Collection)
35. Sarah in B6 Section (© Medmenham Collection)
36. Bespectacled in 'battle dress' (© Medmenham Collection)
37. Family at Chequers (© Contributor: Fremantle/Alamy Stock Photo)
38. Churchill at the Teheran Conference (© Contributor/Fremantle/Alamy Stock Photo)
39. Sarah and Sir Charles Portal (© Churchill Archives Centre)
40. Anna Boettiger and Sarah at Yalta 1945 (© Mortimer Family archives)
41. Sarah, Anna Boetigger and Kathy Harriman by Robert Hopkins 1945
42. (© Mortimer Family archives)
43. Winant, Roosevelt, Stettinius and Hopkins (© Contributor/Everett Collection Inc/Alamy Stock Photo)
44. Sarah with Valerie Hayes and Peter Moore 1946 (© Churchill Archives Centre)
45. Mario Soldati and Vittorio Gassman on the set Daniele Cortis 1946.
46. (© Churchill Archives Centre)
47. Sarah as *Elena* (Author's Collection)
48. Sarah in *The Philadelphia Story* with Pat Crowley 1949 (Courtesy Pat Crowley)
49. Antony Beauchamp in uniform by Vivienne (© Orkney Library & Archive)

# 1

# Waves and Tussles

By the Pacific Ocean where gulls screamed and surf smashed she should have been left to meditate on her sea of troubles, but Sarah Churchill, known to viewers of TV's *Matinee Theater*, wasn't safe from moral guardians. Having studied for her next telecast, a long, salty outpouring to friend Howard Holtzman – a theatre lover and civil rights activist – was a way of unwinding. Their freely exchanged profanities offended the women at the manual telephone exchange and initiated an unwelcome police visit.

'What the hell do you want?' she snapped at the two sheriff's deputies who called at her beach cabin. She reluctantly agreed to their inspection of the premises. What else could she do? They would describe finding kitchen curtains torn down, lipstick smeared on the fridge and the contents of her purse scattered. Her downfall was stepping outside. According to their report she sat inside their automobile, glass of rum in hand, lecturing them about carrying guns. They couldn't move her, they said, and it's this that got her arrested. At the station the real trouble began. Three deputies and four others restrained her. Sarah said they manhandled her so she kicked and screamed and called them 'Fascists'. She was put in a straitjacket after an almighty struggle. How the press was able to take a series of lurid photographs and publish them is a mystery.

Five hours later, in the early hours of 13 January 1958, when attorney Allan Lund paid the $50 bond, Sarah left the women's section of the county jail. *The Makropoulos Incident* was due to go out live coast-to-coast next day. Sarah showed up for rehearsals at 5.30 a.m. Her star billing was omitted from the opening titles, but she gave a perfect performance nonetheless. With photographs from the police station emblazoned across the front pages of national newspapers – some accompanied by sharp words from commentators like Hedda Hopper – it was a juggernaut blow robbing Sarah of her American career overnight and making confetti of her once bankable cachet. On 19 January she appeared before Judge Woodmansee in the court at Malibu Beach charged with being 'drunk in public view'. He determined to impose 'the exact sentence on everyone, nothing more nothing less'. Everyone was equal in the eyes of the law, even the daughter of the world's greatest living statesman. As elegant and imposing as her five foot five inches would allow, she stood before the court, gloved hand rigid and freckled face impassive. The flashbulbs brought back memories of two decades before, from a time she had been a runaway.

Cutting the cord had been a mistake. Atoning for it, she had since presented an ideal face to the world. Now, what ought to have been nobody's business was forced into the open. Just like before, brother Randolph rushed to her side and her mother felt it like a knife wound. Convinced she had been provoked, Sir Winston Churchill followed the case back home, debating strategies with Diana, his eldest girl, as they spread the American cuttings over the floor. Sarah pleaded guilty. Her statement contained these lines:

> I was more ill than drunk. I was alone learning lines for television. I have been under some strain. I realise anyone might have misunderstood my actions. I regret any inconvenience to the public and those I love.

Her bravery affected people. Letters arrived, some hoaxes, but one seems genuine – from a fellow sufferer who says that she too had a Pa she envied and that she had hurt people. She knew what going to the bottom was like: 'There must be some very great confusion or sadness in your life. But believe me, drink will only make it worse.' Then, of Billy Graham, she said:

> I've heard it said 'there are things in his past he doesn't want to talk about.' Maybe only he and Jesus know what he was saved from. He barely escaped some very terrible temptation once.

Sarah wasn't free of demons and shrinking like *Alice in Wonderland*, her introvert nature returned. Friends Marlene Dietrich and Anna Boettiger sent supportive messages and Niki Dantine came to her aid:

> We were here during the Malibu episode and tried to help her as best we could. Sarah was tortured by it, which makes me sad. We talked like girlfriends, discussed our vulnerabilities, tried to solve the problems of the world – you know, 'girl talk'. I was lucky to have had her in my life!

After one further *Matinee* Sarah disappeared to the South of France with the help of friends. On 6 March Randolph appeared on *Night Beat*, ready to fire off his political commentary before American TV viewers. Asked if he thought the press had been fair to his sister, he angrily told John Wingate that this was off limits. He felt a trick had been played on him and said he felt trapped by dirty people selling soap to people who don't want it.

How could the career Sarah had built up so carefully over the last nine years get trashed in the space of a night? It had been a marvellous journey since she appeared with Fred Astaire in a huge MGM Technicolor picture. Arriving in the US just when television was coming into its own, offers of work had flooded in. *The Daily Graphic* on 24 October 1950 lists Sarah as one of the actors bringing distinction to TV and refers to the 52-mile range of the Empire State's TV mast, giving one in ten Americans the clearest reception. She appeared in *Mill on the Floss*, *Romeo and Juliet* and *Witness for the Prosecution* that November, and was a guest on *What's My Line* during its first year. When *Hallmark Playhouse* was still on the radio, hosted by James Hilton, Sarah's vowels and lilting delivery gave dramas like *A Breath of Air*, a fifties take on *The Tempest*, their distinctive feel. As Bernard Hermann's soothing music conjured up an island idyll, her precise enunciation began: 'When I think of Terraqueous I remember my father and me in the garden with the voices of the native and the sea and the wind blending like a symphony.' Threading through each scene were applause, advertising and even staged conversation between Hilton and Sarah; he mentioning Churchill's paintings on Hallmark cards and she saying how delightful they were.

This programme moved to TV as *Hallmark Hall of Fame* and became the longest-running primetime series in TV history, continuing to this day. Sarah got on board in January 1952. Moments of scientific, literary and musical breakthroughs were depicted, as well as events of political and religious significance. Much was period drama, but a Czech girl's choice of freedom in the US over staying behind the 'Iron Curtain' was one modern storyline. Each season had around 40 episodes. Typically, Sarah contributed to 15 per season, occasionally just as host, sometimes narrating but most frequently acting *and* narrating. William Corrigan directed nine episodes, each of which paid Sarah $750. With agent Charles Wick working for her, she earned at least $2,000. Menotti's made-for-TV opera *Amahl and the Night Visitors* broke new ground and saw a second Easter telecast; Sarah's flawless introduction sounding strangely familiar: 'Seldom in the history of music has any composer reached so swiftly and so surely the *Hall of Fame*.'

On 22 June 1952 a modestly gowned Miss Churchill was seen in lavish surroundings in a typical opening. Taking her book to her satin divan, she condescends to watch television, looking at the autocue, not the camera, except for two humorous flashes. Her voice fades as *Forgotten Children*, a story about nineteenth-century educator Martha Berry featuring actor James Dean, begins. A year before getting on the *Hall of Fame* payroll he was a car-park attendant in Santa Monica. Rodgers Brackett, a Hallmark accountant, offered to help his career, soon enabling him to study at the Actors Studio. Dean accepted presents from Brackett, living with him in New York while having a girlfriend hidden away. A close friend of Sarah's, Brackett took Dean to her parties and witnessed her funny imitations of her father. With Sarah's help, Brackett got Dean on board as a stagehand before he graduated to dramatic parts. Sarah began Hallmark's season two as Joan of Arc with director Albert McCleery using the 'Cameo Technique' to convey in close-ups what was going on in the character's heart.

In October 1953 Sarah kicked off Hallmark's season three as Catherine Parr in *A Queen's Way*. The stage directions required little Elizabeth to clutch her protective but reserved stepmother's waist, sobbing affectingly. The child actress playing Elizabeth was Susan Seaforth Hayes – a Lifetime Achievement winner at the Emmys in 2018. Thinking back to that day at Burbank, Susan believes everyone in the cast was English apart from herself and the guy playing Henry VIII, who 'contributed nothing but his girth and couldn't manage the lines, let alone the accent'. Everyone was in awe of the star, as actress Susan Seaforth Hayes recalled:

> *Hallmark Hall of Fame* was a distinguished show and Miss Churchill supplied any class that was missing from the sets and rented costumes. After dress rehearsal and minutes before going live, Albert ruled Sarah's Tudor bonnet wasn't flattering enough. I remember her in front of the camera putting on cap after cap while he made his judgments over a loudspeaker from the control booth. 'Too square, too small, too red, too – just don't like it!' He never asked Sarah's opinion and she endured all of this with a small smile. I vividly recall one scene with Sarah looking through one of those arches at Anne Askew the heretic – somewhere in those black drapes she was supposedly being burned at the stake on Henry's orders. My line: 'To be burned! Oh Kate!' It was all live, live, live.

The camera moved to a close-up of Queen Catherine's face – so close the bonnet hardly showed after all that fuss. Susan admits that the 'Cameo Technique' kept costs down at Burbank Studios.

Sarah's background trebled her mystique, but Susan thought her a fine actress, very approachable, serious about her work and lovely to look at.

She treasures the photo Miss Churchill autographed and remembers the party held in her honour with McCleery springing up to give a toast:

> Which birthday it was for the beautiful red head nobody dared to ask, but there were several questions about her father and Roosevelt. Later that same night, Sarah continued to celebrate in a Hollywood bar and the news made the morning papers. Yes, even in the courteous fifties someone as famous and blameless as she was fodder for the excitable press. Drunk? I doubt it. Delightfully tipsy more like.

With Britain's current Queen seen on newsreels leaving for her Commonwealth Tour on 23 November, the States had their own queen of television: one with American ancestry. They never saw the person beneath the façade. Newspapers corroborate Susan's memory of Sarah making headlines. By 2 a.m. she was having a beer and hamburger in a Hollywood restaurant and the waiter told her that under California law she had to give up her beer. The verbal bust-up resulted in embarrassing news stories. The McCormick papers (often unfriendly to the British) attacked her, while New York's *Daily Mirror* went with: 'Atta girl Sarah.' Mrs L. W. Caufmann of Harbourcreek, PA wasn't impressed: 'I am a high school teacher, fully aware of the effect this type of publicity has on our young people – the reference to your alleged remarks against our fine country will no doubt hurt.'

In the response Sarah prepared she argues that 'she did not break, insult or criticise the law' but objected to the manner in which it was enforced. When J. C. Hall, creator of the Hallmark card brand and the show's sponsor, sent yuletide greetings to Winston, he said it was a ploy for publicity on the restaurant owner's part. Supportive as ever, Hall said that little damage to Sarah's career would come of it. None had been a better ambassador, in his view. By then she had appeared on the stage in a number of touring productions and had recently MC'd at an event celebrating the 50th anniversary of powered flight.

Back in 1949, when her husband Tony also started work in the States, he enjoyed equal success but he tired of America, returning to Britain to make his mark in TV production. They spent far too much time apart. *Hallmark*'s fourth season began in July 1954 after a seven-month gap. Her husband was present for part of her vacation, staying with Hall, but had left by the time she went out on a sailing boat on Grand Lake Colorado. She almost lost her life when it overturned. She and four others were rescued.

Her independent transatlantic lifestyle was not an escape. The constant letters exchanged between Sarah and her mother Clementine were a solid reminder of home. She defined her purpose through the prism of her parents' example. It was a peculiar and obsessive habit. Even her husband, who held Churchill in similar reverence, knew Sarah had to refocus. He could see the anxiety underlying it. Tony had emotional problems of his own but was Sarah's supporter. He wasn't without blame when it came to their marriage breakdown but was trying to save it at the time of the Colorado trip. Direct as ever, he confronted her parents about their attitude. It was going too far for Sarah and she broke off, preferring the oblivion of Manhattan cocktails to a rival master. She found patient supporters in Brackett and his friend Alec Wilder. The latter was a composer and free spirit who scorned Broadway, even if his work featured in shows like 1950's *Peter Pan* (choreographed by Wendy Toye). He lived at the Algonquin Hotel where he hosted Sunday recitals in its third-floor Stratford Suite.

A West Coast friend Sarah got talking to over Scotch-on-the-rocks at Mike Lyman's Bar was writer Charles Hamblett, then sojourning under California's 'reckoning sun'. In London he had been part of the Fitzroy Tavern set but one day said 'I'm leaving' and next minute was hanging out with the Beats on Santa Monica Beach. Charles was blotting paper to everything 'happening' that was new, writing on mass appeal subjects like Brando and Elvis. He knew luminaries John Huston, Gregory Peck, Ernest Hemingway and John Steinbeck. With Americana so in vogue, Fleet Street was desperate for Hamblett's insightful articles.

Friends meant everything to Sarah; her marital responsibilities now apparently relinquished. She styled a Bohemian attitude to life but this was just a Churchill groupie's alter ego. Few saw through the assumed mantle to glimpse the truth.

Her Hallmark output was reduced to three telecasts in early 1955, but radio kept her busy. Her home was the Knickerbocker Hotel. Estranged from Tony and far from her family, this free-living child-woman was unsettled. Beverly Hills support networks were on hand including Rupert Allen (the ex-US naval intelligence officer who became press agent for Monroe, Davis and Dietrich) and his next-door neighbour at Sea Bright Place, Frank McCarthy (former aide to General George Marshall and later a producer at Fox Studios). Only close friends knew that Rupert and Frank were long-term partners. Between May and September Sarah toured New England, Pennsylvania and Illinois, performing at nine theatres. In *No Time For Comedy*, hit comedy writer Gaylord Esterbrook nurses the vain ambition to write a tragedy and only a seductive muse can unleash his brilliance, not his wife, Linda (Sarah). Brackett's cast included Butterfly McQueen (Prissy in *Gone with the Wind*). Still playing maids, she was at least getting the best reviews for the laughs she injected.

At the rustic-looking Matunuck Theatre on Rhode Island Sarah made a lifelong friend in musically gifted Lorraine Merritt – part of the production team. When playing Lafayetteville Playhouse in Syracuse that July, Sarah visited Pompey where her grandmother's father was born and bred. She met relations William Travers and Ella Jerome Huffman (a cousin by adoption). She obsessed over every part of their house, drawing water from the family's old hand pump. A luncheon was held at The Corinthian Club and Sarah talked about the cast's hobby – flying kites – then answered questions about the royal family. She spoke about the warmth of Britain's young Queen and Princess Margaret's personality. Breezes left behind by Hurricane Connie gave momentum to Sarah's kite, swaying and bending and illuminating the sky; a metaphor in her poem *For R.B.*, in which she refers to her mistaken attempt at happiness with Tony. She argues enigmatically that the Eros of classical legend was preferable to a castle in the air. She was the kite: thoughtless, strong and free. (Though kites are tethered.) Ralph Blum, a 22-year-old anthropology student, was her lover. He spoke about the Oracle at Delphi while a 'mist of undefined unspoken things' wooed and dazzled her. Constantly in her company at this time, he would remain a close friend.

She worked Monday to Saturday (with two matinees a week) and went through hell and high water to reach towns on the circuit. At the Poet's Theatre she thrived among mavens Ed Thommen and Molly Howe, joined Constance Bennett on radio's *Town Talks* and didn't give the time of day to critics slating her acting. With Ralph's help she found out about medical developments beneficial to her ailing mother. Whilst at Marblehead's Summer Theatre, Boston, a reporter learnt about the first time she thrust herself upon America – as the unlikeliest chorus girl ever. Now she had a new pastime: painting. But unlike her Pa, she was a neophyte, seven pictures her entire oeuvre.

It seems hard to believe that below the surface of this active life in picturesque surroundings were uppers, downers, introspection, counselling and attempts to stay dry with intermittent relapse. Revealed in a notebook with little red stars on its cloth cover, this chronicle of actress and road shrink – young Ralph or 'R' in the latter capacity – is written during the final part of Sarah's theatrical tour. It begins on 17 September 1955 as she and Ralph pass over the Pulaski Skyway. Taking a look at herself in the aftermath of her life with Tony is a ragged knot to untangle. Armed with a notebook of his own, Ralph makes Sarah comply with this therapy and whether it's Transference or Totemism, he's often 'pushing too hard'. She does her bit, tolerating this 'questing young man' out of kindness and writing down her thoughts about the empty space in her. Interestingly, she questions the motivations of parents. Can they honestly say, she asks, 'I did you in the belief of you'? Or admit that a child isn't begotten for gain?

She writes about wanting one for herself. Ralph seems to be selling the idea as a solution to the void. Sarah knows Ralph is immature, barely having left home: 'What can he know about family life?' She talks introspectively about the relationship between extroversion and success, expressing herself in brilliant language. She feels negative about the restraint in her character and her tendency to hide things. She's had a lifetime of that. She believes the world is suspicious of her 'type', whereas extroverts like Marilyn Monroe are more commercially successful and attractive. And yet, having nothing to say is a good thing as far as she's concerned. Ralph, son of a Jewish attorney and silent film star Carmel Myers, is constantly on at her to evaluate one central relationship: 'In need of reassurance I create my source of inspiration after the initial one of my father. I must learn to be my own root.'

While she infuriates 'R' and is called 'a monumental bore' by him, she concedes he's drawing something out of her. She feels she's been 'shielded from evil' despite growing up through wars, upheavals, upsets and personal loss. Racking her brains and thinking back to the atmosphere at home in the early days, she asks if it's possible to be 'imprisoned' by goodness. 'Nobody ever raised a hand in our house,' she says, clarifying that if mistakes were made, there was only a belief that one could *right* wrongs. 'Reserve is the great law for women,' her teachers used to say and she went along with that until Vic (the first husband) came along. He had told her to leave all this, to go into the unknown. But she rid herself of him. Was this why so much had gone wrong?

Throughout this introspective journey she desperately wants to cry, but this comes at a cost for an actress carrying a show and she can't risk it. The notebook continues as a stream of consciousness as she talks about jugglers, conjurers and being under the influence of something – feeling elated nonetheless. She mentions a panic attack when she runs out of pills. Amphetamines hadn't yet gained their bad reputation and were used by students and beatniks as pep pills. Delysid was another available drug. At the time hallucinogens had a place in therapeutic sessions and Cary Grant and Jack Nicholson were two prepared to use them. Given that Ralph was interested in their psychological role, working with Timothy Leary on the Psilocybin Project at Harvard a few years later, Sarah might have trustingly taken a form of LSD. On reaching Boston her notebook indicates a disturbing episode when the pair occupy a house together. Something evil manifested itself in her room. Ralph seizes on it and asks: 'Was He there?' and harries her to acknowledge if 'He' is still present. Ralph is certain they have isolated the thing she fears. Alarmingly, he asks her if 'He' could be Satan, warning he may destroy her. He adds dramatically that on the demon's next visit she must summon up resistance. 'Pray – do anything' rather than let it happen, he tells her. Was this a bad trip? Was old man alcohol the devil? Coming close to the thing Tony wanted her to face, Sarah doesn't deal with this block to happiness. She's merely obsessive about someone corroborating the spectre's existence. Wilder and Brackett come to the house a little while after, only to tell her there are no ghosts. The notebook continues to early October when *No Time For Comedy* closes. She's still with Ralph at this time, going to wild parties but vulnerable, haunted by the night in Boston when *something* was in the room.

No longer with Hallmark, Sarah joined the roster of actors and directors on *Matinee Theater.* Lamont Johnson, later known for *The Twilight Zone*, directed at least five of her thirteen dramas and acted with her. With top-notch production the show set new standards. The idea was expressly to 'sell' colour television and encourage viewers to buy sets. Housewives whose husbands could afford them watched the show as it went out at noon, believing *Matinee Theater* treated women intelligently. Little did they know the efforts made by Lamont and others to get Sarah through each performance. The stages were gigantic, even though there was no real scenery. *The Book of Ruth* placed her on a ramp for some shots, infinity background to her rear, with a cyclorama for colour washing. *The Others*, on 17 February 1957, received excellent reviews.

She jumped at the chance to do a TV play in Britain. Lorraine came with her and they took a little flat in Bradbrooke House in an enclave off bustling Knightsbridge. Sarah spoke to Tony on the phone about starting divorce proceedings. The next morning at 7 a.m. the chilling news came that he was dead, having taken his own life. Guilt rose up like breakers pounding the shore; a second wave because she had been through this before. Overwhelmed, she didn't want to see anyone except her older sister (at whose Chester Row home she hid). En route to Denver and with a face taut with tears, Sarah was papped at Idlewild Airport.

In her cottage on stilts at 20132 Pacific Coast Highway, Malibu, she gazed at her last photo of Tony, who had reached his journey's end. (Her *Matinee* concerned a woman artist getting a commission from a lady to paint her lover in *The Tone of Time.*) She thought back to that 'nebulous illusive spirit who greatly changed my life'. He was worth it up to a point, but she hadn't stuck it out. She hadn't needed to.

Five more dramas saw her through the year and she started cooking for herself – an extraordinary achievement that prompted Mama to declare, 'You must make me a salad one day.' Sarah survived Tony's death. She wasn't called 'the Mule' for nothing. Friends were at hand, but she liked to sit alone at daybreak, watching pelicans streaming by like bombers.

When those sheriff's deputies arrived, the strait-laced attitudes of the day came at her like earthmovers. The timing of her magnificent, fiery, spirit-fuelled invective was misjudged. She later claimed to have been a victim of wire-tapping, saying the telephone complaint was deliberately set up. A friend to the homosexual elite and to writers and activists, she may have been a target. A frame-up can't be ruled out, even if the era of McCarthyism had waned. Her run-ins with authority had put her under surveillance and as sister-in-law to Britain's Defence Minister it made sense on the political stage that she be put in her place. But 'he that filches from me my good name robs me of that which not enriches him', she told herself. Faced with enemies, the British bulldog stands firm. If she had to, she would fight alone.

2

# Why Am I Alone?

In an interview Sarah Churchill spoke of her inability to be passive. 'Emotions,' she began, subtly alluding to a recent reported indiscretion, 'are not socially convenient things.' She moved on to standing up for what you believe in and risking unpopularity. Somehow the manhandling and assassination of Congolese independence hero Patrice Lumumba on 17 January 1961 illustrated her point. She mused upon her fast-paced life. Where she was running from and where to, she couldn't say. All she was certain of was that she was a passionate person. Admitting she inherited her optimism from her parents, she refused to answer an irritating question about living with the Churchill name during that interview but provided the answer to another newspaper:

> They say children are born happy and free and all my childhood was free, uninhibited and glorious. The only difficulty I've had is that the world continually tries to impress on me that for some reason I'm captive and that things are weighted in my favour.

Never in a million years would she admit that anything in her childhood affected her negatively. To the question: 'Was it tough being a great man's child?' she would give a gnomic reply such as: 'Hercules travelled far when he performed his labours but never did he find an inhibited Churchill.' Yet, her father's work had taken priority when she (and her sister before her) came into the world, his love of the sea and warcraft then uppermost. His firstborn was named after HMS *Diana* (the Eclipse-class protected battle cruiser) whilst HMS *Hermione* (an Astraea-class cruiser launched in 1893) provided one of Sarah's middle names. Father had been reorganising the Navy into four fleets, powering it with oil and modernising naval science.

He and Mama were often absent: he dispatching things to servicemen and she with good causes.

Asked about those early days, Sarah would say that mealtimes weren't formal but they were told not to bring up their own interests unless asked. Her parents might enter the nursery – 'What have you been doing today?' – but this was rare. Their absence was keenly felt and no amount of nannies made up for it. Communication was via letter to Mama and little slips passed under Papa's door. He was unbelievably busy, but Sarah denied that he neglected them. On the contrary, he factored in time for them. These were sacred occasions. In 1969 in a bar in South Africa she got chatting to Iain Kerr and Roy Cowen, then touring in *Gilbert and Sullivan Go Kosher*. Iain played the piano and his musical memory put her in mind of her Pa who drew upon things learned long ago. Iain never forgot what she told him about 'that man':

> If he were busy at such a time, he would insist they sit down until he had finished so he could focus his full attention on what they wanted to tell him. 'I wont be long,' he would say, 'please don't forget as I want to hear *all* the details.' He would show a genuine interest in their news and visibly blub if circumstances warranted. He didn't cuddle them for that was not his style, but his attention to them was genuine.

Churchill cherished those moments spent with Lord Randolph and could see things from a child's perspective. Yet this was an inconsistent relationship and in Sarah's case, time went by before she had his interest. Long ago she had been a tiny, neglected presence gazing up at frozen soldiers on silent battlefields and higher still, cranes and bridges. Her Meccano-mad cousins Johnny and Peregrine (Pebin) had been at work and adults ducked to avoid the horizontal jib of their latest monster. Her cousins and brother and sister told her how a psychotic nurse had hated any child transgressing the law of her domain. For tipping Sarah out of her cot, Randolph had mustard forcibly administered and the heavy-handed way in which Nurse rattled the metal spoon in his mouth took out several of his teeth. Sarah was proud when they told her that she had outwitted the despot. With chocolate creams the prized target in the larder, she was the one whose cunning paid off. Following the theft and a 'terrible hullabaloo' Nurse laid a trap; cruel mustard her vilest weapon. She scooped out the chocolate, applying yellow stuff into the biscuit. Sarah gave herself away, 'howling her head off', but she didn't truly know what fear was. An unpleasant sound (the air raid siren) was a signal for their parents to lead them to Cromwell Road's lowest depths where fruit shelves were transformed into bunks lined with red plush and gold bullion. The adults spoke quietly. Sarah, Pebin and Johnny acted asleep convincingly. Diana and Randolph gave the game away by fighting in their bunks.

In summer they lived in a 'barn' with diamond windows. The adults, who occupied the main part of the manor near East Grinstead, more or less forgot about them. Sarah and Diana kept rabbits in a large hutch whilst Johnny and Randolph trained dogs. A gift from Lord Riddell was a buggy for Sarah and Pebin, who survived after Sarah's brother let it free-fall from a steep hillock. Isabelle, a nice Scottish nanny who later died of the Spanish flu, bent over the bathtub one day preparing their bath and Randolph gave her bottom a shove, causing her to tumble in. Her only revenge was allowing the children to run wild where they could get burnt by stinging nettles, drink from ponds and take milk from cows. Sarah looked to Pebin for protection and they gathered under the cow's flank with their bucket. She got very ill soon after, her glands invaded by tuberculosis. A surgeon came and the bathroom became an operating theatre. She fought like a savage but strong arms pinned her down whilst a thick rubber anaesthetic mask descended over her face.

As children, they knew about fighting in foreign lands: the semi-retired War Department horse that took them to school once bolted with shellshock, Mama gripping the reins for dear life. Peace came and so did a baby born on 15 November 1918 that Papa wished to call Mercy (before they settled on Marigold Frances). The new Secretary of State for War left for Versailles, where he befriended T. E. Lawrence.

One day Randolph asked Papa about a cartoon showing him on the stage of a music hall with Tory chorus girls singing 'You made me love you; I didn't want to do it.' That, he explained, was a joke on him. He'd been decidedly tight about money before he was First Lord but with the new ships and sailors' pay he surpassed the spending levels of his predecessors (his colleagues reluctantly agreeing to this).

Papa had been terribly lonely in the war. At the Admiralty he habitually opened a Bible at random, finding comfort in what he read. Sarah remembered nothing about that building but heard that her frequently unsupervised brother and sister had many goes rolling down the shallow Admiralty steps, making their fluffy white rabbit-skin coats grubby. 'We always do that when nanny is not there,' was Randolph's explanation. They claimed their behaviour was tiptop at Sarah's christening in December 1914 in the crypt chapel of the Commons, when Grannie Jennie (Lady Randolph Churchill) and Grannie Blanche (Lady Hozier) towered like Titans. Sarah heard about a curtain rod that came down on her nose causing an unsightly bump that was to plague her. It held up velvet curtains framing a view onto Horse Guards.

Mr Churchill was dignified even as others besmirched his reputation. Many of his past actions such as fraternising with Kaiser Bill and taking an interest in social security were controversial. His ideas about women's suffrage, tax and diminishing the power of the Lords were all criticised. 'Backward Tories' like Diana Mitford's parents called him an adventurer and a Bolshevik. He was most content re-creating conflict with toy soldiers at 41 Cromwell Road, explaining strategies and sending secretary Eddie Marsh to buy more Meccano for brother Jack's boys. Sarah listened to Johnny's tales of Hoe Farm, the summer escape where Winston absconded and painted Jack's wife Goonie (his first ever portrait). A London friend was Ottoline Morrell, with whom they stayed at Bedford Square during bombings, venturing to the Eiffel Tower restaurant. This was patronised by Diana Manners and artist neighbours like John and Hazel Lavery, who loaded up their Rolls with paints and drove to Hoe Farm where Sarah's Papa and Mama sat for them.

Mr C then put down his easel and volunteered for trench warfare. He and Archie Sinclair ran a unit at Ploegsteert Wood, part of the Ypres salient. Desmond Morton was there before he became Haig's aide-de-camp and led the Industrial Intelligence Centre. Winston was popular with his Ayrshire-born troops. He held Burns recitals with a wee dram as a courtesy, promising his wife not to feign a Scots accent.

Lloyd George formed a Coalition and Mama helped find Papa a new job. In autumn 1917 while war raged at Passchendaele, he ran operations from the Department of Munitions. A colleague was Bernie Baruch, on the US War Industries board. Papa was back in favour.

He and his friend F. E. Smith (Lord Birkenhead) followed scientific developments encouraged by Professor Lindemann (known as 'Prof'). As Lord Chancellor, F. E. defended Ethel le Neve, prosecuted Roger Casement and drafted the Anglo-Irish Treaty. He knew Churchill as a fellow officer, colleague and 'Other Club' fellow. Newspaper barons Lord Camrose and Canadian Lord Beaverbrook were friends, though he periodically fell out with the latter. With so many formidable visitors, just being near Papa felt an honour. Sarah's vivid red hair glowed in the sunshine as she unpacked sandwiches and handed him his Gentlemen's Relish. Good at games, Lloyd George was the earliest friend the kids had outside immediate family.

Her parents moved to Tyburnia, taking 2 Sussex Square, a bobby-dazzler of a house with stables and mews to the rear. Grannie Jennie furnished it and Diana, or 'the Gold Cream Kitten' as she was known, wrote to her in June 1920 (from the Roehampton home of her cousins, the Guests), admiring her work and mentioning Trooping the Colour and Sarah's recovery from tuberculosis. The sisters, aged twelve and five, started at Notting Hill School in September 1920: Diana at the main school and Sarah at the juniors in a villa at 54 Holland Park. 'One didn't ask what went on' in the basement where meals were served. They sometimes boarded at 3 Lansdowne Road (for months if Mama was travelling). When Randolph was home he met Diana for roller-skating or horseriding in Rotten Row, his sister on Snowball, her father's polo pony.

Being a third child, Sarah got left out. Dwarfed by giant adults on the lawn, she had the 'Hatter's Shakes'. A flustered maid emerged with the first of many lunch trays. *Alice's Adventures in Wonderland* made them alert to noise from kitchens. Why didn't the Duchess stop the cook throwing things and overdoing the pepper? Aloof like the Cheshire Cat, Papa said that grinning throughout displays of violence wasn't a bad tactic. The Duchess was indifferent to the Cat, singing about beatings with a chorus: 'Wow! Wow! Wow!' When the adults began swinging croquet mallets the children giggled. Winston forbade whistling but liked animal noises. Some years later someone said it was imitating the bugle sound of the black swans that caused the common Churchill 'Wow' salutation, but it's difficult to replicate a bugle. The mad Duchess of *Alice* might hold the key to it. Papa was the grandson of a Duchess and cousin of Sunny, 9th Duke of Marlborough. The Duke's sons Bert and Ivor (by his first wife Consuelo) were in their twenties, 12 years separating them from Randolph and Diana. To Sarah's brother the most incredible thing about Blenheim Palace was the stuffed lion that let out a roar if a string was pulled. They went with Nana Bessie to Broadstairs in August 1921. Marigold hadn't been well. Leaving her with Nurse Rose, the three older children went to Scotland. Their lonely little sister died of septicaemia. 'Displays' were *not* how one coped and no one could speak of Marigold afterwards.

Churchill was under pressure owing to his actions in Ireland. Allied to John Redmond and the moderate Irish nationalists it was hoped that Ireland might stay in the Empire, but when the Liberals reneged on Home Rule there was a backlash. He then changed tack, sending a brutal lot over to repress rebellion and stating he wanted Republican leader Michael Collins dead or alive. (Churchill as Secretary of State for War had sent the infamous Black and Tans into Ireland on 25 March 1920.) It was extreme for him and even Mrs C criticised his heavy-handedness: 'If you were ever leader you would not be cowed by severity & certainly not by reprisals which fall like the rain from Heaven upon the Just & Unjust.' London played host to Collins and in November 1921 he came to Sussex Square. Randolph and Co perched at the top of the stairs longing to know what it was about but were thrown by the accents. 'You put a £5,000 bounty on my head,' Collins blasted. Winston showed him an image of his Boer War fugitive self, whose bounty was £25. 'At least I put a good amount on your head!' he growled. For better or worse Collins signed the treaty, rejecting de Valera's ideas, so Ireland stayed a Dominion.

Not sensing the tough political battle lying ahead for Papa, Diana and Randolph were full of beans in Dundee, the constituency their father had held since 1908. It was great to lose Nana for a while and appear alongside their parents. Even better was their 1922 summer holiday at Frinton-on-Sea, Essex. Give her a racket and Mrs Churchill acted like a star of the tennis firmament. Now with child, she had to content herself with watching her progeny. Next to the daughters of Mrs Dudley Ward – Penelope (Pempie) and Angie – Diana and Randolph were duffers but Mama always had a kind word. She was Scottish, valued fair play and good manners.

Sarah discovered that even Frinton's Press thought her family newsworthy. Mr Churchill was reported hurrying along the sands clasping a bottle of milk prior to making a spectacle of himself in the waves. The canary yellow jumper Lord Birkenhead was sporting got a mention, as did the screams of Mrs C's sister's little boys, Giles and Esmond. The best bit was Randolph and Sarah's debate on sand architecture: the former's comment 'Thank you, Mr Dog, I'm much obliged!' – addressed to a canine wrecker of grand designs – was made much of. At home Charles Sims did a portrait of Sarah and Diana. The contrast of strawberry-blonde hair, dance dresses and yellow sashes against a hyper-real landscape is typical Sims, whose mental illness was expressly affecting his work. Sarah's high colour from scarlet fever and measles were hard to detect in the painting. (Suffering from paranoia and hallucinations, war artist Charles Sims would commit suicide in 1928.)

The eight year-old scored a whopping 46 out of 50 in an arithmetic exam and no girl could be more modest. When Mummy suggested telling Cousin Sylvia, Sarah remarked: 'Oh no, we must keep these little things to ourselves.' Clementine felt reproved. Sarah was sensitive to Diana's potential hurt, whose grade had been seven out of a hundred. Clementine consoled her eldest girl and told Winston: 'She is a goose but a very good goose.' Perhaps exam papers kindled the fire at Sussex Square that September, when 'spirit came into contact with a flame', devastating part of the third floor. Their father had just secured Chartwell, a 'promised land' for the newborn – 'the Benjamin' – and the rest of the tribe. Suddenly stricken with appendicitis, Winston was forced to convalesce at home with Sarah. Energetically, Mrs C campaigned alone in Dundee. Fishwives spat at her and like Marie Antoinette before the mob, she begged interrupters: 'Do be kind and let me get on.' Sadly, the seat went to the red candidate. Randolph and Diana were truculent and there was nothing for Churchill to do without a seat, party and appendix but rent Villa Rêve d'Or, its terrace commanding a view of Cannes. Sarah guarded Mary's crib whilst her mother, Victor Cazalet and others played tennis. She spoke every day to Papa and he told her that when the Kaiser's armies invaded Antwerp she was his reward for trying to relieve the city, even if his success was slight. 'Set store by resilience,' he said. She prayed that she might be called to duty like Joan of Arc, the woman Father most admired.

Peace was disturbed when more cousins, in fact the entire Mitford clan, were upon them. Lord Redesdale was Sarah's mother's cousin. The Churchill children were guests at Asthall Manor in August 1923 where Sarah went riding with Unity and Pam Mitford before everyone bathed in the river. The shouts and screams were deafening across the quiet water and many young eyes flashed like blue sapphires.

A year later when the Mitfords came to Hosey Rigge, Sarah decided she didn't like invasions. Not only was the noise dreadful, there was a constant pressure to compete – something she hated. She preferred to slip away and read *Peter and Wendy* (J. M. Barrie's 1911 novel). Mama told her that when she was young she had attended a dress rehearsal staged at the Duke of York's and remembered the small light glowing when Tinkerbell entered. She told Sarah about the Mermaids and how Mr Barrie was there to make sure the flying machine was working. Randolph was like Captain Hook, forcing the younger ones into his 'army' and barking orders. For years Sarah put up with punishments. She felt relieved when it was Mary's turn to be 'the whipping boy'. Everywhere in the family were loud and assertive voices. From the terrace she scanned the horizon: looking for a caravan or a knight on horseback.

If a day seemed dull, Papa made it lively. Announcing he was building a tree house, he endorsed her love of make-believe. Dear as his parents had been, they had never sharpened their boys' imaginations. He was righting a wrong, but at the same time he poured cold water on the endeavour: 'Facts are better than dreams. Facts are more powerful and make one live on fully,' he said, adding that tangible results impressed him most. It made Sarah glum.

After her school day in Limpsfield she and Mary acted out a narrative of hunts and balls. Seeing the blinds drawn, Randolph burst in on them, but they were best indoors with Chartwell a building site. A fourth level lake had emerged by the time his schoolfriend James Lees-Milne came and saw Winston 'standing up to his chest in mud and shouting directions like Napoleon before Austerlitz'.

Churchill stood for Westminster Abbey, setting up committee rooms in Drury Lane in March 1924. Intuition made him request Sarah's company. Looking much the impresario in his Astrakhan-trimmed overcoat, he told her that buildings like Drury Lane were made for the spoken word. Bonar Law, who ran the Conservatives, would have kept him out of office had ill health not struck the Canuck down. An election in October 1924 saw Winston win Epping. Stanley Baldwin became Prime Minister and made the author of *The*

*World Crisis* Chancellor of the Exchequer. Britain then owed £900 million and exports were at half their pre-war levels. On 28 April 1925 the new incumbent put Britain on the Gold Standard. Talk of forecasts and shortfalls baffled Sarah, but she got her first pay cheque (£50) that November for handing in a lost necklace. Her luck didn't last and she was operated on when tuberculosis reappeared.

Her prefect sister was embarrassed when Clementine turned up late for a prize-giving and was barred from her school. Diana left for Paris and, aided by Madame Bellaigue, her French came on well. She hoped to be useful to her father like Randolph, who had been his companion in Rhodes, Naples and Pompeii. They had met Pope Pius XI and visited Mussolini. The Chancellor's Gold Cream Kitten was less auriferous after a fashionable bob. She returned to Notting Hill School in January 1927, unsure if there would be anything gold standard about her final grades.

Many disagreed with Sarah's father's policies but Mummie said that when he spoke, MPs packed the House. PM Baldwin and George V thought him the star turn. In 1904 he had switched parties out of support for free trade but now favoured 'Imperial Preference' and imposed high duties on non-Empire goods. Purchasing armaments meant a big deficit. Some claimed he only chose friends who were useful to him, casting others aside. He put up a confident front and so did his children. He liked having Diana there as he held up Gladstone's scarlet leather bag outside 11 Downing Street. An essay she wrote at Notting Hill School, 'The pros and cons of Tariff Reform as opposed to Free Trade', was a breeze. She enjoyed debating and her school magazine mentions one motion, 'That Liberty of the Press is a hindrance to the attainment of World Peace', had Diana as opposer, sustaining her side though failing to convince. The motion was won by twenty-seven votes to two. Despite Diana's misgivings about the press given its intrusiveness, its 'Liberty' was enough for her to take this less popular stance. One young friend she had then was Prof's assistant, Alan Lennox-Boyd, whose mentor had been John Buchan.

A turquoise-streaked sea flashed between each villa on the drive up from Broadstairs in May 1927. Sarah greeted Miss Wolseley-Lewis on arrival at North Foreland School (NFS). She could cope as a boarder in that neo-Georgian domain, having been alone so many times. She asked Mama not to interfere with her room: 'Please don't get me changed mummy as Miss Lewis will not like it.' Chums included Sheila Berry, first daughter of Bill Camrose, Winston's friend. The offspring of both families saw a lot of each other: this book-writing corner of the aristocracy a world away from the toil and grime of ordinary British life. Broadstairs has a Dickens connection, but the Oliver

Twist experience was no fiction for those in workhouses until 1930. People spoke also of the unease among miners.

Sarah and her classmates prepared for their Confirmation papers. Head-girl Prudence Jellicoe was a friend; her Anglican vicar uncle was a social housing reformer who started a 'sensible drinking' pub. The Prince of Wales came by for a nip. Father Basil came to NFS to give a lecture. 'He plays concertina and sings,' wrote Sarah to her interested mother.

In frozen England, Randolph's friend Tom surpassed himself building igloos at Chartwell. Thoroughly traditional might not be a description one attaches to the Mitford clan nowadays, but back then that's how Tom summed up family life, as letters exchanged between these Etonians reveal. In 1928 things perked up for young Mitford during the ten months he spent improving his German in Vienna and at Schloss Bernstein with János Almásy – a man from a family of explorers, diplomats and aviators who understood *things* everyone else was ignorant of. Randolph envied the 'perpetual exhilaration' Tom felt in János's company. The letters show the wariness the Mitford and Churchill elders had with regard to their children's friends and how the younger generation learned to tread carefully. Randolph gets a ticking off from Tom for yapping to Prof. Tom's fear of the adults coming along to crush enjoyment is acute. His sister Nancy warns him against telling the birds about Almásy's weird passions (such as the occult). Prof wore a large gold watch on a chain that everyone called *the turnip*. His Mercedes impressed Tom and Randolph. Earlier, the scientist urged Tom to avoid unsuitably close relationships with other boys, especially since appreciation of his good looks might not be confined to women. Tom cracked a joke to Randolph about not having become so depraved as to pick up boys or go back to the 'old ways' yet. He was mostly into girls and in Vienna a romance was budding with Penelope Cunard, whom he two-timed with Princess Schwarzenberg (the first girl he'd met who smoked in public). Out of the two, he told Randolph, he would marry *the Cunard* since he could never marry a foreigner. That didn't stop him courting a German 'baby' at Castle Kohfidisch. Arriving in Vienna in March 1928 after an immensely tiring journey, Wagner-mad Lady Redesdale went straight to the opera to hear the last hour of *Gotterdammnung* with Tom. Teutonomania's effect on Sarah's cousin Unity is well known.

Sarah received letters from her busy mother telling her about Randolph at the Mimizan Hunt in Forêt d'Eu, Normandy. Nana and Mary visited and they walked past the large houses lining the cliff-tops where the drop to shore was sheer. Keeping a tight hold on the two little ones, Nana let them look down to the crater-like terrain and the steps cut into the rock that could take them to the sandy cove. Thirteen years earlier, these had inspired John Buchan's novel.

While Tom had the 'thrill-factor' for Randolph, Sarah's idol at Broadstairs was Diana Witherby. How she waxed lyrical about 'DW', until one day she wrote: 'Friendship is the most wonderful thing I have ever known but the breaking of it is certainly the most bitter.' While DW was a cold wrecker of hearts, Sarah showed dignity. Her diary reveals how DW was 'rushing about with a new best friend (Betty) this term' and how when Betty left, she returned to her previous favourite and when that failed, asked Sarah to be her best friend again. Sarah was tolerant and kept up with DW, who later visited her to show off a bunch of modern-sounding poems she had written.

The Foreign Office reception rooms held a *Thé Dansant* and Diana danced at St James's Square in a ball to honour Lady Astor in early February 1928 and at another for Mrs Stanley Baldwin. It was her entrée into Society. Leading the Primrose League (set up by her grandfather in 1883 to honour Disraeli), Diana lunched at the Red Lion Hotel and carried a wreath to Dizzy's grave. She was presented at court on 8 May and showy receptions followed at Grosvenor Square, organised by Mrs Percy Quilter. Cousin Diana mesmerised all. Sarah tried to bolster up a sister whose self-esteem was lacking. She had little confidence in herself. Her top teeth were inclined and Miss Lewis said that her conduct was 'very young for her age'. That summer Papa employed her in the building of a brick house on the Chartwell estate. When an observer said part of the wall was uneven, she never forgot Father's reply: 'Any fool can see what's wrong. But can you see what's right?' A visitor on Sundays was financial journalist Brendan Bracken, who helped Papa in campaigns. This wavy-haired carrot-top who 'talked for England' was one of Winston's few real friends. Sarah would use the words 'male household' to describe her environment, admitting she learned to keep silent.

At the start of 1929, Randolph waved goodbye to Eton. His father had recently complained of his son's perverse handwriting, so young Churchill bashed material out using a typewriter. He drank and smoked and became known for his cockiness. His Pa was permissive but Duff Cooper and Lady Astor tried to upbraid him. The latter was his father's opponent in the Commons, throwing monkey wrenches into debates. When Randolph bragged about smoking cigars, that long-time critic of harmful lifestyles predicted he would end up a victim of debauchery like his grandfather. Randolph got a bee in his bonnet and wrote to demand she apologise, adding that if she refused, he would tell Father. It was the earliest example of him suing someone. When Lady Astor's apology came he drew pleasure from having made the Coalition MP crawl, sharing the joke with Papa over a large brandy.

Eton had not been the dream Tom Mitford promised and Randolph was concerned less with Restoration poets and more with politics. Hungrily modern and gracelessly direct, his outlook was miles apart from that of Jim Lees-Milne, a magnet for feminine satellites Diana Churchill and Diana Mitford (as well as older men Harold Nicolson and Eddie March). Tom's sister terrorised the ardent Jim, darkening Botticelli skies over Oxford by flirting with the likes of Bill Astor. Diana C, meanwhile, was a genuine poetry-lover but was rejected by Jim. Lennox-Boyd mainly batted for the other side too. She didn't squander her energy, except to transport Randolph's belongings by car to and from Christchurch. Winston's son knew everyone Evelyn Waugh wanted to know and the two became chums.

When Diana Mitford married Bryan Guinness at St Margaret's in January 1929, Diana Churchill was a bridesmaid alongside Unity (in Valkyrie plaits) and Grania Guinness – both Sarah's friends. Bryan's home, 10 Buckingham Street, hosted a fancy dress ball (with Tom as a respectable Victorian lady) and a crazy reception for a tragic German artist (really Tom in a wheelchair). Randolph and Diana kept dutifully apart from the headline-grabbing fun despite Diana G's 'BEAUTIFUL REPRODUCTIONS' sent as Christmas presents to remind them that her face and form could topple entire civilisations. Their Papa held high office and good behaviour was crucial. A desire to do beneficial things was ingrained in them. Still, raising funds for mothers and babies at the 'Carnival on Ice' (where Hammersmith Palais later stood), Diana was among the gayest of the young people in her velvet skating costume.

Trade was subdued, but delivering his fifth budget speech Churchill was a personal success. New acolyte Harold Macmillan praised him for removing the tea duty and scaling income tax, yet he couldn't guarantee a minimum wage to miners or limit the profits of mine owners. Many were out of work, while the Tories were allergic to spending. LG suggested creating public works to develop housing, roads and the telephone network but nobody trusted him. A General Election was to take place on 30 May 1929 and in the frantic run-up Diana narrowly escaped death in a car accident outside Wood House in Epping. Churchill won the seat but lost his Shadow Cabinet post. He had no government position. A trick was played on him when he went to the US, with the Labour government declaring support for India's Dominion status. This first step towards Home Rule got through unopposed. He could only growl and write; his mode of life bore into his children. When Sarah received a red leather diary from Diana for her birthday, her pen faithfully recorded her life as it happened, except for when she lost its tiny key (later found somehow locked inside the diary). The diary reveals her sensitivity to needy schoolmate Tricia (Patricia Benn) who shows the same love for her she felt for 'DW' and steals off to see Sarah convalescing in sickbay. They get rumbled and 'the old fools' lock Sarah in. One day Sarah and Prudence meet a farmer with a carthorse and take photos of him. It was so hot they took their dresses off, she innocently tells Mama.

A time of spiritual reflection; Sarah was confirmed by the Archbishop of Canterbury on 1 December, then had tea with Father Jellicoe in London and toured his flats. On New Year's Eve she had supper in the nursery with Giles and Esmond before heading for bed. On the landing she heard 'the most awful row going on' and it became clear a pooch was the centre of it. With his 'usual annoying air', her brother had come into the sitting room with 'Gem' under his arm. 'Papa lost his temper,' she writes, describing how he threw his glass on the floor (which shattered into tiny pieces) and stalked out. Sarah notes becoming tearful and embarrassed in case their visitors hear the row. Her reaction reveals who she was then: someone utterly fearful of scenes. Randolph was the opposite. Can the expense of feeding a dog have been so great, or was his attitude so trying? The house was costly to run but its owner enjoyed luxuries. When Jim visited in 1930 Mr Churchill's cigars and brandy gave Chartwell its distinctive aroma. Still there in 1949 on Jim's next visit, the smell no longer exists.

Dining at Chartwell in early January 1930, Johnny thought Sarah's friend Pussy Waring large in proportion and quiet in disposition. Winston was annoyed with his nephew for failing to engage the girl in conversation. Witnessing Amy Johnson's homecoming after her flight to Australia, learning graphology from Major Waring and organising her school garden plot were highlights for Sarah, but life was quiet. She was becoming competitive, viewing each new girl's arrival with terror lest they be better than her. The girls did formation drills on the lawn and gymnastics on a scary pommel horse with Pussy Waring setting the pace. If a Lacrosse equivalent of 'jolly hockey sticks' exists, Sarah's school had it. She could also gavotte, do a croisé efface and even eurhythmics, but thoughts about her future were similar to her exchanges with the Cheshire Cat whilst playing Alice at NFS. She yearned for parental approval. She tried to share in small things that drew Papa's attention, telling him she was rooting for Flamingo in the Derby. Sadly, the Aga Khan's horse won. Her friend Jock Colville would observe later that Mr Churchill paid less far less attention to his daughters than his son.

At Oxford Randolph crashed a Bright Young Things bottle party. He had joined the Balloon Club but a lack of gas scotched one ascent and a party was held for the balloon's husky-voiced passenger, Tallulah Bankhead. Randie thought he 'stood a chance' but surprisingly wasn't successful with the woman the Hayes Committee would accuse of 'verbal moral turpitude'. Hero-worship of F.E. prompted it. Back in 1923, at the time of her first London play, Miss Bankhead caught the eye of the virile ex-Lord Chancellor, who was also Randolph's hero, and named herself 'Lulu Ta Birkenhead'. As kids, he and Diana got to know Freddy Birkenhead and his older sister, Eleanor Smith. A few years older than Chumbolly and Gold Cream Kitten, they formed a gang with the Churchills (including Johnny and Pebin). At Blenheim, when the Duke and Duchess caught Randolph slapping the buttocks of a Greek statue and making suggestive comments, F.E. defended his godson. Nobody came close to him. He could dive into the sea with a lighted cigar and come up out of the water with it still alight. A ladies man, F.E. erred too much for Randie's mother to admire him. She hated his epic drinking, even if he had just wagered a bet with rival wild rover Lord Beaverbrook to lay off drink for a year. The taste of water was supposed to make F.E. keel over.

In North Foreland, meanwhile, Sarah looked out to sea with the Goodwin Sands rising and the beacon twinkling in the evening light. She had written about migrating birds and their manic desire to be free:

> At last they reach the lighthouse bright,
> that tells the ships when danger's near,
> But on they crash with all their might,
> dazzled by so strong a light.

A 'fuming' schoolmistress almost had this bird expelled. It wasn't what Mama (due to meet the Royals that day) wanted to hear. Still, her final report said: 'The school will miss her very much.' Spending August on the North Devon coast, doing what she liked 'free of all conventions', she and Mary stayed with Clementine's Aunt Maudie (mother of Madeleine and Maryott – Nana) at Buck's Mills with the fishing village inspiring her novel, *Tessa*. It was then time for Sarah and other blushing examples of English girlhood to go to Paris to start at the Ozanne School. Recommended by Duff Cooper's niece, Sarah's proficiency in French put her in the top class. Pulling off flouncy bed drapes was an act of vandalism uniting Sarah with Eleanor Sotheran-Estcourt. With Ann Hotham on piano, Eleanor on violin and Sarah with banjo on her knee, they performed in the smelly scullery. Eleanor, who shared her interest in writing, was 'the best friend she had ever had'. Once, when she laughingly whispered 'I love you', Sarah hoped it was true. Sexual and emotional feelings abounded but Sarah was prim in attitude. She writes the maddest letter on 4 March 1932, sparing Eleanor her Chatterton-like sorrows and showing what a child she was. After describing awakening meadows on her misty morning return to Chartwell she's 'shaking silently' whilst servants unpack her belongings. She laughs idiotically; the maid convinced she's some kind of changeling. She was thinking back to a time 'there were bits of yellow egg all over the carpet' (an episode Eleanor knew). Standing by the window her laughter fit grows as she watches the maid pull pyjamas out of her banjo case. She compares Chartwell's butler to a 'clown escaped from a circus'. His name is Inches and Sarah tells Eleanor she's calling him 'foot'. They were expecting Winston, at that moment sailing from America on *The Majestic*. The letter has a cartoon of Papa with a scar on his brow etched in red ink: 'rather attractive ... these sort of scars,' says the caption. With Jock Colville, her escort at the Grand National, Sarah returned to her serious self. Chartwell was quiet except for the time a 'frightfully good-looking young airman' came. The bad news, Sarah wrote, was that Diana had cornered him.

Back in Paris Sarah fantasised about her bed floating out the window and flying through the 'green-skied' night. Attempts by her teacher Mademoiselle Alice to get her paid employment in Paris came to nothing, so Sarah's schooling came to a halt. She was not yet eighteen when she left school. Shy and gauche, she never said goodbye to her literature teacher, Pierre Clarac, a friend of Rostand in his youth and professor of literature at the University of Bordeaux in later years. Surprisingly, she bore the brunt of family purse-string tightening, although money wasn't scarce. That May the family took a Westminster flat at 11 Morpeth Mansions and for his son's twenty-first, Winston spared no expense. Randolph telephoned *The Standard* so its *Londoner's Diary* column was privy to the impressive guest list. The 'Fathers and Sons Dinner' at Claridges on 28 May was attended by Lord Hailsham and son Quintin Hogg and Lord Cranbourne (aka Bobbety Cecil, Winston's ally in the Conservative camp). A dazzling party on 7 July was Unity Mitford's 'coming out' at 96 Cheyne Walk, the Guinness's home. Winston and Eddie March debated the merits of Stanley Spencer's *Unveiling a War Memorial at Cookham*, with Winston a severe critic. Mosley, Augustus John, Randolph, Diana C and Tom were among the guests. Sarah didn't go though she had left school, was in London and could have come. She records meeting Augustus at a party that November. Her Society debut was looming and her parents viewed her as childish enough without Unity putting madcap ideas into her head. Destiny would be kinder to her than to her cousin.

Eleanor visited her at Chartwell that month and years later recalled worrying what Mrs C and Sarah's Aunt Nellie would say about her mint-coloured gown with violets at the belt and high-heeled pumps. Clementine surprised them by being complimentary. Then Sarah was alone, reporting to Eleanor her father's comment that he would have 'lugged her off' to the garden 'painting furiously as the mosquitos ate her alive' had he known she liked art. Sarah had driving lessons from chauffeur Sam. When he married housemaid Olive she moaned that she could 'neither get lunch nor drive the car'. She was less adept playing nine holes at Limpsfield Chart with Mama and

Prof. She mentions some terrific-looking caddies turning up but her game was diabolical and they couldn't help smirking. A white-haired piano instructress taught her *The Blue Danube* and soothed her career angst, advising her to be 'like a tree and have many branches to wave in the wind'. Sarah went with her parents to Cranbourne Manor (Bobbety's ancestral home) and she and Pebin saw a play together in August. With Diana she had her 'first really satisfying giggle', with Papa in high dudgeon demanding to know what amused them. His light-hearted side was uncommon and yet it had been visible many times in the past. If his horse came in or if he was due a sumptuous dinner at his club the atmosphere was frivolous. The house reverberated with his booming baritone and even the soldiers on the toy battlefields seemed infected by his mirth. Secret names were whispered like Little Tich, Chergwin the One-Eyed Kaffir, Marie Lloyd and Dan Leno. Papa became a sentry at a military pillbox with his rendition of George Mozart's parody. As children they had pestered him to know more and got a whiff of the old Tivoli and the Empire, Leicester Square, as well as a rollicking song. He even performed a trick. He hadn't been called 'that expert hat manipulator' by the theatrical press for nothing. He travelled back to times when intrepid Miss Kellerman dived into a tank, or the occasion he and his father watched polar bears on stage in an aquatic spectacle.

Pressure was ramping up on mothers of coming-of-age daughters. Sarah made a trip to Paris to see Eleanor E, telling her the prospect of a husband scared her. Wired in a certain way, her imaginary world was far more important. 'Dreams,' she said, 'prepare people by filling them with courage for the approaching future.' She also hated seeing the past disintegrate. Randolph was the same. He was an usher at the wedding of Charles Sweeny and Margaret Whigham at Brompton Oratory. While unemployment peaked with the government sticking to its minimal intervention policy, guests from the richest families cheered this couple.

Job or no job, ordinary folk were loyal to George V. On 9 February 1933 the Oxford Union debated the motion: 'That this House would not in any circumstances fight for King and Country.' Randolph thought to counter it and delivered a speech. It met with shouts and stink bombs from the left-leaning pacifists backing principal speaker C. E. M. Joad. Randolph held his ground, demanding that democracy prevail. The Union endorsed the motion and young Churchill left – his opponents intent on debagging him.

It was thrilling to hear Papa's speech before the Royal Society of St George on 24 April 1933. The BBC had rigged up the Connaught Rooms for an outside broadcast. Churchill immediately brought up Eric Gill's controversial new statuary (*Prospero and Ariel*) on Broadcasting House's façade, saying how he imagined Sir John Reith sweating at the brow at his every word.

He mischievously asked what Reith might think if he uttered an irreverence about MacDonald, Gandhi or the Russian Bolsheviks. His subject, however, was 'St George and the Dragon'. He mused on what it would be like were that legend to reoccur under modern conditions. A modern St George would have secretaries at his side and scientific formulas to dispense. The League of Nations would propose a round-the-table conference with the Dragon at which it would size up a trade deal. Of course money would be lent to the Dragon and this would be raised from taxpayers. Geneva would decide conditions surrounding the release of the Maiden with the Dragon's 'rights' taken into consideration. The press would get its front-page photo of St George with the Dragon. Winston used the droll tale to steer to the crux of his argument about dangers from within. He glanced at Randolph, seated next to Cousin Sunny. The worst dangers come not from without but from within. The worst threat to Britain and the spirit of St George was the mood of self-abasement that intellectual society was wont to encourage. He fulminated against defeatist doctrines the British people were expected to accept and the supposition that 'England was beyond saving' – one gathering popularity. Sarah paid close attention to his speeches and Randolph's political ambitions. She heard much about the Empire and how, with MacDonald and wily supporters Baldwin and Lord Irwin (styled Halifax after 1934) to deal with, Father could hardly safeguard India. He had lost his brilliant ally F.E. in September 1930.

Sarah put on her white tulle and silver for the ball held by Dorothy Charteris at which the Duke and Duchess of York were honoured guests, the debs admiring the Duchess's red shoes. It was time for her to be presented at court. Her big day was on 11 May during the first court of the season. The gates of Buckingham Palace opened allowing privileged cars to drive direct into the Palace before the Diplomatic Court opened at 8.30 p.m. Ordinary Londoners gathered in the rain to see the brass-buttoned uniforms and dazzling white dresses emerge from shiny black cars. Brazil's delegate headed the procession, then Queen Mary, in aquamarine silk and jewels, took her place on the throne. With the Yorks and Earls of Harewood and Athlone, the Prince of Wales performed duties in his father's absence. Each debutante was led by her mother or by a substitute. A report singled out Sarah as strikingly beautiful and emphasised her 'thoroughly old-fashioned upbringing'. Among her fellow debs were Laura Charteris, Sheila Morris, Rosemary Harding, Elizabeth Scott-Ellis, Daphne Mulholland and school friends Tricia and Sybil Cavendish. Not all the Park Lane residences where Sarah waltzed were to survive those changing times. For all her qualms about an ivory tower existence, she loved her Season. It filled the world with grace – not something you got from 'modernism'.

Alan Lennox-Boyd had attached himself to the pro-German January Club while others from among Britain's aristocratic youth went to Russia to assess progress. Duncan Sandys had made an unofficial trip in July and August 1931. Accompanied by Christopher Fuller, he witnessed the effects of State atheism in the dismantling of Moscow's Church of the Redeemer. Impersonating a school inspector, he gained access to a sanatorium for those the State regarded as misfits. Already an experienced aviator, with Fuller he charted a biplane over some of the most remote reaches of eastern Russia, flying at great height. A year after Sarah witnessed Miss Johnson's triumphant return, Duncan and Christopher encountered Amy and her mechanic Jack Humphreys in Kurgan of all places. She had flown 16,000 miles and was heading for Tokyo. Spending the night with a revolver under her pillow, she continued her journey next day while Duncan and Christopher flew east of Novosibirsk then travelled by road and track. After watching Trans-Siberian trains take prisoners to the gulags they visited the Kuznetskstroy metallurgy complex, an American-constructed plant eulogized by the Soviets. Seeing it was barbarically maintained by forced labour, as was a brick factory in which 20,000 prisoners were put to work under armed surveillance, Christopher typed a memorandum of their journey and would pass this to Britain's Foreign Secretary. Despite the shadier aspects of the regime, they still thought the British should foster Soviet friendship, if only for the purposes of realpolitik.

Other young men believed Moscow was justified in imprisoning spies and seriously believed the posters of sun-bronzed workers crying 'Come join us in the collective farm!' They had no need to visit Russia. Sarah's cousin Esmond, then at Wellington College, was a red schoolboy, a 'Jacobite' and Pacifist. On Armistice Day 1933, his leafleting for the Anti-War Movement annoyed people. He might just as easily have chosen Fascism but hatred for public schools and boredom made him drift towards Communism and Atheism. Esmond secretly convened with left-wing intellectuals and poets in Parton Street, Holborn. A week before Christmas he came to Chartwell, full of Bolshie insolence and hyperactive as ever. Wherever he stood politically, though, he relished conversations with Uncle Winston.

Queen Charlotte's Ball at 16 Bruton Street heralded the Season's new sugar and whipped egg white; with Sarah deficient in air bubbles. Crimped Francis Stonon fussed about, getting debs from last year, like Pempie and Unity Mitford (in her absurdly fake tiara), to form a guard of honour. Whilst Unity loved to shock, taking pet rat 'Ratula' for walks, there was nothing exhibitionist about Sarah. Opening Day at Ascot saw her in a frock of lily leaf green georgette and a hat with a green ribbon. Her clothes were updated each year with her Mama promptly binning old styles. Suspended in privilege as in aspic, never carrying money added to the delay in growing up. Occasionally a feeling of emptiness became apparent. With Mary, Papa, Prof and cousins Pebin and Clarissa, Christmas Day was at Blenheim. When Sarah found out Diana was coming she was relieved, thinking how 'lonely in that big house' she would be otherwise.

Esmond volunteered to use his magazine *Out of Bounds* to radicalise public schoolboys. He ran away when it was censored, attracting public attention. Even *The Stage* newspaper said the best way to deal with him was to give him a good music hall contract – if his headmaster could be persuaded to do a few shows with him (although *Narkover School*'s head might feel his role was being threatened). Duncan and Christopher left Russia behind and talked of reviving Britain's position and spirit. By April 1934 they were devout missionaries of The British Movement, urging organisations to use technology to survive in the face of menacing foreign cartels. Duncan talked of a future 'Parliament of Empire' and thought Indian Home Rule a mistake. He praised the Worshipful Company of Fishmongers whose high standards ensured that no bad fish was sold at Billingsgate.

Meanwhile, a ball each week showcased high-end British merchandise as West End matriarchs paraded their daughters during 1934's Second Season. Royalty was present when Sarah waltzed at Carlton House Terrace and the dance continued at the Ritz on Berkeley Square on 28 May, at Lady Sassoon's Ball, the Derby Ball and one for the Berry girls at Long Cross. Lacking confidence and still immersed in childhood, the fate of this debutante was unclear. In her lineage seeds had been sown for speaking with passion and reaching out to others, but she wasn't quite ready. In the meantime she learned from those around her.

# 3
# We Went to the Arts

Papa had fought 'savages' on the Indian frontier, surveyed enemy lines for Kitchener and been in the cavalry charge at Omdurman – all before the century drew to a close. Now, as a writer and speaker he ranked high and as a statesman occupied posts in the Cabinet. Winter evenings saw the coals glow red and the children's eyes glaze over. They begged him to tell them 'the story' again – about being captured in the Boer War and brought to the Staats Model School (a Pretoria school turned prison for British officers). He escaped Republican forces on 12 December 1899, hid in a flowerbed, crossed the Apies River via a footbridge before jumping into a train to Witbank. Four days were spent down a mineshaft when the Howard family concealed him. What would Diana, Randolph and Sarah do during such an incarceration? Memorise as much verse as possible – that's what! They competed as to who could keep going the longest. Randolph won but storytelling was something they were all good at. Huddling in that two-storey 'house in the trees', located at the end of a steep incline leading to the 'Robin Pool', Pebin sought her opinion on dramas he had composed and cast her as 'Secretary' to his 'Detective'. Sleuthdom was at the expense of safety and, performing a Nijinsky leap whilst blindfolded, Sarah injured her shoulder. Writhing in agony, Pebin's soothing nature bore deep. Their love was such that alarm bells started ringing. Mama and Auntie Goonie conspired to separate them, banning Pebin from Chartwell. When it strikes first time, one never forgets heartbreak.

When Diana complained about days being empty and unhappy, her younger sister suggested acting. Films paid, she said, thinking along Winston lines. In Sarah's 1981 memoir she implies it was the first time theatre emerged as a topic in their home. Yet Shakespeare was a living force there and their Pa was as great an actor as any who walked a stage. Major Morton said Churchill was well aware of this. Grannie Jennie had written plays and her romantic nature made her life a drama. More connections existed in Clementine's family: the Stanleys of Alderley. Cousin Venetia's niece Pamela Stanley (related through her grandmother May Sartoris to the Kembles and Sarah Siddons) trod the boards. Large theatrical personalities like Herbert Beerbohm Tree, along with his wife and eldest daughter Viola (both actresses), were lifelong friends. When Tree enacted Drake's *Defence of Devon*, Churchill wrote him a letter of praise saying he had done so much to spread knowledge of Shakespeare and that the Navy owed him a debt. This message was read out at a Drake celebration dinner. When the stage laid claim to Diana Cooper (née Manners) it made its greatest incursion into aristocratic life. She exploited her name to her parents' dismay and attracted Max Reinhardt's attention with her films. Playing the *Statue of the Virgin* she toured the US with promiscuous Iris Tree, the Beerbohms' youngest gal (who had posed nude for Modigliani). Funding her husband Duff's Parliamentary career and beguiling movie moguls, Lady D would have got *Anna Karenina* had Garbo persisted in being alone. She also introduced Rudolf Kommer (Reinhardt's PA) to the Churchills. Other friends dabbled in acting. Sarah's curiosity was fired as to how these figures came to possess the power they had.

After the May 1929 election, Parliament was hung with MacDonald forming a minority government. Sarah expressed frustration about leaving No. 11 but hoped the wife of the incoming Chancellor would like their decorations. Her father always carried on and 'when he faced defeat,' she recalled, 'he went to the arts.' In early August, Diana saw off Winston, Jack, Johnny and Randolph as they embarked on a tour of Canada and the USA. After counting oil wells in Calgary and buying ten-gallon hats as protection from the sun, they stopped at Lake Louise in the Rockies. Miraculously, Winston returned from a solitary painting trip without being chewed up by bears. Randolph and Johnny did headstands near the Grand Canyon's edge and the party hit California. On 13 September the opulent gates of San Simeon opened and the ex-Chancellor was asked to write for W. R. Hearst's newspapers. Hearst asked Johnny for a list of film stars he wanted to meet and got handed one in record speed. At a banquet Winston sat between L. B. Mayer and Hearst with Randolph on Hearst's side and sixty stars in tow. Chaplin was top of Winston's list. People used to say 'no one knows where Chaplin is' but cousin Clare Sheridan (a motorcycle-riding columnist) both found and bedded him. Charlie read Shaw and Wells and professed to hate capitalism. Ex-Chancellor and Little Tramp couldn't have had more contrasting starts: the former at Blenheim and the latter on a traveller's caravan site in Smethwick. Churchill chatted to Charlie: 'Why not depict Napoleon in your next film?' He would script it. That he saw him in the role is intriguing. Both were obsessed with Napoleon and there are accounts of each dressing up as the Emperor. Nine months before, however, reactions to Abel Gance's *Napoléon* had been poor. The new project was scuppered. Chaplin's mother, whose stage name was Lily Harley, had been attracted to his father because he looked like Napoleon. Lily had died the year before and Charlie was grieving when the visitors lunched at his studio on 24 September. Sarah's Pa stayed on when the boys came home. Five days before the Wall Street Crash he gambled on the markets, losing $50,000. An advance of £20,000 for *Marlborough: His Life and Times* came just in time.

Sarah was also 'going to the arts', tripping out to Margate's Dreamland and enjoying the 'low humour' of a picture variety theatre: the kind Miss Lewis 'would have been decidedly set against'. With Aunt Nellie, Giles and Esmond she wrote and performed *The Perfect Servant* in Chartwell's dining room before 1929 ended. 'It is going to be funny,' she noted. Randolph, meanwhile, socialised at Oxford with Freddy Birkenhead and Seymour Berry. Decanters never ran dry at lunch and dinner with little time spent poring over books. An irresistible distraction was Ottilia, better known as Tilly Losch. Tom Mitford and Randolph were more than acquaintances and competed over who was better placed to call the actress 'my Tilly'. Diana Guinness's bridesmaid Margaret Mercer-Nairne provided more scope for competition. These sporting achievements failed to impress Winston, who saw no industry in his son's second term, not that he revered many 'Great Minds'. Making up one's own mind was more important and words were best spoken instead of festering in books. By way of illustration he sang his old school song:

> Jack's a scholar, as all men say, Dreams in Latin and Greek.
> Gobbles a grammar in half a day and a lexicon once a week.

He had insisted that his children surmount fears of public speaking. Shakespeare's verse with its regular rhythm was practice material. Even Sarah, normally crippled with shyness, developed an affinity with the plays. A friend later said: 'Sarah frequently quoted Shakespeare. My impression was that Shakespeare's words and philosophy had been part of her father's *way of thinking* about life and beyond.'

A tidy mind was Father's by-word. What rankled him was muddle-headedness and mumbling. He taught them not to speak too readily and to *organise*, declaring: 'A good speech is like a woman's skirt. It should be long enough to cover the issue but short enough to make it interesting.' He conceded his son's remarkable gift for extemporising. Bruce Lockhart – *Londoner's Diary* editor and former spy (whose life had hung by a thread during the Bolshevik Revolution) – thought Randolph a miniature version of Churchill on meeting him in April 1930. Randolph's prowess at the Union got him an invitation from William Feakens to do a lecture tour of America, leaving on 1 October. While it meant quitting Oxford after twenty months, Winston didn't talk him out of it. Churchill never sat easily in the 'English gentleman' role. His go-getter nature was thought vulgar by this class but he valued his American heritage. That Randolph could be a success on his own merits tickled him. 'What would his lectures be about?' he asked. 'I'll decide on the journey out,' said Randolph.

As May turned to September thousands of Eastenders trekked to Kent for a 'profit and pleasure' holiday. Families camped by night, picked hops and washed in the open air. Diana, a nurse in the Red Cross's Voluntary Aid Detachment Service, was there to help the Hop Pickers' Army with sunstroke and cuts. Opening Florence Nightingale House (a Harrow Hospital nursing home) she felt she might have more influence *playing* a nurse rather than being one. Joining RADA was partly an attempt to please her father, who hadn't been encouraging towards her marriage suitors to date, among them Alan Bees. Winston's secretary, Miss Moir, who found Diana's gay chatter a happy distraction, said her boss's eldest daughter worshipped the stage. She said how fun-loving and impulsive Diana was, never going anywhere without her portable Victrola. She socialised with aesthetes Harold Acton and John Sutro in Covent Garden. A snooty letter Tom wrote to Randolph expresses surprise that his sister could be Acton's friend. Summertime saw her in the Riviera slumming it with fellow students. When they left, she boarded the Duke of Westminster's yacht for a week's more luxurious r&r. Travelling was not without mishaps. Diana's vanity case flew open at inopportune moments, scattering products far and wide. Another time she travelled by sleeper to Scotland. Forgetting she had left her shellac records on the lower berth she was heartbroken when, in the middle of the night, its occupant, a stout woman, plunged into bed, smashing them. RADA colleague Harold Warren couldn't afford *le Train Bleu* but regarded her with great affection. Debonair Griffith Jones was in her year and achieved lasting success and fame. His daughter Gemma recalls her father talking about a weekend when Diana invited her RADA friends to Chartwell. A working-class man from Wales, Griffith felt intimidated. He remembered Churchill coming down to breakfast in his pyjamas and dressing gown.

While Sarah's diary says her parents objected to Diana going to RADA, Miss Moir talks of theatre being common ground between Winston and his eldest girl. At parties they took turns performing music-hall numbers. Seeing his name in the papers owing to mistaken identities might have caused his objection. The Press fussed about Winston's daughter's new film but in fact it was the debut of actress Diana (Josephine) Churchill. At RADA at the same time but not on the same course, Wembley doctor's daughter Diana J.

would marry Barry K. Barnes and later Mervyn Johns. The two Dianas often returned each other's wrongly addressed mail.

Randolph went fishing in the US but wouldn't hunt defenceless raccoons. He saw Tilly in New York and a tall, slender blonde from Ohio called Kay Halle. She had earned her 'Mata Halle' nickname after a string of conquests including Gershwin. 'One doesn't think of marrying an American, not unless she's rich,' was Tom's advice. Young Mitford's mother had written to Randolph to explain how, flying from Switzerland, her son had had a 'slight' aeroplane accident and was in hospital. He came down in the wood next door to his home at Swinbrook, spinneys cushioning his fall. Sydney Redesdale describes how the plane was 'broken to pieces – wings up in trees'. By letter Tom and Randie discussed the pros and cons of bedding 'ageing virgins'. An admission by Tom – 'I plighted my troth to a lady of 28' – indicates he had been there and done it. Kay's seniority of eight years prompted it. Randolph once asked to see her hair, which was wrapped in a turban. Down came her heavy blonde locks. As she lay sleeping he cut them to shoulder level. She asked why he did it. His reply was that 'it made you seem older than me'. When Randie's mother came to New York in February 1931 to avert the danger of this department-store owner's daughter she ended up having a wonderful trip. Her son's £6000 lecture fee was well earned given the 70 cities he visited, and he sold the Churchill brand. He also made sure to tell Americans how the Red Indian race (allowed to multiply under British rule) had since been decimated and how unlawful lynching of negroes in the South was.

*City Lights* saw its Dominion Theatre première on 25 February 1931. Two days earlier, after being introduced to Mary, Bracken and Winston's former secretary Boothby at Chartwell, Chaplin petrified the atmosphere, launching into a red soliloquy. Ice over, he went into his *Gold Rush* foot dance with bread rolls and a fork stuck in each. Britain, with three million unemployed, came off the Gold Standard. That August in Biarritz the tennis-loving Tramp played with René Lacoste and the Prince of Wales, then dined with Winston. Arthur Coles Armstrong, editor of *Variety Year*, believed politicians were using the film star as a distraction. Wasn't it sick that Charlie only had to 'wave his magic cane to be whisked off to Chequers, to empty the Commons as effectively as a division bell, or have his health proposed by Churchill'? He would return to Hollywood, Armstrong pointed out, 'with a huge pile of English money'. Chaplin received another invitation to Chartwell on 18 September with Bracken, Jack, Freddy B, Tom, Venetia Montagu, Kommer and French tutor Gabrielle L'Honore present. Sarah dashed over from Paris only to be struck by how different the silver-haired, suntanned actor was to his screen image. She remarked how 'one can not fail to be drawn by his charm and personality though he's a complete egoist'. Years later she described what happened:

> She was on her father's right with Charlie to his left. 'I hear you're a very funny man,' Papa said. 'Please do something funny!' Handed Shakespeare's Works, he opened it at Hamlet's soliloquy. No rendition could have been slower with gestures more gratuitous: 'TO BE' (pause) 'OR' (long pause) 'NOT' (pause) 'TO BE,' he began, flicking his nose with his finger with each phrase. Completely deadpan, he picked his nose in the rudest way: 'THAT!!' (flick and delicate lick of his finger) 'IS THE QUESTION' was how he finished – giving a saucy smile and a wink.

Charlie mania was still in the air in the run-up to the October 1931 Election. On the night of Winston's Epping victory Chaplin came to Gordon Selfridge's party where Diana partied with the Dolly Sisters, the Aga Khan, and Noël Coward. His wife and eldest daughter had been a great help, the latter's training used to advantage. Seated on a motor float on 27 October she was like a gladiatrix victorious after battle. Poring over cuttings sent to her about votes and box office takings, Sarah saw how similar the worlds of politics and entertainment were. Amid matchstick men in the margins of letters to Mama she announced that Hermione was her *true actress name*. She yearned to be able to relax in public as Papa had when ragged by Belfast students and forced to don a silly hat. Her school was big on the performing arts but Sarah underplays this in her autobiography. Before 1931 ended, she had been in a chorus line for a charity play, acted a scene from *L'Aiglon*, satirised teachers on stage, met Esmeralda (a child prodigy whose trainer partnered Pavlova) and played an English governess who gets drunk in a café. You would think a girl who could play a tipsy old woman had conquered shyness; but while impersonation was OK, playing herself was agony. Her parents wanted her to gain confidence at the Ozanne's but when virile Monsieur Clarac made Mademoiselle Chu-cheel stand up for an exposé on a Balzac novel, her bashfulness made him wince. She admired Clarac, whose ambition was 'not just to teach silly English girls, but to write'. Her diary bore the command: 'Stop being vain and thinking of yourself.' The pinnacle came when the *professeur* spoke of her journeying with her pen 'through mystic lands'. She imagined their 'grown-up discussions' about 'sin', asking him: 'Is this something God is aware of and can it ever be positive?'

Sunlight flooded Sarah's small fourth-floor room looking south-west across Avenue de Suffren to the Seine. Most prominent in view was the Gare de Grenelle and its scribble of tracks with shunting locomotives. Avenue Octave-Gréard was situated next to the base of the Eiffel Tower. In letters home she mentions it only once but a lovely smell caused her to pass under its lattice where an Italian mama sold hot chestnuts. Sarah and Patricia Berry had singing lessons as well as piano. Affections swung between Mademoiselle Alice and her sister Marie. Seeing Marie bossed around by her sister, Sarah saw the motherly soul who 'liked to spoil the young'. She still asked to move to Alice's floor to be in her idol's orbit. Sarah recorded the dishes they ate, wondering if Clementine might like to suggest some to her cook. Theatre trips were frequent. While appreciating Racine's *Phèdre*, she disliked the way the French actors kept flinging themselves about. The Greeks never would have done that surely? She described Molière as 'horribly coarse' and decried 'fat, greasy French people wobbling with laughter'. Nicer were outings to *Carmen* or to hear Menuhin and Fritz Kreisler play.

A month after Chaplin's visit to Chartwell, Randolph turned up requesting to see Sarah. Her diary proudly states that all the girls were 'struck by his beauty'. The next day he took her to a restaurant with Kay Halle and to the Marx Brothers' latest film. She liked Kay enormously but the glamorous American's offer to take her out again troubled her: 'She isn't on the list,' Sarah reports in sneak fashion to Clementine. Randolph was lecturing to clear debts. He lodged part-time at 3 Culross Street with Surrealist art collector Edward James and John Betjeman, whose poem *The Wykehamist* was dedicated to Randie. Competition over Tilly continued. James married her, then quickly divorced her. When Aunt Nellie wasn't visiting, Randolph, whose father had secured him a job with the Rothermere Press, dined with aristocratic columnist Lord Castlerosse. The latter lived across the cobblestones with his beautiful wife Doris.

Money was an issue during Sarah's Paris schooldays. She barely had enough cash and knew she was there on a term-by-term basis, telling Mama: 'I am so glad you are letting me stay another term.' Papa, meanwhile, had losses to recoup. Encouraged by his son's success he was keen to do 40 lectures stateside for £30,000. Randolph waved off the party, which included Clementine, Detective Thompson and Diana. Mrs Street was enlisted as Sarah's guardian, taking her Christmas shopping on her return from Paris when she chose a baby gramophone for Mary before being taken to Chartwell. Most rooms there were shut up, so in the peace and quiet she began writing. By the fire in the dining room she read her father's article 'Fifty Years Hence' in December's *Strand Magazine*, thinking about the scientific developments he predicted, such as large-scale use of robots. As Nana plaited her hair she dared not imagine where she might be in 1981. She felt subdued and frightened. Even before leaving for Paris, she was harried for news about her Pa. He had been injured in a street accident on 13 December but defended driver Mario Contasino (an Italian living at 200 Yonkers Avenue) telling police he was to blame. Treated by Dr Pickhardt at Lennox Hill Hospital, Contasino visited him twice. The Bahamas restored him and in New York he was touched by the affection shown. Not enough vases could be found for the floral tributes spanning the length and breadth of the Waldorf-Astoria's lobby. In Bernie Baruch's suite, apartment 39A, he interviewed for a secretary.

Sarah later learned how Diana's image became everyone's concern. The 22-year-old old lacked a good coat. Papa couldn't afford furs but sent his daughter and new recruit Miss Moir to the stores. Later Diana entered, not in a coat but in a satin gown that set her hair off a treat. Seeing her poured into that metallic sheath, a strategic dress initiative followed, with his daughter pacing up and down, striking different poses. Puffing on his cigar, Pa checked the satin as if it were munitions material. Behind all this, of course, was the screen test offered to her after Harry Warner (one of the four Warner Brothers) spotted Diana in a newsreel. Then Churchill returned to writing *My New York Misadventure*, and Diana to pursuits like visiting Squadron A Armory. In that setting of towers and round turrets she looked like a medieval princess watching indoor polo's greatest living exponent: cousin Winston Frederick Churchill Guest. She challenged The Optimists' Team Captain to 'show her a New York gangster' and a columnist tells us he 'excused himself from that not very difficult task'. Miss Moir heard that dozens of young women from New York's social elite were inveigling her for news of Randolph. Diana came to the one she had cast as Paul Poiret, imploring: 'Daddy, please take me dancing.' It was 10 p.m. after an evening of tiresome work in a city he didn't know but he gave in, taking her to the place of her choice.

On 28 January 1932 Contasino sat in the front row of Brooklyn's Academy of Music when Churchill spoke of co-operation as a bulwark against Russia and how the British used tax as a deterrent to intemperance rather than 'interference with liberty'. In Chicago at the Union League Club he addressed world finance. Clementine came home in March after seeing the Empire State and following Diana's test.

Hollywoodland was in depression so Warner Bros leased Teddington Studios for income, showing flexibility over film content to attract German money (opening themselves to later accusations that they were appeasing Nazis). Diana's test proved unsuccessful but Warner didn't give up and in his letter to Mrs C said he would supervise a re-test at Teddington, adding that it was necessary for a 'proper story' to be found. Diana's parents' encouragement indicates it was a hedge against Winston's financial losses. Huge fortunes were being made in the pictures and no Churchill turns down such an opportunity. Winston probably initiated it on the suggestion of Spyros P. Skouras, manager of Warner's theatre circuit. When the story leaked, Churchill denied that Diana was going into films. He said the test was just for fun. In her diary Sarah mentions her sister's 'hectic time out in America trying to get into films' but interestingly writes how preferable it would be for her to marry instead. When Diana saw her father and Miss Moir in Washington she was alarmingly high-spirited, possibly having had one dram too many. She treated onlookers at the Embassy to a Highland dance and chattered away nineteen to the dozen. Lecturing in DC, Winston was open about ring-fencing the Empire, stating that in India the British had maintained law and order more than they got credit for. Regarding deaths among Muslims and Hindus, he doubted that many more had been killed since Gandhi had been gaoled (certainly no more than New York and Chicago criminals imprisoned in the same period). Russia's great strides, he argued, were achieved through slavery.

With scotch and soda ('perfectly legal, diplomatic stuff') to fortify him, Winston and Britain's Ambassador tripped to Gettysburg and on 27 February he delivered his lecture, 'The Destiny of the English Speaking Peoples', to the Murat Theatre, Indianapolis. His first US broadcast aired on all Columbia Stations at 9 p.m. on 10 March with Edwin Hill interviewing. *The Washington Journal* hoped he would comment on UK censorship given the BBC's monopoly. At Hobcaw Barony they stayed a week with Bernie in his new fireproof house. His daughter Belle, who, on her horse Toto, had received a perfect score in a 1931 Paris show, showed Miss Moir, Thompson and Diana the South Carolina plantation. Saddling up, Diana told the mannish equestrienne that the expense of lessons had stymied her riding career. Belle's relationship with her parents was good, although nobody was open about that other kind of love.

The scaled-down liberty on the Île aux Cygnes made Sarah think of Papa. His silly investments are subtly referred to in her poem *January 1932* – also a comment on the level to which Britain had sunk. She desired to earn a living with her pen – not in journalism's masculine world but in novels, as F.E.'s Bohemian daughter Lady Eleanor Smith had with *Red Wagon*. The author showed guts living among circus people and gypsies. At a circus near Bournemouth she stood in for an equestrienne while Johnny C did double somersaults with the clowns. They talked of making a film of Lady E's book. Sarah's niece Arabella would, in years to come, display circus passions at Glastonbury. People praised Sarah's writing: but what had she produced? Grannie Jennie's exploits encouraged her. She had not only run a hospital ship in the Boer War but, upset at London's lack of a National Theatre, had organised a Shakespeare Ball in 1911 to begin paying for one, enlisting Shaw and Chesterton to furnish a brochure with their wit. 'There is no shame in exploiting a name!' Winston growled as he talked about Jennie: 'Leave no wire unpulled, no stone unturned, no cutlet uncooked!' Maxine

Elliot (the actress and businesswoman with whom he stayed in France) had also built a theatre herself.

Sarah sought to prove her worth with *Tessa*, about a girl from a fishing village with a modern mind. Mark is a visiting Bohemian. Tessa won't just hang up her nets and run off with him, even after a night blissfully spent 'talking philosophy'. Tessa torments him for drinking but in the end loses her inhibitions, jumping gaily into his two-seater and speeding off to London. She got 'historical', creating a saga crossing centuries, although the basic theme was how it hurts being young. Sarah frequently went to the cinema, noting up-and-coming stars like Dietrich.

Surprisingly, Diana seemed to lose interest in stardom. Harry Warner stated in a letter to Clementine that he would be in London around 15 March for Diana's re-test but it was days later when the reluctant starlet came home. Sarah abandoned *Tessa* around this time, yearning instead to 'bring laughter or tears to an audience'. Her diary at this time has her musing that acting was her 'great dream', reasoning that only through applause can one experience what its like 'to be really living'. If she made it as a writer she would give up her thespian dreams but by Gad, the stage was profitable!

Her sheltered background cries out when she writes: 'I love Pebin.' She refers to a play she, Pebs and Johnny were filming that summer and the dread of a love scene. She hoped it would be Johnny she had to swoon over. In January she had posted Pebs a letter – the kind you send and rue the day. Poems about him can't be found in her later verse collections. In one she pleads: 'Have you forgotten? Was it in vain? And of the past shall nothing remain. But like some melodie – faintly die, sobbing with pain – as a long-drawn sigh.' She also wrote a lot about death. To Diana, she asked what the 'point' was of all this 'fooling around with men'. Her sister said: 'It isn't natural to exclude men from your life or hate them.' But Sarah didn't hate men. She just found deeper meaning in art and writing.

Diana was herself in the slough of despond. Whilst at RADA she had an apartment in London but came down to Chartwell to 'vegetate and take a rest cure'. Her banjo-playing sister lightened her mood. Eleanor E. wrote to Sarah saying that her sister, too, was starting RADA and Sarah wished she were going. 'I want to act. I want to write. I want to dance,' replied the prisoner of Morpeth Mansions, whose notebooks held painful lines about restraining one's natural creativity.

At Chartwell Sarah found a Rupert Brooke volume among her birthday presents. He had been in Antwerp at the time of her birth, usually given as a Wednesday (7 October 1914) but her death certificate gives 6 October as her birth. People always said she was 'full of grace'. For her first 'grown up' cocktail party she put on a backless evening dress worrying about her knobbly backbone. A conjurer whipped £1 notes out of lemons and a mystic foretold the active life she would lead and that she would marry at 21. Her husband (connected with films and liable to leave her alone as he travelled) was apparently already familiar to her. At another party, in between shrimps and a 'thrilling' talk with Augustus John, a second fortune-teller told her 'a new era was opening'.

Her brother was now a *Daily Graphic* columnist writing presciently on 3 March about a hypnotic new leader espousing revenge and getting astonishing support. That May in Berlin one couldn't fail to observe this party's presence on Charlottenburger Chaussee. Randolph checked into 22 Regentenstraße (now Hitzigallee) alongside journalist Philippe Barres. He pulled a stunt in the lead-up to elections of 31 July, hiring a Ford Trimotor, the same aircraft Hitler used, to fly between cities. As a boy Randolph ran headlong into danger. He had been the first Churchill to get arrested (aged about ten) but he had Eleanor Smith's circle as models so it isn't surprising. Supposedly studying in Sloane Street, the girls were really writing a column for *The Weekly Dispatch* and achieving scoops pretending to be other people. Baby Jungman's *Anna Vorolsky* – a refugee from the Bolshevik Terror with pearls artfully spilling from her bag as she sobbed about the cost of her son's education – was one story people fell for. Eleanor and pal Allanah Harper went one further, dressing in men's clothes and taking the bus way down East to Limehouse to report on opium dens. Zita Jungman and Eleanor capped it with a night in the Chamber of Horrors. They influenced young Randolph, but when he came up with similar ideas it triggered his mother's ire. Descending on Sandroyd and catching him in mid-mischief with school chums, she gave him a mighty slap in front of future playwright Terry Rattigan whilst Sarah looked on. Mama never removed his desire for stunts or roving tendencies. Now in Karolinenplatz, Munich – the Nazi HQ – his ear was to the ground. Hitler, in power on 30 January 1933, had given his Brown House an anti-modernist makeover with a life-size portrait of Henry Ford, a bust of Mussolini and the blood-spattered NSDAP banner from the Beer Hall Putsch of 1923, lovingly revered as a 'blood flag'. When Sarah penned her next letter to Eleanor E she was less than ten minutes away.

Prof Lindemann had arranged a peregrination for her father to see where Marlborough won his victories and she and Mama came along for the ride. In Brussels, military historian Packenham-Walsh joined them and Randolph greeted them in Munich. They stayed three days at the Grand Hotel Continental on Max-Joseph-Straße. Sarah reported to Eleanor how Malplaquet and Ramillies were enjoyable but Germany's landscape of 'gigantic rolling waves' took her fancy most. She looked forward to *Blindheim* (Blenheim). Writing on 28 August she argued that the Teutons had more in common with the English than the French, apart from being vengeful and proud. She predicted France and Germany would go to war 15 years hence, with 'Old England' forced to 'trundle in' for France. Spending the night in the walled town of Rothenburg, she was awoken by strolling singers. She scrambled to the window but they went out of view and she 'wished she could have stopped time' as that moment felt 'immortal'.

Her father said he was willing to meet Herr Hitler so Randolph did his best to set it up, contacting Hanfstaengl (Hitler's Foreign Press Secretary) and inviting Hitler to dine at the Continental. In Hanfstaengl's memoir he states that Hitler was reluctant to come: 'What on earth would I talk to him about?' he said. Hanfstaengl turned up at Hitler's apartment at 16 Prinzregentenplatz to persuade him a second time. The Führer vacillated, doubting the significance of Churchill (then out of power).

Bob Boothby had observed after meeting the Führer that his English was riddled with mistakes. When Debo Mitford had tea with him five years later it hadn't improved. Self-consciousness might have made Hitler decline, although Clementine spoke German and would have been able to help him. The Press Secretary sat down, apologising for his absence. Sarah talked poetically about Germany and her father asked the German how his boss might feel about an alliance 'between your country, France and England' (even though, he stated, anti-Semitism was a 'bad sticker'). 'Transfixed' at this suggestion, Hanfstaengl gave his chief the lowdown. Sarah could so easily have dined with Hitler.

Just when Churchill had sufficient imagery for his book, the 57-year-old was struck down with paratyphoid and was put under Dr Petschacher's care at the heavily disinfected St Johann's Sanatorium. Sarah longed to escape the Salzach, the cathedral and the dull concerts. Her poem *Salzburg* expresses her love for England. Back at Chartwell with her Daddy not a well bunny in his invalid's chair, she wasn't a sensible nurse and when cousin Anita Leslie visited they surpassed themselves in the titter stakes when Randolph's £8 8*s*-a-night suite at the Mayfair Hotel was brought up (about £650). He was dining at Boulestin with H. G. Wells, discussing the hostile environments that meet writers with roving commissions. Wells took a shine to him and put him in *The Shape of Things to Come*, although the pacifist speeches his character gives hardly reflect the Randie everyone knew.

One young man her brother befriended in early 1932 was John Farrow. In the autumn of that year the Australian had adapted *Don Quixote* for a film directed by Pabst starring George Robey as Sancho Panza. Randolph's older sister seems to have been involved when scenes were shot in Nice, with a newspaper referring to her 'doing a little film acting'. Farrow might have been the one Harry Warner spoke of enlisting to provide a story for Diana. Newsmen speculated on a romance, though Churchill denied it. Then, after Robey and the Aussie clashed over how Panza ought to die, Farrow stormed off to Tahiti and Diana returned to London. Farrow's ambition and spiritual writing may have appealed to Diana. He had written about Catholic Father Damien who ministered to those in Molokai's leper colony. If the beginnings of a love affair had been cut short with the young lady's hopes dashed, it might have caused her to marry on the rebound. Sarah's obscure comment in her memoir about her sister being woefully in love with a sailor points to Farrow, a sailor before a producer passing through Tahiti got him a job in Hollywood.

Then an alternative suitor appeared: John Bailey, stockbroker son of family friend Sir Abe Bailey (gold mine operator and Boer War veteran). Nine years Diana's senior, John was eligible. To Eleanor, Sarah confided: 'I hope he will make a useful brother-in-law,' perhaps anticipating the literary career he would sponsor. Diana's engagement was announced with a wedding planned within a month. In late November 1932 the Baileys' townhouse at 38 Bryanston Square opened its doors to Sarah, her parents, Randolph, Jack and Goonie, the Duke of Marlborough, Ivor Churchill, Eddie Marsh, Lord Wimborne and several other Churchill intimates. Diana's theatrical associations can be seen by the presence of Reverend Basil Bourchier, Rector of the Actor's Church, Soho. Instead of a wedding bouquet she opted to carry a tiny prayer book.

Much planning went into the gowns, the bridesmaids wearing copies of the frock she wore at Diana Guinness's wedding with silver lamé instead of gold. If only the same thought had gone into the logistics of exiting St Margaret's. Footage shows the couple scurrying out only to walk into a mob blocking their way, forcing them down another path. Events like these saw the participation of local celebrities and peacock-plumed 'Prince Monolulu' (Epsom betting tipster) proved a life-saver, distracting the rabble with his cries of 'I got an 'orse!' The apartment the Baileys took at Hereford House, Marble Arch, was crammed with presents. John was close enough to her family to come to the funeral for Aunt Maudie, but differences soon emerged. His face betrayed someone prematurely aged by alcohol and in her straightforward way Diana Guinness simply referred to him as 'boring'. He hadn't been unattractive to Barbara Cartland (enterprising author, businesswoman and darling of F. E. Smith, Noël Coward and Beaverbrook and sister of Conservative MP Ronald). They enjoyed flirtation and fun in Deauville casinos and country houses. Before John married Diana, a letter he wrote to Winston refers to the 'patience' shown to him. Doubts necessitated a trust reassigning Diana's inheritance in the event of divorce. This was days before the marriage.

As Sarah's first manager, Clementine hoped for a return on investment from the Season. The notion, therefore, that Sarah might study dance was laughable. Having plotted to get Diana's film career off the ground, Mr and

Mrs Churchill's objection sounds hypocritical but this wasn't Hollywood and she would be starting at the bottom. Artist William Nicholson had planted the idea while painting her parents in early 1933. When he said his granddaughter Jenny was training at a London school he saw Sarah's eyes widen. A begging campaign commenced. She later claimed that 'we were brought up to be individuals, to stand on our own feet', but the truth was more a case of people being sick and tired of *Someone to Watch Over Me* played endlessly on the turntable. She had to go to one school or another before she married. She started out a Kitten, but everyone realised Sarah had been mistaken at birth. She was really a Mule. When permission came (obligations to the Season pending), the sound of great joy emanated from the nursery. While the slight prospect of Mrs Worthington's daughter ever getting an engagement triggered Papa's schoolboy humour, he admired a go-getter. In August the family went to Cannes for a fortnight. Inspired by Chanel's stylish villa and Maugham's Art Deco palace, Maxine Elliott's Chateau de l'Horizon provided guests with a water-chute to slide down. Sarah and Mama swam in a piscine perfumed with Eau de Cologne while a false moon lit al fresco diners. They had rooms in the villa but Randolph and Doris Castlerosse (swiped from Culross Street) stayed at the Carlton Hotel, Cannes. Winston loved these holidays, although a year later Mrs C and her dancing daughter chose to stay with the Carnegies in Arbroath rather than see Maxine.

The de Vos School, located above a bathroom store at 11–13 George Street and entered via Jacob's Well Mews, had been new to the area when William's Jenny first studied there in 1930. Ten de Vos branches had been established since. Audrey and Kathleen de Vos taught the Russian traditions to students with an average age of nine. Late starters like Sarah, who began in October 1933, got every encouragement and took exams accredited by the Royal Academy. Climbing three flights of stairs to the studio she suddenly felt at home. Dance was about *honesty*, even ecstasy when something was achieved perfectly. Audrey de Vos did everything to spot a dancer's faults. Knowing about sculpture and pathways of movement, she was ahead of her time. Dance was Jenny Nicholson's lifeblood. Her grandfather saw this quality and she appears in lively illustrations for his book *The Pirate Twins*. Miss de Vos loved Jenny and in 1960 had a photo in her office of the dancer striking a pose. At fifteen, Jenny formed The Patchwork Players with Doreen Seely, Sheila Melville and Kit Marks, choreographing dances to *Rhapsody in Blue* and other works. Sarah was in Jenny's ensemble playing a 'Gentleman' in *Cherry Stones*, but being so new, acted as the troupe's manager. Clementine worried about her adolescent daughter's gloom given her gothic poems and plays like *The Hand in the Dark* concocted that December with Esmond and Nellie.

Sarah still respected her peers. She shared ancestral ties with many of them but was happy to challenge what was perceived as her destiny. Duty meant bloodstock in the eyes of society elders. Along with Pam Mitford and Baby Jungman, Sarah had been a bridesmaid when cousin Cynthia (Lord Wimborne's daughter) married Thomas Talbot that December. After hanging out with the Asquiths and visiting the large country house of Panshanger near Hertford, she saw 1934 in with the Heathcoat-Amory family at Chevithorne Barton in Devon. Tom Mitford, she reported to her mother, surprised her by being less of his usual 'standoffish' self although Bill Astor was 'horrid, facetious and stupid'. The grandsons of Earl Wemyss, David and Martin Charteris (later Private Secretary to HM Queen Elizabeth II) were so shy she could barely talk to them. Their second cousins Ann and Laura Charteris were far easier to get on with. Sarah's favourite girl was Asquith's granddaughter Cressida. The toff she fell for was Sidney Herbert (later the Duke of Kent's Equerry).

Already forging a professional career, Jenny understood what it was to live in the shadow of a famous father, not that hers, the classical poet and writer of historical novels Robert Graves, had much of a place in her life. She hadn't seen him since she was eleven. Jenny liked fairytale actresses like Diana Cooper whilst Sarah stressed that her own calling was serious: 'My father and mother said that if I wanted to dance then it was all right, I could be a dancer provided I make a good one.' In Paddington Street Gardens with coats spread out on the grass, their conversation switched to love. They gossiped about Elizabeth Vyner Brooke. Hailing from the only English family to occupy an oriental throne (ruling Borneo for fifty years), Didi, as she was called, paid no lip service to killjoys. Unbelievably, it was her unconventional mother who wanted her to be an actress. She was now romancing bandleader Harry Roy. Sarah's experience in this was was lacklustre. She repeated to Jenny Pebin's solemn line: 'There are times when men have to be alone,' explaining how he bowed to pressure.

She heard about Jenny's 'liberal' upbringing and her feminist mother, Nancy Nicholson, who didn't take Graves' surname when they married, making Jenny do the same. Few knew she was his daughter as a result. Jenny's grandpa had eloped to marry years before and her Oxfordshire childhood had been artistic but she hated going about in dirty rags and clogs like an Augustus John gipsy. In 1926 a poetess came into her Pa's life causing him to bolt and set up in warmer climes. Graves and Laura Riding made a home at Deià, Mallorca, in 1930 on the advice of Gertrude Stein. By late 1934 when Korda bought the rights to his *I Claudius* novels, he wanted to make amends with Jenny who had received erratic support, contacting Nancy (then living a fiercely independent life on a houseboat at Hammersmith). The Spanish Civil War would bring him back.

Sarah was aware of another wife and husband living apart. Diana was now at 8 Gerald Road with John at Hyde Park Street. Measures were in motion to extinguish ties. John made it easy when the divorce was set down, sending her a receipt from the De Vere Hotel, Kensington (scene of a staged adultery). Then John proposed to Miss Cartland (then between marriages) but Babs, though proud of the fact that John was 'madly in love' with her, refused. She dreaded seeing Mrs Churchill and Diana. Sarah would look back on the Season saying that many married under pressure with devastating results. While good friends Ann Hotham and Sheila Berry married Tony Bazley and Freddy Birkenhead, she remained *mulish*; likely to eat the Castle Howard tulips that came in every colour at Geoffrey Howard's ball at 21 Hyde Park Square. Her mother found divorce odious. Having no choice but to put up with it, she clashed with her eldest girl. Being the first to take that dreadful action, Diana had broken a taboo. Her brother and sister would find divorce less of a millstone.

'Dianas of Modern Days' was a ballet routine put on by the de Vos girls at a ball at Nottingham's Highfields Park in November 1934. Over Christmas and New Year, the Churchills went to Blenheim except for Clementine, who was in tropical climes on Lord Moyne's yacht. Sarah wrote imagining her chasing butterflies with her attractive fellow passenger Mr Philip running after her shouting, 'Hi not so fast, I can't keep up!' Sarah went to the Glamorgan Hunt Ball at Cardiff's Drill Hall, dancing with Harry Llewellyn (later Grand National and Olympics champion) and there was cricket with Dick 'Bolshie' Sheepshanks, a rival to Harry. Lithe on the dancefloor and urbane in conversation, the Reuters ace was the cousin of Anthony Blunt. Only older Sidney Herbert, with whom she dined at Violet Bonham Carter's, gave her a thrill. She wore her new evening dress from Miss Munn's for the occasion. In the run-up to the Wavertree by-election Randolph stood as Independent Conservative, opposing the party line on Indian Home Rule and challenging indifference regarding rearmament. Lady Houston was his angel. Horrified at PM MacDonald's failure to strengthen the Navy and Air Force, she used her fortune to help develop the Rolls Royce S-6 seaplane, direct predecessor of the Spitfire, and threw money at Randolph's campaign.

In early January 1935 Sarah threw aside leggings and pumps. After dancing late into the night at St James's Square with Victor Cazalet, she was bright-eyed setting off for South Liverpool. In the suburbs Diana and Sarah chatted to housewives and attached a huge Vote Randolph poster to his Rolls. Her sister seemed a little less highly strung but Sarah still pondered: 'I hope she will meet someone soon. She seems to have so little in her life.' Their brother barked commands and fought a fierce campaign. He knew his photogenic sisters increased public interest so off went the trio, charming potential women voters including factory workers and laundry girls. Randolph's ability to put down a speech at lightning speed and read it without prompts left people in awe. His father, by contrast, slaved over speeches making the home atmosphere Stygian until they were complete. Randolph got the crowd laughing and his sister wrote how, after asserting the right to free speech of every Englishman, he was 'literally worshipped'. Cries of 'Randolph 'ope and glory!' said it all.

Growing up, Churchill's children had learned not to flinch at earfuls of verbal abuse. Violence was another matter. At Liverpool's docks a brick missed Sarah by inches. Responsible for their safety, Randolph entrusted a writer on *The Post*, Bill Deedes, to take his sisters home. When Diana stepped off the train carrying a huge bouquet from a function she had earlier attended, there were cries of 'She's got married again' as Deedes and Diana were mistaken for a couple. The Beaverbrook Press called Randolph 'The Fat-Boy of Wavertree' after a speech annoyed them. Political pundits knew he would split the vote and cause Wavertree (a Conservative stronghold) to slip over to Labour. Winston was against the candidacy but spoke on his son's behalf at Liverpool's Sun Hall. A week before polling, Randolph got the jitters, asking Sarah to amass admirers to canvass on his behalf. He overestimated her capacity to vamp. All these men excused themselves, except Harry Llewellyn and his brother David.

It was a case of *I told you so* when the result came in. Randie was a gallant loser. Despite admiring him, Sarah observed wryly to her Mama that, had he won, 'he would have been impossibly conceited'. Diana was the focus of Winston's sympathies. He took her to the cinema and they discussed Sarah's chances of acting success. Helping in Papa's constituency, and in a second campaign by Randolph funded by Lady Houston, lessened Diana's twentieth-century blues. In the Norwood by-election her brother fielded an Independent Conservative, Richard Findlay, whose brief flirtation with the British Union of Fascists (BUF) muddied the waters. Lord Rothermere had been pro-BUF but withdrew support and Randolph was doomed. He challenged the Conservative Unionist candidate Duncan Sandys to answer questions about India. Once the driving force of The British Movement, Duncan wouldn't tie himself down over Indian Home Rule as Randolph had. Findlay lost Norwood, Duncan won and on 24 July 1935, a month after Baldwin replaced MacDonald, the Government of India Act got assent. Winston sighed, knowing the bugbear had been fought to please him. The one who did best was Diana. She had only seen Duncan from a distance during the campaign but he was tall, handsome and had red hair.

The pacifist voice remained strong regardless of Mussolini's flagrant subversion in Abyssinia. Winston's talk of continental tyrants and 'dangers from within' got him labelled a warmonger. Baldwin never offered him a post in 1935 but he was put on the Air Defence Research Committee, allowing him to oversee developments in defence technology with access to the Admiralty. Despite Prof Lindemann's drubbing of technology and prickly relationship with former Berlin colleague Henry Tizard, new Radar Stations were springing up. At Chartwell, Winston's ingenuity conquered the forces of nature. His swimming pool was heated so even on horrid rainy days they could cavort in lovely warm water. That summer he could be a devil, pushing unsuspecting people in the pool. When not diving Sarah was pirouetting on a low wall, silent in an Eleusinian Mystery.

When Eleanor E came on 10 May they discussed Sarah's Bassano portraits to advertise her for stage work. Hearing a noise, they looked out the window and saw Lawrence of Arabia on his large motorbike. Eleanor thought it quaint the way his tin mug hung from the handlebars by a shoelace. His blue eyes shone and he was small and thin. When he was lent one of Sarah's father's dinner jackets later that day, the girls giggled seeing his hands disappear in the sleeves. There was more engine noise when Randolph pulled up in his silver sportster. He insisted on taking them out and soon they were winding through country roads at 100 mph with Randolph chatting incessantly whilst negotiating blind bends. White-faced, they rejoiced on seeing the house again. With the night air so lovely they pitched camp beds on the terrace and couldn't help but overhear Winston and Randolph in the room above the verandah. The former spoke harshly but offered to pay an overdraft and the conversation ended lovingly. Later that evening Eleanor was surprised to find Lawrence sitting at the end of her camp bed. He liked to watch the stars. He spoke of things they had never before conceived; hours passed and they were still travelling in their imaginations. Eleanor was so gripped she hardly noticed Lawrence stroking her toes tenderly. They fell into a blissful sleep when he left. A week later Eleanor heard of Lawrence's death when he went over the handlebars of his Brough Superior SS100 in a collision near his cottage in Clouds Hill, Wareham. This was the man Mr Churchill regarded as a genius. Sarah wept copiously, telling Eleanor how much she had loved him.

'Mr Churchill's Daughter To Marry "Baby" of the House of Commons' was how Diana's engagement to 27-year-old Duncan was announced on 24 August. When the Sandys marriage was blessed at St Ethelburga's the ceremony was held up pending the arrival of the bride's sisters, one rushing from an audition. Despite rumours he was retiring, theatrical impresario and talent-seeker C. B. Cochran always had a bunch of musical comedies and dramas on the go. By the end of October, the theatrical press learned that *Follow the Sun* would see a Manchester Christmas season before going to London's Adelphi Theatre. Fast-talking comic Vic Oliver was in its list of principals and the Cochran Young Ladies were to number 25. Desiree Moore, one of the Patchwork Players, was hired, plus Jenny, who had already been in *Anything Goes*. Sarah requested an audition at the Palace Theatre. Under bright lights on a stage with one of the steepest rakes she did three dances while CB watched, noting how plain her costume was. A tap to *Smoke Gets In Your Eyes* was followed by an acrobatic routine and finally she proved herself en pointe. Learning that Cochran had spoken to Papa before agreeing to audition her, she tried not to let it bother her. Winston wrote on 22 October giving approval. The draw of having a Churchill in a West End revue was huge and CB was relieved she didn't opt for a stage name. Engaged at £4 per week, the chorus had sessions in the Stoll Theatre, Kingsway. November came and cast and crew left St Pancras for the frozen north. At the Opera House in Manchester's Quay Street, Sarah was determined to make a success of it.

An instinct keeps living things in pursuit of the sun and Cochran's biggest revue to date developed the theme of being 'led by the dance'. It caused Sarah Churchill's satellite to smash into Vic Oliver's star. Cochran saw Vic at the Holborn Empire in November 1934 and, while his overuse of the word 'lousy' grated on his nerves, signed him up on account of his faultless timing. The biggest name was Claire Luce who had filmed with Bogart and Tracy in *Up the River* and been Astaire's stage partner in *Gay Divorce*. The applause Claire got after 'Dangerous You' (her closing dance) held up the show every night. Ravishing and recently divorced, she counted Randolph among her legion of admirers. CB indulged her and every strop was forgiven.

A contrast to the huge Opera House where the show opened on 23 December was Sarah's digs in Chorlton-on-Medlock. Little backstreets running to the rear of the Church of the Holy Name brimmed with life before demolition in the 1960s. There were two theatrical boarding houses and Sarah's was Mrs Thomas's at 16 Ackers Street. A hot dinner was served each night and the children outside bid the russet-haired young lady 'Good morning' before resuming their skipping. As well as Cochran's Young Ladies, fifty dancers were hired; some with no qualms about nudity and one who liked to compare the end of the guide rope to a penis, teasing Sarah for being a virgin.

One young lady, Pamela Gordon (daughter of Gertrude Lawrence), said of Sarah: 'I thought she was charming but a bit aloof. Then I discovered the reason. She was terribly shy.' The theatre folk were kind, but Sarah sometimes returned to Ackers Street in tears. She was determined to prove herself. One thing she never anticipated was striking up a friendship with a man twice her age. *The First Shoot* was a short ballet by Osbert Sitwell about countryhouse life with music by William Walton and Fred Ashton devising choreography, in between bedding partners of different sexes. Cecil Beaton designed a backcloth of swirling mauves and pale greens for the scene when Lord Charles Canterbury points a gun at Lady de Fontenay (Claire Luce in a Parma violet gown) mistaking her for a prize game. 'The Pheasants', among them Sarah, Jenny and pretty Ann Clare (daughter of actress Mary Clare), performed an intricate routine with fingers curled in a claw-like manner.

It was during these rehearsals that Vic Oliver became aware of Sarah. Fred loved to mimic and at a party did a Cochran Young Lady parody that could only have been aimed at Sarah. Only she wore her skirt on her hips, revealing her navel. When it became rude, off-duty Vic got uppity and leapt to her defence. He called at Ackers Street and asked her out. She wondered if it might be a prank but the twinkly blue-eyed six-footer seemed sincere. The schtick was nowhere to be found and his European accent only emphasised his earnestness. She accepted his curious invitation, noticing his cleft chin and well-kept hands. He wasn't handsome but beautifully dressed, just like he was on stage. At the Midland Hotel he told her about Ashton's parody. Allegiance is a good tactic in getting close to shy girls. On successive assignations she would hide in doorways and get scooped into his car as they rode off to Buxton and other villages for tea. Vic took her to *Tonight at 8.30* with Noël Coward and Gertrude Lawrence before it left Manchester. Its characters had that frivolous manner then in vogue; a quality Diana possessed but one that didn't come natural to Sarah.

Oliver's experiences in America fired her fantasies. She spoke about her grandmother's family and her bloodline to Princess Pocahontas; a fanciful claim seeded by the siblings in childhood. Touched by her breeding and strong sense of right and wrong, Vic grasped her latent energy and fire, recognising it as the same that allowed him to break his own confines. Sarah had an outlet for her creativity and felt far less alone. She yearned to be loved and protected. Vic succeeded because for the first time in her life she placed someone above her parents. For years she had hidden things, fearing hurting Papa and Mama. She still appeared introverted but she had undergone a complete turnaround. So blinkered was Mule, a likely collision course with her parents meant nothing to her. Vic thought her bold choosing the arts. To educate her further he took her to Grosvenor House's Annual Variety Ball on 14 November. Many famous names were present including Mary Brian – the star of an early Peter Pan film. 'It's my favourite story,' she told Vic as he squeezed her hand. It was polling day for the General Election. To the rear of the band were four thermometers (for 'Labour', 'National', 'Liberal' and 'Other Parties'). 'National' with its Conservative majority won, staying in power until 1945 and Stanley Baldwin became PM. Sarah surprised Vic by revealing her practical experience of politics. It dawned on him how untypical her family was.

He promised to help her when the show ended – the kind of offer only a fool turns down. Everything happened fast and it was still November when, on a weekend trip to London, she introduced Vic to Diana and Duncan. The four dined and went to a play. The following month the foursome made a trip to the circus. Diana's approval meant everything. Vic and Sarah secretly became engaged on the lead-up to opening night – the maddest time. A rebel spirit took hold and she girded herself against the coming intimidation.

Mrs Churchill was expected at the Opera House première on one of the foggiest nights of the year. She was there a couple of days prior to her skiing holiday with Mary. She admired Pamela Stanley, who had performed Shakespeare and portrayed Queen Victoria before marrying Sir David Cunynghame and leaving the stage. Privately, Clementine didn't think Sarah shared her talent and hoped her experience would be chastening, as Diana's stab at films had been. In scene 12 it took her time to recognise Sarah in Mozart's Vienna with all the eighteenth-century wigs. Another Komisarjevsky-directed tableau was the festive 'Three Holy Kings' in scene 5. Glyndebourne soprano Fräulein Eisiger was the voice and also sang 'Love is a Dancing Thing', the show's big number. Scene 13 had the 'Young Ladies' as a gulp of cormorants strutting around a ship's deck with their backs to the audience before bending to fly off and revealing frilly knickers. 'How High Can a Little Bird Fly' caused a few more gulps.

On the second day, over dinner, Sarah came clean about her hope to marry Vic Oliver. Clementine took a deep breath and considered Sarah's youth. It wasn't a surprise that she should fall in love with an actor, but she suspected that the snake-like comedian had been married before and was fuelling Sarah's foolish dream of stardom. Visions came of an ugly slave driver lining up undignified work. She and Sarah faced each other like two figurines wrought from the thinnest crystal, mother paler than an Arctic sky and daughter with head bent. Clementine said how she had come to like Duncan and how they had first been staggered to learn of Diana's choice. He had no money. Vic, at least, was a high earner. They said goodbye and Sarah was told not to worry. Winston's letter from Hotel Balima required a response, but his wife didn't answer. Appearing serene, she invited Vic and Sarah to Chartwell on the only day they could spare, Sunday 29 December, to give the situation her fullest assessment. The impeccably dressed man felt honoured to be there and Sarah gave him a tour. As soon as they left Mrs Churchill took out paper and pen to brief Winston, her composure dissipating.

# 4

# He Who Divided Us

In Clementine's day, one ignored actors who stepped over the footlights and into the drawing room: but Anne Seymour Brokaw had married Henry Fonda, Sandra Shaw was now Mrs Gary Cooper and Phyllis Baker Livingston Potter was Mrs Fred Astaire. England was different. Traditionally, if an officer in the Guards married an actress he was expected to resign. Mrs Churchill was more inculcated with ideas of birthright and preserving the stock than her husband and a far cry from Sylvia Brooke, who rejoiced when Didi married down, although when their youngest gal married wrestler Bob Gregory in 1938 this was going too far.

Winston was at Hotel Mamounia as he opened his wife's letter. Seated by his easel, his alarm was expressed in violent reds and oranges. A mind troubled by social-climbing villains and Samaritans seeking salvation created 'Sunset Over the Atlas Mountains'. Clementine's next letter on 30 December suggested he write to Sarah without being too severe. At New Year the lovebirds came to London. Sarah thanked Mama for the day at Chartwell, apologising for setting her holiday back a day. She was aware of the stress created: 'I hope the time will come soon when you will forget the misery of the last few months – I hope too that I shall be able to forget that I caused them.' She admitted that Duncan and Diana knew and that the four of them had gone out twice. Vic was often at the Mayfair cabaret and fellow denizen Claire Luce was sympathetic, so Randolph knew.

The public, meanwhile, were still entranced by *Swallow the Fun*, as the girls had started calling the show. Whether announcing 'Innovations of 1945' or as Claire Luce's sarcastic Footman, Vic held the audience rapt. Scene 10 had the loudest music from Ciro Rimac and his Rumbaland Muchachos (discovered in Holland by CB) offering demoniacal movement and Cuban rhythm. The theatre woke up to the flashing eyes of Carito, Ofelia and Cuncita and their bare stomachs. The only flaw was seeing English cast members in the same attire. 'En masse, English stomachs are pretty forbidding, don't you think?' one theatregoer was overheard saying.

Perhaps the only 'Young Lady' whose Pa didn't have means was Jeni Le Gon. In Hollywood she sang and danced with Bill Bojangles and Fats Waller and was one of the first black actresses at MGM. It didn't get her far, so she joined Cochran's show. Touted as the new Florence Mills, Jeni was doing toe stands and spins fifty years before Michael Jackson.

*Follow the Sun* opened at the Adelphi on 28 January 1936 a week after the death of George V. One critic wrote: 'Never has so much dancing of so many different kinds been offered to the London public under one roof.' The revue cost £20,000 and boasted the most completely dressed chorus ever on a London stage: 1,200 costumes and 800 pairs of shoes. Vic's sister Lilly, whose life had been dominated by textiles and *Jugendstil*, had set up a clothing business in London. Costumiers Barbara Karinsky, Ada Peacock and Reville put work her way. Her staff included Islington-born Alice Luckett who had a husband invalided from a wartime mustard gas attack and two teenage daughters, Elise and Phyllis, but she was widowed soon after getting the job with Lilly. Phyllis begged her mother to let her go on the stage. Alice had been proud to see her girl dance in local events but was set against it. Phyllis kept asking and Lilly and Vic, whom the Lucketts knew well, got drawn in. Vic said he'd act as her guardian and keep an eye on her. Aged fourteen, Phyllis became a Sherman Fisher girl at the Palladium, appearing by Royal Command.

Everyone gasped at the Hogarth-inspired 'Strolling Actresses in a Barn' with the cast in eighteenth-century dress. By a clever metamorphosis they changed from sepia to showgirls in a modern dressing room. Clementine sighed. anticipating her baby's Hogarthian fall. Winston came a month later and Sarah went through her 36 costume changes. Viola Tree never forgot her father's 1906 production of *Nero* at His Majesty's when the then MP for Manchester North West joined the Trees in their box. Seeing Constance Collier on stage, Winston remarked: 'What wonderful hair she is wearing.' The funny thing was Miss Collier was wearing her own hair. Outside the Adelphi, Sarah told reporters: 'I've great dreams for the future. I'm going to work as hard as I can.' To friends she spoke about keeping one's feet on the ground: 'I have large feet. It's the only thing I have in common with Garbo.' Untypical in looks, she had to prove her talent too. She was soon understudying Claire, performing 'Dangerous You', flitting between suitors: a poet, a man-about-town, a soldier and a tough. Her colleagues' praise touched her more than anything although Claire's refusal to allow the dress to be fitted to her figure caused umbrage. Sarah got the dresser to do it all the same. 'Ah those blue sequins,' she later sighed. 'They were quite something!'

At Morpeth Mansions on 1 February Papa summoned her and got assurances that she would not act hastily. Diana, who had come to know Vic and liked him, was made to highlight her hastiness with Bailey. Winston's meeting with the man in question was on 15 February with Sarah present. Refusing to shake his hand, he then heard the worst: that Vic hadn't gained US citizenship. The Austrian owned up to having been married twice (the second a marriage of convenience, he claimed). Immediately, Mr Churchill launched into why they shouldn't marry. He demanded they separate for one year, having no communication throughout this time. If they wished to marry after he would not oppose it. If they refused he would make their lives difficult. The threat was calculated to hurt and it was a triumph seeing Vic perturbed and ousted. 'It's who the person is as a human being, not marriage, that draws me,' Sarah cried out pathetically. She ran after him. Without Vic she couldn't grow. She would be stuck.

Winston was fluid in emotion in a three-page letter he wrote to his daughter on 18 February. In almost religious terms he explained it was his duty to guide her and made no secret of his concerns and that an investigation was the only way to elicit facts regarding Vic's heritage and past. Over ten years later this letter went missing, emerging at auction but forever eluding the family's efforts to get it back. Winston was busy with his articles for the *Evening Standard* but couldn't stop worrying. Getting her away from Vic was his aim and appealing to her ambition was worth a try. He enlisted Brendan Bracken to pull strings to get her an apprenticeship. Pempie Dudley Ward was at Liverpool Rep and Bracken, her secret admirer, asked her about Sarah. Winston didn't know that his daughter resented his interference. She was making her mark single-handedly for the first time and this self-reliance would forever be important. 'Of course I have benefitted from my father's position,' she said decades on: 'but I also think what I have done professionally I have done on my own.' New York lawyers Chadbourne, Stanchfield & Levy (CSL) had represented Maxine and provided legal assistance for Winston's lecture tour of 1931–32. Their job was to dig up court records on Oliver's past.

So far Vic was down a few points, but a sportsman doesn't give in. Opposition can be a great motivation. He went for her like a dog after a bitch; or was it bitch after dog? It was the kind of thing a father couldn't control. That first year Vic beckoned and encouraged. Conventions were to be cut through. He pointed to a way of seizing life guilt-free.

He held the cards. He had 'It'. He wasn't 'common as dirt'. He was the opposite, despite a chequered past. Sarah listened to his talk about music lifting people into higher states – even those with the basest characters. And he could play! He wasn't 'a fiddler of the ordinary stripe' either. He thought with his heart and was courteous and kind. He had weathered the storms throughout the 'lives' he had lived, which Sarah suspected were many. Ever the 'aristocrat', one thing was certain: if the world were coated in dirt you could guarantee he'd come up shining. He was the first one who cut through the tripe, the one who saved her.

He came from culture, was a musical aesthete, but there was an alienated rebel below the surface. Staying one step ahead makes you lonely. It paid to be fearless in late-imperial Austria. As an 11-year-old in his *Gymnasium* he took risks nobody else would, creeping into his master's room and forging his exam paper with seconds to spare before certain discovery. Vic apparently had a university education, continuing music separately with courses in orchestration, counterpoint and conducting at Vienna's Conservatory (although he never claimed to have completed lengthy studies). An interview reveals that he studied under violinist Otakar Ševčík for three years. Ševčík was director of the Violin Department at the Vienna Music Academy from 1909 to 1918. His pioneering method of teaching violin, études and exercises was published widely and is still used today. No records remain of Vic in Vienna's universities. They elude the archives of the Academy/Conservatory and Neues Wiener Konservatorium, although there might have been a later cull of records relating to students with a Jewish heritage. In his memoir Vic mentions private tuition (in violin from Karl Knoll and piano from the brutal Moritz Rosenthal). He could write out musical scores by ear after visiting the Opera. He says that at Baden bei Wien the resort's orchestra let him conduct his own scores and offered him an assistant conductorship. Ševčík was concertmaster in Salzburg so Vic might have been here, too. Not everyone needs a long stint at a school. Besides, few among Vic's contemporaries could turn cartwheels while playing violin as he did at the Hackney Empire during his long summer as one of Britain's finest comedians. In 1945 he formed the British Concert Orchestra (BCO) and while he did variety, pantomimes and made recordings, he was the only man who achieved pre-eminence both as a humorist and a conductor. In July 1963 at Croydon's Fairfield Halls he was supported by Eileen Broster, whom he knew from BBC concert broadcasts. Eileen played piano with Vic conducting the BCO, which was not a chamber ensemble but a full-sized symphony orchestra:

> There was nothing he did to distract from his conducting – no desire to tell jokes. He was fully engaged concentrating on music and points of expression. He had an intimate knowledge of the pieces we played such as Mendelssohn's concerto and the Schumann concerto. There was never enough time for practicing prior to performance. It was a tense experience – lots of anticipation. Vic was a very sensitive conductor and very good at

> conducting a concerto. You got his undivided attention. He was courteous – the sort of man who wouldn't raise his voice. If someone repeatedly made a mistake he took them aside, never humiliating anyone.

A little while later Eileen was asked by Vic to perform works by Grieg with the BCO at Portsmouth Hippodrome. The Henry Wood Prom Circle was a club where prominent artists gave recitals and spoke. Eileen heard Vic speak here. He talked about Churchill. He was sad the establishment weren't interested in music, believing that all children should learn an instrument. He singled out Eileen in the audience so she never forgot the evening. One of Vic's last stage partners (who acted as his secretary) was Vanda Vale, whom Eileen remembers as 'very actressy, very glamorous, very nice'. In a radio programme Vanda says that Vic's presence in cities and towns touring with the BCO exposed ordinary people to classical music for the first time. In her cutglass, almost Sarah Churchill voice she concludes: 'If you can do two or three shows then jump in a car and drive 300 miles, if you can rehearse for hours without a break then you should apply for a job with Vic Oliver!' Vanda was a regular on *This is Show Business*, a frighteningly live TV show that ran between 1952 and 1957 (with Vic in white tie and tails beside a full orchestra) with star guests such as Zsa Zsa Gabor. Robb Wilton forgot his lines, said 'sorry' and somehow got back on track. Vic was kind, saying, 'Come back any time, Robb.' It ended with the guests saying goodnight to the doorkeeper. Vic was the last to leave. Vanda was the 'nuisance' character to 'Oliver' (which is how she addressed him – by his surname only). That they were annoyed with each other was the running joke.

Gavin Doyle toured with him in *Let Yourself Go* in October 1951 and wrote about how Vic's women had well-bred accents, played Canasta, had flat chests, wore twin-sets and took spaniels for walks. Two among the ever-changing singers in the 'Girlfriends of Song' spot in Vic's line-up were Sylvia Campbell and June Oliver, who began working with Vic aged 16. The entourage went everywhere in a chauffeur-driven Bentley. One thing that's clear about Vic is he needed loyal, dependent women. For each of his wives he chose a woman much younger. A mother who flits back and forth like a butterfly until deciding one day to leave the family might have contributed to this, were one to ask Dr Freud (operating in Vienna all the time Vic lived there). In *Mr Showbusiness,* Vic's memoir, he mythologises his 'ballerina' mother from the moment his father sees her at the opera. His stepmother's mother was the only noted ballerina in the family and he seems to have substituted her in his book. He adds that his mother was young and of a lower rank, embodying all that was frivolous about Belle Époque Vienna. Obstacles stand in his parents' way. But what do obstacles matter? When Vic fell for Sarah they didn't. Viktor Samek senior, Vic's father, is blinded by his love for Josefa. 'Come to Monte Carlo,' she says. Like a lamb he follows, losing heavily at roulette. He never blames her.

It was near that joyful place, their summer home at Baden bei Wien, that Vic Oliver came into the world. 'Viki' was the name most people knew him by. His grandfather Jakob Samek and his brothers, after living for generations in Bučovice, founded a factory in Brünn in 1863, specialising in cloth for formal and military suits made from the finest black worsted yarns from the Cheviots. The Sameks, along with other German-speaking Jewish families like the Löw-Beers, played their part in what was then a thriving 'Moravian Manchester'. Things hadn't always been so good but Napoleon's emancipation laws and Bismarck's measures to weaken Austria benefitted Jewish businessmen. The Sameks imported technology and skilled international workers from Britain and Holland. Their weaving mill became a state-of-the-art factory at Cejl 70, the building still standing in the street in what is now Brno. Jakob, who also ran a savings bank, was given the right, in 1872, to use the Imperial Eagle on the official seal of Bruder Samek Brünn (BSB). The boom ended when the new states created after the Great War began protecting their industries. Although Jews owned half Germany's textile firms and were the biggest players in Austrian ready-to-wear by 1929, Czechoslovakia was a limited market and BSB's future was in international sales. When Viki was ten the business had branches in Vienna, Berlin, Paris and London and exported to Australia, America, Amsterdam, Portugal, and Poland. British Samek Ltd was at 2 Saville Row. Another company, Wain Shiell & Sons Ltd of London and Huddersfield, was closely linked to the family. Viki's uncle Robert (Jakob's eldest son) sat on several trade boards and developed the brand in the decades of its greatest influence.

The Sameks had a position, and reputation counted. Josefa was a distraction to Viktor in 1892 at exactly the time that he took a senior role managing the family business. Being an individualist with a love of theatre and actresses, Viki's father, the second eldest, left BSB's board to 'devote himself to other ventures'. While Robert's younger brothers Karl and Hans supported him on the production side, Viktor senior later ran the retail business in Vienna with seven salesmen. Comments Vic made about having been to Huddersfield and Manchester long ago suggest he accompanied *Vati* on trips here aged 17 (1912–13). A newspaper ad shows Viktor senior could pay generously for an English shorthand typist at his 'American Accountancy' while another has him seeking a recruit to reside full board at Alsersgaße 12. The business would pass out of Samek ownership in 1926. It underwent 'Aryanization' in 1938 and a restitution process after 1946. It remains a gentleman's outfitters to this day. Vic's father's expertise was trusted and matters sartorial obsessed him, as did personal hygiene. He took his meals in the bathroom. Hans also had one or two peculiar Germanic traits. Viki enjoyed a lot of privilege during his first 25 years, but that world where snobbery and double standards were rife was crumbling.

The Sameks were typical of the secular Jews of Moravia, superficially embracing Christian worship whilst seeing themselves as Jews and marrying Jews. Only family elders went to the synagogue. Viki's family were outwardly Christian. Lilly was two years older (born in June 1894). His parents didn't marry until April 1896, three months before Viki was born on 8 July 1896. One might think that Viktor's having a child out of wedlock would have caused a scandal in Old Vienna but mistresses with children were common and the family wanted Josefa to stay one. One detects that the clan's deep-rooted hostility to her caused the delay of Viktor's marriage until it became unavoidable. But the dislike had much to do with her being Roman Catholic. By not marrying in the faith Viktor Samek Senior broke ranks. There were plenty of other reasons to dislike Josefa. She was a gold-digger and free spirit. Perhaps the family's objections had more to do with her indiscretions than her religion, artistic leanings, or class. Viktor did the honourable thing in making his children legitimate, not that it stopped Josefa scandalising him with her flirtations. Before five years were up they were divorced. Vic brushes over all these issues although he admits that when *Mutti* left, mealtimes became dour.

Josefa's singing talent and charm gave her a means of independence. She sang in public under her maiden name 'Josefa Rauch'. The few accounts of her in the press have an air of fin-de-siècle extravagance. She morphed into the lady singer from late 1902, travelling where the money was, between the resort of Łańcut and fashionable Vienna suburbs. While on board ship she is reported (under the headline 'Latest Thefts from the Rich') as carelessly leaving 190 Kronen and a case of jewels valued at 1000 Kronen unattended. These were all stolen. Josefa had already made the Vienna papers in 1900 named as the lover of temperamental businessman Karl Hölst. 'Mark this, Josefa!' he apparently shouted, vowing to shoot her after she refused marriage. Vic was only four at the time. In 1906 she remarried. Paul Johann Grüssner was a keen sportsman, alpinist, cyclist and automobilist. Despite the scandalous way she had behaved, she came to Graz's Christian Women's Federation in 1907 to sing songs.

Josefa was punished for bolting and forbidden from seeing her children until limited access was granted. Viki had the makings of a tragicomic outsider. He and Lilly suffered for their mother's conduct. He longed for his mother and struggled to make sense of the world. Added to this, patrilineal Jews weren't recognised according to *halachah*. Nevertheless, pride in their family is seen in the essay Lilly wrote about sheep's wool for her exam at the

Mädchen-Lyzeum. In Vic's memoir, his condemnatory family hangs over him like a spectre. He never mentions the talented Sameks who succeeded in fields like sport and music. Uncle Hans (youngest sibling in his father's family) was a world-class golfer and writer whose influence enabled Viki to contribute to *Sport im Bild* – the first German illustrated sports magazine.

Vienna was the centre of Viki and Lilly's world. Newspapers from 1912 mention the success Viki O. Samek had in lawn tennis tournaments. The 'likeable player' won the men's singles and doubles. At the same time his football team – the High Gamblers – thrashed the Vienna High Club at Graz. He even played Sunderland FC when they visited Vienna as part of a tour of Hungary, Austria and Germany (late in the 1913 season). A regular visitor to the Spanish Riding School at Michaelerplatz, Viki and his sister (married to Georg Berger from 1915 to 1921) loved horses. Although Vic shares origins and a Catholic conversion with Mahler, the story that he had tuition from him seems unlikely as the latter left for America when Viki was eleven. Unlike Mahler, Viki had little exposure to the poor. Perhaps this is why in his act he played a character both pompous and manqué. After a violin warm-up he would go off-key at the vital moment, throwing in a gag: 'I once played for Toscanini (pause) – just once!' A social conscience is perhaps hinted at in the name 'Viki Oliver Samek'. He talked of the name Oliver coming from a certain Oliver von Loudon, apparently his godfather, but Dickens' *Oliver Twist* is a likelier source. The novels were popular in German-speaking countries, with several translations. Vic's sympathy for orphans ran in the family. Grandpa Jakob's humanitarian gestures included a Widows and Orphans Fund.

He entered the Imperial and Royal Dragoons and was a non-commissioned Officer in November 1915. There's no truth in the claim that he served alongside Hitler (who failed the Austrian Army's entry exam and joined the Bavarian Reserves, serving in France and Belgium). The Austro-Hungarian Army needed to be entertained and talent didn't go unnoticed. A news item from December 1915 highlights the celebrity of two army comics who did recitals and songs whilst Archduke Heinrich Ferdinand photographed them keenly. His older brother Archduke Peter, a war hero, thanked the raconteurs. With a similar performance, Vic won their praise too. So special was Peter's regard that he ensured his protégé was never placed in danger. The same age as Vic's father, Peter thought Viki's contribution unique. The dynamics of the friendship is uncertain. What Vic mostly did for most of the war was raise funds for Homes For War Blind by entertaining and selling badges; the sums regularly reported in the press. In early 1916 he was stationed at Teschen where he entertained men including Heinrich Benedikt. The latter became a historian and mentions Viki in his memoir, saying that before the Great War Vic had been to America – 'as was usual with a good-for-nothing'. How else could Vic produce something 'unknown to our continent' at the piano? Vic's Great War history goes hazy when he becomes personal adjutant to Prince Rene Bourbon of Parma. His claim that he was friendly with the Hapsburgs is probably true, as Lilly moved in these circles. A newspaper confirms Vic had a flat in Vienna and a small stable with horses. Despite the war, he ran an enterprise storing and selling automobiles, aged only 20. He was imprudent and ran up debts. Viktor Senior, impressed by the names in his son's circle, overlooked this. Vic tells us he hated being 'protected' while friends were getting killed and entered the fight, receiving a small wound. Years later he would come on stage wearing showy medals and begin an engaging story about 'how he earned them in 1917' … cue *Stars and Stripes Forever* getting louder and louder until its so DEAFENING, he's drowned out. The whole time he's talking German gibberish.

Viki married in September 1916. Both Viktor Senior and Lilly opposed it, but Vic got round them. Elisabeth was the girl and might have been an orphan: how else would such a young girl have won approval from her family? If Elisabeth's date of birth (16 August 1903) is correct she would have been fourteen. This marriage sounded the death-knell of Vic's rise in society. Reasons are unclear as to why it was scandalous. The Archdukes abandoned him. He was demoted and the couple was shunned. Surely with defeat and the Proletariat on the prowl, Viennese society had more to worry about? Vic tells us that the only option was escape, initially by obtaining Rumanian passports on the black market. It involved a trip to a gangster's den where the racketeer demanded luxury goods in return for forged identities. In *Mr Showbusiness* Vic writes: 'The next day we left Trieste for Milan where we sold Elizabeth's silver-fox cape for 4000 lire.' He doesn't mention how he acquired the goods. A small entry in a newspaper from 23 March 1919 under the headline 'Fugitive Couple' fills in that detail. It says Vic and Elisabeth ('very elegant and blissfully pretty') left town earlier, having perfected a means of obtaining merchandise on credit, exploiting the fact that they were 'well-known in Vienna's rather fractured society'. Their method involved pulling up outside an elegant shop, asking for delivery to their apartment at 14 Wickenburggasse, then vanishing. The vendor who parted with the silver fox (costing 28,000 Kronen) and a blue fox (21,000 Kronen) was fuming. The police were called. The king of spending sprees was taking his biggest risk. The plan was to get to America. The fugitives ended up in Rouen, the industrial port on the Seine where, for two years, Vic had to make do with being a 'fake American' or more specifically a Rumanian who had 'lived his life in Salt Lake City'. Saving for their passage, he played piano in dockside cafes, then turned a crew of motley French musicians into a snappy 'American' jazz band with him as drummer. He writes that when Vienna settled down he came clean about the fake identity. Why then does 'Cuban' appear scribbled over Vic's Austrian nationality on the passenger list entry for the day in December 1922 he and Elisabeth left Southampton on *The Ansonia*?

Vic talks of working the lowest dives during his early days in New York. In fact, by July 1923 he was tinkling the ivories for WEAF, the first commercially licensed radio station, just four months after it started. He and Elisabeth were apart: he in Chicago and she keeping house at 106 West 74th Street. Before Laurence Olivier came 'Victor Olivier, Orchestra Leader' – one of the 'Nine Knights of Jazz' with 'originality their keynote'. With his extra 'i' the first signs of a comic showman emerged during a New England tour. Vic met Margot Crangle, a 20-year-old dancing violinist from Kansas City; the leading light of Westport High's School orchestra two years before. Her vivacity made up for her short stature. She played jigs and reels, loved contra dancing and took him under her wing. New Year 1925 saw 'Crangle and Oliver' on a Kansas vaudeville bill with Vic at the piano and Margot combining violin and Russian dance. She was on the roster of a travelling radio station and introduced Vic to impresario C. L. Carrell. Prior to a big picture and in between turns, a John Doe in Ohio could jump on the stage to deliver a message to his mother in Wyoming. Publicity tells us: 'A new entertainer has been secured in Victor Oliver, pianist and violinist, who played many times for President Harding.' Vic's playbills show even then what famous associations (even fake ones) meant. Tiring of radio frolics, he and Margot left for Chicago where he played the Kedzie Theatre. His accented drawl made 'Alabamy Bound' vastly different from Jolson's and he was called 'one of the cleverest piano entertainments ever presented'. They appeared with Efrem Zimbalist senior, the man who popularised Russian music in the US.

Where was Mrs Vic Oliver Samek? Vic says his wife had never learned English. She would stick her head in a magazine to avoid talking. It can't have been fun being Rumanian, then Cuban, then American. In Vic's version, Elisabeth returned to Vienna, but evidence from divorce documents reveals a different story. Her landlord stated that the young wife was deserted in 1923 with Vic 'eloping to Chicago with *the girl*' (Margot) and adds that 'Bessie Samek' didn't go back to Vienna. She remained in New York until late 1925, during which time Vic had known his stage partner a year. Vic divorced Bessie in February 1926 claiming she had deserted him. Two witnesses testified: one being Miss Crangle. Margot was dying for him to be single and on 15 May married him. They set up home in Chicago. A report tells us the new Mrs O was unlike most stage brides: 'she wears her wedding ring all the time ... she thinks it bad luck not to.' Six months later an Austrian paper noted that Elisabeth was filing a civil lawsuit against Vic, although the reason isn't clear.

The newlyweds spent a week in Florida where Margot enjoyed the sun, sea and sand of Palm Beach with friends from Tin Pan Alley like Louis Bernstein. They toured New Orleans, Philadelphia, Brooklyn, Saratoga, then Troy in April 1927. Viktor Senior died on 13 November 1926 with his only son far away. There is, however, evidence of a Victor Oliver present in Europe for a month in the summer of 1926 before crossing back on *The Lancastria*. He returned five months before his father died. He probably saw Elisabeth but there was another member of the Samek clan worth seeing, not that Vic mentions her in his memoir. Aunt Beatrice resided in the finest districts and, being closest in age to brother Viktor, was part of Viki's childhood. Married for the third time in 1903, her husband's status of *Reichsgraf* (Count of the Holy Roman Empire) was absorbed by Viki and Lilly. Vic never acknowledged his connection to Baroness Triangi von Latsch und Madernburg, while happily encouraging rumours of his links to Austrian nobility. Lilly married into it in 1922, becoming the wife of Georg Münzer von Münzbruck. Viki and Lilly drew comfort from the fact that Josefa's faux pas were trifling in comparison to Beatrice, who began flouting convention prior to her husband's death in 1926. Viktor Snr left his money to his second wife, who bequeathed it to their servants. An interview with Beatrice in 1932 corroborates this. Answering questions in court, she refers to her dispute 'against the servants of her deceased brother, the great industrialist Viktor Samek, to whom he left all his fortune'. She was interceding for her nephew and niece, although it has to be said, Countess Triangi used the courtrooms for publicity.

Like other Samek ladies, Beatrice was accomplished musically but Laura, Marie and Else (spouses of Robert, Karl and Hans) would never dream of wearing five rings on each finger or wrist ornaments of brass and malachite. None would be seen with cheeks made up, or go out with a liberal décolleté and bizarre oriental veil. Like an under-dressed version of Mozart's Queen of the Night, she climbed onto her ancient *Fiaker* with its two white horses. Glimpsed by passers-by, Beatrice was certainly unforgettable. Taking a bow, the 58-year-old raised skirts to reveal thick wool stockings, then began on her flute. She played piano and harmonica, danced and recited Schiller, her wasp corset defying nature as it separated bulging hips and bust. Making Vic's strait-laced father cringe, she had no hesitation stating 'I am the most beautiful woman in the world. Men have died for me.' The spectacle attracted Christian Schad, a painter who annihilated social niceties with studies of boys frantically kissing. His almost bare-breasted Triangi sits knees apart, an ostrich feather lewdly in between. Her shows were well attended and she was once presented with a bouquet of Frankfurters. Her popularity paints an interesting picture of a society before intolerance took hold. This 'real 'Viennese original' splashed colour into a drab world. She was in demand at the opening of buildings, for posing next to muscle-bound Teutons during summer *Strandfest* or at *Blumenkorso*, a spa-town tradition where VIPs waved from Daimlers and, in Triangi's case, her *Gummiradler* (state carriage). Vic's aunt had turned professional and her flamboyant, perhaps delusional qualities sank into him.

His own tour work was tough, as Evelyn Dall (who started in American Vaudeville at 15) knew. She spoke of journeying 400 miles only to find a wooden shack for a theatre and '"out-for-what-they-can-get" lumberjacks' as clientele. 'Hoke' acts (old routines done with pace and a new twist) were all the rage and the Ohio pair Clark and McCullough, whose work can still raise a laugh, inspired Vic, as did Ed Wynn, Milton Berle and king of radio Jack Benny, whose inept torture of the violin was his trademark. Vic's *Rhapsody in Blue* gained a dance section and Margot's *Amazing Grace* followed his jolly *Washington Post March*. They duetted *Eine kleine Nachtmusik* and for *Hungarian Rhapsody*'s middle tempo had the stage in darkness with the spot on Margot's fake diamond-studded gilt violin. Still more was required. They added interruptions and bashed out a script. Work was steady on the Keith-Albee-Orpheum circuit before Joseph P. Kennedy grabbed the whole shebang in a hostile buyout. Radio fuelled growth through advertising. Kellogg's, Standard Oil and Ford relied on big-money acts. People at home stopped going to the theatres and these advertisers cherry-picked acts for broadcasts, letting the rest go to hell. Vic wrote a 'grievance' letter to the *Vaudeville News*:

> Dear Friend: We worked the Keith-Albee Theatre in Boston last week and besides our regular act 4 times daily, we also did a special N.V.A. act, in which the writer took up the collection and with the assistance of Miss Crangle did 15 minutes of comedy, music and song... This was done on No.4 on the regular bill; also four times a day, making a total of 8 shows daily — and 15 minutes to every act. We were in the theatre from exactly 10:30am to 10:30pm daily 56 shows a week. But it was for a good cause! Sincerely, VICTOR OLIVER, Oliver & Crangle

They made it onto the bill at Proctor's 125th Street Theatre New York. Self-mockery was now part of the act and late 1927 saw them calling themselves 'Aristocrats of Variety'. It's a testimony to hard work that Oliver & Crangle caused one critic to call them 'one of vaudeville's most diversified acts'. Yet the financial nous of Joe Kennedy and other tycoons sounded the death knell for pure vaudeville. Kennedy's new RKO required that its buildings convert to cine-variety. In August 1929 Vic was at Loew's State Theatre in Times Square, which would eventually be the last venue there to book vaudeville acts. In Montreal he applied for permanent residence, facing a five-year wait. The Depression had begun and Vaudeville champion E. F. Albee died, marking the end of an era. In early 1930 Vic and Margot appeared at New York's Palace Theatre with Adelaide Hall and Bill 'Bojangles' Robinson. April 1931 saw them in San Antonio where Martha Jane Heath, home economics and psychology guru, gave a 'food demonstration' and designated Vic and Margot 'Cooking School Entertainers'. Acts like Eddie Cantor, Doctor Rockwell and Helen Kane were keen to come to Britain where the genre wasn't in decline. Henry Sherek gave 'The Aristocrats' the chance.

*The Performer* thought their debut at the London Palladium on 13 August 1931 registered well alongside Max Miller and Roy Rogers, even if the dance 'wee Margot Crangle' did defied description. Their next house at Holborn Empire on 24 August 1931 saw Vic as MC. The British liked his self-deprecating humour and aspersions cast at Margot. Back they went to the US and picture-variety: watching Will Rogers play a cowboy ambassador to a European court. Hiding his own buckaroo status, Vic said: 'I may not be so good but, by gosh, I'm different!'

He was in touch with Lilly, who, with her manufacturer husband, left the chi-chi life revolving around Vienna's Schwarzenberg Riding Centre for Bielitz, south-west of Krakow, where assimilated Jews once made up a high proportion of the population. The former territories of Austria-Hungary were changing fast with frightening things condoned. The Münzers settled in Britain in 1933. Through Lilly, Vic got news of Hans's sporty son Stefan. Fourteen years Vic's junior, he considered his parents Czech and his nationality German by domicile. An accountant at Price Waterhouse, he had credentials for American citizenship and, like his father, planned to emigrate. Internationally, BSB (Bruder Samek Brünn) had done well with an exclusive arrangement with Adrian Inc (the Beverly Hills company owned by Gilbert Adrian, couturier to stars like Garbo). Like Vic, Stefan composed scores for European films such as UFA's *The Rascal*, in which he appeared. Vic had another relation (in uncle Robert's family) who went into films. This was Franz Lederer who played Romeo in Reinhardt's European Shakespeare and succumbed to the erotic power of Lulu in Pabst's *Pandora's Box*. Lederer, then on the stage in *Volpone*, might have met Vic in London in 1931. Vic and Margot were back in Britain at the Liverpool Empire on 14 August 1933 and at the Palladium a week after. That December they divorced in St Louis, remaining partners.

Then everything almost ended in a muddy bog. Travelling through Jackson County where rivers flow into the Mississippi bottoms, they hit roadworks and their Cadillac whirled into a ditch, breaking the arm of Vic's Hawaiian chauffeur and capsizing in the gumbo mud. An 'unspoiled son of the river' came to the rescue, unhooked them and drove them to Chicago. His generosity allowed the fiddler and dancing violinist to take London by storm again in February 1934. Staying in separate hotel rooms, they played Birmingham, then the Palladium. They worked frighteningly hard in the big theatres and in Kine-variety at the Trocadero, Elephant and Castle, 'turn-working' to and from the centre of town, as in the week commencing 16 April 1934:

| | |
|---|---|
| 1.25 Trocadero Theatre | 9.15 Trocadero Theatre |
| 3.30 Palladium | 10.00 Palladium |
| 5.15 Trocadero Theatre | 10.30 Mayfair Hotel |
| 7.30 Palladium | 12.15 Mayfair Hotel |

Vic's involvement in charitable causes began in the Great War but his early days in London saw him embrace theatrical traditions. On stage at The Prince Edward Theatre in aid of the Norwood Jewish Orphanage, Vic joined Dick Henderson, Hutch, Lupino Lane, Randolph Sutton and the players of Portsmouth FC (fresh from playing in Wembley's FA Cup final). He was welcomed back. The orphanage was a long-term commitment of Anthony de Rothschild and Vic began a lasting friendship with the philanthropic banker whose passion was horse breeding. The Rothschilds, along with Mrs Israel Sieff, Lady Sassoon and Lady Reading (widow of Liberal MP Rufus Isaacs) were significant in developing the Central British Fund for German Jewry (CBF), assisting Jews after the emergence of Hitler. In February 1936, £7,000 of the takings from *Follow the Sun* were donated to the Fund for German-Jewish Women and Children. Vic thanked everyone from the Adelphi's stage.

Jewish comedy wasn't obvious in Vic's act, apart from his mixed-up phrases. It was a time when homegrown Jewish acts took goyim names like the comic who made a living not as Chaim Reuben Weintrop but as 'cockney' Bud Flanagan. Fine-voiced Issy Bonn ('My Yiddishe Momme') embraced the stereotype but nothing Hermione Gingold, Hughie Green nor Alfie Bass did confirmed their heritage. Vic talked like a streetwise American and looked like a suave international playboy. Discussion about culture back then was along simple lines: *foreigners* and *Englishmen*. Immigration was a sensitive issue with memories of the East End prior to 1914, when Jewish immigrants apparently unable to assimilate congregated in large numbers. The Jewish quarters of New York seemed acceptable but ghettos never rested comfortably in the British psyche. Whitechapel had no-go streets, although a few East End halls reflected integrated communities.

Margot left early in 1934 so Vic worked alone at the Palladium with Gracie Fields and at the Alhambra with Nina Mae McKinney and Teddy Brown. He did another charity show with Max Miller and Lance Fairfax. He knew the right people. Travelling stateside, his pal was Val Parnell who was on the Board of Moss Empires, the circuit that ran the top British theatres.

In New York that November Oliver & Crangle danced their last dance. In *Mr Showbusiness* his partner of ten years who truly helped him gets a mere mention, and he ignores their marriage. Margot carried on in the business. She and her sister Beula (forty years musical director at Radio City Music Hall) were still working in the 1950s. During the first half of 1935 Vic returned to New York's Palace but in early July was at The London Palladium. His infectious grin and 'cod' violin went down well in Manchester and he broadcast for the BBC that December. His listeners stretched from northernmost Scotland to the Blue Mountains of New South Wales. Wireless was why people came to see him in the flesh. As comedian Wyn Calvin, who later worked with Vic, explains: 'Radio filled theatres whereas TV started to empty them.' He worked hard, placating the hands that fed and greasing palms. He was one thing on the outside and another on the inside. Pathé filmed him that October. Looking at the camera he describes finding a 'big blonde girl' in his room the night before. He was so angry he yelled: 'I don't know who you are but I'll give you just twenty-four hours to get out!' In another film a girl runs off screaming when he indignantly declares he can economise, whipping off his dinner jacket to show he's nearly naked underneath.

Night and day, Sarah thought about the places Vic had travelled to, the people he'd met, the polished act and the bucks made. The thought of losing her chance of adventure was unbearable. Papa had forbidden them from seeing each other, with no exchange permitted apart from the purely professional.

Some time after Vic's inglorious retreat from Morpeth Mansions, Sarah was summoned to Papa's study. He emphasised one outcome she hadn't grasped. Vic's American citizenship was way off and she might find herself on the enemy's side by marriage. This seemed to sink in. Satisfied, Winston didn't take Sarah out of *Follow the Sun*. He even mentioned to his wife that if she played ball he'd say something friendly to Samek. He hoped it would cool off. She promised to obey the 'one year separation'. An Astaire fan, she had Astaire's photo on her bedroom wall. Her father gave it a withering look, reiterating his line: facts are better than dreams. Vic left Southampton on 21 July 1936 on the *Ile de France* to head a revue that was painfully modest compared to *Follow the Sun*. He had the ship's photographer pose him, sending the flattering image to Sarah.

Privately she was bitter, comparing herself to Elizabeth Barrett-Browning. She didn't like the way they never spoke of Vic. He wrote to her about his film, *Rhythm in the Air*. It was a tiny role but any Manhattan tale fed Sarah's imagination. What was really happening beneath the skyscrapers was that detectives were finding stuff and passing it to CSL. When they asked questions at the Simon Agency, Samek got wind of it, being director of the firm. Most of what CSL found failed to make Vic look bad. He paid his bills and H. B. Elmer of Eberhard-Faber Pencil Co testified that 'Mr Oliver is of high moral character'. In June 1936 CSL identified the place and time of Vic's St Louis divorce. It was a blow to Churchill that Vic was free but he shrewdly asked if Vic had legally notified his first wife after divorcing her in 1926. CSL found that notice had been 'served' only in that the *Chicago Law Bulletin* published the suit. There was no 'decree' in Vienna, it gleefully reported via *Hindenburg*, the superfast media vessel. The next tack focused on the 'criminality' of re-marrying without a decree (giving inadequate notice to Elisabeth). For private investigations CSL used John Broady, whose clients included Joan Crawford, John Jacob Astor III, H. W. Schmahl (who stole and sold photos of Hitler) and Buick. He was a strange choice, given that he had recently been accused of seducing a woman on the promise of marriage. He would later be convicted in 1949's City Hall Wiretap Plot. Broady relied on Viennese lawyer Max Kulka. If Elisabeth appealed against the decree within fourteen days of it becoming final in December, it might scupper Samek's plans.

In April 1936 the Saville Theatre staged the fruity *Follow the Daughter*. It was topical that an ex-Chancellor's daughter could go on the stage and that an ex-PM's daughter could open a pub. Ishbel MacDonald, daughter of Ramsay, had recently opened The Old Plow near High Wycombe. That June while Clementine partnered Dick Sheepshanks for mixed doubles, her husband worried about Hitler's Rhineland coup in March and civil war in Spain. He was frustrated with proposals for rearmament that had stalled in Parliament.

A glamorous representative of disobedience arrived at Morpeth Mansions on 18 August in the form of Diana Guinness, whose divorcee lifestyle wasn't exactly respectable and whose sister had followed her Munich education (alongside Pempie Dudley Ward) by befriending Hitler, speaking at rallies, and acting as unofficial attaché for Brits dying to meet him. Knowing Winston was keen to hear her opinion, Diana didn't mind trudging over from 2 Eaton Square to Morpeth Mansions. Her suggestion that Winston meet the Führer didn't go down well. Sarah was more intrigued by the freedom Diana possessed: young with no husband but a small house and servants. It prompted Mama's idea (expressed in veiled language) to extend Sarah's independence, allowing her a flat to 'develop freely'. Sarah shuddered at this progressive gesture and felt embarrassed that Mama should go to such lengths out of antipathy to Vic.

Her Pied Piper Vic provided her with a ticket to sail on *The Bremen* and she began making plans for her relocation. For Sarah it was a case of either taking the plunge or never being with Vic. She broke her promise to Papa but always held that she hadn't deliberately timed it for when he was staying at

Maxine Elliot's in France. She knew how distracted her mother would be by Diana, whose baby was due. The plan was to be at Morpeth Mansions on the afternoon of Monday 15 September when she would slip out to get her hair done, doing her best to avoid their suspicious housekeeper. Her mother and younger sister were at Chartwell. Her loyal 'Miss Smith' (as Sarah called Mary) had been briefed. Sarah felt guilty that Mary's birthday, coinciding with the day of the escape, would be ruined. Jenny was Sarah's other confidante, if that word's definition might be stretched to include her blabbing about her friend's plans to her family. Robert Graves had only recently returned and his diary for 14 September tells us: 'Jenny had phoned Laura about a wedding present for Sarah Churchill who is running off with Olivier the Cochrane [*sic*] *Follow the Sun* humorist. Laura to Selfridges to get it.' The elopement present was a cigarette lighter. Graves knew Winston but didn't intervene when he heard about it from his mistress, though he did get involved when Jenny's actions led to a sensational story. He smoothed things over with the Churchills. His journalist brother, whom he didn't care for, had been encouraging Jenny in her career, mentioning her in his *Daily Mail* column.

The day before she left, Sarah confided in Jenny, who agreed to see her off. Carrying a huge mascot doll, the kind female stage stars pose with when getting on boat trains, wasn't exactly a subtle move. She gave Jenny a letter to take to Diana, having earlier left one at Chartwell. As her carriage pulled away reporters suddenly filled the platform. Sarah tells us that she overheard through the hiss and chuff Jenny spilling the beans and that the story immediately broke. In fact, Jenny saw her friend depart happily, parried reporters as best she could and delivered Sarah's letter. From the boat Sarah sent her two joyful telegrams saying how much she liked her lighter. She suggested that Jenny tell the press nothing or say her US visit was to see friends. She had no idea that Jenny's links to Fleet Street via Uncle Charles would mean that two days later the *Daily Mail* ran the story about Sarah escaping to meet Vic quoting Jenny's words without her permission. While Vic would later talk about Jenny being cynically on the make, she hadn't blabbed for material gain. Conway, one of the reporters, had wormed it out of her. It would take more than this single wrongdoing to cause a grudge lasting decades. Jenny's family believes Vic caused it. Sarah's own guilt for putting her family through hell coloured things, hence her use of the word *treachery* in her memoir written years later.

Mary never expected her mother to sob so much on opening the letter. She owned up to knowing about the getaway but her mother never once reproved her. Sarah's tone echoes that of a chippy young Winston. With each word piercing her mother's heart, the brief note explains how 'last minute' it was. She knew 'hearts and minds' opposed it and believed that had they waited until January any 'blessing' that might follow would be 'very hollow'. Winston was crushed.

She had, however, been a child too long and only this could wrench her free from the hold her parents had. Everything would now change permanently. Seldom did she confront the loneliness and unhappiness that produced this action. Years later there was a moment of what seems like honesty. She explained: 'Before Vic, I couldn't put a foot right. I left my castle and joined the real world. If it hadn't been for him, I don't know where I'd have ended up.' She wouldn't enlarge upon this any further.

# 5

# Life with the Magician

Winston obtained a list of passengers on *The Bremen* and finding Lady Astor and her daughter Virginia Brand (dating Sarah's ex-beau Harry) on it, arranged that they 'guard' Sarah. On 18 September Britain's *Daily Herald* ran a headline about Mr Churchill hurrying home from France. Randolph was now on *The Queen Mary* halfway across the Atlantic, like a minister plenipotentiary in hot pursuit. In truth, he was already going to cover the American elections before Papa told him to remonstrate with Sarah in New York. Reporters waited until *The Queen Mary* reached the Hudson and was in quarantine. The pressmen were 'on their best behaviour', which was apparently as unusual as a bolt of lightning from a cloudless sky. Here was a story embarrassing for the aristocracy. They baited Randolph, watching him nervously attempt to smoke. The flashing cameras and shouts bothered him: 'Hey look this way. Smile.' First he locked himself in his cabin, then made a dash for it, press-hounds snapping at his heels. In the dining room Randolph sipped tea, a pile of newspapers before him. The press attributed the slow red flush rising from his neck to the roots of his ash-blonde hair to the lurid coverage in the dailies. Evening papers remarked how he was turning out to be a whole British Olympic team – leading the field in a quarter-mile run around the promenade, even managing to hurdle over deckchairs to their cries: 'How about this Oliver fellow? Where does he come in?'

'I don't know him and I don't want to know him.'

Randolph said he could hardly comment on something he knew little about until he saw his sister. On 21 September *The Bremen* arrived late. Ship officers had been ordered not to divulge Sarah's cabin number but her predators located it and fifty were skulking outside. When Vic boarded they dived on him and he was initially reported as saying he was flattered to join a dynasty and that 'if the family were willing [he] would be very honoured to become connected with the name of Churchill'. Another comment was: 'Mr Churchill is not exactly opposed to a marriage.' Sarah later said these were inventions. His first statement was actually that he was not marrying anybody. He stressed that he wouldn't dream of going against her father's wishes. He said he presumed she had come on her own accord but was forced to explain his business letter offering her work. He blamed an energetic publicity agent for this, making a gag out of it: 'She is engaged – but only to dance.' It was a transatlantic mix-up, that's all. The headline was: 'Is Miss Churchill eloping or job-hunting?' Not once did Vic admit to having sent the ticket. He was quite good at working columnists up into a lather only to rinse them away. Newsmen were welcome to find him, he said, between 6.30 and 7 p.m. at the Dorset Hotel. Until her brother arrived next day, he told them, he felt it his duty to hold the young lady in escrow.

The US papers described him as being about forty and 'very Broadway' in his brown suit. Less appreciative hacks called him 'foreign-looking with side-burns'. Vic's greatest hoodwink was saying his real name was *Joe Blotz*. The US media swallowed this misinformation and a story ran about Sarah receiving a cable from *Herr Blotz* advising her that everything was in order for their engagement, only he didn't say whether it was theatrical or matrimonial. 'Never let it be said,' this paper concluded, 'that a Blotz can't make up his mind.' Walter Winchell suspected that the whole Vic-Sarah story was a con to bring in oodles of stage and screen offers. 'Do you love Miss Churchill?' came a question for Vic from a lady reporter. He went into his dance protesting that he merely admired her.

Everyone got excited about the imminent meeting between Vic and Sarah. Vic was allowed to make use of a small cabin on *The Bremen*. He saw Lady Astor and they had a whispered conference. Some reports claimed that Lady Astor kept the lovers apart, but in reality Vic was the first person Sarah saw for five minutes in her cabin. He had a man with him ready to sort out her passport and luggage. The plan had been to slip off and get married. It changed only on account of Randolph's arrival. They didn't want to humiliate him. Harry Llewellyn got a message to her emphasising that the Astors meant well and that she needn't feel worried.

Lady Astor penetrated Sarah's refuge when Vic and his lawyer left, persuading her to face the press. Sarah admitted a few reporters into her cabin saying she hadn't authorised any of the statements attributed to her. She said she was 'very happy to be in America', mentioning her American grandmother. The newsreel shows Sarah on deck walking provocatively towards the camera swinging her hips, left hand in the pocket of her jacket as she passes startled men. The vigilant-looking man several paces behind is Broady, who *The New York Post* says was there to ensure Sarah maintained silence. Some said he was a friend of the family. Vic must have been facing her because it seems he catches her eye. Sarah bears a look of love and for a split second you see the torture that comes from controlling impulses. She crinkles up her nose to smile, then looks down. It might be the frilly collar Sarah wears but the moment brings to mind the artless Diana Spencer walking down the street to the door of her home in Earl's Court in 1980, smiling but responding little to questions from Carol Barnes. Sarah leans against the ship's superstructure for her disappointing newsreel speech. 'There is nothing I can say until my brother arrives on *The Queen Mary* tomorrow.' Vic slouches defiantly before repeating the same line. Both have the shameless air you see in children beyond discipline.

'It simply won't do, you know,' Randoph said when *The Queen Mary* docked and he hurried down the gangplank. He didn't know those awful Americans were eavesdropping as they spoke after embracing: 'What about it?'

'Nothing settled yet.'

'Well, we can't discuss that here.'

'What does father say?'

Next day one journalist observed a ring on Sarah's engagement finger. Another tracked down 'former Kansas City Society Girl' Margot Crangle. Now a platinum blonde and Hotel St Moritz resident, she said: 'I have nothing but the kindest attitude for everyone involved. I wish them both the best of luck.' *Blotz* didn't show up at the Dorset Hotel as he said he would. On leaving the pier brother and sister headed to Bernie's penthouse 'for a wash and brush up', as one of the dailies put it. The following day, 22 September, Sarah and Randolph parried questions. Sarah's joyful look was because Vic was part of the meetings (although none admitted it). They disappeared into a room at the Waldorf for a two-hour conference. Sarah wasn't smiling when she came out. Her father's masterplan to wreck everything using details about Vic's divorce was plain to her. The trump card (which Vic was noticeably perturbed by) was that a marriage bigamous under Austrian law guaranteed bad publicity. Sarah was appalled that Levy had tried to bribe Vic's first wife to contest the divorce and she felt tricked by Broady. She was livid, liable to do anything in that heightened state.

Vic had to leave to join his new show, *Shooting High*, but not before he had taken Sarah to dinner at the Colony restaurant, where they sat in a quiet corner. The following evening, Randolph, cousin Raymond Guest and Mrs Tommy Hitchcock (wife of the polo star) were expecting Sarah. She entered wearing her tailored suit with a spray of gardenias at the lapel, a little black hat, black-red lipstick and an aura. The fashionable diners gasped and whispered, 'Look – the Churchill girl!' If a love poem Sarah later wrote didn't recall the night when she and Vic left the Colony and stole a few precious hours before saying goodbye, it ought to have done. The title is '45th Street New York City'. It sounds like a disguised reference to West 54th Street, where no. 30 was the Dorset – Vic's hotel, once the epicentre of showbiz deal-making until its demolition in 2001. The couple in the poem are so giddy with love they barely notice traffic or the stares of passers-by. Their universe is the street they glide down, and if disaster looms they sure as hell don't care:

> I found speech again and words that for a million years
> I dared not to utter... Shamelessly I clung to you, oblivious

From Vic's point of view, he was reliving his escape with Elisabeth. He had aimed high and here he was with this chorus girl-aristocrat-actress. He had won over his opponent. How they got into the Dorset and out is a feat. According to *The New York Daily News*, a gang of reporters waited day and night to snare their prey in the lobby, creating such a nuisance the management didn't like it. The couple avoided them by a masterstroke. Vic was the man to know if you wanted hotel staff working for you. Examples exist of the understanding he had with bellboys, chambermaids and kitchen-staff. They were charmed into getting them in and out, via surreptitious entrances. Hotel escapology was second nature to Vic.

On 24 September Randolph left and Sarah went with the Raymond Guests to Long Island. She hadn't come all this way to watch polo and spend evenings at the Country Club. The crunch point came when Ciro Rimac and his band turned up. Sarah greeted her friends ecstatically and committed an undefined faux pas. Vic was called and Sarah never felt more relieved than when the chauffeur-driven car arrived with Vic to usher her off. Early the next day Sarah was in Schenectady, chaperoned by Vic's secretary Bette Willner. His three-day booking at Proctor's Theatre was starting. She passed the walnut box office and took her seat. When *The Daily News* traced her it asked, 'Is this Churchill-Blotz business just a tank town vaudeville act?' It had taken all this time for them to be alone. She saw MC Oliver appearing and disappearing closely on the tail of the Bebe Barri's Dancing Comets – a sixteen-strong chorus line. He was performing with acts from his agency. It was sad returning to the Waldorf. She began thinking about Jenny – now in trouble on account of her comments – and her father – eager to improve military rifts with France. She studied his speech in praise of freedom: 'Three kinds of nations exist in the world: those governed by Nazis, those governed by Bolshevists and those governed by themselves.' Nations must come together, he urged. He was probably thinking of Vic Oliver with his line about the time being nigh to 'beat the pride out of' the aggressor. Randolph, she knew, had supplied his 'For or Against Roosevelt' article for the *Daily Mail* with Bernie giving him contacts. Randolph was anti-Roosevelt politically but warmed to the man who said to tell his Pa he loved his latest book. He painted a homely picture of the President, his mother, wife and family at their home, Hyde Park. In another article, Randolph predicted that Britain would help the US if she were ever 'done in' by Japan in a war. As for Hitler, he added bluntly: 'We are all mugs if we let him make a world issue of Communism and Fascism. Both are dictatorships.' Randolph announced he was staying in the States until the end of the year. He made no further references to his sister but was frequently in the audience when she appeared on the US stage. Each time he duly reported what he saw to his father.

Vic's 'very dear' friend was there to study American showmanship and he spoke of her success essaying Claire's role in *Follow the Sun*. There was talk of a part for her in *The Show is On*, a Bea Lillie–Bert Lahr revue, but she ended up making her debut with Vic seven days after the Schenectady visit. Her parents had been her original agents, but in a seismic shift she let a stranger supplant them. The glaring flaw was that he was the star. Sarah's participation in Vic's Boston show on 1 October wasn't a chance decision. Spadework had ensured that permits were prepared and theatres factored in that would see them through before returning to England. The word 'probably' never featured in the plans of top-liners. When your earning capacity is high and many rely on you, where you'll be months in advance is set. Already, Vic's Mayfair Hotel engagement for January 1937 mentioned Sarah booked for the same. The poster for his Boston show just needed one of Sarah's photos from *The Bremen* stuck on with a previous star's face yanked off. 'Startling and Romantic English Beauty' served as bill-matter. Still shooting high, Vic renamed it *Follow the Stars* to cash in on Cochran fame.

Although variety has seen many overnight sensations, it was some leap coming from nowhere one day and sharing top billing the next. The chorus loathed the English arriviste. They had to strut out the old torso while she wore a skirt with 18 red ostrich plumes and an orchid satin bodice with modest straps. On came Mule, on her toes before an audience of 3,000 with Vic announcing her. The sight of this ethereal redhead in front of American girls with thrusting hips and false smiles was incongruous. *The Boston Post*'s verdict was that her two minutes doing mildly pretty ballet steps 'didn't exactly electrify'. In fairness, stamina was needed to rapidly choreograph a routine with an ingrowing toenail. In the finale Sarah and Vic walked on arm-in-arm. Those who came for curiosity's sake applauded, although *The Post* asked why nobody from Boston's social register was there. Just as she said in an interview, Sarah was studying showmanship; they watched Fanny Brice and Bobby Clark on 5 October, for example, when she and Vic were caught on camera like rabbits in the headlights. This was at the Winter Garden during a performance of *Ziegfeld Follies*.

On her birthday Vic brought a cake. The cast needed the calories as two days later *Follow the Stars* opened at Loew's on Broadway. The headline 'Churchill name packs the State' made it clear that the sensation hadn't much to do with dance. The most extraordinary artiste in the line-up was Barbette, 'Female Impersonator on the Flying Trapeze'. With Botticelli looks and known for closing 'her' act by tearing off her wig, Barbette used the ladies' loo. Sarah recalled that Vic wasn't too happy about that.

Ballet slippers were cast aside on Vic's orders because of her painful feet. Abandoned too were the ostrich feathers that rivalled Barbette's. At short notice Jimmie Struthers was elected from the Four Hundred's dancing set as her partner and he danced like a dreamm, although he went on with a black eye one night after falling on a washstand. Randolph joked to his Pa how the family name was up in marquee lights and that the Great White Way had seen another dream come true, with Sarah getting $750 a week for looking pretty. He had no doubt that the elopers were in love and knew the odds of ousting Samek were slim. His father's thoughts were of older elopements. William O'Brien, in David Garrick's company, had shocked the world in 1764 eloping with Lady Susan Strangeways, daughter of the Earl of Ilchester. They escaped to New York and were later forgiven, so a precedent existed.

Sarah's comment about her family congratulating her on her birthday and on her Broadway debut is disingenuous, but she only had to wait a day before hearing from her mother. The telegram was icy. She hadn't been there for the birth of Julian, Winston's first grandchild. Whilst at Loew's, Vic found a hotel suitable for a lady, the Lombardy on East 56th Street, with a sweet-natured maid, Marietta, to look after her. Sarah wrote to Clementine on 12 October using words like 'stalwart', 'considerate', 'attentive' and 'gentleman-like' in describing Vic's character. Showing signs of anger, she claimed it had been tough living in an atmosphere where one couldn't speak about one's emotions.

*Follow the Stars* went to Baltimore and in that city Sarah commented on another couple, saying that 'only Americans with "romantic notions" are interested in the friendship between Edward VIII and Mrs Ernest Simpson'. She went on to say that in England one 'hears little of Mrs Simpson's activities and that no one pays any attention to them'. Seldom did she venture opinions like these. It was out of loyalty to her King. He would cease to be so when he abdicated on 11 December. To her mother she mentioned they would go on to Chicago and Montreal. Vic had a different story, saying that Sarah was going to New York to study musical comedy. He made vaudeville appearances while she explored the Big Apple. A friend they made was fair-haired Peter Willes, an ex-Stowe boy who had arrived with actor Frank Vosper. Five months later, returning by ship with his young lover, Vosper died in mysterious circumstances, giving rise to the saying, 'Never get on a ship with Peter Willes.' Peter would become Vic's tour manager in the 1960s. Sarah mentions to her mother they'd met Willes at Maxine's a few years before, subtly alluding to him being gay. She was newsy, full of it, unrepentant. Clementine was curt in her reply of 25 October, telling her it was necessary to wait for Vic's naturalisation before she married. She cuttingly added that she had won the fame she craved. She didn't show her true emotions. These went into another letter that bore every trace of a mother's heartbreak, referring to the joy of holding her as a baby and her distress that Sarah could accuse her of not feeling things. Pride stopped her sending this.

For Clementine, this brought back a trial they went through in the first year of Sarah's life; a time when destroyers met the enemy under smoke-filled skies at Dogger Bank and when Gallipoli was her husband's undoing. With the Turks lacking ammunition, destroying their forts would have taken them out of the war. Later describing it as 'the only imaginative strategic idea of the war', Sir Ian Hamilton led it, but when they delayed, everything went wrong. The Turks gathered arms, mined the straits and a bloodbath followed. Winston was made to carry the can (even though he wasn't the campaign's only champion). He was demoted, experiencing a déchéance on a par with that of his father Lord Randolph. A music hall satire, *Three Blind Mice*, made fun of Churchill, Lloyd George and John Redmond, all of whom saw fortunes reversed. Clementine helped her husband. They got through it.

Irrational fears connected with shame had played on her unconscious four months before Sarah was born. She was in Dieppe when she had an awful dream about her child vanishing soon after the birth. She found it in a darkened room following a desperate search. Looking at it she noticed it wasn't as perfect as she thought and asked her doctor to kill it. He refused, taking her baby away. Clementine's guilt was relieved when she found she had been dreaming, but the dream and her terror returned: Tuesday struggling against Wednesday, Belgians against Germans. Amidst the strife came her bonny baby covered in golden down: Mama's own *bumblebee* that she couldn't love more or feel a greater need to protect.

Sarah's passions were always pure and innocent, but enormous, as her early love for Pebin made clear. The thought of her tears should things go wrong was too much for her Mama. Vic had supplanted her. Her baby had been taken away. The two would not be close until the Oliver marriage ran out of gas. They exchanged few letters over four years. Nevertheless, she put pain aside to help Sarah over her hurdles. Sarah wasted no time, asking her to get Papa's lawyers to expedite Vic's naturalisation. Clementine did this, cabling Randolph to take it up personally. Bernie Baruch also helped. It was in place by 22 December.

Randolph was amazed by the role radio now played in political campaigns. At a diner he was less impressed by developments in cuisine: 'What? Does one eat syrup on a sausage? Why they're diametrically opposite ideas.' On 5 October he gave a nationwide radio talk challenging the US to show common sense in the event of war in Europe. Germany, he claimed, was armed and unafraid of war. Each day more Germans were being brainwashed into feeling like victims. Russia, meanwhile, was hesitant to engage in war. His own countrymen were pro-peace but unable to defend democracy alone. If America evaded the issue he predicted utter doom. He travelled far and wide, arriving in Topeka to interview Roosevelt's opponent. He had a regular column in a Pittsburgh daily, was a *Toledo Blade* writer and voiced similar views to his father in many other papers. He has not been sufficiently credited for informing America about the threats. The excitement surrounding his wayward sister got Randolph listened to and that had long-term consequences. At the time, his rescue mission on *The Queen Mary* hadn't been what she wanted, but American awareness of Britain's plight at the end of the decade owes something to this unwanted publicity. Randolph dropped anchor in Tinseltown. Because he was still handsome, his cutting comments, like those to actress Mary Astor, were forgiven. Having failed to enter the Commons, there was consolation in donning false muttonchops to play an MP in MGM's *Parnell*.

Churchill telegraphed his son, telling him he was withdrawing opposition to Sarah marrying Vic. The last hope died when Elisabeth refused to contest the Vienna decree. The lawyers could do no more. Randolph told her just after the King's abdication (a story that British columnist Hannen Swaffer said knocked Sarah and Vic from the front page). Sarah wrote to her Papa saying: 'I know that you acted out of love – I am sorry for the pain and shock I must have caused you and Mummie – and I do thank you from the bottom of my heart.' Matters pending included the financial settlement Vic was asked to make. On 18 December, after all the denials, the comic announced to the US press that they *were* marrying. On Christmas Eve they tied the knot at City Hall and on Boxing Day left on RMS *Aquitania*. Stepping off the boat in Southampton, the newlyweds looked super cool for Paramount News with Vic saying, with emotion, how proud he was to have an English wife. Most the British press, however, treated the Olivers like nobodies. Sarah had to open her trunk and pay duty on her wedding presents. 'I must unpack?' she said, horrified at the thought. If the British had any 'romantic notions' they were barely perceptible. The country was bereft of a wayward King and gripped by cold weather. Here was an ungrateful daughter one shouldn't pay undue attention to.

Last-minute deals and frenzied efforts by secretaries to bash out contracts were aspects of the business now apparent to Sarah. Vic was at the Holborn

Empire and sometimes ate in the nearby Holborn Restaurant, cheaper than The Carlton where they were staying. The staff at the latter loved Vic and bellhop Frank Cox became part of his entourage, staying with him for 30 years. On 4 January 1937, confident that a pair of thick-rimmed spectacles was an adequate disguise, Sarah bought a three-bob ticket and made her way to the stalls fourteen rows from the front. She was mobbed and took refuge in Vic's dressing room. She didn't pose as a member of the public again. In a red knitted beret she stomped around backstage instead. A reporter compared her to a comedian's wife, loud in her verdicts: 'The milk gag went well, Vic. *Out* the one about the liner – didn't get over well.' Whilst seeing traces of her Pa's ability to drive a point home, he called it the talk of 'a hardened trouper'.

Her husband was so popular that over-enthusiastic fans left him bruised and shaken at the stage door. He was at the Mayfair Hotel most nights following Billy Bisset and his Royal Canadians in their lensless octagonal spectacles (a new look for band boys at the time). At Holborn his fiddle playing featured prominently. He had two: one he would later donate to charity and the other was 80 years old and made by Vuillaume. The next week Renée Houston was on the bill, interrupting the singing of new partner Donald Stewart. The couple provided a crash course in crosstalk for Sarah, who joined Vic at Columbia on 12 January to record *Knock Knock, Who's There*, the comedy springing from Sarah's insensitivity to jokes. 'I married you for life – well show some!' Vic's records usually include muscular piano playing or the violin piercingly going off key at the worst moment. He was identified as the man who, practising violin on a sea voyage, would find that even the stowaways came out to protest. The BBC rushed to book him and a week's Radio Luxembourg booking would last eighteen months. Ciro Rimac's band was back too, joining Vic, Hutch and Evelyn Dall at a fundraiser on 14 March for a home for aged Jews and to provide clothing for poor kids.

'There are few opportunities for ballerinas,' C. B. Cochran warned before Sarah left *Follow the Sun*. When she came to see Papa on 6 January he was glad that she wished to regain his trust and touched by the things she said about her mother. She also hoped to find an apprenticeship in legit theatre. It would take time for Clementine to forget Sarah's selfish action. Churchill's reconciliatory nature shows itself in a letter penned to his wife after Ralph Wigram's funeral, in which he compared Sarah's predicament to Edward VIII's. Sarah had made her bed and had to lie in it, but he shuddered at the idea of that bed being in a hotel. The next time Sarah saw him at Morpeth Mansions on 19 January, Vic was by her side. Winston wrote to Clementine telling her about Randolph's suggestion that Sarah and Vic take the vacant flat below his at Westminster Gardens. Winston would buy furniture as a wedding gift. He writes touchingly about sleeping in Sarah's old room at Morpeth where the 'hard-soft-springy bed' was nicer than his. It settled his feelings. With their common love of Shakespeare, it was natural for Winston to ask her opinion about his speech for the 'Shakespeare Down the Ages' exhibition in March 1937 at 16 Bruton Street. Michael Redgrave did a short scene as Romeo while Lord Feversham, Brian Aherne, Edith Evans and Laurence Olivier also performed.

Sarah and Vic were in a diorama including publicist MacQueen-Pope and Vivien Leigh at the Criterion's Gallery First Nighters Club dinner on 7 March. Olivier gave the biggest, bolshiest speech about how the theatre mustn't bend to what it believes public taste is but should leave the public to follow where it leads. Oliver gave a short speech recalling his own days as an 'Olivier'. Sarah was well aware of an old chum who had caused far less havoc pursuing an acting career and was even translating German plays for producers at St James's Theatre. Penelope Dudley Ward's *Escape Me Never* with its gorgeous locations attracted Diana Guinness and Unity to its première. A new film meant a great deal then and *Fire Over England* in February 1937 brought Winston, Clementine, Duff and Diana Cooper, and Merle Oberon. As historical advisor, Churchill made sure his 'Think twice before you mess with England!' message was clear to any modern-day dictator who saw it. After Spyros Skouras gave Chartwell home cinema equipment, there was something to see there every night.

Vic's eagerness for Sarah to get into pictures had awkward consequences. With Mr and Mrs Churchill adjusting to Sarah's new status, this risked a setback. Casting an ex-deb as a domestic servant was intended as a shocker, but whoever was responsible hadn't consulted her Daddy. An Austrian newspaper was the first to reveal that *Der Herr ohne Wohnung* was being remade (telling readers Churchill's daughter had a part alongside the nephew of the Viennese performer Reichsgräfin Triangi). Vic and Sarah had agreed to it prior to leaving the States and to being reconciled with her parents. It was a tricky subject when raised at Morpeth Mansions. The Churchills disapproved but production of *Secretary in Trouble* started that spring at Ealing, with Carol Reed directing. Renamed *Who's Your Lady Friend*, it was finished in June but didn't reach cinemas until December 1937. Hardly any publicity was generated. The filmmakers were hesitant. Like another film Vic made in 1940 where he appears in drag, the film has mysteriously disappeared. To protect Sarah's father from adverse propaganda some years later, copies may well have been recalled.

Vic's Plastic Surgeon rotates his tabletop of ceramic heads with every nose to choose from in his shiny rhinoplasty showroom. His male assistant (the Secretary) is sent to collect his boss's client and picks up the wrong girl: sex-mad French Cabaret Artiste (Frances Day) instead of the genuine client, volatile

French Society Girl (Marcelle Rogez). After depositing the Cabaret Artiste in a hotel with the surgeon (accidentally encouraging her belief that he's a willing sugar daddy), mishaps abound with the Secretary's Fiancée (Margaret Lockwood) and Surgeon's Wife falling out with partners on account of the Cabaret Artiste. Frances Day, who danced in New York speakeasies before coming to Britain, had top billing with Vic. A scene was changed to present Vic and Sarah together. Her Domestic Servant has to complain to the Surgeon and his wife about the French Society Girl staying at the house. Despite her melting eyes and good legs Sarah isn't well photographed. Acquiring a celluloid aura takes time. Margaret Lockwood said that her own appalling performance almost stopped Reed working with her again, but maybe Sarah's acting was to his liking. The multiplication of French girl parts was idiotic. After filming, Marcelle Rogez eloped to Las Vegas with freshly divorced director Wesley Ruggles. Sarah and Vic's escapade the previous autumn was contagious. Cousins Esmond and Jessica Mitford eloped to Spain on 2 March.

Vic had to be content with his father-in-law getting better ratings when Winston became Luxembourg's newest star on 9 May talking about George VI's ascent to the throne. There were changes, too, in the make-up of the government. Baldwin stood down as PM with Chamberlain taking his place. The Olivers' entrenchment in theatrical life is reflected in their participation in the Actor's Orphanage Garden Party. Sheltering the offspring of theatrical pairings since 1912, it had just moved from Langley to Chertsey. Noël Coward had Ruth Chatterton and Joyce Carey on either arm and Ivor Novello presided over the thesps. Shaw advocate Ellen Pollock ran a 'Gift Shop' with René Ray. Graham Moffat was at 'The Tuck Shop' while Sarah and Vic served at 'The Listener's Inn' with fellow tapsters Renée Houston, Bryan Michie, Gillie Potter, Hermione Gingold and Henry Hall. It was a chance to network.

They settled into their residence on Marsham Street where, after travelling eight floors in a fast lift, you could scratch the face of Big Ben with a gunful of gramophone needles. Papa was only a chime away from Westminster Gardens, while Randolph (producing items in serious and frivolous vein for *Londoner's Diary*) had a phone in every room of his top-floor powerhouse. The Olivers in Flat 66 had a massive lounge/dining room that could be divided into two rooms with country house furniture in white and red, tapestries and modern paintings brightening the walls.

One guest was Tina Mitford (Sarah's closest confidante then). Lord Redesdale's elder brother had daughters. Had Tina been born a man she would have got the title that passed to Tom Mitford. Studying German at the Foreigner's Institute of Berlin University, she had Vic to practise with. Tina, who loved modern art, disliked the way the Nazis condemned it, as their infamous 'Degenerate Art' exhibition made clear. Tina wondered if detractors in Britain, of which there were many, had the same mindset. She met the Führer with Unity. Randolph hadn't given up on a Hitler scoop and pressed his cousins frantically to wangle an introduction. Knowing that some were bullying Jews into leaving their homes, Tina was sensitive to Vic and was surprised at how little Sarah knew of her husband's past. Vic sheltered his wife from bad news. Sarah met Lilly, but the dangers faced by the Samek family seem not to have been obvious despite her family's sensitivity to the plight of the Jews. Vic was cautious of letting anyone know about his family. Racist comments were barely acknowledged as such back then. Friends were too polite to make them, although some were less tactful, even telling Sarah she had shamed her class. Vic's love of horses made him acceptable to country types and being great at tennis, golf and croquet, there was common ground with Clementine and family friends. For the wedding of William Harris and Elizabeth Coates on 15 July (when Pussy Waring was a bridesmaid) Vic pulled out all the sartorial stops in his top hat and tails, looking like an ad for Harrods' Ascot Shop.

Making the gramophone record was a sassy move. Sarah wasn't a bad 'stooge' with her deadpan seriousness. Her friend Eleanor recalled how she was so in love with Vic she even 'forced a change upon herself', trying to tell jokes. Audiences might have enjoyed the novelty of seeing her in his act, but it would have been professional suicide for him. Besides, Clementine would have died of shame. Sarah's fate was legit theatre, though there's a part of her character that regretted missing out on variety. Later in life a need to wipe away her serious mien and enact her forfeited *turn* would be rekindled. She did a little acting in mid-July 1937 in court of all places, having been the victim of a cheque-forger. In the Old Bailey's witness box she examined a cheque and passed it to the court, her face covered with a veil.

An initiation into repertory was fast approaching, but not before Vic spoiled Sarah, taking her on the trip of a lifetime. In their earliest days in Manchester they talked about America. Papa had never taken her there. They left on 28 July, made friends with a Spanish tennis champion and his wife and arrived in New York, checking into the Dorset Hotel. They left for Chicago where, from 8 August, he played the Palace Theatre. Despite tugging the bottom of his coat (a habit irritating by the 198th tug) his act garnered universal praise. He couldn't holiday without graft and was paying tax as a US resident. Their trip resumed and after a lot of driving they saw the Golden Gate Bridge. Vic caught up with his Spanish friend for tennis while Sarah and the Señora took in the sights. They stayed at the Beverley Hills Hotel. Vic could secure little work there (despite knocking on doors and name-dropping aplenty) but Tinseltown left a good impression. Sarah explored the razzle-dazzle and places off the beaten track such as Chevrolet's automobile dealership, with Felix the Cat smiling down on passengers on the freeway. Asked her date of birth, she would later reply that she was born in the sign of Felix in remembrance of a joke she and Vic shared. Sarah described her vacation to Marie Ozanne. Gossip in the letter concerns Patricia Benn (little Tricia of Broadstairs). She had followed Sarah to Paris and was presented at court the same day. Her next move was to find her own Austro-Hungarian in Baron Toni Dirsztay, an aspiring matinee idol. Her City merchant father cut his daughter off without a penny. Reports in the press have Tricia down as going to the Registry Office on 18 August, having second thoughts before going with Dirsztay for a conference at 66 Westminster Gardens, National HQ for eloping couples. In reality, the Olivers neither encouraged them nor attended their wedding. They lent them their flat while they were away. Sarah knew she'd get called a bad example but said: 'If Tricia is as happy as I am, I'll gladly take the blame.'

These were relaxed, happy years, with Vic trying to make a singer of Sarah. Opinions were sought whenever someone wrote a speech. Randolph and Seymour Berry gave feedback on one Duncan made about the declining birth rate. Sarah was a fan of her brother's work, avidly reading *Londoner's Diary*. Having lost the backing of Lady Houston, Randolph's political ambitions were on the back burner. Instead, in just a few inches of column-space, he could highlight the crux of an issue and amuse with his observations. He exposed the widening gulf between British and German military strength and his 'Guns Over Gib' article in July 1937 (about the Germans intervening in the Spanish Civil War) was an attack on government ministers. His talk of Nazi police 'in our midst' was less convincing. He drew on Tina's help with German when covering the visit of the Windsors to German cities in October. As they toured a Nazi Welfare HQ, Randolph reported that only sick people of pure German blood got cared for. He observes how, at the Krupp Works, Dr Krupp neglected to show the Duke the production line for armaments (which Mussolini saw) and how, at a factory where 'Strength Through Joy' organised concerts, the Windsors' attaché, Dr Ley, let slip that managers who did not do their job well were removed – never to be seen or heard of again. He writes how, after the visitors were told how *wunderbar* the canteen was, the Duke embarrassingly asked why many brought their own lunches. Randolph keeps constant watch in case the Duke succumbs to a Nazi salute. On 14 October the Duke gave one but only, Randolph tells us, because he was saluted in the middle of the National Anthem and had to out of courtesy.

Winston's son obsessed over the latest doings of Hitler. He told people how Hitler never wore a uniform in Munich, regarding himself as a private citizen there. Returning to Westminster Gardens from Germany with a stash of material, Randolph needed only to pop downstairs to get a quick assessment from Vic as to what the Germans were saying. For variety performers, daytimes were fairly free and Vic obliged him with quick answers. He talks warmly about Randolph in *Mr Showbusiness*. Close to the same philanthropic gentry in the CBF, Randolph put his neck on the line: 'I have always been a pro-Semite and Zionist,' he had stated two years before, and that persecution was disgusting. He repeated LG's line that 'Anti-Semitism is a good starter but a bad stayer.' He thought the BUF didn't pose a menace and believed in the freedom to debate with Fascist or Communist alike. In his younger years Randolph liked the works of Disraeli, whose line that 'Every country gets the Jews it deserves' resonated. He believed his country treated them better than any. The Nazis, however, thought Randolph active in a conspiracy, claiming he was on the board of the British Maccabi Association. Records do not support this although he might have spoken at its meetings. One of his best friends, Henry Mond, was a prominent supporter of the 'Strength Through Physical Education' movement devoted to building up the Jewish race. Mond had taken part in an Eastern European Maccabi tour. That Randolph's Nazi critics were quick to bite isn't surprising. For years he had pilloried their ridiculous mind-set. Wasn't it inconsistent, he asked, that *Camille* (the Garbo film Hitler saw six times) passed the German censors when its director was a Jew? He tells the tale of the 'Aryan Horse', which begins when a friend (probably Unity) took a Nazi to a Marx Brothers picture. This Nazi was hugely entertained until something clicked. He asked with pallid seriousness: 'They're not Jews are they?' The friend nodded. The guilty German was tight-lipped until the end. Suddenly, he was laughing again. His justification? Well, it was the horse that was funny, not the actors!

Countless actors trained in repertory, the machine that turned out the talent that made British theatre in the twentieth century. Even in the early 1960s, 87 rep theatres were still working. Sarah Churchill was at Brighton's Theatre Royal in November 1937 in *Victoria and Albert* with Joyce Redman and Ronnie Waldman. She worked very hard and was humble about where this lark would take her. 'One of my greatest ambitions,' she said, 'is to play Peter Pan.' She was also found at weddings. She joined a motley bunch of actors throwing confetti at Peggy and Wallace Douglas in their plain little ceremony at Chelsea Old Church. On 10 December when Eleanor and Phillip Morris-Keating tied the knot at one of St Margaret's most lavish weddings, she and Vic were in high society. Stepping between worlds became second nature. On Kilburn High Road Vic felt he was looking up at the Empire State building when he performed at the Gaumont State's opening with Henry Hall, Gracie Fields and George Formby. That Christmas, with several Churchills on the slopes, Sarah's Mama reported how happy she was to see Duncan and Diana tobogganing and having fun. She worried about the Sandys marriage, with

Parliament claiming much of Duncan's time. Sarah was another concern. She could have been a society hostess but caught trains and stayed in common boarding houses instead. At least in London she had 'Jeff' (Ada Jefferies) as seamstress and lady's maid. News came in just after New Year that Dick Sheepshanks, whom Clementine had wanted Sarah to marry, had died in shellfire in Spain. Oddly, all the correspondents in his car were killed apart from Kim Philby. Clementine ached to think of her strapping tennis partner. Winston developed misgivings about both sides and saw the conflict as a foreshadowing of a worse war. When Duncan suggested taking Diana to Barcelona for a trip, he forbade it outright.

Clementine was on civil terms with Vic, who didn't pose in photographs with the family and, being a teetotaller, was a safe bet. You had to admire his musicality and he wasn't common, like Harry Roy. Clementine predicted that given their careers, rivalry would affect the Oliver marriage. Sarah came to St Bride's on 7 January 1938 for the service for Dick, then returned to Brighton. Working alongside Waldman and Ernest Clark, she was the nurse in *The Amazing Dr Clitterhouse* where a medic turns to crime. She became friends with Judy Campbell, fresh from *Anthony and Anna* at the East End's People's Palace and the two girls took *People At Sea* to Northampton that May, where Sarah described her impressions of the town: 'It is so clean and so unlike one imagines a manufacturing town will be, that one cannot help but comment upon it.' Asked if her family would come to see her perform, she timidly said that most of her family were busy but Mummy, who loved plays, might see it. It was an indication that the relationship was repairing.

It is the dream of many actresses to play Juliet and Sarah was due to play her opposite Arthur Lawrence's Romeo. The cast included Waugh's friend John Fothergill. Any Juliet's worst nightmare is to fall off the balcony. Dream and nightmare happened on the same night – mercifully the dress rehearsal. With her thickly bandaged leg she didn't miss a performance at the Royal Theatre. The theatre's colourful safety curtain was a notable feature. Such theatrical details were not lost on Winston and he was a judge, along with Kenneth Clark and C. B. Cochran, deciding the best design for the Old Vic's new safety curtain.

Vic returned to Holborn Empire on 20 April where 'The Three Rays' rolled and somersaulted as only American gals can. At Grosvenor House's High Spirits Ball (for a victuallers benevolent fund), Vic and Gracie headlined. He was spearheading a fashion for droll jokes. Whilst the older music hall was uproarious, there had been little malice. Vic's high-energy act, however, had a touch of evil. Long-limbed and balding, his one-liners came out innocent and sweet and were downright suspect when the penny dropped. A typical line was: 'I like girls with glasses. You blow on them and they can't see what you're doing.' He hotfooted between halls and film studios and became a cartoon personality care of Anson Dyer (Britain's Walt Disney) in advertising a Bush radio. He played an agent hired by a film magnate taking a star round London to book acts in *Around the Town*. At Welwyn Studios Vic lived up to his catchphrase 'I'M COLOSSAL!' as a 'Department Store Midas' whilst humble clerk Penny (already a character on radio) enjoys the peace of his allotment. When Vic's enterprise builds a warehouse on top of his runner beans, a rebellion of the Great British kind causes a boycott of goods. By the time *Meet Mr Penny* came out, boycotting German goods was something Sarah's Papa was calling for.

Chamberlain's 'positive' attitude to Mussolini and Hitler and Britain's lack of preparedness was polarising the Commons. In January 1938 Bob Boothby demanded that compulsory National Service be introduced as well as an increase in the frontline strength of the Royal Air Force. Chamberlain rejected both ideas. Winston, Anthony Eden, Bobbety and Sir Robert Vansittart upheld a firm anti-appeasement position. They faced the powerful Cliveden Set that refused to admit the dangers. Eden resigned that February. Attending a press ball at Berlin Zoo on 12 February, Randolph became aware of Nazi brainwashing, with the Germans too scared to address anything that discredited the regime. He badgered Unity and fascinating nuggets found their way into *Londoner's Diary*, such as how Hitler sobbed when things didn't go his way, how he was an insomniac, liked a fresh shirt every day, might have married Frau Wagner and had a lot of respect for 'muddling through'. Randie talks about the culling of Austrian statesmen and how Unity, protected by her 'autographed' Nazi badge, rushed to Vienna to be at Hitler's side for his triumphant visit. He left the last word to his father who wrote his own piece in the *Evening Standard* claiming the majority of Austrians wanted their country independent. This prompted Unity to reply to Winston on 5 March arguing to the contrary. Austrians were longing for *Anschluss*, she claimed. Knowing what it was like to bring shame on one's family, Sarah sympathised with her cousin. She was used to her jokey style and recklessness. Knowing the Mitford utterances were great copy, Randolph took up the story of Unity's badge after a mob tore if from her on 10 April. Lord Redesdale thought young Churchill was worsening Unity's infamy and complained to his father. Randolph retreated to the topic of what had become of the actresses of the Edwardian era. He was an effective PA for his Pa, ringing up people Winston wanted to speak to and arranging meetings in his apartment at 70 Westminster Gardens. One was with Russian Ambassador Ivan Maisky, who visited on 23 March.

The oddly named *Idiot's Delight* had a gala performance that same evening at London's Apollo Theatre, with young ladies of the Season collecting for the National Birth Control Association. One of them, Pamela Digby, would soon be drawn into Randolph Churchill's orbit but others currently held centre stage. As well as Claire, Laura Charteris began a long, loving friendship and Mona Harrison Williams, with her silver hair and aquamarine eyes, was an unobtainable love. Playwright Robert Sherwood, former movie critic for *Life*, had won the Pulitzer Prize for this play. Set in a hotel in an Alpine region that might any hour be fought over, guests are from Germany, France, Italy, Britain and America. Raymond Massey played the comedian representing the latter country, Harry Van, stranded with his chorus of high-kicking blondes. There's a German doctor, a French communist (returning from an International Labour Conference), a British couple on honeymoon, a dodgy arms sealer and a histrionically fake Russian countess. The most notable feature of *Idiot's Delight* was of course its timing. When it appeared on Broadway, Italy had just invaded Abyssinia and it reached London's West End as Hitler's forces were marching into Austria. It's been called a Pacifist play with an anti-war theme. However, it is Pacifism for pessimists: remote isolationists looking into a glass snow globe with bombs falling as well as snow. Any member of the audience expecting some deep meaning must have come out of the theatre strangled by Sherwood's puppet strings. Remarkably, it earned huge box-office receipts and was described as 'London's most talked about play'.

The staging coincided with the first two weeks of Joe Kennedy's tenure as American Ambassador. For raising huge sums for the campaigns of Franklin Delano Roosevelt (FDR) he became the first Irish Catholic appointed to the Court of St James's. Soon after arriving, his eldest girls, Rosemary and Kathleen 'Kick' Kennedy, were guaranteed presentation at court. Thousands of American debs applied each year but never more than 20 could be accepted. When Kennedy made his Pilgrim Address on 18 March, he never offered the slightest hope that help from across the pond would be on offer, should Britain be in peril. Sworn to appeasement, the doors of Cliveden opened wide for him, and Kick, loved for her insouciance, dazzled Lady Astor et al on the tennis court and started a new fashion for throwing bread rolls down the table.

At this time, Sarah's brother-in-law Duncan was a Lieutenant in the Royal Artillery as well as an MP. Discovering evidence showing how inadequate the country's anti-aircraft defences were, he made a noise about it. Secret Service officials suddenly turned up threatening to prosecute. Despite ridiculous attempts to put him behind bars, it was observed that because he was an MP his disclosures weren't subject to the Official Secrets Act 1920. This brought into being a new version of the Act. Duncan got off and Sarah's Papa rejoiced.

Winston had had a busy day at Chartwell with the new Golden Orfe. Another person he looked kindly on was Vic, whose music took him back to the evenings Jennie would play piano after dinner. He said: 'I have come to like and esteem him greatly.' Sarah looked happy but he was concerned about what might happen if Vic repatriated. Feeling settled after banker Henry Strakosch paid off his recent debts, Winston intervened to get Vic British citizenship, liaising with Alex Maxwell at the Home Office. Vic went through the hoops even though he wasn't sure he wanted to lose his hard-earned US status. The process wasn't simple. Where Maxwell came up trumps was giving Vic exemption from compulsory re-applications at the end of each visa period. The relationship between father and son-in-law was transformed.

In Tavistock Square Diana's friend Miss Moir was a guest of Leonard and Virginia Woolf and writes about how depressed the Munich Agreement on 30 September had made them. These relics of the Bloomsbury Group expected freedoms to vanish. Drawing little comfort or sense of hope from their vague world of muted chintz, Miss Moir left for America; not that there weren't Nazis there too. In 1937 *The Nation* referred to 20 Nazi camps for kids existing in Ohio, Texas, New Jersey and Pennsylvania and listed flourishing organisations like the Committee for German-American History and the German-American Bund.

When Harry Van admits that he sells 'phoney goods to people of meagre intelligence and great faith' it sounds like a Vic Oliver aside. Only a strong lead like Massey (co-producing with Henry Sherek) could carry the London show, and when Lee Tracy took over in August a touring production made Vic the provincial show's Harry. Sarah, whose name guaranteed business, had a part. Judy Campbell was Countess Irene while Michael Gough and Sarah were Mr and Mrs Cherry, the couple showing British restraint in times of conflict. Heron Carvic and Phyllis Luckett were cast, too. Following Chamberlain's 'Peace In Our Time', a sizeable anti-appeasement protest went unreported and tension was rising in the populace. Kennedy was forever telling Washington that the prospect of Britain surviving a European war was bleak. Harry Van's 'freedom to sneer' was a fragile entitlement held by Churchill's son-in-law, but *The Daily Express* marvelled at Vic's star status. Normally, Moss Empires required performers to tour the provinces. Not so Vic. A new contract let him stay in London for the whole of 1939, provided he graced the Holborn or other prominent London theatres once a month. He could go to America, make films or reserve touring for revues with his wife. In music-hall terms, it was little short of a coronation.

There was scope to aid relatives, even if he had broken from his continental family. How he intervened is unknown but one thing counted: contacts. Lajos Lederer's involvement in a failed scheme to make Lord Rothermere king of Hungary in 1937 shows the kind of networks that existed. When Lajos was arrested as an alien in late 1941 and sent to the Isle of Man, Randolph got the Home Office to release him and the Czech went on to write for *The Observer*.

Sarah's brother could fast-track paperwork for friends like Virginia Cowles, but influence inside enemy territory was negligible. Whenever strings could be pulled, Vic had enough standing to put in a request. Immigration rules had been tightened with hefty paperwork (sponsors, tax information and affidavits) required to go to the US. Franz Lederer, in faraway Hollywood, was unable to save his mother from Nazi brutality. Perhaps Uncle Hans's slogan – 'Anything worth doing is worth doing urgently' – said it all.

Intriguingly, a woman is listed as resident in Paddington in March 1939. It was Elisabeth Oliver Samek, Vic's first wife. How long she had sought refuge there is unknown and sadly, this is a death record. As for Josefa, he skirts over the subject in *Mr Showbusiness* saying the SS had her home watched and that he brought his mother to Britain after the war. There is little evidence of this. Besides, Josefa was doing fine. She didn't require Home Office help to leave the country. It's true that the SS enquired about Vic's whereabouts for their black book, but she couldn't be officially criticised. She was still in Vienna, as records show, living with her husband at 4 Favoritenstraße 22. A kind of schizophrenia would ensue where Christians had married Jews: one side of the family suffering racial persecution with the other sometimes linked to the persecutors. It left families numb for years after.

Hans Samek and his wife were now in New York where he ran the business from 400 Madison Avenue. Stefan was in San Pedro. Doom hung over those left behind. Only weeks after the *Anschluss* Jews were publicly humiliated. The days either side of 10 November became a blur with *Kristallnacht* in Germany and Austria, allowing mob violence to reign. It was at its worst in Vienna because Nazi daily *Volksicher Beobachter* indicated the location of Jewish synagogues for the thugs. Vic's 70-year-old aunt Beatrice seldom left her apartment in the Landstraße district fearing *Anpöbelung* (discrimination and taunting, or 'mobbing'). Her daughter lived there too, waiting each day for papers to offer an escape. Between 1938 and 1940, 117,000 Jews left Austria. Vic may have assisted in the case of younger members of his uncle's family. Robert died in 1928 but the lives of several relations still revolved around the factory in Brünn (now Brno). They had briefly enjoyed democracy under T. Masaryk only to see the democratic leaders exiled and a right-wing government installed that was unwilling to cross Hitler. The factory was part owned by brothers Hans and Karl Samek and part by the Esslers, the family of Robert's widow. A law imposed the right to seize such property. A local Nazi, Appeltauer, had BSB erased from the commercial register and Karl was transported to Terezin, dying in Riga in January 1942. Robert's daughter's husband was called in by the Gestapo and interrogated on account of Vic's connections to the Churchills. The family were desperate enough to naïvely ask Robert's granddaughter, Maria, to go to England to talk to Churchill to see if they could get their factory back. It didn't happen but this brave young woman survived interrogation by the Nazis and even managed to escape from Ravensbrück. Many members of this family of industrialists were to perish in concentration camps. Of the survivors, none returned to their country. Maria's son believes that it was owing to the failed attempt to get access to Churchill (and the fact she was Vic's cousin) that Maria received a passport right after the war, which was unheard of.

Churchill set great store by first-hand accounts. Prague journalist Sheila Grant Duff and Jan Masyrak provided these. The latter was Vic's neighbour at 58 Westminster Gardens. He, too, was ex-Austrian Army, a pianist and broadcaster. Vic's own intelligence was beneficial to Winston, who was delivering a devastating verdict on the Munich Crisis to all the non-Fascist European newspapers every two weeks, assisted by Jewish publisher and friend Emery Reves.

Vic took Lilly and Georg Münzer-Münzbruck to Southampton on 18 January 1939 where they departed on *The Ansonia*. They hadn't tried to get British citizenship. America was their best bet and they were fortunate having Hans as a sponsor. Phyllis Luckett, Vic's 'charming and pretty' assistant at Holborn (able to supply 'a few shots of crosstalk whilst otherwise doing little else'), was close to Lilly, while the connection between Sarah and the formidable Austrian-aristocrat-modiste was vague, possibly sour. Vic's wife helped in other ways. As the *Evening Standard* on 18 November records, Churchill was enjoying a roll and butter and a glass of cream when spotted in a restaurant with his wife, Maxine Elliot, Mrs James Beck and Lord Alington. Sarah was there too in conversation with Dr Kommer, Diana Cooper's friend. Winston's chat with Naps Alington was possibly about land on his Dorset estate used by the RAF, but Naps was also a patron to Polish composers and sympathetic to cultural exiles. So was Dr Kommer, who actively helped them leave Nazi Germany. Kommer and Sarah had Viennese theatre director Stefan Hock in common. Hock had joined the Kommer circle when Reinhardt took over Josefstädter Theater. Hock was allowed exile in Britain and given a job at Chester Rep. An Austrian newspaper says that 'Sarah Churchill was among his favourite students', which indicates a Viennese chain of influence linking Sarah, Vic, Kommer, the Arts, and immigration.

Apart from charity commitments such as speaking before the Jewish Board of Guardians in Hull, in the months following *Idiot's Delight* Vic was back in variety. He spoiled Sarah – giving her a brand-new Jaguar two-seater for her birthday. Her scarlet SS100 Coupe was the latest in speed and chic. Years later, Sarah disingenuously referred to it as a standard model. The luxury of the old life obviously gave the mature Sarah some discomfort. She and Vic were 'at home' that Christmas and in January she appeared at a film première and a party at the Savoy. Vic paid for another gift in February 1939: rhinoplasty. A nagging concern about her image had been there since childhood. Chattering innocently to Cecil Beaton a year later and stupidly trusting him, Diana provided anecdotes about Winston's reaction to Sarah's 'op'. Beaton tells us that she was a gruesome sight for weeks, hiding out at her London flat. If anyone called she held a fan against her face. Lowering it to show Diana the swollen patches, her sister shrieked: 'Oh Sarah, you have been going it!' A week or so later the nose was ready to be scrutinised by the Great Man, shown in by the Westminster Gardens maid. According to Beaton, he stood quietly facing the chimney breast preparing himself, then addressed her with the words: 'Whatever happens ... I shall always love you more than anything on earth.' Turning to see her, for a short time his eyes were full of joy and he exclaimed: 'Not my old Sarah, of course, but still – very nice,' before his customary tone resumed: 'Now then, what were we discussing? Victory, of course...' It shows that Sarah had the wholehearted support of Papa in her showbiz aspirations. *Chateau de L'Horizon* was also handy for slipping off with him to recover, even if she had to suffer women like Maxine and Daisy Fellowes. She told Diana how much she loathed them. Still, few other convalescing patients in 1939 enjoyed such perks.

While 5,000 Jewish children had arrived from greater Germany with 1,000 more coming, Vic and Frances Day offered comic relief with *Black and Blue* at the Hippodrome. 'Acrofunsters' Cass, Owen and Topsy and Max Wall were turns, with Phyllis a junior. Vic did a radio sketch and Frances stole the show as Scarlett O'Hara and as Marguerite to Vic's Mephistopheles in *Faust and Furious*. The critics were sold and a joke went round the theatres started by variety stars Dave and Joe O'Gorman: 'Forty beautiful girls in London Hippodrome Show – Vic Oliver still fiddling.'

Vic took credit for Sarah's 'modern' face. With her chiselled features and noble air she was called a female Leslie Howard. She told a reporter how her husband, 'being American', took 'a lot of interest in her clothes', always noticing when she wore something new. He 'liked red fingernails'. She wore countless tiny charms on her wrists and favoured tailored suits and flowing skirts for evening; her favourite dress being a striking one in royal blue with a chevron pattern. It was seen at 1939's orphanage event, where British Movietone News caught Vic off-guard. It's a rare example of him looking awkward. His job wasn't to be 'himself'. Sarah was part of Coliseum history, being in its first full-length straight play, *George and Margaret*, that afterwards went to Wood Green Empire where Winston and Clementine turned up together to see her. This warmed her heart. They followed her successes with great attentiveness.

The National Government bore deeply entrenched suspicions about the Soviets, but calls to cut a deal with Stalin came from Winston, who wanted Chamberlain to consider a triple alliance with France and Russia: 'It should still be possible to range all the States and peoples from the Baltic to the Black Sea in one solid front against a new outrage of invasion.' He was sickened when *Time* announced the Nazi–Soviet Pact on 28 August 1939, a deal so disturbing that an Emergency Powers Act had to be passed. Sarah shuddered at Vic's talk of land grabs and about Jews and intellectuals being the victims of *both* aggressor nations. Chamberlain might guarantee Poland's independence, but could he pledge territorial integrity?

The Third Reich's press went on the attack. Sarah's career had been derided in February 1937: 'Once Papa sits down in the theatre and sees me, he'll forgive me,' went one phoney quote. The tabloid *Der Stürmer* distorted Sarah and Vic's *Follow the Stars* photo with their noses made bigger. 'Proud England' had fallen into the mire with daughters of the nobility marrying nouveau riche Jews. *Österreichischer Beobachter* had gone over to the dark side with its hate-filled articles and cartoons. Married to a 'sire of the brother of crazy Countess Triangi', Sarah was a target. When Churchill returned to the Admiralty on 3 September, attacks in *Der Stürmer* worsened and Unity couldn't deflect them. The two countries she idealistically dreamed would be friends were at war; she shot herself in the head in Munich. Aunt Beatrice's creative disposition played into the hands of the propagandists. She had willingly posed for photos depicting her 'çonversion' to Protestantism. She may not have been of sound mind at the time – five months before, her daughter had finally managed to get passage to New York, leaving her behind. In September *Der Stürmer* used the histrionic images to create their cruellest pages to date. She was also pictured next to Churchill: 'Minister und Jüdin'. Finding Beatrice confused in her apartment, the Gestapo detained her in February 1940, taking a mugshot and attaching the label of senile mania. She was sent to Am Steinhof psychiatric hospital where she died on 28 April, apparently of pneumonia.

Sarah didn't know how vile the German press was. It was Vic's role to take innocent 'Trilby' and transform her into a star. Myth, artifice and luxury should surround her and she should be kept a child. Alongside her own scrapbooks, Sarah proudly kept ones dedicated to Vic's career. The marriage was one of parent-child affection, gifts, light-heartedness and loyalty. On stage she was a wife manipulated to the point she doubts her sanity, which was strangely prescient. Critics thought Sarah a dab hand at conveying terror without 'laying on the paint too thickly', but few came to see *Gaslight* at the Coliseum. For her next play, *Quiet Wedding*, the first night on 4 September 1939 attracted a house of four. The previous day, Chamberlain's declaration of war was broadcast. There were blackout curtains to put up and supplies to stockpile. People dreaded separations.

The Churchill family had a topsy-turvy life with Morpeth sold, the chauffeur's cottage at Chartwell only part-occupied, Clementine redesigning the Admiralty rooms, Duncan at his Anti-Aircraft Battery and Diana a welfare officer on Kingsway in the Women's Royal Naval Service (WRNS). Vic's uncanny ability to fit in with the clan caused his wife to compare him to a magician. Their flat was a nexus and Mary, at college and helping the Red Cross, was given a party there when she turned 17. That October, Robert Morley's *Goodness, How Sad* was at Wimbledon Theatre. A Hollywood idol returns to a small seaside town but no one recognises him when he performs once again at the local theatre. Critics said that Sarah, with her gleaming eyes and copper hair, compelled one to follow the agonies of young actresses going through the hoop in Rep. With real-life Rep doing well out of her name, she insisted on privacy, only signing autograph books left at the box office if a small donation was placed in her Red Cross box.

London's 'legit' theatres shut their doors but nightspots thrived with couples making the most of time left together. *Tatler* reported that the blacked-out facade of L'Apéritif in Jermyn Street concealed not only the fascinating actress Margaret Vyner but also Randolph Churchill and Pamela Digby – a vivacious redhead – now his fiancée. Sarah and Vic were there along with 'Creeps Library' editor Charles Birkin and Bridget Dunn (her hair in a pink headscarf). Horror fiction wasn't Randolph's thing but Birkin, brother of Freda Dudley Ward, appealed to Sarah, who wrote short stories when she could. The extra theatre downtime wasn't empty, given the countless six-inch woollen squares to join together for army blankets.

Pamela later recalled that this evening was two days after she first met Randolph (now a junior officer in the Queen's Own Hussars). When not training on Salisbury Plain he got jobs like escorting the Duke and Duchess of Windsor back to Britain. It was shyness that made him turn away from Pamela and engage in quick-fire conversation with Birkin, seated at his side. He was acutely aware of her presence and every now and then flipped around to tell her how ravishing she was, only to quickly resume his dialogue with the editor. People tried to put her off Randolph (his best friend Ed Stanley being one) but Pam felt drawn to this scion of a political bloodline. Listening to Randolph, not for a moment did one believe the war could be lost. The Dunns, Philip and Mary, brought them together telling her what great fun he was, despite being a bit fat. Pamela was staying at their flat near Victoria Station. (Bridget, Philip's sister, had married Peter Metternich and was soon to be widowed and stranded in Germany.) Pamela's season ended and in those uncertain times there seemed little point in waiting. Within days the couple set a date to marry.

Pamela already had a bubbly friendship with Sarah and Diana. A hiccup occurred when Mary thought one of best man Seymour Berry's gifts for the bride was for her. Mary started wearing the contentious little clasp. Seymour prised it off and it rankled. A newsreel shows the couple leaving the Admiralty with the enormous quill in Pamela's beret negotiated through an arch of swords. The happy faces outside St John's Smith Square show how much the Churchill family warmed hearts. Vic was first to arrive from the Liverpool Empire. Sarah was 'Gaslighting' at the TR, Bournemouth, but was magicked there and back.

The newlyweds moved to a semi-detached house in Driffield near Hull, close to Randolph's unit. Feeding him meat pies, Pamela discovered her hubby came complete with unpaid bills from his tailor, from Berry Bros & Rudd and for gifts delivered to Mrs Harrison Williams. Her talent for home economics was soon tested to the limit. 'Gentlemen exist by credit' was young Churchill's explanation. Teased about being out of shape by colleagues, he wagered £50 that he could walk 50 miles in a day. He employed his wife as coach and started training. He began the trek late at night from York with Pamela trailing him with her car lights. He won the wager at great cost to his feet, hoping it would help with bills (despite these being greater by a factor of ten), but his colleagues never paid up. A gold pen was nevertheless found for Winston for his birthday. Churchill loved Pamela's easy wit and warmth and signed all his wartime documents with her pen (it became Randolph's later). He got *Roses of Picardy* rendered correctly on violin by Vic at his birthday celebration – a change from the off-key version at the Hippodrome.

Vic's new show was *Black Velvet*. Below a sign bearing the legend 'Silence is Golden', he was seated at a camouflage-painted desk in the sketch 'Censored by the Ministry of ?' in which he was a sarcastic Minister. The Führer arrives and delivers a monologue. With Jack Morrison the absolute spitting image in this early mockery, some emotional detachment was required on Vic's part, given the persecution affecting his family. He managed to perform the scene 620 times up to September 1940.

There was somebody else in the *Black Velvet* audience with a memory that went back to Vienna. This was Heinrich Benedikt, who had known Viki Samek in the Austro-Hungarian Army. He was intrigued to see that the 'good-for-nothing' was now king of London's West End. In his memoir he recalls Vic's comment on stage about his 'grandmother' having come home from Egypt 'forcing him to perform'. Egyptian slaves came on quick as a flash carrying a sarcophagus. What went through Heinrich's mind was that Countess Triangi would suddenly come out of that box, complete with flute. However, the lid opened and an adolescent girl in an abbreviated costume toppled out. There were more prods at the enemy: satirical acrobatic turns in '*Achtung! Achtung!* We all Fall Down'. The feminine content included 'overnight sensation' Pat Kirkwood and other lovelies. Finally a mise en scène harked back to Leicester Square's Empire Theatre. It was 1939's take on its 'Promenade' (or second-floor room) that Winston had known in 1896. Back then he led a group of rioters from Sandhurst, disrupting the efforts of moralising crusader Mrs Ormiston Chant to fence off rooms where the demi-monde and sodomites were rubbing shoulders with gilded youth. Cadet Churchill told stunned crowds: 'I stand for Liberty!' In *Black Velvet* antique turns like the Vernon Sisters and Gus Elen were impersonated, with Pat Kirkwood as Vesta Tilley. The First Lord's daughter beheld that 'Cosmopolitan Club of the World' from the wings.

In December a further revue at Holborn boasted the talents of two Americans: Bebe Daniels and Ben Lyon. In *Haw Haw* the former did an Eleanor Powell dance. Putting Max Miller in sketches didn't work and here he donned a variety of guises including a 'Blitzkrieg Hitler', while Ben was a Nazi in another scene. Not many folk knew then what was happening abroad owing to censorship (and lack of interest). The revue took its title from the words of British Fascist William Joyce (ex-Black and Tans) who announced himself nasally on the wireless with 'Germany calling, Germany calling' in a fake cut-glass accent. It was obviously Nazi propaganda but 60% of wireless owners in Britain used Reichs-Rundfunk to get news rather than wait for the interminably slow British news. The ideas Lord Haw Haw perpetrated, such as 'Churchill's Lies' in December 1939 and 'Britain's Cowardice in War' in August 1940, were enough for letters to be sent to *The Times* calling for the broadcast to be jammed, but no official denunciation was issued. There were so many tricky subjects requiring censorship, like the masses of Jewish refugees. The London borough of Hendon alone had received 145,000 and a repeat of problems faced 50 years earlier was feared. An 'alien takeover' was expected and an opinion poll showed that the idea that Jews were associated with money prevailed, with only 18% considering Jews deserving of sympathy. Even Orwell remarked, 'For the time being, we have heard enough about the concentration camps and the persecution of the Jews.' Some Londoners, however, were proud of their cosmopolitan city. In Knightsbridge 50 East End Jews were among 90 residing at Lord Redesdale's house, the place where Unity Mitford and her pet snake once caused havoc.

Machiavelli's satire *Mandragola* opened at Notting Hill's Mercury Theatre on 19 December with Sarah portraying an adulterous Florentine plotting to murder her husband (John Laurie). Casting Churchill's daughter as the one whose wicked 'code' wreaks havoc on figures in public office made little sense. She was also 'bored-looking' on stage. Her looks suggested 'a modern

English girl', so a different play was tried: Shaw's *Misalliance* at the Embassy, Swiss Cottage. That failed. She wasn't 'jolly' enough. She contracted measles and by early February 1940 had shelved the Shavian and the esoteric and was back in plays with popular appeal. She toured the North alternating *Gaslight* and *Quiet Wedding*. When the *Yorkshire Evening News* came to interview her she was knitting scarves for Randolph and Duncan. Homemade scarves were not what you gave Vic. She joked about how unpopular she would be if she tried singing in one of his revues. Stacked up with blue wool, her dressing room was like a Royal Navy scarf factory. The men needed woollens and she had, after all, adopted a minesweeper. New benevolent funds resembling those for actors were springing up for the Services. Sarah became a champion for knitting, with Liberal women giving her a scarf for Papa. The press said how different she was to the pampered wife you expected one of London's highest-paid entertainers to have. As well as her lack of 'side', her voice was far less 'deb' sounding; a conscious change influenced by friends like Judy. The Olivers adopted two lion cubs, helping London Zoo's Adopt an Animal Scheme. Most venomous or dangerous animals were killed but not the Komodo dragon or the huge python, kept in bombproof cages. A splendidly besuited Vic let Sarah and Phyllis play with the cubs. Phyllis lived close by at 65 Marsham Court. She had changed her name to Langford Oliver.

Vic was at the core of *Black Velvet* and in a Services skit as Shakespeare's Malvolio. In March he tried straight drama in a pilot revue, *Plays and Music*, a new packaging of Coward's *Tonight at 8.30* that five years earlier paired Noël and Gertrude Lawrence. The 1940 version chose three playlets only: *Hands Across the Sea*, *Fumed Oak* and *We Were Dancing*, adding variety-style turns. Phyllis had several parts and in the interval belted out the hit tunes of 1940. *Plays and Music* benefitted from original 1936 cast members Kenneth Carten, Joyce Carey and Moya Nugent. Robert Sansom and Hugh French were recruited; the latter compèred Vic and Margot at their first Palladium date in 1934 and later became a Beverly Hills agent. Sarah had a stumble-proof Juliet balcony. They went on to a hospital in the West Riding of Yorkshire where wounded troops got a vicoliverish *talking to* before being led in song.

Vic rushed back to the Hippodrome and Sarah to Norwich's Theatre where she heard cries of 'Good old Winston!' and gave prizes at the RAF's Joystick Dance. *Gaslight* went to Torquay, then to Bath, where her performance was called 'a triumph in emotional acting and skilful restraint'. All of a sudden she was stopped in her tracks at the reaction her father was evincing from people around her. Seeing how lost and fearful they were, she noticed them looking to him as a kind of saviour. She wrote to Papa conveying this and began to feel the pull of destiny.

During a week at the Grand, Luton, she and Phyllis were guests of Sir Felix Cassel at Putteridge Bury. Francis Cassel, a boy after Sarah's heart, was theatre-mad and a great concert pianist. Whither he went came Clarissa Borenius, also musically gifted. Since moving to London in 1909 her father Tancred had gained a reputation as an art expert. Sotheby's and members of the aristocracy consulted with him. His country, Finland, stood on its own in the 'Winter War' following the pact between Germany and the USSR. Now, as Secretary-General of the Polish Relief Fund (PRF) – one of Britain's largest charities – he wanted to preserve both countries' sovereignty. Concerts and dances raised money at venues like the Hungaria Restaurant. Sarah longed to help nations her father regarded as friends. It was at Putteridge Bury where the idea of a way to help the Poles came to her.

When Germany invaded neutral Norway, Churchill was quick to send a combined Anglo-French-Polish force to provide warship cover of island bases and forestall capture of the ports. He worked like a dynamo, leaving many Chiefs-of-Staffs in the shade. The war felt close to home when Giles Romilly (reporting for the *Express* in Narvik) was captured. Randolph vanished, too, during a 48-hour leave; but only to the Savoy. Duncan Sandys faced off enemy aircraft and guarded RAF airfields. He wrote to his father-in-law about his gratitude for the faith his colleagues had in his command. They bought time to stop Norway's gold reserves falling into Nazi hands, but the Allies had to withdraw and at home there was severe criticism. While he accepted blame, people drew inspiration from the 'warmonger' at the Admiralty. Bracken ran around town looking for Winston on 9 May 1940 to persuade him not to second Halifax after Tory MPs voted against Chamberlain. Halifax might just have supplanted him. He found unexpected support in the Labour Party and in the atmosphere following Hitler's ultimatum to Holland, King George VI sent for Churchill.

Vic was thrilled, writing to express his belief that nobody was better suited to being PM. 'May you be completely successful! Yours, Vic and Sarah.' When asked for a comment about her Pa's new position, Sarah 'smiled soaringly' then struggled to think what to say. It dawned on her how difficult it might be for her to discuss him. Three decades on, she reflected on this. Asked if he was a stern parent, she replied, 'Not to me, but he probably was to his country. Else why did we go on the long journey with him? We believed in him.' Jock Colville became a myrmidon in the PM's Private Office and initially found his boss intimidating. Winston's dictation continued to be taken by good-natured Kathleen Hill (a skilled violinist). Clementine's opinion was sacred enough that Winston gave her his drafts – such as his 'Blood, toil, tears and sweat' speech on 13 May (channelling Byron and Garibaldi). He simplified phrases she thought pertinent. She showed disapproval if his treatment of others became tyrannical. She was a warrior too, settling scores he would sooner let go of, where those who had undermined him were concerned.

Sarah toured the provinces, organised collections and arrived at friends' houses in her Jaguar. She wished she could be in more things with Vic, then appearing in a Mrs Doubtfire type role in *Room For Two*. She told a newspaperman her home life was non-existent. Only when she and Vic took vacations was it normal and he was on her mind every day. When his schedule allowed, Vic travelled to be near her. Later that month in Coventry, husband and wife were spotted cosying up at a café. Pumped up with happiness, the Oliver marriage suffered sharp pricks when Vic began talking about returning to the US. He could lose his US citizenship by being away too long. The truth was he was staying only because Sarah begged him to. 'Could we not help Britain more in the US?' he asked. The prospect of American aid seemed non-existent with Kennedy talking to Göring's economic advisor about a gold loan to Germany. Ten days after Churchill's appointment, US diplomat and isolationist Tyler Kent was found to have stolen thousands of documents at the US Embassy, some of which made it to Germany.

Sarah was the daughter of the man whose grave words a nation clung to. 'The whole fury and might of the enemy must very soon be turned on us,' the unmistakeable voice intoned on 18 June. Her wifely and daughterly loyalties were divided. Doing something worthy mattered. In her dressing room at Brighton's Theatre Royal, she confessed that acting was 'just a job ... it can help people keep their spirits up, remember their sense of humour and through their laughter find new confidence in themselves'. She was braced for duties. 'Consolation,' she said, 'must be found in the knowledge that our routine jobs are as important to the country as the more satisfying and seemingly more practical war work.' She emphasised the value of cheerfulness, which makes 'passing through the valley of the shadow of death bearable'. She stated she had no intention of leaving for America. She wouldn't under any circumstance bring her family's patriotism into question. Never mind Vic.

Clementine (acknowledged for her beauty in the family and beyond) traditionally advised her daughters on their clothes. Now it was Sarah's turn to tell Mama how a PM's wife ought to look. Sarah was in and out of outfitters helping Vic and ran into Renée Houston, then choosing a fur for her entrance in Korda's *Old Bill and Son*. Wondering if a little of the Houston sister's magic might rub off on her constantly photographed mother, Sarah asked her if she could tell Clementine about the lynx Renée had chosen. 'You tell her, ducks! Don't mind one bit,' said the star to her wee friend. When *Old Bill* premièred on 1 March 1941 a newsreel ran before the film. Renée was in the cinema with John Mills, who laughed when Mrs Churchill was seen in the coat before the actress got a chance to debut it. Renée didn't expect Sarah's mother to wear a replica and steal her thunder, but Clementine's glamour, whether inspecting the Home Guard, or dressing the lynx down with a turban for war-torn streets, did much for morale and Sarah could perhaps take a little credit.

Randolph's actions caused a major row on his next 'forty-eight hour'. He was expected at Downing Street to lunch with Sikorski (Head of the Polish Government in Exile) and Lord Halifax. He told Pamela he was seeing Spanish Civil War reporter Cholly Knickerbocker for an hour at the Savoy Grill but his place at the table was still empty at 5 p.m. Next day he stumbled in dead to the world at 6 a.m. and his wife had to put him to bed. Randolph had military maps in his possession and had left them on the seat of Pamela's Jaguar, which he had borrowed. Sgt Thompson notified his parents of the security risk and they were livid. Randolph's mother summoned Pamela to her room, sitting upright in bed wearing white gloves. She reduced her to tears and ordered Randolph to leave immediately. Sarah had sympathy, having had the white gloves treatment herself. These were slipped on when things were *bad*, she told Pamela. Her sister-in-law was intrigued as to what Sarah had done to trigger them.

The Battle of Boulogne had gone awry and General Gort ordered withdrawal via Dunkirk, the only port offering a chance of escape. Leaving behind 7,000 tons of ammunition, 120,000 vehicles and 90,000 rifles, it was a bitter blow, but the amazing coordination and fellowship beginning on 26 May 1940 that enabled rescue was a miracle. A new show, *Hi Gang*, coincided with this extaordinary operation. The format Ben Lyon and Bebe Daniels proposed to the BBC revolved around the lives of Ben, Bebe and Vic Oliver. It became the most popular wartime radio broadcast. Soon, the Austrian could quip: 'Well Bebe – you won't have to busk in front the theatres to keep Ben and me.' The public got to know Vic as the 'other person' in the Lyons' marriage. Devious as hell, he messed up their plans, trying to lure Ben back into a crap vaudeville act they did long ago – trying to prise him from the clutches of Bebe. 'Don't be a lion in a Daniels den,' Vic would plead in his Malaprop way. The Lyons' enterprises would come crashing down because of Oliver's hare-brained schemes. Miss Daniels called him a 'rat' and a 'twerp' and he retaliated with a sneering 'Are you undressing me?' People loved the new phrases like Bebe's 'Oh take a powder Vic.' You had to be listening close to *Hi-Gang* with its mastery of pace and pitch. Some critics disliked the gabbling voices. Could this 'atmosphere of unblushing vulgarity' really help the Forces? 'Every time I open my mouth I put my foot in it,' was Vic's explanation. He made topical gags, too: 'You wouldn't understand it – that's occupied French,' he told gullible Ben. The Lyons sang with the help of Jay

Wilbur and his orchestra aided by the Greene Sisters (a trio rather like the Andrews Sisters) with solo numbers by British baritone Sam Browne.

Mussolini entered the war. If Sarah thought she was a wayward daughter, she wasn't half as bad as *Il Duce*'s Edda. As pro-Nazi as Unity, Edda married Foreign Minister Galeazzo Ciano. She often accused him of Germanophobia, as his diaries testify. He was distrustful of the Nazis and became their victim. Churchill had made a perilous flight to France on 3 May, concerned about military deficiencies. 'We shall fight on the beaches, we shall fight on the landing grounds…' came on 4 June, after the Dunkirk evacuation. While the Churchills were moving into 10 Downing Street the Germans rolled into Paris. France collapsed like a pack of cards. The family made themselves comfortable at Chequers, but not a moment was spared on idle subjects as telegrams went out to FDR and the Dominion leaders.

Diana Mosley, Hitler's opera buddy at the Wagner *Festspiel*, was, like her husband, imprisoned shortly after her son was born under Defence Regulation 18B. Hearing this on 29 June, the Churchill children felt sad for the Mitford family. George Pitt-Rivers, husband of Sylvia Henley's daughter Rosalind, was also locked up for his eugenicist beliefs. Out of the 150 prominent people arrested, the first two were cousins. One had to laugh at the irony. As age-old country signs came down, hikers asked directions and were met with, 'Dunno, I've just been evacuated.' People wondered if the clocks might advance two hours ahead of GMT so folk might awaken at dawn when invaders usually arrive. It would assist the theatregoer to get home before dark. Home Secretary Sir John Anderson was considering it. For safety, the *Hi-Gang* team moved to the underground Paris Theatre at 12 Lower Regent Street. The scarcity of writers meant that Vic, Ben and Bebe wrote scripts in the safety of the basement of the Lyons' Paddington house, 18 Southwick Street. Vic had amazing energy. He did this on top of two West End shows a night.

Sirens screeching, guns firing and bombs falling obliterated any trace of ennui between 10 July and 31 October. Nerves were frayed in the Battle of Britain. What chance did 650 British Spitfires and Hurricanes have against Germany's 2,500 bombers and fighters? A weekend sanctuary was Ditchley Park in Oxfordshire – difficult to spot from the air. On 14 July 1940 Diana Cooper, Noël, Bobbety and Betty Cranborne gathered there. Winston formed the Special Operations Executive (SOE), specialising in sabotage and coordinating with British security. Great War air ace 'Little Bill' Stephenson was a key player, as were Canadian newsman Campbell Stuart and propaganda expert Dallas Brooks. Bruce Lockhart was in its ranks with a safe house in Caxton Street, seeing the recruitment of Ian Fleming, Leslie Howard, Niven, Roald Dahl, Korda and Cary Grant. Noël joined in late July. Posted to places crawling with Nazis such as South America, his celebrity served as a cover while he tried to gauge what the enemy would do next. Sarah was inspired by Noël's ability to rally American friends to the cause of Allied relief, ignoring a suspicious FBI and a communist cabal in New York. Fanny Holtzman, legal advisor to L. B. Mayer since 1926, secured refuge for Noël's reportedly spoilt orphans at the Edwin Gould Foundation. 'We never knew how this miracle came about but we thanked God, Gould, Gertrude and Fanny,' said actor Brian Aherne.

Jock Colville thought Sarah a great girl, although he considered Mary the better looker. On 25 July he took Clementine and Mary to dinner and joined the Sandyses at the Q Theatre where Sarah was performing alongside Peter Glenville in Novello's *Murder in Mayfair* (so 'pre-war' you forgot present troubles). Aware of the bad rap Sarah got, Jock wrote that he was 'agreeably surprised' by how good she was and that with her striking hair she 'looked much lovelier than she in fact is'. With the Churchills he dined at Vic and Sarah's, levelling a large dish of cherries. Teetotaller Vic had water and munched on a sandwich while everyone else 'swilled champagne'. Vic rushed off to broadcast to the US, allowing the clan quality time. Sarah and her mother were at the Apollo on 2 August as Kennedy's VIP guests for the first night of a play. Its author, Clare Boothe Luce, was present. Sarah had met her six years earlier when, with Bernie Baruch (Clare's secret lover), she had spent a few days at Chartwell. Randolph picked her up at the station and something clicked, accounting for a passing affair. Within a year of this visit another rich old man, Henry Luce – publisher of *Time* and *Life* – proposed and Clare accepted.

Over the years Randolph never tired of commenting on Clare's exploits. The writer of *The Women* had concerns about her country's isolationism. 'How would America cope with the Third Reich?' was the theme of *Margin for Error*. A New York Jewish cop is ordered by the Mayor to protect visiting Nazis. Luce's anti-isolationist stance made her popular with Winston, desperate for an alliance with the US. Joe Kennedy writhed in embarrassment. One of the lines, that America was a free country on account of the British Navy, drew huge applause.

The other Claire Luce – stage star – saw less of Randolph. After *Follow the Sun*, she was in Broadway's *Of Mice and Men* before taking Steinbeck to London's tiny Gate Theatre. She stayed in Britain throughout the war. A Pathé film featuring Claire is a relic of the Oliver marriage. The trio publicise a horse-drawn trailer ambulance supplied to Britain, starting with a little dumb talk with Vic's elastic features twisting into a funny smile as he distorts meanings. 'A horse is a friend's best man ... I mean a man is a horse's best friend.' In her 'English' voice Claire says: 'Sarah, I think Vic's getting a bit muddled.'

The newsreel ends with Vic at the reins but you don't hear the Cockney in the crowd shouting: 'Thet's the Prime Minister's daughter, thet is!'

Sutton Vane's play about passengers discovering they are disembodied spirits was Sarah's play at the time she filmed this. Having attempted suicide, she is semi-living as a 'Halfway' (to heaven or hell) in *Outward Bound*. It had its baptism by air raid the day Clementine and Vic came to Golders Green. It was harrowing enough to see Sarah running around the stage crying pathetically for help. Critics were complimentary apart from one who unkindly commented that she lacked 'the warmth and light of life and love'. Excerpts by the cast were on BBC's *Theatreland* on 23 August, one of Sarah's earliest radio broadcasts.

De Gaulle (of the Free French), Pug Ismay (Winston's chief military assistant), Prof, Morton and Halifax were at Chequers on 18 August. Sarah, along with Duncan and Diana, listened to discussions. With heavy casualties at sea and in the air, everyone rejoiced as enemy losses increased. Ramping up aircraft production was Beaverbrook's responsibility. For four weeks Moss Empires presented all *Black Velvet*'s receipts for the purchase of Spitfires. The PM did them the honour of coming to a performance. Despite the Blitz, Sarah insisted on staying in the West End, seeing each new play at the Arts Theatre.

Her obsession with high art annoyed Vic. With the heavy bombing and limited transport, he wished she wasn't waiting for him. Where you laid your head each night was a life-and-death matter. Cousin Johnny, now designing camouflage, cadged a bed at the Downing Street shelter. Bracken's next-door neighbour in Lord North Street opened his basement to the public and the Dorchester's 'Turkish' shelter welcomed celebrities. A writer on *Vogue* identifed MPs, Diana Cooper (in full evening dress), Vic Oliver (in serious mood), Sarah (sound asleep on the floor) and actress Leonora Corbett (trying out hairdos). The elite made the 'Dorch' their base, installing treasured items in suites. Victor Cazalet took his modern art whilst Lady D's room had the sketch Queen Victoria did of her mother. The Savoy shelter, situated under eight floors of luxury, had comfy cubicles, water services and a medical corner with Red Cross staff. The 'have-nots' took umbrage and a hundred Cockneys burst in one night so the authorities might take notice of their deprivations.

Even if the American President wanted to help, the Neutrality Act made this difficult. While his Chief of Staff General Marshall predicted Britain would fall and warned against sending supplies which might end up in German hands, FDR was trying to secure Britain military goods and raw materials and get around the fact she lacked currency to pay. It took guts to champion Britain and sail against the wind. After a RAF raid on Berlin Hitler ordered the Luftwaffe to concentrate attacks on London. Buildings were prised open and silhouetted by fire. Inside the Holborn Empire the ground shuddered, but Max Miller and songstress Vera Lynn weren't deterred. The Cheeky Chappie's sketches included one of him as a Home Guard, one as a parachutist and one in an exchange between PM and son-in-law Vic Oliver. A few days later, FDR signed an agreement whereby the US gave the British 50 obsolete destroyers in exchange for 99-year leases to territory in Newfoundland and the Caribbean as bases. Churchill had hoped to get them for free but Congress put paid to that.

Randolph was selected to represent Preston when the seat fell vacant on the Tory incumbent's death. Next door to him, his father used 67 Westminster Gardens (acquired by Diana and Duncan prior to the Blitz). Neighbour C. B. Cochran was planning star-filled radio broadcasts for Saturday nights and persuaded the Olivers to do a sketch; Sarah professing a desire to be a comedienne and Vic wanting to be a dramatic actor. This was on the first *Cock-a-Doodle-do*, live from the Paris Theatre on 14 September before they skedaddled to Chequers for a party for Mary. CB had always been in love with Sarah's speaking voice. He got her to read Juliet with Leslie Howard as Romeo and at the height of the Blitz Sarah enjoyed national fame, as shown by the publicity created by Donegall of *The Sunday Dispatch*. The day after her broadcast, he announced he had selected a number of lovelies to advertise his Red-Heads Spitfire Fund. Sarah was 'Red-Head No 1'. Earlier that month *Tatler* featured two full-page photos by young photographer Antony Beauchamp with the caption: 'Two of the Premier's Beautiful Daughters: One an actress, the other a Charming Debutante.' Sarah and Vic were in the last *Cock-a-Doodle-do* on 5 October when listeners heard her read Rupert Brooke's *Old Vicarage, Grantchester.*

When St Paul's took a hit, Diana Sandys was terribly upset. She and Duncan were great admirers of the City churches and had been married in one. That same night Pamela went into labour at Chequers. She had intended to have her baby at Middlesex Hospital to save money but, with bombs falling, changed tack. Her bargain basement doctor took ages to arrive and when he did his presence made Clementine awkward. Into an inexplicably violent world, little Winston was born. No one could find Randolph. Cecil Beaton later recalled a joke played on Mr and Mrs C when Pam's Pekinese was wrapped in the baby's smock.

Vic and Sarah were to begin *Plays and Music* (the revue piloted seven months before) touring the 'safe' provinces. Sarah pulled out after landing a part in *Spring Meeting*. Husband and wife saw each other in between her time at Welwyn Garden City and Vic's tour dates, borrowing homes for short periods from obliging friends. Enid Bagnold (introduced to the Churchills by Sickert) and her husband Sir Roderick Jones (formidable head of Reuters) gave them Dale Cottage, across the pond from their Rottingdean home, for the weekend of 12 October. There was a high demand for their properties and in a letter Enid wrote to Beaton (also vying to come) she doesn't sound happy about the Olivers' visit. Scenes were being witnessed with wife accusing husband of betraying his pledge to stay in Britain. At Sarah's party in the Savoy's River Room they were saving face. He breathed a sigh of relief when the cast of her film was told to remain at Welwyn. Pleased that the work hadn't come through Vic's offices, Sarah was blown along on a gust of independence, regretting not having done enough herself. Her husband's guidance no longer suited her. More stimulating was the acceptance of colleagues and technicians who were crazy about what they did and weren't in it for the money.

Sarah was holding her own against experienced film actors including Henry Edwards (as Sir Richard), Enid Stamp-Taylor (as Tiny Fox-Talbot, out to snare a bride for her son) and Basil Sydney (as butler James – full of the Blarney and fond of the brandy). Nova Pilbeam was scatty sister Baby – fellow inhabitant of a crumbling Irish pile. Michael Wilding was the nouveau riche Tony, in love with Baby. Margaret Rutherford had played eccentric Aunt Bijou on stage and TV. With its slightly farcical parallel to Chartwell life, *Spring Meeting* has Sarah as Joanie. Her acting is studied. She didn't possess the confidence yet to relax; her face coming alive with an intense thought only to go sad and cold when it passed. There was scope for romantic playing alongside Hugh McDermott. She's in love with Michael: 'perfect son-in-law material', only he's the stable-hand. They confront Sir Richard but 'round one' fails when the stable-hand's courage wanes. When Sir Richard loses what's left of his fortune, 'round two' of the Joanie stakes sees Michael standing up to the old man and threatening to elope. Sarah shines using quickfire dialogue, telling father how she's no longer afraid of him. Ironically, the actress was wishing she could dump her current manager and get her fearful one back.

# 6

# Re-claimed and Re-educated

Vic was in Blackpool on 14 October 1940 playing one half of a not very successful music-hall act; Bea Lillie his viper-tongued other half. Performing *Red Peppers* was a physical feat but headlines like 'First Rate plays Third-Rate' made it worth it. His straight role as Henry Gow, exacting revenge on an ungrateful family in *Fumed Oak*, surprised people, but his breezy stand-ups made critics call him 'the best story-teller we have'. Sarah saw *Plays and Music* in Bristol. Reading notices like 'What an asset the Churchill family are', with the PM's son-in-law named its popular frontrunner, made bittersweet reading. Little limelight was falling on her – just bombs. These left Leicester Square deserted and 10 Downing Street blasted and without gas. None was more defiant than family cook Mrs Landemare, believing the PM's supper took precedence over the siren. One story has Winston scolding his staff with the unlikely 'I shall prepare my own dinner', only to find his chop served the way he liked it. Another has Mrs Landemare waiting for his mousseline pudding to rise when the PM saves her life. When the family gathered for his 'Hommage à la France' speech (21 October), Clementine was so nervous she broke the dial of the radio. They trekked up to a servant's room to hear the rest of the broadcast.

To a journalist Vic said: 'I would never run away from England,' silkily assuring fans: 'I am completely neutral. I don't care who kills Hitler.' He admitted he was wealthy, pointing out, with regret, that it paid to play instruments badly. On 10 November, while on tour promoting war bonds, he broadcast from RAF Sealand, then left for Oxford where he and the Duke of Marlborough (Cousin Bert) were to start the bidding at a farmer's auction to benefit the Agricultural Red Cross.

He passed Coventry and, like every pilgrim, saw its cathedral. Londoners prepared for a raid on 14 November but, as it turned out, Coventry got it, with St Michael's ruined. British Intelligence could now decipher enemy messages via ENIGMA decrypts. Codenamed 'Ultra', some say the system showed Coventry was the target for the big raid but that no steps were taken to put citizens on high alert in case the enemy caught on that Britain was ahead of the game. Eyewitnesses reject this, saying the PM genuinely believed London was the target. Years later, when Britain's success in cracking German codes was publicly revealed, Sarah privately admitted to her father being aware of the situation a few hours before. Her father had once told her: 'Truth is a precious thing but it must sometimes be surrounded by lies.' She admitted how difficult it was but clarified that, when millions depend on one person's integrity, this happens. She recalled his choice to sanction human sacrifice to protect the greater good:

> A few hours before Coventry was bombed there was a tip-off but to switch defences would be to let the Germans know we had broken the code and it would impact the next major set of offences. It meant letting it go and sacrificing a beautiful cathedral in exchange. The decision brought tears to his eyes.

That November Sarah joined Vic on *Hi Gang* but reminders of the day she eloped, like Jenny Nicholson (now at the BBC and mentioning their friendship to plug the drama she had written), made her shudder. In November Pamela and Randolph moved into Icklefield House in Hitchin. The huge rectory had room for Diana, her children Julian and Edwina, the Sandys' Irish maid and Pam's nanny. Visiting Randolph, Ambassador Maisky noticed that Sarah was living there too. Sarah and Pam travelled to Downing Street to dine with Lord Moyne (Minister Resident in Cairo). As well as running the rectory Pamela ran a factory canteen.

Cecil Beaton was all ears on 20 November, recording that Diana worked for an interior decorators. Telling Papa she didn't think much of its dull premises, he remarked: 'Dowdy? Why, all England's dowdy!' Randolph gave his maiden speech, referring to his grandpa's Progressive Conservatism, then returned for training with Battalion 8 Layforce, the formation named after Bob Laycock. His friends Philip Dunn, Robin Campbell and Peter Fitzwilliam (known as 'Blood') were there, each in charge of a troop. The 2,000 tough boys due to serve in the Middle East resented being commanded by idiots from Whites Club who knew little of warfare. Despite the fact that weapons were being bombed off assembly lines, Vic spoke to a large crowd, promising to tell Mr Churchill about Huddersfield's excellent performance in War Weapons Week: 'If we don't win the war the money won't be worth anything anyway, so why keep it? Lend everything you can and the war will be over quicker.' When he said America could be relied on he received euphoric applause.

The Olivers were now Jimmy de Rothschild's tenants at The Homestead, close by Eythrope Pavilion on the banks of the Thame. For a while they stopped bickering. The entire Churchill clan gathered round the font when baby Winston was christened at Ellesborough Parish Church. Godmother Virginia Cowles arrived to see tears streaming down the PM's face. Asked to speak, he began: 'In these days I begin thinking of Our Lord,' then sat down and remained muted all day. Not having a phone at The Homestead annoyed Sarah, who pestered John Martin about an installation. The Secretary requested that she be patient given demands in the wake of Coventry.

Bea Lillie was leaving *Plays and Music* and Sarah sped off to join her husband at a Cardiff fête. She was joining the show at Manchester. For publicity's sake they played up the Opera House's romantic connotations. 'This is a place of memories for us y'know,' Vic said, pulling his wife's arm through his. Sarah was Juliet, but the only playlet she did was *We Were Dancing*, a satire set in 'Samolo', a South Pacific colony where if you faltered in the heat the National Anthem revived you. Modern times invade the elite enclave when, at a dinner-dance, 'Louise Charteris' and 'Karl Sandys' (both married) fall in love, astounding British expats. The coincidental surnames surprised the Churchill family, but these were in Noël's original play. Louise convinces Hubert Charteris to let her leave for Australia with her lover. Day dawns, enchantment passes and Louise and Karl become strangers again. Many times had the Olivers shared a stage but they hadn't acted together. Having them shrug off consequences in planning a future was clever casting. Sarah needed a boost from the Press. The *Manchester Guardian* judged her approach to Juliet scrupulous but said her etherealised Shakespeare was 'not at all impassioned'. It felt her talents had more scope in the playlet. Vic kept Sarah on her toes in December 1940. There's every indication they enjoyed working together, making *We Were Dancing* fresh for each performance. They took it to York, Hull, Glasgow, Edinburgh, Newcastle, Bradford then London. What always brought a stir in the audience was the moment when Vic kisses his wife. Fay Lenore, a legendary performer from the London Palladium, worked with Vic many times, famously as principal boy Nemo the Gypsy in *Old King Cole* at Glasgow Empire, with Vic doubling as the king's wicked brother. Fay practised épées prior to the pantomime. In one energetic scene Nemo and Rollo fight sabre to sabre. She remembers what it was like being on stage with Vic Oliver in 1953:

> Vic played a kind of devil character – he made it harder for me. There was a cheeky laugh and glint in his eye that told me he would do something

> slightly different that wasn't rehearsed. It made the work more fun – slightly unpredictable. It was really good working with him. Vic was not severe at all – never pushy. I knew he was very shrewd and serious-minded off stage. I got the impression he kept people at an arm's length. As a colleague he was a perfect gentleman. I respected him.

Vic only occasionally tried out jokes on Sarah. She would later admit: 'If I don't laugh, he uses the joke. I'm rather slow.' He was a studied comedian who kept abreast of public affairs and newsworthy items, learnt about every new town he appeared in and saw scope in the vagaries of the lives of ordinary men and women. Some gags suited the wireless:

> The other night I overheard a boy and girl talking in a corner. The boy asked: 'Is it true you have a penchant for flirting?'
> 'Oh no,' she told him, 'I do all mine on an old-fashioned settee.'

Others were OK on the Glasgow stage:

> Do you like my trousers? Lovely aren't they? Made by a lady tailor. She felt me all over – must have been Australian as she kept wanting to get down under.

His promise to stay in Britain now they had a wonderful home should have pleased Sarah. Why didn't it? They appeared united but the jury was out as to whether 'Louise' and 'Karl' could sustain a future. Far away from Noël's Pacific, the German battleship *Graf Spee* marauded and losses were heavy. Mary told Sarah about a Europe of the future. Papa visualised a Britain linked to it but not inside it. Jock, de Gaulle and Morton saw him cover a map with marker pen, creating nine democratic zones with Poland a *Mitteleuropa* focus. They knew that when night fell and the No. 10 black cat jumped on his bed he wasn't above asking that darling creature's opinion. Nothing was certain except that the Empire couldn't carry on fighting alone. The President remained out of reach.

Vic had no need to look at the world through rose-tinted glasses. His eyes, he said, were 'naturally bloodshot'. He was at the Bristol Hippodrome with a festive message to his 'dear Fans and Fannies in the Services', asking them to 'Think of me once in a while, as I'm constantly thinking of you and don't say "*With what*?" either.' In December 1940, he and Sarah opened up their flat to the family with Sarah transforming Vic's dusty alcohol-free larder into a fine liquor display. Then it was Chequers for Christmas and Vic got tinkling with Sarah trying out a number. Papa danced to Viennese waltzes and before the season was over, a glint of light appeared at the corner of the blackout curtain. The following month the Churchills would welcome Harry Hopkins (unofficial assistant president) and something, just something, gave them cause for optimism. History might have been different had Hopkins failed to click with them. A New Deal architect, he hated hereditary privilege. He'd heard about the sour impression Churchill made on FDR when he'd been a visiting US Navy official in 1918. Arriving in England in 1941, Harry's first evening was spent at Soho's Black Cat with CBS correspondent Ed Murrow. With nine live mics, Ed told the folks back home about the Blitz, starting his show with 'This is London!' Hopkins enjoyed every comfort at No. 10, Chequers and Ditchley Park. There was pheasant, champagne and the gleaming Michelin Man gave him cigars whilst questioning him from the tub. 'Whither thou goest, I will go,' Harry was soon heard saying and his stay extended to six weeks. He grew fond of the family, particularly Clementine and Pamela.

Partial to a wisecrack, Harry admired Vic and was impressed by the warmth between the PM and his self-made son-in-law. Harry knew what Vic had experienced, having had a clandestine, interfaith courtship himself prior to marrying Jewish Ethel Gross. Vic was admired for the links he fostered. The American Home Guard in Britain, now integrated with the Services, was a motorised squadron made up of US citizens, many of them Press correspondents. General Wade Hayes, its leader, was Vic's friend. Well established in the US, the William Allen White Society (WAWS), named after a progressive media mogul, reached out to Middle America with a message of 'All help for Britain short of nothing'. It retaliated against the message of America First – a body that hated the idea of the US being dragged into Europe's war. The nucleus of WAWS was the non-isolationist White Committee, personally backed by FDR. Vic and Claire Luce were closely involved and at the end of 1940 helped establish a branch for motivated US volunteers. Vic served as its vice-president with Claire on the committee. He highlighted WAWS, speaking to Blackpool's Rotary Club: 'Pro-British propaganda hasn't gone far enough' was his opener, and he vowed it wasn't too late to kick up a stink. Asked if America would enter the war, he said at present she wouldn't but 'before long, planes, guns and tanks will come, not in dozens but in hundreds' – enough for the PM to need a good 'chartered accountant' given the assets and liabilities. Asked if America could do more, Vic replied she could, blaming the 'Nabobs of industry' to whom FDR 'is tied ... hands and feet'. He became grave, asking those assembled not to be 'lulled by false security', citing France as proof of where that leads. The fact that Vic gave further speeches signifies Churchill's approval. American aid needed to be on people's minds. The more frequently it was talked about, the more normal it was to expect it. The folk across the pond sent parcels, horrified to hear of the bombing of London.

Churchill wanted his family to appear strong. For decades his children had been in the public eye and Sarah's transition from deb to actress had been closely followed. She was a unique means for the British to glimpse a private Churchill world. She didn't act supercilious and her parents seemed open-minded given the way they accepted her career and husband. Clementine was always smiling and leaving a trail of good feeling wherever she went. This happy family embraced modern life and there was mileage in the starry Vic and Sarah saga. A song they had jointly written was dedicated to the average couple and the lyrics to *I Give You My Heart* are Sarah's. The sheet music carried Sarah's portrait by Beauchamp and Vic's by Angus McBean. The song told lovers not to despair and to await the light that will shine in. Its message sadly applied to its composers no more. She had once given Vic her heart but now just being a dutiful daughter sufficed. On *Star Time* on 11 January 1941, however, they seemed a pair of lovebirds telling listeners how they met. They had their revue to publicise. Critics said Sarah's Juliet at York's Theatre Royal should be worked up a bit. Phrases like 'clever elocutionist' were applied to her 'Golden Reign of Queen Elizabeth' scene (written by Clemence Dane and featuring Bess's stirring words at Tilbury) but few real tributes. Vic outshone her.

The threat of an invasion lay heavy and Pamela's father-in-law gathered the women of the household to tell them that should the enemy pay a call they should reach for a carving knife and take out the nearest German. Randolph left for Egypt via the Cape of Good Hope. He played for high stakes on board and soon owed thousands. He sent word to his wife, pleading with her not to tell his father and asked if her £12 a week canteen pay combined with the proceeds of pawned jewellery might see him through. Pam got into her Jaguar and went to see Beaverbrook to ask if he might discreetly advance the money. They agreed she could rent Icklefield House and send Nanny and baby to Cherkley (Max's Leatherhead home where visitors complained of hunger caused by its owner's austerity). Pam in fact wouldn't let him pay the debt and begged for a job. Her role, connected to Royal Ordnance factories, was so boring it was a relief when bombs destroyed the office. Pamela then took a room at the Dorchester.

A concert Vic gave at Fulford Barracks in York was so packed that many had to be turned away. Watching him, Sarah thought how easy it was to idolise this unobtainable man. She came on to wish the men well, apologising for not having a 'turn'. The revue transferred to the New Theatre, Hull, with the Olivers getting star treatment from the mayor on 31 January before Vic picked lucky numbers at an Air Raid Fund dance, joking about the silk stocking prizes. Their next stop was Glasgow, the most Americanised city in Britain, as Vic described it. The Glasgow Empire saw them in *Idiot's Delight*, but Vic hadn't taken *Plays and Music* to the city with Bea. He would give it a shot with his wife. Prior to opening at the King's Theatre, a writer on *The Evening Citizen* was downbeat, saying he hadn't liked Vic's straight acting and that Glasgow was sick of Coward plays. But when the freshly renamed *Tonight at Seven* opened, the same critic, Jack House, changed his tune, calling Vic 'one of the funniest men who ever stepped on a stage ... My hands were so busy wiping my eyes that I feel I owe him some extra applause.' A dour critic on the *Evening News* early edition said the show was 'swollen with good things, yet conscious of a meal missed', but by the later edition he was ecstatic that Vic could 'air piquant gags which wouldn't normally be aired on radio'. Sarah's work was also admired. Glasgow's *Express* said that 'the words are Shakespeare but the voice is Churchill', adding that her 'half-boyish gallantry' suggested Rosalind.

People went Vic crazy. He spoke about cranks wielding Heath Robinson-like inventions – all of them boasting solutions in war-torn times. 'Would he use his influence with Mr C to get government go-ahead?' they asked. He said opportunities to spend time with the PM were 'restricted'. After his February 1941 success, the Glasgow Empire booked him on 10 April. Despite its tough reputation, the Empire (known for its difficult patrons who reacted badly to artistes like Jewell and Warriss) always welcomed Vic (even letting him revive *Fumed Oak* in November 1954, which in any other circumstance would be unheard of).

Sarah loved showbusiness. She would move through theatre's many-branched tree but always scampered back to Vic. It was necessary to milk 'the name', he told her. Keeping your foot on the pedal of commerce was the idea. It wasn't an ordinary marriage but mutual support sustained it. At first when Vic said they should be in America, where she was sure to get work in pictures, she appreciated his pushiness. But he wanted her to succeed by the easiest route without rating her talent highly. When she took risks, he got the credit. This crowd-pleaser with a polished exterior was restraining her. She *wasn't ready*, he would say, stifling her displays of boldness. His tone resembled the way her parents used to be: fearful of openness. The early romance gave way to a business-like friendship and Sarah went from loving 'pupil' to unsatisfied accomplice. In *Mr Showbusiness*, Vic points to Sarah's obsession with the stage and her constant thoughts about perfecting her art while he was focused on the money. The comment is disingenuous. He eventually went from star comic to less lucrative conductor, remaining as perfectionist as he was in comedy.

Vic loved Sarah and tried to make her happy. His failure was not seeing how dissatisfied she was. He had no wish to change the status quo. His marriage ensured entry into the topmost circles and he was gambling it would last. He and Sarah had dared to dare, but her inhibitions remained despite the liberties unleashed early on. They had a close trust and that was enough. He was made in a certain way and couldn't help it. Spending a lifetime inventing a character to present to the outside world comes at a cost. Liberal-minded friends ensured a safe environment for anyone exploring aspects of life and love. One source implies Vic was on such a journey. The evidence is uncorroborated but credible, casting light on his motivations. But the informant has to be treated with suspicion. Can you trust someone with morals so corrupt they could rob their own family and hate and subvert beneath a superficially helpful face?

Many would find it disgusting that a man given a life sentence for murder could publish his memoirs. The author refers to his early life in Glasgow when a chance meeting with a well-dressed man led him to obtain a position as a servant to the *bon ton*. Roy is the author's name. He wasn't a murderer then, but was to all intents and purposes a chancer, a heartless thief, a dominating sexual partner and a maverick. In his prison-dictated memoir he refers to his first meeting with Vic, who was staying alone at Glasgow's Central Station hotel. Roy didn't recognise him but thought his European accent distinctive. The conversation allegedly turned into a sexual opportunity and thereafter they saw each other intermittently in London (after the outwardly straight but pansexual Roy saw business opportunities down south). While Vic's identity became clear, one thing Roy wasn't (surprisingly) was a blackmailer. Gentlemanly rules seemed to apply in this case. To commit a gross indecency carried severe penalties, so people were skilfully covert. The young man was liked and trusted enough to be given access to a highly privileged circle of VIPs over a long period. He was, he claims, lent out for waiter duties with 'sexual services' on the side. The first encounter would fit in exactly with the time Vic was knocking around Glasgow giving interviews. Where Oliver was concerned, the liaison sprang from an unfettered impulse. Even Roy's account implies that the older man was new to the game. It might have lasted two years but wasn't a close association. Roy found he could no longer contact Vic. With his supportive nature, Vic had all kinds of friends and was vulnerable in his own way.

Roy served a witty, all-male set, always in private houses, sometimes at Terence Rattigan's. Terry's brilliance then reigned supreme: the characters in his plays appealing, deep and isolated by an inequality of passion (critics interpret some of his female personae as gay men). In this space, myriad friendships were tolerated but the last thing any man would do was to acknowledge publicly what was in his nature. Rattigan was seen as one of Britain's most eligible bachelors. Sometimes the club met at Ivor Novello's place; he eventually got into trouble with the police but powerful friends rescued him. The parties had frightfully respectable VIP attendees like Lord

Mountbatten (mentioned by Roy as an occasional guest). Fear and formality were left at the door. Not all the guests knew what could be on offer in adjoining rooms but many did and few cared. Tallulah Bankhead's line – 'Here's a rule I recommend: never practice two vices at once' – might apply to some of the gentlemen in those rooms. That Vic was part of this elite shows how liked he was. In the darkest days of the war this trusting and accepting bunch kept good faith.

Flattering theatrical honchos to further Sarah's career might be a reason why Vic was there. Added to this were the insecurities that come with age and getting over one's fright with birds of a feather. If he had another side to his nature it seems surprising that after five years Sarah was ignorant of it. Yet, no matter how non-judgmental she was about the sexuality of Ivor, Terence *et al.*, all of whom she knew well, the idea of her condoning Vic's walk on the wild side is unlikely. This was the 1940s and it was enough to send the former hero-worshipper into shock. The age difference between husband and wife also counts against this. Honesty would have destroyed Vic's moral authority. A married man's choice to have a liaison with a person of his own sex is often a way of exacting revenge on his wife. He might have had a giant axe to grind. Ironically, just when Sarah wanted 'action' Vic was pursuing the same. However, that's *by the by* because she was calling time on the marriage.

She was in Glasgow at the time Roy Archibald Hall reared his criminal head, and was trustful or neglectful enough to let Vic stay in a separate hotel when they toured. Oddly, Sarah stayed with Phyllis Luckett and the other actors. Phyllis was the only woman in the cast near to her in age. The two were close but there were limits to how far Sarah could open up to this 'adopted daughter' whose loyalty was to Vic. In a naval hospital, wounded Canadian soldiers gathered round the piano as Vic hammered out an off-key 'Roll Out the Barrel'. The joy he brought was immense and Sarah knew she had done nothing to warrant the bouquet she accepted. The play went to the Kings, Edinburgh, on 11 February and then Newcastle's Theatre Royal. Outside of work and charity events, Vic led an independent life.

Over at Ditchley, Winston worked day and night with a break for films. He saw *Escape* where Robert Taylor's mother, played by Nazimova, faces execution in a concentration camp. The other, *Quiet Wedding*, brought the play Sarah helped popularise to the screen where Margaret Lockwood, beloved of Hitchcock and others for her 'undoubted gift in expressing her beauty in terms of emotion', inhabited the role. No one thought of casting Sarah. Winston cried in both films even though *Quiet Wedding* was an upbeat comedy. A few months before, Ambassador Kennedy (who believed that FDR, Churchill and the Jews were leading the US into Armageddon) asked to be relieved of his duties. Kennedy's departure left a vacuum. The appointment of a new ambassador, John Gilbert Winant, failed to excite, despite news of his royal welcome at Bristol on 1 March. No one expected big doses of charisma. Yet, after speaking to Bracken and Prince George, the American made an unexpected statement: 'I'm very glad to be here. There is no place I'd rather be at this time than in England.' Neither his manner nor words bore any resemblance to Kennedy's. His hushed but manly voice disarmed the listener. Whilst his predecessor nailed his isolationist colours to the mast, people quickly felt Winant was different. Asked if America would come into the war soon, his response was plain: 'That is my belief.' Throughout that first year he emphasised the effectiveness of common action. His ideas harked back to the League of Nations but he wasn't pacifist and spoke about the fight being worthwhile if it preserved a way of life. 'We can never call back the gallant dead, but we can see that they did not die in vain,' was one comment made to British schoolchildren. He knew how to use a gun and believed that fighting oppression should be every nation's concern: 'It is not enough for those who love peace to talk peace,' he said. 'A lover of peace must understand war, its causes and its course.'

That evening, Winant's first in London, he and Johnson dined with Churchill in the No. 10 Annexe. Seeing Downing Street, Winant noticed how the facade had been trussed up to withstand bombing. He met the Cabinet and discussed the risk to the Suez Canal and the question of American bases in the West Indies. Talk switched to war materials sold, lent, or leased. Winston's inner circle included Sandys, Robert Menzies (former Australian PM and staunch imperialist) and de Gaulle. Harry Hopkins was on the phone confirming they had the go-ahead for 'Lend-Lease'. Congress passed the Act on 11 March. It felt like the Magna Carta: a long-awaited redemption. Despite the fact that the President decided the form repayment took (which Winant clarified as 'anything he deems satisfactory') and that questions were raised about what property might be exchanged, the PM was ecstatic as he coughed away with bronchitis.

Sarah and Vic received CB, Evelyn Cochran and Francis Cassel at Eythrope. It was then back up to Bradford Alhambra. At the Great Northern Hotel Vic addressed over 200 people. The *Hi-Gang* star said the US would not enter the war unless they saw their own possessions threatened and warned the British not to expect an immediate influx of materials. He could offer news about a new 'American bomber' due to be shipped here, powerful enough to make night bombing a thing of the past. Hitler and Mussolini, Vic said, were scared stiff by Lend-Lease. His 'America and the War' address was thought a first-rate political speech.

Neither Vic nor Winant (or Gil as his friends knew him) was the real spokesman for Lend-Lease. This was aid expeditor Averell Harriman, the fourth-richest man in the US, who arrived on 16 March, immediately meeting key Cabinet staff before checking into the Dorchester. (Historian Max Hastings adjudged him to be 'cleverer and better-informed' than the next President, Truman.) His daughter Kathy, an Olympic-level skier and brilliant horsewoman, was fresh out of college and set on being a journalist. On arrival she got a Savoy reception and a job with Hearst's International News Service. Gil, who formed an unlikely friendship with Harriman, came from a privileged family but had a different outlook to the businessman who hadn't fought in the Great War and had profited from shipping interests. FDR rated him highly enough to refer to him as 'Averell', a gesture not extended to Winant. It was hard not to fall for the hustler of Lend-Lease, but men on the Labour side of the Coalition raved about Winant, whose work with the International Labour Organisation (ILO) was noted. This helped countries set up social insurance, factory inspections and youth training. In Geneva Gil had befriended Clem Attlee and economists like Ernest Penrose. Churchill joked about the folly of socialism and it took him time to appreciate Winant, who harked on about social justice. FDR called him 'Utopian John' behind his back. A great fan of H. G. Wells, Gil made friends with the author. Winston, who had known Wells since 1902 and liked his fiction, didn't share the Ambassador's enthusiasm for *The Rights of Man*.

With help from Harvard President Ben Cohen, Gil won the day when he made his Pilgrims Address on 18 March. 'Everyone was agreeably surprised,' wrote one convert, adding, 'We have been told that he found speech-making a trying ordeal ... actually he spoke extremely well.' He said the Nazis had 'stolen and run amok with the great inventions of free and inquiring minds' and were now 'using them not to liberate but to enslave the human spirit'. Churchill addressed His Excellency with:

> You come to us at a grand turning point in the world's history. You hold and embody in a strong and intense degree, the convictions and ideals that, in the name of American democracy, President Roosevelt has proclaimed in the past few months ... You, Mr Winant, share our purpose. You will share our dangers, interests and secrets.

That same day, Sarah and Vic performed *We Were Dancing* at Golders Green Hippodrome. Sarah was thought 'first rate' in one review but *The Times* urged her to stick to cool modern intellectual comedies (with fewer emotional demands) and dismissed her Juliet. *The Sunday Times* derided her facial expressions and called the vocal range in her speech deficient. Vic, of course, got a rave review. This was upsetting reading at the end of *Plays and Music*. Sarah cried out for her own identity and was sick of the way Vic reeled out comments to reporters that ranged from well meaning – 'Sarah would like to be playing the Katherine Hepburn type of part' – to easy shots – 'To those people who keep on asking me whether I have seen *The Great Dictator*, I wish to say that I have not only seen *The Great Dictator* – I even married her.' Each comment felt patronising. He was also rubbernecking on conversations with the PM – ingratiating himself with her original master.

Winant took a leaf out of the publicity-savvy Averell Harriman's book, allowing a photo of him smiling with cigar in hand to grace *Picture Post*. His face underwent a transformation when he smiled. His typical demeanour was tense and rigid. Sarah had seen FDR's glamorous American visitors on a weekend when people were coming and going at Chequers. Sunlight flickered through the branches of the huge tulip tree, lighting the faces of Pamela, Mary, the Duke and Duchess of Kent, Menzies, John Anderson (who dictated that back gardens across the land would have corrugated iron air raid shelters), Pug Ismay and Bobbety. Jock Colville recalls Sarah leading himself, Clementine and Thompson on an excursion to see 'her new and luxurious (but very film star)' house. Winant and Harriman must have been getting out of their cars while Sarah's party were sweeping into theirs. All they got from the actress was a quick smile. Mrs Oliver's new home, they were told, was a half-hour's drive away. There would be time for introductions later. That day, 29 March, and throughout the weekend, Sarah exchanged little more than a word with Winant, who was barely audible when he spoke. His bushy black brows hid away his eyes when he was thinking. Looking up, his eyes shone with hope, captivating anyone watching.

The following evening, a party was held for Ave and Gil chez Emerald Cunard, the hostess famous for her barbed exchanges. 'Do you mind if I smoke?' Lord Birkenhead had once asked her, taking out his gargantuan cigar. 'Do you mind if we eat?' she replied. 'Not if you do it quietly,' retorted Birkenhead. Randolph had long aped his style. With a passion for trailblazers, she filled 7 Grosvenor Square with lions from the political, literary and music worlds. If you were talked about, like the former Mrs Simpson, you were on her guest list. Pamela entered in a shoulderless gold lamé gown. Admiration for this young lady preceded her, with Hopkins advising Ave to watch out for her. Pamela didn't break the ice with Gil. Harriman was, as she rightly judged, quite randy.

Late March saw Vic at Bolton's Lido but he was back at Eythrope on 9 April, bringing Ben and Bebe. Another guest was the US intelligence officer and CBS reporter Paul Manning who later scooped the attempts of Martin Bormann and others to hide Nazi loot. Manning called The Homestead a 'really swell unit'. Few people had access to the PM then and Vic's recent Lend-Lease intelligence meant journalists were hot on his trail, too. He also knew what was happening in the Third Reich. Vanishing, Vic reappeared at the Glasgow Empire, telling them how much he 'enjoyed playing to English audiences!' Sauchiehall Street was too fond of vicoliverisms to be outraged. Also keen to question Vic, Reuters' Roderick Jones wrote to Sarah in flattering tones asking if they might do lunch. Satirist Arthur Mertz in *The Performer* gave his predictions headlined '1960 News Reel'. He forecast that in twenty years Vic would not just be in the government but also First Lord of the Treasury in Washington.

In early April, Constance Winant stepped off her Pan Am Yankee Clipper to be greeted by a joyful Gil. Work swiftly separated them as he accompanied Winston, Clementine, Mary and Menzies to South Wales and Bristol. Gil got first-hand experience of people with lives turned upside down. Before they left, dense crowds gathered and Winston did his music hall trick, holding his hat high up on the end of his stick. Gil was astonished to see pictures in newspapers of Sarah receiving instruction from Wing Commander Hodsoll about how to put on a gas mask. 'Hitler will send no warning – always carry your gas mask' cried the posters, yet people were unsure how to wear them. Gas bombs were feared though none would be dropped. One story focused on Sarah's combined handbag and gas mask container. Knowing how disorganised she could be, her family joked about her remembering the bag and forgetting the mask. Gil congratulated Winston on Sarah's war work. Magazines satirised it as *The look of 1941*, but Clementine found the image of a girl's features hidden inside an ugly mask alarming. Work done by Sandys at Aberporth (an RAF centre developing anti-aircraft projectiles) came to a shuddering halt on 10 April when a driver fell asleep and Duncan received injuries to his feet and spine. Pamela's little son was being cared for while his mother dedicated her energies to extravaganzas such as the May Day Eve Ball for English-speaking POWs. With Randolph in Cairo, she played hostess to Ave and a romance ensued. Gil asked where Sarah was and Diana told him that the Olivers had just completed a gruelling tour. Their long-awaited film *Ring o' Roses* was to begin production soon. Renamed *Call Me Lucky*, John Paddy Carstairs was to direct. Work began at Riverside Studios in Hammersmith. A full-page photo by Cecil Beaton of a sad-looking Sarah modelling a Strassner black and gold dinner dress appeared in April's *Vogue* to aid promotion.

Mr and Mrs Winant's home was Flat 30, 3 Grosvenor Square (opposite the later Saarinen building – now a hotel). Gil liked the polished furniture, waxed floor and the shrapnel-cracked glass on one of the windows. They had four rooms. Gil and Constance (or Connie as she was known) hadn't carried much luggage to Britain. Months later, Gil was wearing the same brown boots he wore on arrival and apart from Connie's 24 pairs of stockings and the huge photos of her children, which she displayed on the mantelpiece, she had little else. She had been practising what to do if she heard bombs. Gil told her to throw herself flat. On 16 April, this was put to the test. 1,100 Londoners were killed. News came that their friends Ed and Janet Murrow narrowly escaped death. Gil went out at dawn, just avoiding a bomb blowing up close by. Impervious to danger, he started going out during night raids to assist people on the streets, accompanied by aide Theodore Achilles. Twenty years younger, Ed had known Gil since the early 1930s and shared his political outlook. Both had introspective natures and were 'similar brooding Lincolnesque figures'. Ed preferred Winant to Harriman, whom he knew from CBS. Gil's sense of duty to help the underclass was one Mrs C shared. For Winant she went out of her way to alter a schedule so he might meet Rachel Crowdy, a social reformer he admired. Mrs C planned it for 8 April when Winston wasn't there. That way Dame Crowdy and herself could savour his company.

In the wake of raids, Britain's Women's Voluntary Service (WVS), staffed by a million women, provided 'hands on' aid. American organisations did sterling service. Prominent was the American Red Cross (administered by the WVS) and Bundles For Britain (which Janet Murrow and Connie were a big part of). Lady Abingdon and Mrs Crawshay ran Refugees in Great Britain, funding a home for Belgian kids and rehousing Breton fishermen. Gil opened one of their hostels near the East End docks on 5 May, playing dominoes with 'lonely husbands' whose wives had been evacuated. In weather-beaten clothes he blended in. That said, he would don a dress suit to hob nob in Pall Mall clubs with MP friends Eddie Devonshire (brother-in-law of Adele Astaire) and Anthony Eden, his junior by eight years and his closest colleague. The bombing reached a climax when the Commons was blown to smithereens on 10 May. That same explosive weekend, Gil and Connie were at Ditchley Park, where one of Winston's quibbles was why Americans refused to take proper mustard with meals.

Mary Churchill's love life had enlivened Chequers talk the previous weekend, giving FDR's two VIPs respite from war matters. The youngest Churchill was in agony about an engagement hastily entered into. Gil saw another side to Sarah when she told him about Clarissa, Jock and the Dashwoods from West Wycombe convening in the Long Gallery to discuss Mary's issue, dismissing the whole thing as humbug. When Gil told her she could be more sensitive, she was apologetic. Seeing her speak to Vic in her cold, business-like way made him feel sorry for her husband. He seemed a sensitive soul. His conversation about the old watches he collected and recommendations for antique shops impressed Gil. The Mary business caused Clementine to enlist Harriman, also at Ditchley Park, to talk to her daughter. His cool logic struck a chord. Thoughtful as ever, Gil got Hopkins to send a little message 3,398 miles to boost the girl's confidence, which he delivered personally.

It was hard for Gil to understand why Vic had lost his place at the centre of Sarah's life. She had tears in her eyes next time she spoke to him. Both the Olivers seemed lost and Gil was desperate to comfort her. Some corner of their pounding schedules was found for a private encounter and release took the form of mind-blowing passion; alleviating sorrow and lost *amour propre*. What else could prompt the poem she wrote with a Blitz backdrop: 'I'm detached, I'm aloof, I'm on top of the roof!' It wasn't entirely unexpected. It was destiny. The protagonist in Sarah's poem claims first not to be in love, just playing games of mockery with the moon and stars. She later finds she's falling and realises she must be alone no longer. A letter, with its first page missing, is a relic of this passion. The phrase 'the only complete and shadowless happiness [and] ecstasy I have known' suggests what had sprung to life and was now burning. She talks about loving him and thanks him for being there when 'conversation silly or grave' was much needed and for leaving her when she needed to be left. Minus its opening paragraphs, the first phrase on the orphan page is 'So ends this episode.' The letter goes on to philosophise about moving forwards, even though good and bad things will be part of life's tapestry. This undated partial missive written on hotel stationery (dated accurately by the Savoy's historian using its paper and McKnight Kauffer logo) is a haunted love letter. A private guest at the hotel, Sarah's thoughts returned to the words spoken by a gypsy in 1932: she would upset her marriage by rocking the boat after five years. It would fail because she was 'strong-willed ... Tactful but lacking in confidence,' she would meet 'someone interesting'. Something momentous was required to shake up a settled partnership that had until recently been happy. Yet she hadn't felt alive until that moment with Gil. The *magician* was drowning her. She had decided to leave him. Winant was the catalyst.

A lot of Sarah and Vic's time was spent filming what was now re-titled *He Found A Star*. One scene appears to have been shot at the Kit-Cat Club on London's Haymarket. Another was inspired by Charlie Brown's, a legendary café in West India Dock where African masks, a two-headed calf and a mermaid were some of the macabre souvenirs displayed on the walls. It's here we meet the real 'star', Uriel Porter, singing the Negro spiritual 'Goin' to Sing all over God's Heaven' with his earth-shattering voice. The producers had spent weeks combing England for a new Paul Robeson. By chance, Porter's voice was heard on the radio. Early in the film Sarah's character reluctantly lets 'boss to be' Vic come to her home. She takes us not to Chartwell as cinemagoers expect but to her tumbledown family home where, amidst chaos, dishes are sloppily piled on the draining board. 'Ruthie Cavour's' home may be next to the rickety Bermondsey Stairs but she's made something of herself. She's drifting west of Tower Bridge and won't be washed into the sea, not that she's ashamed of her working-class Dad and squabbling siblings. Sarah is so interesting in the film. Her light movements seem to have come from some fairy ancestor and despite a serious face, she's changed from who she was in *Spring Meeting* and is instead someone transcendently real. Vic is 'Lucky Lyndon', a first-time agent who gets Ruthie to be his secretary. She gives up a better position to help him and eventually Lyndon's Agency is on the up. The song scenes feature croonettes Gabrielle Brune and Evelyn Dall. The latter, as Suzanne, performs a 'Coster' Rumba number. Lucky is blinded by their charms. Casting aside a tatty possession of the early days with Ruthie, a weather house (with a husband and wife coming out of little doors), it's handed back to him: a metaphor of the true home versus the false.

Ruthie confronts Lucky about what a user he is. Sarah made the most of it. Critics who said that her voice was incapable of notes of passion were wrong because she is inflamed at being taken for granted. The camera moves to his astounded face as she tells it straight. Had Sarah and Vic not been at loggerheads in real life, the scene would have lost all thwack. There's a tender moment after Lucky deals with Ruthie's good-for-nothing brother and comforts her. Soon they are back trading quips. Sarah handles dry comedy expertly. As guardian of the cashbox, Ruthie is hilarious; smashing it shut when wisecracking blonde Suzanne comes in with her usual 'I'm in a jam' line (knowing Lucky will be taken in). It's Ruthie who helped her boss on the way up and who now saves the day, appealing to Suzanne's vanity when she doesn't turn up for his big show – something that'll ruin him. Skirt-chasing Lucky realises Ruthie is the gal for him. In answer to his declaration that he's giving up the agency, Ruthie's speech captures the spirit of the British perhaps, as she refers to the little people who need someone to fight their corner and how it's they that struggle on with courage and determination. As a security measure Vic addressed his wife in letters as 'Dickie' and her letters to Paddy were signed 'Richard'. Her director would later say of her: 'She was a strange combination: a girl of enormous sensitivity whose instinct was to withdraw into herself, yet full of enthusiasm for a business in which one has to live in a shop window.'

When Sarah and Vic re-emerged after filming, the war had taken a queer turn. Deputy Führer Rudolf Hess had parachuted down south of Glasgow, anxious to speak to a Duke. Had he really come with hopes of peace and an Anglo-German alliance? Was he an imposter? Was he mad? In America there was a rumour that Britain would enter peace talks: a move that would play into the hands of isolationists. While Downing Street maintained a silence, the US response was that Hess had no peace plan.

J. M. Keynes poured cold water on the idea of a German financial paradise with every industry privatised (touted as something Britain could emulate if

Hitler was given the boot). The fruit of late-night discussions between Gil and Keynes at Grosvenor Square was a reconstruction fund to finance post-war Europe's repair with open markets, fluctuations of employment and prices controlled. The impact of economic policy on working people was Gil's concern (bearing in mind the mistakes after the First World War). In late May, Keynes went to Washington to allocate resources for Lend-Lease. He irritated FDR, Churchill and Bracken, although Gil and Eden liked his ideas. The ambassador was liable to take a hard line at Chequers on matters such as opposition to conscription in Northern Ireland. Sarah was always present, eyes shining, with her puckish smile a comfort to the bashful visitor. Questioned by her Pa or one of the chiefs, Gil stared at the floor for what seemed like ages. He looked up and Sarah wondered if those eyes had burnt a hole in the carpet. Nobody else had his eccentric powers of concentration but his silences commanded respect. She imagined the room where he stayed. Observing this tall, lanky, lantern-jawed, loose-limbed man lay bare his sincerity, her heart ached. A mysterious bond was deepening. Her wishfulness and magic had prompted it.

It was a 'blip' in Gil's case: a risky action he felt compelled to take. For once he left high principles at the door. A rumour could jeopardise the relationship with Churchill. Sarah's father knew nothing. By the time people suspected, her status served as a guard. Any other woman would have been a security hazard. How did a man like Gil become a master of subterfuge? He had a mind that could drill down deep into a problem. He was extremely cautious when gathering information, once using detectives to find out about a man who had murdered someone close to him. His security team were trained in damage control and at the onset were incredibly loyal. Secret lives were refuges for lonely men at the top and par for the course. Not letting fear obstruct you from your path registered with the man who had fearlessly travelled to France during the First World War.

Back in 1925 when he told his folks he was running for Governor of New Hampshire, Gil's father tried to talk him out of it. It wasn't what Winants did. Gil trusted his instinct. He knew his shortcomings as a husband and father. Traces of rebel spirit emerged in his 20-year-old daughter Constancia who, the year before (studying in South America), had eloped with a scientist. Now Gil took drastic action, exciting the passion of this English girl. Sarah had been unhappy and Gil couldn't say 'no' to her because he never failed anyone. As Governor he received troubled visitors in his home late at night. His wife said that it was a blessing she had married him at 19. Otherwise she would never have become accustomed to his peculiar ways. Gil met Connie Russell just before he served in France while studying Government Problems at Princeton. Connie and Mrs Russell (who counted Mrs Roosevelt among her friends) helped him stack pamphlets during an anti-capital punishment crusade. His sweetheart then was Dolly Black. When Connie's fiancé didn't return from the war, they decided to marry in December 1919. A mansion at 274 Pleasant Street, Concord, New Hampshire, surrounded by acres of land, became their home.

He tried being a sheep farmer, an oil well owner, a newspaper proprietor and head of a lumber business. The Winants' greatest difficulty in the 1920s was deciding what to do with Connie's $11 million inheritance. Whether it was for her pleasure or his own, Gil took a large home in Georgetown. He kept a string of Arab horses. Her great interest was breeding dogs and getting 'best in show'. She even came to London in the mid-1930s as a judge. She turned this into a business and at any one time 70 pedigree West Highland terriers were barking or digging up the ground at Edgerstoune (her kennels, named after a town where her Scots family came from). Connie told a reporter that one of Gil's horses stepped on one of her scotties and to prevent accidents he gave up the Arabs. Perhaps the real reason was Gil's terrible financial sense. He might have protected New Hampshire depositors by reforming banking laws but he fell into debt after borrowing to cover life insurance holdings. He lost his entire investment and could no longer afford the Georgetown house. Giving luxury a wide berth, he took the pledge. Later on, in the right company, his enjoyment of expensive cigars and good claret returned.

He was the first governor of New Hampshire to be voted in three times. A Civil War veteran told young Winant that the Republican Party originally put civil rights above property rights. Hence, it was as a progressive Republican that Gil administered to his flock. He devoted his life to improving the lives of the less well off. In 1931, every third worker in the state was unemployed. Gil brought in a four-day week. In 1933 his outlook was similar to that of the governor in neighbouring New York (before FDR was elected). Gil impressed him when he settled the Textile Strike in 1934 and made breakthroughs with the Townsend Plan, which became Social Security. He alleviated hardship among the elderly and unemployed and as Chair of the Social Security Board (SSB) eliminated political patronage. The rights of the disaffected blacks and problems of housing, nutrition and medical care gripped him. Gil's first ever visit to Britain had been to study the Insurance Act for Workers so he could propose free insurance benefits at home. 'All my life,' he would later say, 'I have believed in sufficient rations for every one.' During the Depression, he had the Concord police distribute food to the homeless and picked up the bill. He handed out change outside the State House. Strictly speaking, the money wasn't his. It irked Connie. Many times she thought of leaving him. She stayed because she loved him.

Gil met Maurine Mulliner, former personal secretary to Senator Robert F. Wagner, and hired her as his Girl Friday. Familiar with fixers like Harry Hopkins and New Deal legends like Frances Perkins, she became the SSB's executive secretary. She would compare Gil's humanitarianism to a caring mysticism and when he told her that reading Dickens in his youth had made him this way it came as no surprise. Moving to Switzerland with the ILO, Gil observed the changing European situation. When the Nazis seized the Sudetenland he flew to Prague as a gesture. With Hitler on the rampage, the ILO relocated to Montreal but Winant was to leave in early 1941. Just before, publicity photos were taken of the Winants in Concord. Gil sits in his chair with carved armrests. Connie has a sardonic smile in one photo. In another they gaze into each other's eyes. On the mantel is Gil's collection of small dancing figurines. Classical 'household gods' or *Lares* influence all that happens within a house's boundaries. Master and mistress of the hearth left their protective gods. From the State House on the east side of Concord near the Merrimack River, Winant made a tense speech about standing by England, not asking but giving. Connie, Constancia, John and Rivington Winant waved as he left Pleasant Street. In Britain, he navigated the new committees in the Whitehall machine. His wife secretly dreaded her role and nervously attended a Dorchester gathering. She was apt to get lost in the background and they had to search for her at speech time. Cecil Beaton took this girlish figure in hand and a high-cheekboned Mrs Winant emerged on the cover of *Country Life* in May. Whilst Mrs Churchill undertook fire-watching duties high above the Annexe, a nervous Mrs Winant stayed indoors at Grosvenor Square. Her English-born housekeeper Orol Mears didn't trouble her mistress with the coping methods her London relations had taught her. Connie formed her own opinions and hated to be called weak.

Thought vulgar in its early days, the *Hi-Ganger* style was now so huge it was satirised in a West End revue, *Lo-Gang*, while a common spoof, *Oi!*, ran in the theatrical press (taking the form of a dialogue between Ben, Bebe, Vic, Flanagan, Allan, Arthur Askey and Richard Murdoch). The trio who leased-and-lent their talents were megastars and guests who came to the mic, like Gielgud, Ralph Richardson, Coward and Valerie Hobson, got wild applause. Sarah was there in May 1941 humming the melody of 'I Give You My Heart', with Vic at the piano then Bebe took the mic with her sensuous contralto. *Hi Gang* would go out in a blaze of glory on its 52nd episode. This night the Paris Theatre audience was composed of celebrities. When the first show aired (when Churchill became PM) *Hi-Gang* featured a message from Kennedy. Now Ben Lyon read one from Winant: 'I am glad to hear England laughing,' he said, 'and to know that Americans have been able to help.' Sarah, Claire Luce, Valerie, Diana Wynyard, Georgie Wood and Nellie Wallace were among many doing short turns on stage while Bebe's 'blitzed but still beautiful' joke became a catchphrase. The glamour continued at the Dorchester on 22 May with 200 guests. Sarah and Vic invited the ambassador, who conferred thanks for what constituted the finest American aid so far. Connie was also all smiles. It was then announced that *Hi-Gang* would be back that autumn.

The mirth evaporated on 24 May when HMS *Hood*, Britain's fastest warship, was blown up with only three surviving crew. As Churchill listened to Vic's playing of Beethoven's *Appassionata* Piano Sonata No. 23, he kept insisting it was the Death March. He lashed out, ordering him never to play it. Sarah had to intervene and suggest Vic play an old favourite instead.

Gil travelled to Washington to consult FDR's team and see Keynes, still in DC. When the Hess business came up he said he believed the Nazi wasn't insane and had come because he feared for his life. Returning to Britain by B24 bomber, the ambassador joined Eden at Chequers on 22 June, helping the PM with part of a speech relating to the US's condemnation following Germany's attack on Russia. Winston's large-scale Help Russia drive began with planes and tanks sent to the Soviets, along with £10 million credit at 3% interest. The war on the Eastern Front at least gave the British respite from the Blitz that after nine months had killed some 40,000 civilians. After observing Clydeside's war effort and spending time among her 'ain folk' in Jedburgh, Mrs Winant (a descendant of Sir Walter Scott) went to Buckinghamshire, joining Mrs Churchill and Lord Nuffield (of Spitfire fame) at Colworth House. Transformed by Lord Melchett (son of the ICI creator) it was now a rest home for heroic nurses.

At the film industry's gesture to War Weapons Week at Cookham's Moor Hall on 27 May, Vic compèred and told jokes. Victor Cazalet (liaising between the Government and Poland's Government in Exile) asked Sarah if she and Vic might step in with fund-raising. 'Victor, you can rely on us,' she assured the man she had known since childhood, at whose home the PRF committee met. Thanks to Polish and other European intelligence sources, Bletchley Park had received the original device to break the ENIGMA settings in 1939.

Polish fliers were thought the very best. Winston told Hugh Dowding (commander of Fighter Command) that 'one Pole was worth three Frenchmen' and many held the view that Britain owed them a debt. Now Germany had seized the Poles' most fertile land and was using starvation to get them out. The PRF aid did not get to its intended recipients. The aim was now to concentrate relief on the 8,000 refugees in Britain. A concert was arranged on 2 June at Oxford's Town Hall with coupons arranged for the Olivers' journey by road. Clarissa Borenius came to Eythrope to travel with them and they met Francis Cassel en route. In that wedding cake interior Clarissa's father Tancred (PRF Secretary General) welcomed guests who included Poles and

Finns (whose independent voice the BBC's Finnish Service communicated to those back home). The Finns stood against the Soviets with the Germans as allies. Vic wondered whether to jibe at Russia or Germany. Each was morally contentious. He knew that Mr Borenius was in a curious position. He hoped for peace with Germany under certain conditions. It is now known that four months before the Oxford concert Borenius went to Geneva, helped by MI6, floating proposals through Carl Burkhardt (former Governor of Danzig and Red Cross executive) that Europe be redrawn to accommodate Germany in return for peace after Hitler was replaced. It's thought by some that Hess came to Britain to establish the process as a result of this meeting.

Borenius's mission was top secret. Sarah knew nothing, even though her family had known the art historian for some time. Tancred waved his pudgy hands in the air and introduced 'the daughter of the greatest living Englishman – the man who will lead us to victory and ... the best friend Poland ever had'. The writer John Harris asks if Borenius was a 'spy' plotting with an anti-US, anti-Churchill 'Right Club' but Borenius's links to Sarah and Vic suggest otherwise. The Finn looked forward to an alternative German regime but wasn't eager to remove Churchill from power. Sarah began her address reflecting on the difficulty of interpreting wars when you're so close to current events. She referred to the 'hateful German occupation' and the 'greed and megalomania' of Hitler. She felt people should remember 'it was Poland who first stood firm. They were the first to know the incredible onslaught of the German army.' She pointed to the Poles' 'stern refusal to co-operate', saying their 'heroic resistance' made them a noble race. The local papers reported how she maintained 'the family tradition for eloquence' but these were her words. Referring to those inside enemy lines she said: 'We are, unfortunately unable to do anything for these brave people until we have won final victory ... In the meantime we can do much to help these civilian refugees.' She mentioned the 60,000 Poles fighting for us, 'our brothers in a brave cause', and how it was an honour to give them 'all we can spare'. Borenius kissed her hand as they parted. Stopping at Putteridge Bury, a fine Bedfordshire house built in the style of Chequers, she remarked on the fact that its template was her home.

The presence at the Oxford concert of Royal Navy Officer Sir William Crawford (PRF Committee Chairman) was 'one in the eye' for the Nazis. Less than a week before, Crawford had been a gunnery officer on the *Rodney* providing cover to Atlantic convoys. They sighted the German battleship *Bismarck* and Crawford found the correct range to torpedo it on the third salvo. He was awarded the DSC on 27 May. The revenge Churchill desired for the loss of *Hood* was rendering the *Bismarck* a wreck of twisted metal. It's doubtful Crawford had time for an Anglo-German deal, causing the Nazis this huge setback. At Chequers Winston enjoyed a preview of *That Hamilton*

*Woman*. He had advised the filmmakers on the historic sea battles. It was his favourite film. Laurence Olivier and Vivien Leigh brought Nelson and Emma to life. Everyone was blubbering.

Gil had received backing as a potential presidential candidate in 1936 but chose to support Roosevelt's re-election. He never lost his White House ambitions and, like Eden, remained in the wings. Both put up with accusations of not expressing themselves clearly. Winant regarded Eden (a highly skilled linguist and Dickens disciple) as one of the most able diplomats he had ever met. Both men had wives they respected but had grown apart from; their children providing unity. Neither Beatrice Eden nor Connie Winant was willing to be an ever-present help in public life. Beatrice hated politics and Connie's views were quite different to Gil's (although she made it appear as if she supported him). In the case of the Edens they loved each other but excused each other's affairs (having an agreement that, should he accede to the premiership, she would stay with him with no divorce). Fuelled by work, Anthony and Gil each threw temper tantrums but could unwind. In an after-dinner speech Eden reveals how 'almost every evening' at the end of a long day 'the Ambassador is good enough to come down to the Foreign Office [for] the excellent custom of refreshing our thoughts from time to time with the produce of Scotland. Though it may be a most unorthodox method we do not feel that it works too badly.' The two cracked jokes when they met the King's Royal Rifle Corps (established in America in 1755) and Winant was a guest at Binderton, Anthony's home near Lavant in Sussex.

Although America was not in the war, Churchill was keen to fly the flags side by side on 4 July, Independence Day, the new federal holiday for Americans created by FDR. In the crypt of St Paul's, Gil attended the unveiling of a tablet to honour the first US citizen killed in the Battle of Britain. He joined Connie at the American Society's luncheon at the Dorchester with Harriman, Kathy, Drexel Biddle Jnr (ambassador to the exiled European governments) and Mrs Biddle (director of London's two American Red Cross clubs). Charles Sweeny supervised imports of sub-machine guns and automatic rifles and helped form the American Home Guard Vic had links with. Honorary Americans were Sweeny's fashion icon wife Margaret (later to become Duchess of Argyll), Australia's High Commissioner, New Zealand's PM, and Sarah Oliver. Shaking the hand of granite-profiled Mr Winant, she was ecstatically happy. 'How slim is a sylph?' was a question a critic once asked; and she was alluringly sylph-like. Vic was present but showed little of the cheeriness one associates with that nation. Based on the observations of Kathy Harriman, he was sulking in a corner. He was probably experiencing pangs of rejection, though he knew nothing about the alliance his wife had entered into. Three days later Kathy wrote to her sister about the Olivers:

'I don't think much of her husband. She's got guts enough to stick with Vic on account of her father. Going on the stage is the one way she can keep from going mad.' Kathy's letter might indicate that Sarah had already proposed leaving Vic before July, with her father blocking it. The line about Sarah sticking with him sounds like gossip from Pamela – the one Ave had nominated to look after her, whom she now knew to be his paramour. Kathy swung between fascination with and distrust of Pamela. Once she bluntly told her that she wasn't going to leave her father unsupervised at the mercy of a narcissist.

For the first week of July 1941 Sarah was in J. M. Barrie's *Mary Rose* produced by Esmé Percy. Her character vanishes twice on the same uninhabited Scottish island. She was taken there as a child and reappeared three weeks after disappearing (insisting that just an hour had elapsed). She comes there as a young wife and mother and vanishes again – this time for decades. Again, she springs in to see her family, oblivious of time and not a single day older. The pain faced by her husband and fragile parents is unimaginable. 'Would you mind telling me why everyone's so old?' asks Mary Rose. Frozen in time, the mother fails to recognise her son. But where had she been in the time she was away? It was like Sarah to escape to a secret world with a friend to play with.

Gil was close to Papa in age and made Vic seem like a boy. The workload of an ambassador is immense and at first sight it seems impossible that space and time should avail itself during those busy days in 1941. But Sarah was a 'Barrie' girl. The ability to create a private life in a timeless empyrean was easy for her, unfathomable to others. A complimentary ticket to a play was liable to be extended to a family friend. It's credible that an ambassador might venture out to the Q Theatre and into its low-key surroundings, catch the second act and escort her home.

Barrie was out of fashion in 1941, yet Sarah's success confounded the critics. Cochran saw it and so did Cynthia Asquith (Barrie's devoted friend) and the verdict was that Sarah was 'lovely' as Mary Rose, apart from the 'dance' movement of her arms as she left the stage.

The weekend before the opening Pamela was at Eythrope. Part of the discreet *one of us* club and admiring Sarah's damn-everyone attitude, she was a breath of fresh air. If Pamela knew about Winant and Sarah about Harriman, neither pried into the other's business. Other whispers on the grapevine enlivened conversation. Pamela would say: 'Sarah was my friend – I adored Sarah – Sarah was darling.' Vic didn't come into it, although Pamela had no reason to dislike him. He was filming the *Hi-Gang* movie at Gainsborough Studios. The screenplay featured Bebe's attempts to adopt London evacuees with Vic upsetting one plan after another, going to *other woman* lengths to break up the Lyons' marriage.

Randolph's Layforce unit was to fight in Crete but the Nazis won the battle after ten days. Probably deliberately, Laycock sent Randolph to Cairo to see Eden and he escaped the German attack, living to trumpet angry opinions about the army in the wake of Rommel's successes. When Churchill sent Harriman to Cairo to assess army intelligence, Randolph was assigned as his escort and the two had a 'fascinating time'. Winston's son suspected nothing. Convalescing at Chequers, Duncan wondered if Randolph's wife and FDR's expeditor might be enjoying more than friendship. As for Sarah, she was having a mysterious time on a lonely island.

Diana and Duncan came on 21–23 June to Eythrope. Churchill intended to make Sandys Under-Secretary for Foreign Affairs, but even when he settled on making him Financial Secretary at the War Office there were cries of nepotism. Pug learnt that on the evening of the announcement Vic Oliver was using this in his act: 'I am expecting a call to Downing Street at any moment,' he said. The PM didn't see the funny side.

Vic, Sarah and Randolph had the 'consolation' of being Churchill's 'henchmen' in an international Jewish conspiracy linking Roosevelt, Churchill and Stalin. Nazi scare tactics on posters produced in Munich might influence gullible Continentals but were washed away at England's shores where such silliness didn't count. With Russia 'in' and Lend-Lease in full-throttle, Chequers had an upbeat atmosphere on 27 July with Hopkins, the Harrimans and Winants in a large party. Pamela cracked a joke, asking if Winant had modelled his look on Abe Lincoln with his shiny suit and bushy eyebrows. The 52-year-old, whose Brooks Brothers get-up was on the shabby side, liked the comparison. He repeated Lincoln's line of 'malice toward none with charity for all'. Pamela was quick to involve Gil in her 'own' charitable activities, getting him to be a patron when organising a ball for POWs in April 1943 and always telling him how welcome he was to visit her and baby Winston. Gil was busy visiting Canadian soldiers and touring Scotland, Wales and the North. Accompanied by Attlee, he would give a good speech, such as the one before 5,000 at Abertillery. Often with Lady Reading, Connie dropped in on hospitals. One duty was opening the New England Service Club at Reigate in August 1941 with Mrs Churchill. Gil's wife became very capable in her role. In early August, after receiving a grateful letter from a fireman's wife, she hosted a party for City firemen and their spouses. Sarah Oliver attended. Thankfully, there had been no air raid since May.

On 14 August Attlee announced that the PM had met the US President and that the eight-point Atlantic Charter was agreed. It put people's rights at the forefront and was hugely significant to Winant, who looked forward to a Lincoln-style reconstruction plan similar to the one after the American Civil War. The less idealistic Churchill didn't accept self-determination of the Colonies, having fought against this his entire career, but agreed to the elimination of trade barriers.

The big disappointment was that America hadn't entered the war. Gil gave Churchill little consolation. His suspicions about him and Sarah coloured Winston's feelings. Gil sent Winston an example of the gramophone put to good use to advertise Defence Savings but the thanks he received were lukewarm. Winant saw Winston's ire at Chequers on 30 August – the day Germany began its siege of Leningrad. He was with Anthony and Beatrice, Melchett and Halifax. Winston pressed him about his country's commitment and pointed out how Europe's civilisation was vanishing every day. When Winant gave his best estimate of March 1942 for entry, the response was torrid.

'Victory Oliver', meanwhile, was auctioning goods at Morecambe's Happy Mount on 13 August, providing a framed photo of the PM in bulldog mode that sold for £30 and bottles of rare champagne brandy. £1,123 was raised for the Royal Lancashire Infirmary. 'I am American by passport but British by heart,' he told crowds, promising that 'any time that I can do any good for this nation I will gladly'. Although Viki and Dickie made appearances in the run-up to the release of *He Found a Star*, Sarah didn't find his promises sincere.

Borenius was grateful to the BBC for its launch of a new radio appeal on 31 August. She read her speech from Oxford and the *Week's Good Cause* raised £3,200 for the PRF. The last time she saw Tancred was on 25 September when he chatted with H. G. Wells and Gil at a Savoy luncheon to herald the Conference on Science and World Planning (at London's Royal Institute over a three-day period). Scientists from free countries drew up a charter; the first time an event of this calibre had been held. Wells spoke about men's place as 'servant-masters of the world', Eden about science and statecraft, and Herbert Morrison about scientific truths diminishing vested interests. A message was read out on behalf of the PM concerning 'intellectual darkness' contrasting with the freedom to develop science. Sarah watched as Gil put on his spectacles for 'Science and Human Needs'. The transcript of the conference was translated into 37 languages.

To the younger Churchills, Gil was a kindly uncle and teacher. On 29 August Connie boarded a Pan Am seaplane bound for New York. She missed her teenage sons John Junior and Rivington badly. This visit turned out to be a nine-month stay where she coordinated relief supplies to the British. She had no suspicion of Gil's attachment to the owner of the voice that had read elegies by Brooke and Shelley on the wireless on 31 July. Sarah's reputation was good. One critic said: 'Broadcasting women usually sound like domineering governesses but she's a notable exception.'

*Rise Above It*, at Panton Street's Comedy Theatre, auctioned gifts with lots of audience participation. Sarah and Vic raised funds to buy a box in the theatre for RAF boys. In August 1941, Cochran wanted Sarah for the first British production of Enid Bagnold's *Lottie Dundas* and she was also due to tour with *Garrison Theatre*, a radio variety show first broadcast in November 1939 and transferred to the London stage after a year. Unbeknownst to everyone she was calling time on this magical life. She had altered course in 1936 and would do so again. This time it was about duty, even hardship. Others were doing dynamic war work like Paddy. Mary had joined the Auxiliary Territorial Service (ATS) to support anti-aircraft batteries. Sarah's 'look' at that time had the severity of square-shouldered jackets; a step away from a uniform although underneath, she favoured shirts in rationed silk from Jacqmar, allowing her to 'wear' her father's inspirational wartime speeches. Normally seen on scarves, the print found its way onto other clothing. As an actress with youth on her side and offers coming, throwing up six years of preparation to join the Services was absurd. Her career would suffer and she underestimated how long the war would last. She knew she wasn't getting the film roles she desired, which were going to actresses like Rosamund John and Deborah Kerr. With her father facing the worst crisis ever, she believed that carrying on as an actress undermined the serious nature of his work. She sought to remove the eloping daughter stigma forever. Her motivations were in this order of urgency: to leave Vic, be true to the Churchill name with its reputation for fighting, serve her country usefully – and have time for her new champion and inspiration.

The last visitors to Eythrope in October 1941 were Toni and Patricia with their daughter Diane. Both couples had overcome severe objections to their marriages, but the once-defiant Oliver marriage was fractured and not blessed with children. Sarah couldn't express her dilemmas to Tricia. Seven years later she told a friend that to leave Vic Oliver she had to 'adopt a sudden cruel course and just bolt'. A day or so after seeing the Dirsztays, she heard her island calling and disappeared like Mary Rose.

Scant evidence remains in the form of letters between the Olivers. One exists where we discover that Vic has returned at 1 a.m. and writes to 'Dickie' who is nowhere to be found at Westminster Gardens. Vic's nickname was '*Cocliquot*', meaning poppy, or maybe rascal. It's a sad letter, written in the second week of October 1941, Vic talking of the things their flat had witnessed throughout the years and what secrets it could tell. He admits he is responsible for her leaving. He didn't listen to her, insisting that she always hear *his* side. He was often wrong too. He realises that over the years he was blind to what she had attained by her own merits and chides himself for his 'constant subjugation'. 'To me – you didn't grow up!' he says, not once but twice. He sees the cruelty of putting her on a pedestal, patting her on the cheek like a child, buying her clothes, sweets and other presents and then scolding her when she did wrong. If only he could return to 1936, he says. He feels that loving her the way he did eroded her equilibrium. The last five paragraphs of Vic's letter are an apologia for her accusation that he never believed in her. He blames the hard line he took on advice from Cochran and others that Sarah shouldn't be allowed to get comfortable and stop improving. Vic questions this approach. He argues that his support for Sarah's professional career has been constant, citing as proof a letter he wrote three years before to Sherek, in which he vouched for her abilities. All of us at times injure others in the heat of an argument. One of Vic's nasty comments about her acting ability had caused a deep wound. He says how regretful he is. When he talks about his deep joy seeing her use little tricks he had taught her, his warmth and sincerity comes over. He pleads for her to accept that he 'always thought and still does' that she has 'the ingredients for becoming one of the greatest actresses in this country', adding that someone had to take a firm hand as well as an interest in her. Vic believed they would get through this. He talks about preparing for a new phase where she can come and go as she pleases. He accepts he's on probation and asks for one more chance, aware of what must change. She'll see a *new* husband, he promises, having no idea her departure is for good.

Sarah moved into the Goring Hotel at 15 Ebury Street. She tells us in her memoir that her father called her a bitch. It's obvious he had genuine regard for Vic. It's unlikely that Diana and Randolph approved and it was kept from Mary for a while. She requested that her father set her up in the Women's Auxiliary Air Force (WAAF) to allow her to separate from Vic and avoid confrontations. Her father, as he so frequently did, gave into the 'redheaded little monster'. He pulled the strings and she acquired what would be a new identity. She intended to cut off from Vic in a neat and tidy way. Two days before her WAAF interview she started a letter exchange with solicitor William Rollo about how to divorce an American citizen. Rollo reveals that Sarah and Vic met and agreed to do nothing about a divorce for six months in case Vic had to go to the US to retain his citizenship. Rollo tells her a future divorce might be lengthy and difficult should Vic leave and advises Sarah to use 'personal indignities' as her plea, although he adds it will mean little in an American court and suggests she reach a solution with Vic. When she disappeared into the WAAF Vic was hopeful of her returning. Being cast aside had cut through when Josefa left all those years ago and the pain never went away.

Work was his distraction. In *Get a Load of This* at the London Hippodrome Vic headed a cast of 80. Celia Lipton sang Judy Garland numbers and Charles Farrell played the villain. The set had a cocktail bar in one of the boxes and supper tables in the pit and members of the cast astonished the audience, jumping up and becoming prowling gunmen. Leaving his speakeasy at the end of November, Vic indulged in a little retail therapy, purchasing a new horse, Indian Tea, for 100 guineas. He already had Colorama and Treasury and a yearling called Richard the First.

In a Germanic tale of cosseted imprisonment, the princess only had to mention not possessing a pair of gloves for a pile suddenly to appear. When she spoke of Vic she sometimes sounded flippant, talking about how this relationship blighted the one with Papa and Mama, but in her heart she knew how special those years were. Hearing anything harsh said about him hurt. 'Whatever has happened,' she sighed, 'he has meant much to me in my life.' At times this fantasist got a grip and it crossed her mind she was ditching one American she could have for one she couldn't; but on the whole she didn't regret bolting.

Vic was one national treasure noticeably absent from Mr Churchill's 67th birthday party on 30 November. Photographs taken on the garden steps at Chequers show Winston in his siren suit, cigar in hand. His steely control and steadfast determination prevail. The news offered little to cheer him. Clementine, in a dark dress and knitted snood, smiles quizzically, keeping Rufus, the reddish-brown French poodle, on a slim leash. He could easily free himself from her grasp. In the back row Peregrine stands with his father Jack. Pamela, Sarah and Duncan make up the middle row. Diana is in front with her parents. Thompson, Maryott Whyte and Lord Cherwell (Prof) join them in other photos. Pamela's legendary allure isn't apparent. Duncan is bolt upright and smiling, the injuries of six months earlier invisible. Sarah couldn't be less like the white-frocked, long-haired Juliet on a cardboard balcony. Uniform and square bashing had left her with a robust and slightly scary appearance but she was back in Churchill-land where she wanted to be. Mary, stationed with the ATS, was not present, organising a change of barracks for the girls in her unit following an outbreak of deadly meningitis.

# 7

# Like Father I Fight Alone

A young woman flicking through a magazine in 1941 couldn't ignore slogans like 'Am I clever enough to join the ATS?' Or be unaware of the typist turned Morse slip reader or shop assistant raised to Equipment Officer by the WAAFs. Mrs Oliver came to Victory House for an interview with Felicity Hill who suggested getting her terrific pageboy hair restyled rather than let someone at camp ruin it. Top-coated and laden with bags, Sarah went to Morecambe where she was billeted and singled out for having been on the stage. A good sport, she entered the line-up of a RAF concert at the last minute, reciting Rupert Brooke's *Soldier* and a passage from Shakespeare. After rounds of inoculations the queasy Special Duties Clerks had to name equipment, respond to instructions, drill, salute and march-past. Military life is not for the faint-hearted, being tough on the feet and allowing little peace. Homesickness was rife but Sarah was resilient. The marvel was seeing girls with slipshod ways transformed into servicewomen, coiffed and kitted out in serge. 'The Style for You is Air Force Blue' shouted the posters.

Officer Training at Loughborough was better, apart from the freezing huts used for lectures. In a letter to Paddy, *Richard* said it was like being back at school adding that they saw two information films he had directed. She was serious about training in land intelligence, thinking back to T. E. Lawrence's descriptions of surveying in the Middle East and the time Papa and Major Packenham-Walsh interpreted the movements of soldiers. She had sought expert advice from friends and had gone to the top to ask questions. Jane Trefusis Forbes (Director of the WAAFs 1939–43) told her that Photographic Interpretation (PI) had possibilities for quick promotion in the ranks.

The Aircraft Woman Second Class (ACW2) made friends with Molly Upton and Hazel Furney, the latter proud of her Sergeant Butcher accreditation earned in Farnborough's WAAF quarter. They found Sarah surprisingly clued up about the Central Intelligence Unit (CIU) located at RAF Medmenham where they expected to be based after exams. Her knowledge of other centres of wartime intelligence was enough to make Hazel and Molly nervous. She went to Medmenham for an introductory course on plotting: pre-assessing the photographic material that came back from airmen on sorties over enemy territory and identifying geographic positions. It was nifty work if a 'pilot's trace' made comparison with an equivalent map easy, but bad weather or pilots getting lost made the job difficult. There was much anticipation by the men in the Station about this vamp married to Vic Oliver. Technical Control Officer (TCO) Douglas Kendall recalled how, when they were dining at camp, the red-fingernailed owner of a long cigarette holder made an entrance. Gentlemen from the RAF swarmed, spinwheel lighters in unison ready to oblige. The daft thing was it wasn't Sarah at all but a flirty redheaded recruit who fitted the bill for the imaginary Sarah. The real Churchill – an invisible figure, makeup-less with hair rolled out of sight – unfairly got blamed for the other's conduct, getting a talking to. Kendall tells us she took this on the chin, a comment that sums up Sarah.

Churchill's daughter's poem *ACW2 to Pilot Officer* suggests the real Sarah had admirers, whilst it was actually inspired by the experience of a girl married to a Belgian reconnaissance pilot. Remorselessly as the dawn, a bulletin board printed the names of pilots missing presumed dead and Sarah's words convey the choking suspense. The young flyer is a complete flirt but his personality rubs off on her. 'You're the ruddy blinking tops' is her first line, perfectly capturing that elite 'officer talk'. The young buck in the Irvin sheepskin jacket is her opposite and something of a 'son of a ---', who comes out with things wild horses wouldn't drag out of her. She's hooked despite his reputation and might weaken before this 'no lark top-line winner' and 'straight-up proper smasher'. Yet she holds back before he flies off and now wishes she'd told him how she felt (concluding all the same he was vain enough to assume it).

When that lyrical ACW2 in the plotting department put stylograph aside at 2 a.m., lying in wait in the canteen was *The Lynx* (or more accurately a writer from the in-house magazine 'written by index-finger typists'). In this mock scoop, the interviewer adopts an attitude of worship, hanging on to every utterance of this new personality at camp. We learn how after two cups of NAAFI tea 'her eyes shone and [we] find her comment on the tea being "SOOOH sweet" a veritable *screamer*'. The article isn't coy about mentioning Churchill and her husband. She's asked how many bricks she managed in a hod when helping her father. She speaks of the US road trip with Vic and admits never missing her Pa and hubby when they are on the wireless. She used to cough at inopportune moments behind the mic but late nights and early mornings in studios have prepared her for shift-work. Here she demos going cross-eyed (the screen actress's nightmare). *The Lynx* tries estimating her rep performances to date but gives up, concluding, 'Sarah nor I can do maths.' Sarah becomes nostalgic about the stage, telling her interviewer that if there were good parts she didn't care if it were London or a seaside pier.

Most of Sarah's colleagues genuinely liked her and would speak about her quiet and gentle manner. They gathered with her round the radio at 8 p.m. on 29 January 1942 when Vic was Roy Plomley's first guest on *Desert Island Discs*. Proceedings began with him opening a telegram from Ben and Bebe, the message regretting that he hadn't been sent to a real desert island. He dismisses them as 'a couple of third-rate stooges'. Vic's eighth music choice was 'I Give You My Heart' with a snatch of Bebe's gramophone version. He and Sarah wrote it to keep the wolf from the door, he says, to which Plomley asks whether the wolf might be able to hear it. Another choice was 'Roses of Picardy' – a haunting tune he'd been 'murdering for years' – and there was 'Ride of the Valkyries' (one Sarah hated) and 'Love Is a Dancing Thing' – another reference to Sarah he would include on a second exile to the Desert Island thirteen years later.

A week before, a letter from Charles Evans at the Air Ministry informed Sarah that she had been commissioned with the rank of Assistant Section Officer and within days she set off for Nuneham with Molly and Hazel, where they shared a dorm and undertook an officers' course in PI. Sarah frequently suggested trips to the pub and her two friends struggled to keep up with this fast walker. She arranged for a tailor to come to the pub to measure her for a bespoke uniform.

There was much to learn. Aerial photography had been used from 1915 but the first air reconnaissance mission with cameras attached to fuselage had only taken place in March 1939. Australian inventor, pilot and MI6 agent Sidney Cotton had taken the first photos. Sarah's cousin Tina was making these air reconnaissance cameras as war work. Now married to Alfred Beit, her husband was at Bomber Command. The 'kindness and even temper' of Douglas Kendall, who delivered lectures, was greatly appreciated. A mathematician and surveyor, he was one of the brains behind photographic intelligence linking CIU and Air Ministry. Soon the Officers were 'on the job' at Medmenham. In a large white house dating from 1901 WAAFs beavered away in workrooms damp enough to make the metal in their suspenders rust. When the sound of scurrying mice announced it was dinnertime, colleagues trooped down to the galleried banqueting hall used as a mess.

Using the tech of the day to aid interpretation, the Photographic Interpreters (PIs) employed techniques of scaling and measurement. Frequently, they compared a current image with one from a previous sortie to gauge changes. With photographs taken from different focal lengths, procedures might have to be followed to get the two images on par. Photogrammetric tables, trigonometry tables and slide rules were handed around. The practical Ursula Powys-Lybbe created a *Child's Guide to the Use of the Slide Rule* – a bible for Sarah and others. Four years older, former freelance photographer Ursula had spent time in Cairo. Planning everything visually and claiming she never took snapshots, her artistic composites in *Tatler* (showing fashionable folk at home with pets) were technical feats.

Hazel remembers the agony Sarah went through when they were tested on interpreting an aerial photograph, calculating ratios between an object from the air and on the ground. Hazel put her right when Sarah made a mistake but noticed later that her friend had vanished. She found her blubbing in their room, saying how shameful it would be if she failed. Hazel saw the angst caused by having that name to live up to. Sarah's panic is understandable. Her survival depended on being able to do the work. Her only home was the one she shared with Vic.

February was a depressing month with the capitulation of 60,000 troops (the largest in British history) to the Japanese in Singapore. For five months the saviour status of the US hung in the balance as its Navy fought a treacherous air and sea war. In Romania a newspaper viciously attacked the PM, declaiming that his daughter had risen from the harem like Queen Esther to take down Haman and spare the Jewish race. Just then Evil King Vic was at the Palladium with Vera Lynn raising funds for Civil Defence workers. On 28 March St Nazaire, the only Atlantic dry dock big enough to house a battleship like the *Tirpitz* (doggedly resilient to Allied attacks) was blown up. At Chequers with the Mountbattens, Sarah was proud of her model-making friends who had helped plan it. David Brachi was one of those 'V Section' boys who could use PI to spot a new class of naval destroyer, get exact ship measurements and even assess a convoy's purpose and level of threat. 3-D models were informing raids like the one on Bruneval by the SOE, allowing Britain to snatch foreign intelligence.

Only returning occasionally to make a speech as Preston's MP, Randolph was based in Cairo. Editing *Desert News* alongside correspondent and jack-the-lad Alaric Jacob, he called for measures to improve the lives of desert servicemen. While leading a sociable life at the Shepheard's Hotel and Mohammed Ali Club and generous to girlfriends (sending makeup, perfume and stockings), his gaffe raisonné about the Egyptians got reported and Miles Lampson (Lord Killearn, Britain's ambassador to Egypt) gave him a ticking off. The Egyptians were a sensitive bunch, Randolph was told, though Miles thought young Churchill had 'very good stuff in him'. Alaric, who saw Randolph as a cutter of red tape, met a man who remembered Winston in the days he was in barracks at Al-Azbakkia (Cairo's colonial centre) before going to Sudan. This old boy said he had been a 'cocksure young upstart' too. When Randolph left Cairo in April 1942 to join the parachute regiment of the Special Air Service (SAS) his men missed him. He later told Sarah that he actually hated jumping out of planes and that it got worse each time. It made his mother furious because his father worried for him. In May he penetrated enemy lines at Benghazi in the Libyan Desert, dislocating vertebrae when his truck overturned on the journey back. At home Mary was annoyed at him and begged him to save her mother's woes. She got a scolding from her father who defended Randolph, only for the young man to turn on his Pa for 'condoning' Pamela's affair. With no income from Randolph, the Harrimans had let Pamela stay in their spacious flat. Winston was soon wondering why he selflessly paid his son's bills.

In early summer 1942 Sarah was making strides in second-phase interpretation. An object photographed at 30,000 feet looked like a speck and she had to judge the photo's significance. An eye for detail and good concentration made a good PI. Mary Grierson, later a botanical artist, believed a 'curiosity for the unusual' was equally important. Ground Intelligence or 'Z Section' (divided into subsections relating to geographical areas) had Sarah studying Kiel Harbour, a major enemy naval base and U-boat dock repeatedly targeted by Bomber Command. The last Spitfire reconnaissance had yielded more photos taken with frames overlapping by 60% that under a stereoscope provided 3-D qualities of height, contour and depth. Poring over them, she counted gun turrets and shipping features, divining ship movements such as when a smaller craft was being moved to make room for a battleship or destroyer. Her memorisation skills were put to use and the work provided her greatest sense of achievement to date. Charlotte Bonham Carter, one of the department's permanent staff (whose ancestor William of Wykeham had coined the phrase 'Manners Maketh Man'), had been in MI5 for years. A vegetarian, Charlotte's lack of snobbery, individual way of wearing a uniform and love of the arts made her stand out. Also there was George Dury who later published a work on climate change. Grania Guinness (Lord Moyne's daughter who had known Sarah all her life) was in Z1 Sub-section, responsible for the Baltic. Grania was a good friend and her son remembers his mother's face 'lighting up with pleasure when Sarah's name was mentioned'. Archaeologist and Cambridge don Glyn Daniel, also in Z1 Sub-section, knew Prof and had personal contact with the PM.

Ft-Lieutenant Villiers (Peveril) David had recourse to contacts in MI6. The 'knowledge' in 'Z Section' meant officers might get asked to attend interrogations. Villiers sat surrounded by maps, POW intelligence, trade directories and pre-war period handbooks concerning continental companies. The 'Grand Maester' presiding over this card index library had an off-putting manner. People began by disliking the balding, bespectacled man but barriers came down and their opinions changed. In later years, he would say his violent father made him this way. He called his wider family (Sir Sassoon David, founder of the Bank of India and Percival David, famed for his Chinese ceramic collection) 'carpetbaggers from Baghdad'. An earlier career at the Bar was undertaken 'without enthusiasm' until he became a journalist at *The London Mercury*, illustrating books including one by Gide, *Amyntas*, fragments about North Africa with erotic homosexual undertones. A self-taught painter, Villiers trained as a pilot in 1932, then inherited wealth let him travel. Ann McKnight Kauffer (daughter of the artist) described the nightmare that befell Villiers when he exchanged Rolls-Royce for motorbike. He couldn't stop it and whizzed past guards at the front gate countless times until the petrol ran out. Hazel witnessed a man calling him 'My Jewish friend'. He replied: 'I am a Jew, but I am NOT your friend.' Villiers derided friendship as mutual appreciation – 'Sooner or later familiarity and habit exhaust both' – but his wit consoled Sarah. His home, Friar Park at Henley-on-Thames, had medieval gardens, caverns and a stone crocodile in the lake. Inside, door handles were shaped like monk's heads and light switches like monk's noses. His sister Elaine operated a small farm next door. Sarah, Hazel, Glyn, Brachi and others came to his tennis and croquet parties and when they did Scottish dancing he sprang around the room in red braces. His Song Dynasty alter ego was that of the drunken poet: 'I love alcohol, food, all kinds of pleasure.'

Frequently Sarah would rush off to greet her Daddy late at night. Service girls faced severe reprimands if they got stranded. There were only 15 hostels for young women operating nationally and just a couple in London. Clementine, who sat on the YWCA committee, aimed to change this: 'We want ten times as many,' she said, adding that Mary and Sarah had never been able to get into one when they tried. Mrs Oliver needed a crashpad given her summonses. Flat 157A, 55 Park Lane was a snug modern apartment two miles north of her estranged aristocrat. On 20 August, the evening following her father's return from Moscow, Sarah was dining at the Ritz with Randolph and Pamela late into the night. Bob Laycock and wife Angie, née Dudley-Ward, were present, as was Evelyn Waugh, who annoyed Sarah by calling Vic a joker. Waugh had just completed a PI course, his at Matlock.

Section Officer Oliver hid her inferiority complex and in August 1942 was doing critical work for 'Combined Operations' – a small inter-Allied team led by the TCO and Philip Hayes. Requiring the biggest use of PI so far, masses of aerial photographs scanned the terrain of Gibraltar, Malta and North Africa. Measuring bridges and roads to inform commando ops of dropping zones, this was part of Operation TORCH (the invasion of French North Africa). Surrounded by boffins of the highest order, Sarah, whose academic credentials were lacking, felt cowed. She was working with eminent archaeologists Dorothy Garrod and Peter Murray Threipland, plus St John's College organist Robin Orr. Dorothy's skills in Arabic were highly relevant. Ursula Powys-Lybbe was a liaison with Ike's TORCH team at Norfolk House, St James's Square. Hazel recalls that Sarah's proficiency with the slide rule improved but there were limits. Reconfiguring it to its former setting after use was a bind. Sarah found her own solution by trotting down to the cellars of Medmenham's Danesfield House to see David (her friend in model-making). From him she obtained a second device that could be kept permanently on one setting. She carried both around and got on with the job. Clued up about TORCH, she could swiftly correct her father regarding ship numbers heading to North Africa. Winston was impressed.

'Now there is such a thing as security,' Sarah reminded Papa (assuming he wouldn't leak the info). After the PM told Mrs Roosevelt, this reached Sarah's superiors and she got a bollocking. Two months later the time-sensitive task of finding roads and beaches for landing was pressured; a Halloween fancy dress party organised by the Americans offered respite. The officers' table offered unghostly fare such as *Polet Roti President Roosevelt*, *Tarte aux Pumpkin Abraham Lincoln* and *Creme des Tomates MacArthur.* During a concert soon after at which Moiseiwitsch went pink when a string snapped on Charlotte's piano, Sarah recited a poem, its tone semi-atheistic having faith not so much in God but in 'The Bombers'. Ignored by subsequent World War II poetry anthologies, it received cheers from genuine flyers of the day. Peter Portal (a star at Bomber Command and now Air Chief Marshal) appreciated it. Writing to thank her, he mentions C. S. Lewis's *The Screwtape Letters*, a book they admired and one he was lent Mary.

Unlike the Russians who had no qualms about sending women to bomb the Finns, Britain didn't fly women in combat in the RAF, though five women pilots won their wings. WAAFs might do Air Transport Auxiliary flying between factories and depots or get taken up in a Tiger Moth to understand the pilot's perspective. This happened to Sarah, Hazel and Molly and they got the shock of their lives when told they were in control of the aircraft as it rapidly lost height. Sarah was feeling the strain with the long hours. She looked ill in early January 1943 when Laura Charteris saw her at a dance in High Wycombe at which many Americans were present.

Russia was now dealing Germany what would be seen in retrospect as a fatal blow and Britain's War Cabinet was consulting with scientists, second-guessing how a German rocket attack might be carried out. On 17 March Duncan shook things up by speaking about the threat of long-range weapons, initiating a scientists' debate that didn't help the PIs. Prof asserted that a liquid-fuelled rocket was beyond Germany's capability – a massive miscalculation.

A month later Pug Ismay urged the formation of a committee and Duncan, from his HQ at Shell Mex House, headed it. Given the range of these weapons, he called for concentrated surveillance over a 130-mile radius of London. Until July 1943, one of the towers of Danesfield House saw Sarah and her 'F Section' buddies analysing enemy transport infrastructure with before and after photos; judging the extent of repair since the last attack and determining when a new razing was due. Hazel, Geoffrey Stone and Constance Babington Smith were colleagues. Constance was the daughter of a Bank of England director and cousin of Rose Macaulay. She had written satirical articles for *Aeroplane* magazine and designed hats for garden parties including one with a bomber on it. Her artistic bent made her adroit at identifying aircraft from tiny specks on photographs. 'Babs' would later receive a US Legion of Merit for services to Allied Air Photographic Interpretation.

Maintaining the Sunday night tradition of seeing family was hard, given the restrictions on transport and fuel. Sarah wasn't averse to dropping the name. When she got a lift from young PI Len Chance, he overheard her telling the garage man: 'Give him two of daddy's!' When Sarah wasn't at Chequers or making clandestine trips, she was a cheerful face at the Station. Her TCO appreciated her generous spirit. She would take her turn on the 4 p.m. to 8 a.m. shift. She patronised the Dog and Badger and Hare and Hounds and ate her dried egg omelette at Marlow's Dutch Cafe. All the RAF and WAAF got a boost on Wednesdays, doughnut day. Sarah never pulled rank at the Station but being Officer Class, ordinary WAAFs called her ma'am. While ordinary WAAFs fetched their wood to keep huts warm, officers had a batman for menial jobs and enjoyed accommodation at Phyllis Court on Marlow Road. Sarah found conditions trying, whether it was there or a Nissen hut. Geoffrey Stone recalled that some folk unkindly treated her like a 'nobody' and believed this was the first time in her life that she had experienced this. Her London flat was a lifesaver. On 48-hour leaves 55 Park Lane was a place where friends and colleagues like Elliott Roosevelt (commanding the US reconnaissance wing) congressed en route to parties. Winston's daughter might have been spied on because a story was floated in a number of Austrian newspapers about her dancing with a GI who, after swinging her around in a Lindy Hop and calling her Baby, stepped on her foot. Sarah is said to have slapped him. The report adds that the US presence was eroding English manners and that Papa Churchill had issued a handbook of manners for English women regarding the correct way to deal with Americans.

At the beginning of 1943 spies identified a Luftwaffe test facility on the Baltic Island of Usedom and sorties brought back photos with curious objects that pointed to the weapons the Nazis were developing. Duncan, who had a model of Peenemünde on his desk, made a visit to Sarah's RAF station on

9 May. It was a boost having his sister-in-law there, helping him reach out to the team. Cousin Johnny came to the mess, as did Winston on 16 June. Myra Murden, one of the WAAFs who did typing for Sarah, thought he came to 'see what Sarah was doing'. Churchill saw the powerful optics of Medmenham's Wild (pronounced *Vilt*) machine in action. It took stereo shots and computed data connected with the terrain such as angle, height, depth and weight. The Wild machine analysed the suspected production site at Peenemünde. The PM loved the finishing touches to the models of tiny buildings achieved with Perspex. Bending down to get a closer look, gold pencils spilled out of his pockets.

In July, Poland's resistance army, the *Armia Krajowa*, hauled rocket wreckage from a river and later that year passed MI6 information about rockets hidden by dense forest in Blizna, south-eastern Poland. Sites in Cherbourg and elsewhere were identified as launch sites. On 18 August Operation HYDRA attempted to bomb Peenemünde. Winant, too, came to Medmenham several times, he and Sarah acting formal. Initially, Gil didn't grasp the benefits of an inter-Allied team despite the successes. He supported Elliott Roosevelt's break-up plan, whereas TCO Kendall thought it misguided. Gil called a meeting at Claridges, inviting General Spaatz (USAAF Strategic Bombing Commander), but Air Marshal Sinclair intervened, supporting Kendall. Elliott's plans were soon dropped.

Ted Wood (fondly known as 'Woody') was Chief Entertainment Officer and driving force of Wings For Victory weeks. Henley had a number of these. Summer 1943 saw Sarah put together a concert at the Odeon, Marlow. She had a small spot in the show and enlisted a choir and WAAF singers. She got Vic to compère and 'Lucky Lyndon' got her Jack and Daphne Barker from *Get a Load of This*, platinum blonde singer Sylvia Saetre, a dance band, a tenor and a lightning caricaturist. With rousing songs and a 'God Save the King' finale, the show raised £755 13*s* 6*d*.

Meeting his wife after being cast aside wasn't easy. Vic saw Sarah a few times after, noticing her confidence had grown in leaps and bounds. Having helped win the right for performers to give free Sunday performances to HM Forces, overturning the Lord's Day Observance Rule, Vic had been recruited by the Office of Strategic Services (OSS), the agency that later became the CIA. His job was to broadcast propaganda from 'fake' radio stations to Germany, kidding listeners these were live from a Berlin station. He admitted this in 1959 after Agnes Bernelle revealed that OSS head Bill Donovan had recruited them to broadcast from fake German stations (in Milton Bryan or Woburn Abbey). Agnes was 'Vicky of the three kisses' on 'Radio Atlantic'. Using names from intercepted letters they misled listeners, persuading a German U-Boat captain to surrender (telling him his wife had given birth), or stated that Allied saboteurs were dressed in SS uniforms (causing SS in France to arrest each other). In 1945 Berlin-born Agnes married Desmond Leslie, Winston's second cousin, then in the RAF.

When Vic wasn't being a secret agent or making films with Margaret Lockwood, he was busy racing (opening Coventry's Horse Show) and travelling with the Air Ministry's Lord Willoughby de Broke (in charge of the RAF's PR and broadcasting). Lord de Broke's son remembers meeting Vic who, to a seven year-old, seemed 'ancient'. While Sarah claimed she had done everything to 'part with mutual respect and as little bitterness as possible', Vic twice appealed for a marital reconciliation. Myra Murden recalled he had been telephoning Sarah at Medmenham at regular intervals ever since she started. Myra speaks of 'tears on the blotting paper' after these conversations, though her colleagues did not know that she had rejected him. She was always guarded about her private life.

In September, Sarah was back measuring enemy sites for re-targeting. She got corralled into finding out which 'Progressive Training' talks appealed to WAAFs. Nobody could match her Egyptian Dance (demonstrated in the mess) or her contacts drawing big names to concerts. In 1944 Sir Malcolm Sargent came. The Medmenham Rep Company exploited those with performance skills such as Pauline Growse (formerly in rep at Wigan). The networks of these players outlasted the war. For *Out of the Blue* (the pun being the 'blue' of the WAAF uniform) the programme cover showed girls doing military drill on one side and in their undies on the reverse. If that wasn't saucy enough, the men of Henley found themselves a little hot under the collar at the sight of ambassadresses summoned by ex-Windmill Theatre stage director Lt Ken Bandy, now one of the Social Secretaries who determined that nude statues feature among the cultural highlights. Sarah had a scene in the revue doing a comedy monologue at a looking glass before performing ballet with a wedge of cygnets. She had an ally in Bill Duncalfe, who directed and acted in Medmenham Rep plays such as *Saloon Bar*, sometimes enlisting Sarah as director.

# 8

# Our Secret Place

On 13 November 1941, John G. Winant and Winston Churchill were at Bristol's Grand Hotel when their waiter came in from firewatching with his scorched shirt hanging out at the back after dousing flames. It made Gil's tough words to the press two days before about 'not accepting the ground the enemy elects' sound a little lame. The Great British armchair was threadbare. Whatever stuff was stiffening it there wasn't enough of it. During the first week of December Margaret Sweeny ran into Averell Harriman who confessed he was unsure about the prospect of the US ever entering the war (at least not actively). A turnaround came when Ave was at Chequers with Gil, Kathy and Pamela. Late on 7 December Winston's valet Sawyers came in bearing the radio Harry Hopkins left as a gift, followed by the PM in his dragon-embroidered dressing gown. The Japanese had attacked. The news of America coming into the war created a surge of excitement. At the Foyles luncheon celebrating Cochran on 17 December Sarah sat next to H. G. Wells – knowing that the man she was giddily in love with regarded him a prophet. In great secrecy the PM left for Washington. Ave, Gil, Dudley Pound (First Sea Lord), Portal and John Dill – Chief of the Imperial General Staff (CIGS) – accompanied Winston, remaining with him until he sailed away on the heavily armed HMS *Duke of York*. Gil left Winston Christmas cubanos at Chequers to find on his return.

When Gil taught at St Paul's in New Hampshire his lessons were characterised by discoveries not from books but free conversation. It made him popular with his pupils. On New Year's Eve he addressed the British Association of Head Masters referring to a 'world of justice' with the youth of America and Great Britain working alongside each other. After MP Arthur Jenkins played host to Gil, young Roy Jenkins landed a research job at Winant's office until February 1942. He recalled how obvious it was during those four months that his boss was 'ethereally in love' with Sarah Churchill. It was an unorthodox union cemented in wartime. During Sarah's leave and outside Gil's official duties they relished their forbidden fantasy. 'You are making new opportunities where none ever existed before,' was a line from Mrs Winant's address to mobilising British women before she left Britain in August 1941 for ten months. She could not of course have seen the irony.

Four months earlier, during the Blitz, Connie went out of her mind. She was relieved when Gil took her to The Ramblers. They got value from the country cottage he had use of. There are few references to this hideaway, except that it was a masculine retreat where friends (US colonels and generals) came to smoke, drink Scotch and 'chew the rag' with Winant. In a letter to Gil, Sarah mentions Penn Farm in Penn, Bucks, a short distance from Chequers and Medmenham. Some years later Gil took Clementine for a walk at a farm near Beaconsfield. The Ramblers might be the same place. Nowhere else was better suited to stealing a few hours together. This was their 'bower', reminding Sarah of a chapter in Granny's memoir about the first time she came to Blenheim and chanced on the place where the 'other woman' Fair Rosamund hid her royal amours. A couple of centuries before Jennie Jerome, Sarah, Duchess of Marlborough had heartlessly reduced that romantic site to rubble as part of her modernisation campaign. No wonder that imperious ancestor (after whom Sarah was named) was branded 'the Great Atossa'. Being with Gil, Sarah knew she was more like the vandal and less like Fair Rosamund. Would Connie sniff out the 'bower' and confront her, just as Queen Eleanor did? Sarah told herself she would willingly take poison were that to happen. Perhaps the secret kept by John Churchill (before he rose to become the first Marlborough Duke) applied too. He never compromised the Duchess of Cleveland. Poor John once had to hop it out of the window but wasn't reproached for being naughty and was paid for his discretion. Years later, Connie showed her husband's colleague Maurine Mulliner photos of that country place. Looking at them brought back fond memories. Connie wondered why he had insisted on maintaining The Ramblers when he was never there. She grumbled to Maurine about the credit he had run up at Gumbiners Jewellers on Madison Avenue, observing that many of the items purchased hadn't been for her.

That *Heaven for Two* had open countryside to protect them. The fallen leaves and delicate elderflowers marked the path to her independence. Gil was her first true relationship, in that he couldn't gain anything publicly out of her name – his diplomatic role locking them into a state of secrecy. Above all, he wasn't a thespian competing for the limelight. He cared little for fame. He was liable to say something dour about the cinema, such as 'Too many people by far have been influenced by the screen flash of easy living. That is not America.' And yet, at times he watched in suspense when something rose from within her and she replenished herself with theatrical balm. Typically, she was her plainest self; uniform carefully hung up and one modest change of clothes. He told her it was a special time when rich and poor stood side-by-side defending liberty. Sarah agreed that severe inequalities ought to go, but she was never a socialist. Thankfully, there was much Gil wanted to preserve. Sarah told him about her grandfather living for three years at Lord North's house at 50 Grosvenor Square and an emotional Winston (aged twenty) running across that square in the snow on learning of his father's death on 24 January 1895.

Gil was the man whose life experience came nearest to her father's. He was idealistic and had served nation, wife and family. Electra could settle for this paternalistic protector. As if invited to become like Mr C, he responded intuitively. People noticed Gil doing his work before he got out of bed in the morning or striding around the room when receiving visitors, unaware he was in his dressing gown or pyjamas. Father figure though he was, the bond was simple and mutual: someone to care for and to sympathise with. When they could seize an evening or a day, he was devoted to her, drawing sustenance from that secret place. In typical Winant fashion, he forgot time and Sarah had to think for him. Unlike the set-up with Vic, she became a genuine giver and he selflessly listened to her, not confronting her when she sounded like a complaining neurotic child. This man with quaint New England ways could also be childlike; he might suddenly panic after hearing a radio broadcast, ordering her to get herself into the frikkin parlour. She didn't have the capacity to take on Gil's problems but thought she was helping him. Living in the moment, they didn't need to consider a future.

The President had invested in Gil. So had the British. A blind eye was turned to private dealings so long as these were discreet. Harriman used Robert Sherwood's house at Great Enton in Surrey and it was here that Pamela came. Sherwood had owned it since 1929 and he was a close friend of Harriman and Hopkins. International diplomacy and security were at stake but all this could be managed and watertight. Besides, the Churchills had too high a wall around them. Sarah's actions, like Pamela's, might be regarded as patriotic, but Winston's reaction was complex when he found out. Knowing each day was a godsend, he didn't begrudge those who grasped happiness and, though only 15 years older, was quite paternal towards Gil. He wished it hadn't happened but thought of his daughter as a soldier who had left a formation to ride alone, survey the scene, reach the outpost and report back. Admiration took the form of a knowing glint whilst whisky glasses clinked. It was never discussed in the family until 1945 and then only obliquely.

After staying three weeks at the White House, Winston returned to England. Gil spoke at a Dorchester luncheon, saying the US was raising an army of 7 million. American sea, land and air forces were taking up stations in the British Isles: the first step 'on the highway to ultimate victory'. When it came to GIs, he announced that 'idleness had no part of America's national life'. After seeing FDR again, Gil came back on 1 May 1942 accompanied by Commander Stark (head of the US Navy) and Connie, whose next stay in Britain would last seven months. She attended a Claridges lunch with Gil, Eden, Bobbety and Bracken, and in early June went to Durham with Deputy PM Attlee. The angry miners were set on nationalisation. The Cabinet had long ignored the mine ownership issue and many bore a grudge against Ernest Bevin, Minister of Labour, for selling out after the General Strike. Now they were striking again, angry at essential work orders imposed to deal with absenteeism. The ambassador brought their future to the fore, his address centred on the idea of preserving people's democracy. Against the odds the miners went back to work and *The Herald* branded it 'Gettysburg in Durham!' Gil's years of reaching out to people set him in good stead. His friends the Murrows had a Welsh maid called Betty and Winant always insisted on Betty's father attending so he could hear about real miners' lives in Britain.

On United Nations Day on 14 June he donned his natty suit and Homburg, ecstatic about the 27 countries standing together. Sarah met Gil and his wife at the Hoare Memorial Hall where the Commons was convening, any familiarity between them imperceptible. It was shortly after 20 June when news of defeat at Tobruk revealed Britain's vulnerability in the Middle East. As Cairo rep, Richard Casey's job was to mobilise rearguard services. Defiant in the face of criticism, the PM ordered weapons including Sherman tanks on his swift trip to the US. Mary, stationed at a mixed anti-aircraft battery, absorbed her parents' angst. Her moral outlook underwent a crisis of faith serious enough to warrant a minor breakdown and a stay in camp hospital. She came through, determined to face the blackest days. Having arrived at Chequers on a borrowed motorbike, Sarah listened to Mary's concerns before venturing a husky word of wisdom. She was reminded of her erstwhile career when, next evening, after a dinner for Bomber Harris, they saw the film *Kipps*. Mary said the girls at Enfield enjoyed hearing her WAAF sister call up Lt-Commander Ralph Richardson in the spoof *Happy Landings* on the wireless. She had no inkling about Gil and told her sister about Vic's hopes for reconciliation, having seen him in the interval of *Get a Load of This*.

Independence Day 1942 was a bigger affair than the previous year with a Grosvenor Square garden party with marquees and deckchairs. A hundred thousand young American servicemen had entered Britain. As President of the American Red Cross, Gil opened The Washington Club in Curzon Street (now the Washington Hotel). The Red Cross had added dorms, reading rooms and an opulent lounge. Gil said that here they would 'find rest, comfort, good fun' and 'comradeship'. A week earlier, he spoke on air on the first *Let's Get Acquainted* and a few days later was at The Washington on a platform with Connie, Charles Sweeny and General Dwight Eisenhower, a soft-spoken Kansan. Appointed to command the European theatre of war, 'Ike' had just moved into 20 Grosvenor Square. Young flyers were being recruited from all over the US. Sweeny's initiative led to the first Eagle Squadron, flying alongside the RAF and equipped by the US. In early July Mrs Winant talked to WVS assemblies and visited Edinburgh's Paderewski Hospital (its staff and patients all Polish). She and Gil were heroes in Devon, American flags lined the streets. On times like these with gratitude spilling over, Gil drew his greatest satisfaction. He afterwards told fans: 'I do not think there could be a happier welcome even at the gates of heaven.'

Mrs Winant was recovering in a nursing home after a minor facial operation and cancelled her Caledonian Society dinner on 21 September. She was at her husband's side in early October at a luncheon for Maisky where Leslie Howard was a guest. Surprisingly, she isn't mentioned a few days later when the PM showed off Dover's defences to Mrs Roosevelt, her secretary Malvina Thompson, son Elliott and Harry Hopkins (with his son Robert). Winant, Sarah, Eden, Prof and Mary were present. Hopkins called on Pamela at 49 Grosvenor Square where she surpassed herself as an all-expenses-paid femme d'intéreur. In late October 1942 Sarah got her flat back from Randolph (who had requisitioned it for months), Miss Buck promising his belongings would be removed. The charlady Mrs Burran cleaned it in time for Diana Cooper to visit and declare that Eleanor Smith would 'pay a good rent' for it. The Mule put her hoof down. She invited Hazel and Molly over after a night out (taking them backstage to meet Ben and Bebe). Hazel hoped they would meet Vic at the flat. Sarah's subterfuge meant her friends were not only unaware she lived in a separate apartment but also that the Oliver marriage had died a death.

Halted by the Axis under Rommel, the Allies' campaign started badly. The PM felt renewed hope as he walked alongside Montgomery, who replaced Wavell as Commander. The Second Battle of Alamein that November and Monty's leadership turned the tide of the war. Vichy France was an enemy until Ike did a deal with a çollaborationist (with Winant forced to defend it). Gil's brother Fred arrived as US rep of the Middle East Supply Centre, the shipping regime the British had set up a year before to prioritise supply lines for military use and allocate cargo space for imports (to avoid famine). It would be a stepping-stone to US influence. On 26 November there was a Thanksgiving service in Westminster Abbey, parades and special children's parties at USAAF bases; each GI responsible for five children's entertainment and off-ration goodies. Winston's daughters were at the Annexe for his birthday, the room decorated with candlelight and flowers.

Harvard lecturer-cum-theosophist Colonel Conger (Pershing's Intelligence Officer) had instilled in Gil his passion for Lincoln and Grant. Gil arrived (without Connie) with a gift for Winston: *I Rode with Stonewall* by Henry Kyd Douglas, a soldier who had fought for the South. Stonewall (Jackson's youngest aide) had surrendered to Grant ending the War but was admired by his enemies. Like Lincoln in 1863, Churchill had seen a low in his campaign that picked up with a change in General. Gil envisioned Sarah in the role of the 'Belle' who evaded Union soldiers, smuggling resources to blockaded Southern troops, Hetty Carr Cary. With her auburn hair and perfect figure, Kyd Douglas called her 'the most beautiful woman I ever saw in any land'.

The awkward Winant communicated his feelings to the PM through the narrative and romance of combat. Churchill enjoyed his views on Gettysburg and the Great War, in which he had progressed from Lafayette Flying Corps to commanding a squadron. For Armistice anniversaries, he and fellow Legionnaires had made visits to Europe. Gil's brothers' adventures (Fred in the AEF and Cornelius in the French Foreign Legion) intrigued Churchill. Cornelius deserted and the Armistice saved him from reprimand. He continued an army career and wrote a memoir.

Roy Jenkins implies that Sarah's hold over Gil 'helped attract him to the Churchill family ... to the British cause'. Could she really have influenced international relations to any extent? In the case of North Africa the British and American weren't singing from the same hymn book. Gil had a problem with GYMNAST (later called TORCH) at the time Sarah was involved in the intelligence underpinning it. She was second-guessing disguised enemy positions. Medmenham's 'X section' supplied 'true landscape' information to the SOE and to bodies reporting to the FO like the Political Warfare Executive (PWE) specialising in 'sibs', or rumours, with Bruce Lockhart at the helm. The PIs helped equivalent American agencies like the Office of War Information (OWI) headed by Robert Sherwood (latterly screenwriter of Hitchcock's *Rebecca*), who wrote FDR's speeches and would outrage Churchill in 1948 owing to his candid book about FDR and Hopkins. Most WAAFs weren't told the reasons for the work assigned to them but Sarah knew the ins and outs. She could have brought her massively influential friend in line with military angles favoured by the British. He had FDR's ear. Later, when a Second Front was debated, Churchill and Alan Brooke (who succeeded Dill as CIGS) wanted to extract the Axis from North Africa and take Italy out of the war prior to invading Western Europe. Winant, Ike and the US generals disagreed, yet America bowed to British strategy. The over-careful Winant was actually opposed to the principle of inter-Allied intelligence; but where Churchill's daughter was concerned, it is possible he made an exception. Through her inter-Allied work she was informed about positions held by Ike's Staff, as well as having Gil's insider view. Her own views on strategy were entirely in line with her father's.

The Virgin Queen had her Lords Burghley and Walsingham, and the championing of this modern Bess was no less impressive. Her court held forth beneath Danesfield House's dreaming spires and while the idea of the PM's daughter sharing top-secret information with her American devotee and vice versa seems romantic, this might not be so far-fetched. They were trusted allies. The harvest of information reaped by the OSS and the cryptological yield that owed everything to the experts at Britain's Code and Cypher School were now Gil's for the taking. Since mid-1941 Sarah's father had been receiving the most important decrypts daily. With fast-changing developments following on the back of them, how could Sarah be ignorant? Her work in Ground Intelligence exposed her to plans originating in the Secret Intelligence Service (SIS).

Withholding a thing useful to the other is a tough call for lovers each bound by their country's code of honour. Where work entered the parlour it was best not to go there. Winant's stubbornly cautious approach clearly rubbed off on her, as did his skill at letting people talk: reading their character before drawing conclusions. Sarah exercised a degree of independence and when Papa brought Bomber Harris's idea to her that she switch to PI at Bomber Command she refused, saying she was best off in her current location. As for Gil, he didn't always toe the American line, backing the argument that Montgomery was the best of the commanders (something no other US spokesman did). He gave the British the benefit of his nearness to FDR when hardly anyone got close to Roosevelt, given the odd way he had of keeping even his closest aides separate. Eden's comment that relations between Britain and the US wouldn't have been the same without Gil was one the PM had to agree with – but who acknowledged the bond between Sarah and Winant? Wasn't that the closest point ever in the Special Relationship?

'All Care Abandon Ye who Enter here' were the words etched above the gate at Chequers and the war failed to dampen the fun of Christmas for young Winston. Gil arrived on Boxing Day with Mary. The ambassador, who recently spoke about 'Youth and the Fight For Freedom', had a meeting at the White House before going to Johns Hopkins Hospital for his bursitis. Connie had returned to the US in December 1942. Sarah might have joined Gil (leaving for Washington after Boxing Day and returning alone on 2 January 1943). Clementine thanks him on 3 January for the lovely gifts, mentioning how Sarah was so much better for her 'adventure'. Sarah was away again, writing to Gil four days later from sunny North Africa before returning with her Mama (whilst Winston stayed for the Casablanca Conference). Elliott

Roosevelt joined his father there. The Allied attack on Axis-held Tunisia hadn't gone well owing to lack of cohesion between British and US troops. The Roosevelts listened to Randolph's talk about the Balkans but didn't take what he said seriously. Winston was another matter; on 23 January FDR let the PM show him the view of Marrakesh most dear to him. His wheelchair was lifted up the tower of Villa Taylor to see the city at sunset. It didn't take long for him to agree to the PM's plans to prioritise HUSKY (the Allied invasion of Sicily under the command of Ike). Despite victories by the US Navy, the Asia-Pacific War was his gravest concern, with Japan a tenacious and implacable foe.

In Washington at a ceremony on 12 February marking Lincoln's birthday, Winant told America: 'If Britain had fallen in the summer of 1940 after ten countries had been overrun with the Japanese planning to bomb Pearl Harbor, all present hope for our American way of life would have died.' He was there when the British Parliamentary Union made a gift of the Charles West Cope painting *The Embarkation of the Pilgrim Fathers* (which used to hang in the Peers Corridor of Parliament). Gil set up a committee whereby the US, UK and USSR cooperated on the restitution of works of art, historic monuments and records affected by war. Eden joined him for talks about emergency relief with Cordell Hull and Sumner Welles. Gil wrote a preface to Julian Huxley's book on the Tennessee Valley Authority, praising that public work that revived a poverty-stricken region. More transatlantic flights took him to the Washington Conference, even though flying wasn't safe. On 1 June a Douglas DC-3 was attacked by eight German Junkers and crashed in the Bay of Biscay, killing all on board including film star, producer and propagandist Leslie Howard. Back from North Africa, Winston had been struck down by pneumonia.

With her genius for organisation, Pamela was handpicked to run a club where top military brass from America and the Dominions could rub shoulders with British Officers. You had to be elected to get in. A dull looking 'Churchill Club' sign above an archway leading from the playground of Westminster School (empty after evacuation) was the portal to drawing rooms that breathed history. The Inigo Jones staircase and landing of Ashburnham House led to a library, rest areas, lecture room, bar (never out of whisky) and an American cafeteria. From July 1943 the Churchill Club celebrated culture with H. G. Wells lecturing on 'The Natural Rights of Man' and Pulitzer Prize historian Herbert Agar offering a 'Blueprint for the Postwar World'. There were discourses by Eden and Hugh Gaitskill and by literary figures Edith Sitwell, Rose Macauley, Kenneth Clark and Desmond McCarthy. Attendees included Stephen Spender, Graham Greene, David Niven, James Stewart and Clark Gable.

Connie Winant returned on 8 June after a six-month absence. Gil's proximity to the Governments in Exile allowed him to voice their concerns but Poland's fate worsened on 4 July when a plane crashed into the sea just sixteen seconds after take-off from Gibraltar. Only one person survived and the dead included Sikorski and Victor Cazalet. It was just a month after the Leslie Howard crash. From mid-August to late September 1943 Chequers was quiet because of the First Québec Conference, where delegates discussed the post-war world. One suggestion from FDR, that the British improve how they cook Brussels sprouts, led Clementine to request that Gil obtain appropriate recipes from Belle Roosevelt. The last person to know about such things, Gil confronted FDR, demanding leave. How else could he advise Mrs C about cordon bleu cookery? Writing to his aunt in Canada, Johnny reported on another British problem. Sarah had been terribly ill and was recuperating at Chequers. The reason isn't known but a few months earlier, 'deplorable kitchens' and lack of cleanliness at Medmenham had made her lodge a complaint. Georgina Landemare looked after her. Thirty years later Joan Bakewell asked the cook what the family were like and was told they all were wonderful – 'especially Sarah!'

Gil stood next to Harriman when the latter swore an oath as FDR appointed him ambassador to the USSR. The Flying Fortress piloted by Winant's son hadn't returned from flying over Münster. It was John's thirteenth raid having attacked the Messerschmitt plant and other assembly sites. In the days after 9 October 1943 the Churchills were distressed for the Winants, as were many ordinary people. Sarah felt like a plaster saint writing comforting words to Connie. Leaving Prestwick on 21 October, the Winants headed home, Connie staying in New Hampshire until July 1945. Five terrible weeks passed, not knowing if John was alive or dead. More bad news came with the sinking of HMS *Charybdis*. At Chequers, Noël Coward's mind was a leaden weight that neither food nor gossip about Sarah and Vic divulged by Clementine during croquet could lighten. Weeks later the Winants heard that John Junior was alive but the downside was he was a 'VIP' at Colditz, alongside Giles Romilly. Gil and Sarah were then drawn into the International Conferences.

In late November Winant had public relations issues. Ground for GIs to train in amphibious landings caused the evacuation of age-old coastal communities, creating ghost towns. British servicemen saw newsreels of The Washington and heard that at 100 Piccadilly and 23 Shaftesbury Ave (Rainbow Corner) GI boys had juke boxes, pool tables, pinball, showers, Coca Cola and doughnut rings threaded on forks. British troops got one beer a week while the Yanks got four. One embarrassing side effect of wealthy young men amassed in London was the increase of prostitutes outside the clubs. British observers were also shocked at segregation and racism in the US Forces. When it came to the manners of

GIs, perceptions varied. Some families were dying to invite these paragons of decency to stay at Christmas. Other, like George Orwell, believed 'the only Americans with decent manners are the Negroes'. Gil tried to address these concerns but his proposals were largely rejected. At Medmenham attempts by Americans stationed near Wycombe to ingratiate themselves with WAAFs were frowned upon, with bananas and stockings hurled back at them. One GI there shot his British girlfriend and was hanged. The 'Cleft Chin Murderer' Karl Hulten took the prize for most notorious GI.

From La Marsa, where Sarah tended the PM, she wrote to Gil on 22 December describing how 'the real battle' was to make her 'very naughty' Papa rest. She wished Gil a Happy Christmas and enclosed cufflinks and a little soft toy to keep him company. She enquired after Orol Mears, sending her handkerchiefs (gaudy ones so hanky thieves like Gil would think twice before spiriting one away). Sarah asks if his job is going well and if he'll send word that he's OK to 10 Downing Street (where she can safely pick it up). Something between them needed resolution. She writes enigmatically about happy endings, saying, 'My heart failed me,' but it's her Papa's health she's referring to. Sarah can be playful with Gil but a sombre respect predominates. A poem, *Christmas 1943*, may be from Gil's point of view. She writes the word 'Chequers' below it but she wasn't there, just imagining its 'dim-lit room' in which Gil wasn't 'left for laughter'. He was at Diana and Duncan's party opening presents round the tree FDR had shipped. When Clementine returned from Carthage a letter from Winant awaited her. Inside was an early spring flower, incongruous and touching. Only four years older and in sympathy politically, she replied saying how valued he was by her family. Over the years Clementine received many a fragrant violet or gorgeous bibelot for Mary and others.

A European Advisory Commission (EAC) was set up to get a clear policy on Germany's surrender, dividing its landmass into occupation zones while avoiding another Versailles. Based at Lancaster House, Gil, Philip Mosely, William Strang and Gusev got to work on this in January 1944. In March they defined the 'instrument of German surrender', ensuring the Allies had a legal pretext to exercise full control over a defeated nation and begin a denazification programme. Unfortunately, the US Military didn't like EAC going into such detail and restricted its functions. The Commission was so hampered by bureaucracy that clearing any document was next to impossible. The Russians also weren't wired for compromise and he couldn't get a joint contract the Allies would agree to. FDR also hadn't shared information about the occupation boundaries he favoured. Paralysis beset EAC and everyone deplored it.

The poetess seemed to be shedding her ethereal wings. A letter to an unidentified young man is a marked contrast to those to Gil and reveals her silliest, flirtiest side. Writing to 'Jack', she's madcap and longs for him to prattle on, carelessly referring to those in their circle: the 'Contesse de la thingimmybob who paints' being one. Jack had been raving about what a great dancer she was and recommended that his mate, Tommy Jenkins, take her on a date. Sarah says how the friend 'rang Mummie up at Number 10 and wanted to take me dancing. Well, Mummie passed the message on and I thought well, any friend of Jack's is sure to be nice,' so she went (bringing another boy and girl along). As Sarah's letter reveals, Tommy doesn't stop talking about his heroic deeds. Sarah questions 'why anyone else bothered to fight at all!' The 'said charmer' was so unlike Jack, he might have been an imposter. The relationship with Jack lasted at least a couple of months. He must have been important for her to beg him to stay in touch. What stands out is that Sarah was going out with men her own age. She could be as unchained as she wanted. But Gil was her anchor, beginning his letters with a 'Dearest Sarah' and ending with a 'Devotedly G' in careful, tiny handwriting.

Sarah learnt how proud Connie was of Gil's Freedom of the City paraphernalia. He claimed that his wife was obsessed by finance and loved gambling on anything. They shared a love of European culture. He said his wife was more comfortable in High Society than he was, but Sarah wondered if it were true because Gil liked beautiful hotels and good food. When she met Mrs Winant her outlook seemed modern on some counts. Her husband advocated birth control and was criticised by Catholics at the ILO for these views. Connie's Church approved of family planning on the grounds of welfare but she wasn't a free spirit. She disliked divorce and felt uncomfortable with unconventional lifestyles.

Despite being lonely at the 4th of July celebrations, London had a profound effect on Gil. Even in the Churchills, he saw Dickensian qualities. There was Winston's taking up the cudgels to fight Tory stupidity and Sarah's mix of Esther Summerson and Fanny Dorrit. If an opportunity arose to repay courtesy, Winant did so. For Pamela, he chaired lectures such as Professor Trevelyan's 'How the English came to Britain'. He cut through bureaucracy to help the Churchills in personal matters. An example was passing them a message from Peter 'Gerry' Koch de Gooreynd (formerly of the Ditchley Park Set and colleague of Stewart Menzies). The ex-POW was in Paris seeking repatriation. Randolph possibly wished to help Laura Charteris (pregnant with Gerry's child, although she lost it). In late August, inter-Allied top brass came to the opening of the Stage-Door Canteen at 201 Piccadilly. Bing Crosby, the Astaires, Bea Lillie and Jack Buchanan made it a starry affair. As President of its Welfare Fund, Gil was present and Eden was given a big hand when he came on stage. No way would Sarah have missed this.

Why was Gil talking about divorce when he had gone out of his way to mediate in the Eden marriage, persuading them not to separate legally? Divorce messed up plans to get the top job. Anthony and Beatrice had an arrangement to put his career first, allowing each to be a free agent. In late 1944 Beatrice went to live with C. D. Jackson (on Ike's staff). Gil told Sarah that he and Connie acknowledged each other's 'special friend'. If Gil tried to make her believe that a future marriage was a possibility, she was lukewarm. She sensed Connie would never condone an affair. Gil's course couldn't be altered. She guessed right because Connie had already refused to give Winant a divorce. The Winant–Sarah affair was an escape, not a union. Sacrifice, duty and saving face were part and parcel of their lives. She liked the love and care of a father figure but balked at any obligations placed on her. She never envisaged marriage and assumed Gil felt the same. The delirium that had characterised the onset of their relationship had worn off. The danger signals were there and she should have given him up just then. She didn't.

Instead, with Connie in the US, Sarah came enough times to 3 Grosvenor Square to become fond of Orol, who mothered Winant and said what a joy it was to devote her life to him. With him two decades before his time abroad, she nagged him and lent him spare change. She felt honoured to cook for Mr Churchill's daughter who was so enthusiastic about their water bubbler and kitchen gadgets. Sarah played hostess too, although it was her trusted maid 'Jeff' who prepared supper. 55 Park Lane had a discreet staff entrance in South Street and she collected him and showed him tender loving care. He brought his fervid excitement edged in doom to her chambers. He knew a package store and his briefcase never failed to produce something *wicked*. He would unwrap and she would pour and he felt relieved, eyes shining in the candlelight. It was an outlet never shared with Vic, who turned grey at the mention of a drink. Gil had been teetotal until joining the ILO. While Connie drank little, Sarah enjoyed a snifter and Gil could put away a few.

She didn't see Gil throughout October and the first part of November because he was in Washington helping FDR in his presidential campaign. On election night he called asking if she would spend the evening with him given the importance of the election. He said he would be alone otherwise, since Connie detested FDR. They stayed up until 3.30 a.m. to see Franklin in for his fourth term.

FDR's vagueness about partition didn't help Gil with what was to happen after Germany's surrender, so he returned to London with Maurine Mulliner, his loyal colleague of ten years. He was upset at not being included in FDR's delegation to Russia but threw a party on 14 December 1944 inviting Phil

Mosely and John Corson (from the SSB). Maurine notes in her diary how everyone drank scotch. She joined him at Claridges three days later and in a subsequent letter his affection is obvious. He talked about divorcing Connie without naming the woman he wanted to be with. Maurine didn't know about Mrs Oliver and had never met her. She hoped to deter him from such action hoping he might run for president. Putting her own feelings aside, she only thought of what was best for him. As a young woman she had run away from Idaho Falls to dance in the ballet. Like Audrey de Vos, she was a student of Laurent Novikoff before touring in Washington and Chicago. She dressed elegantly and had a dancer's frame. Eighteen years Gil's junior, Maurine was another woman he opened up to. He told her he was the eldest of four brothers and about holidays at Monmouth Beach, NJ, where the family had a second home. When Gil and brother Clinton shared a room at 103 East 71st Street it was traumatic seeing their folks separate. Winant's biographer Bernard Bellush says his mother considered him the light of her life, letting him do as he liked, which explains the adult Gil's overspending. Maurine says Gil's mother neglected him despite giving him material resources. His unmarried aunt, Sarah Gilbert, who lived with them in later years, offered far more affection. His Scots-English mother's family was significant enough for him to want to be known as 'Gil'. The other side of the family were Dutch and building sailing vessels in Brooklyn is how the Winants started, although the next generation went into the New York real estate business.

Gil's floppy forelock suggested permanent boyishness. He was achingly attractive and years later Sarah wrote how she was 'madly in love with him – madly madly whispered across the formal atmosphere'. Then, it was love at first sight. But can it truly be love when you quit when the fun's over? She initiated the affair and Gil helped her become self-assured. By the time her worship was declining, his needs were soaring. She didn't know what she wanted apart from total freedom. Though married and 'separated' she thought of herself as free. The saddest thing about the affair was its never being open.

Gil was welcome at Ed Murrow's, 84 Hallam Street, where Navajo rugs draped the walls, even if he frequently ruined Janet's cooking by arriving late. What a shame that he couldn't have taken his special lady there! Years later Sarah felt nostalgic when she saw Ed, regretting the times she and Gil had declined invitations. Despite the distance of time, their secret love affair feels only marginally less secret now. Letters were burnt and weeded out of archives. It was not until the 1990s that contemporaries made mention of it. Jenkins' observation that Sarah drew Winant into the Churchill camp makes her motive political. Yet it was a real love affair, as books by Lady Soames and material in Sarah's hand confirm. Pamela abandoned an autobiography and Christopher Ogden wrote his own book in the 1990s using taped interviews, without quoting her directly. Mostly it's about Pam's *Dynasty*-like life but she let the Winant–Sarah business slip, implying that Sarah had no intention of getting into fourth gear whilst Gil was hopelessly in love. Familiarity and the acidic taste of reality caused disenchantment. At one time Gil was the greatest passion of Sarah's life and she felt no guilt for being involved with a married man. Later on, she felt deeply troubled by it.

Sarah had been at the Russian Conference and in February 1945 told Gil she was thinking of him and that her father felt his absence. Pointing out how 'things happen for the best' she seems to be referring to a discussion about not continuing in the same way. She got a surprise when Winant joined the President on USS *Quincy* on 15 February. Sarah and her Pa were aboard and when she saw Gil's smiling face, her heart missed a beat. She tried not to show it, sitting on one of the homely wickerwork chairs Franklin had for enjoying the sun. Her letter to Mama talked of seeing 'The Ambass!!' and how she had been knocked sideways. She responded to her mother's news about Gil taking her out for a country walk with mock jealousy, saying that Mummy's losing a shoe and getting ankle-deep in mud served as a lesson to femme fatales. Clementine didn't tell her that during the hailstorm she had confronted Gil about his relationship and that he had admitted he was serious about marrying when this became possible. Mrs C's attitude was nonetheless warm, despite her misgivings about the age gap and doubts about her Mule's future. Sarah didn't know Gil had come clean. That summer at The Ramblers when it was discussed, it probably affected their relationship. She didn't like her private business being outed, whoever was doing the outing. She wondered how this ritual sacrifice ever came about: loving in secret, dowsing for rockets (at Medmenham) and making votive offerings (to foreign dignitaries) in foreign lands. For all the goodness of the countryside, it's folly maintaining secret relationships and fumbling around in the dark.

# 9

# I Shake Hands with Uncle Joe

'Of course we had no idea what went on in the Conferences,' Sarah told interviewer Maureen Cleave in 1981. She was there to observe and chronicle events. But had she forgotten taking up the cause of the Poles (much discussed at the International meetings)? Did the words 'bracelet' and 'brooch' ring any bells? What about in May 1942, when a fox viciously savaged the black swan at Chartwell? That's when the business started. Ave Harriman had typhoid, Connie had flown back and Sarah was coming by motorcycle to Chequers. Molotov and his retinue had been and gone, the 'All Care Abandon Ye' spirit lost on them. Eden's attempt to negotiate Poland's future had fallen on deaf ears and the Soviet Foreign Minister's communiqué to secure a Second Front had gone unsigned. Her father was reaching out, though. For a year he had been supporting Russia in terms of Lend-Lease. For a while every new tank was sent, at Britain's expense, to defend Leningrad, Kiev and Odessa. War expenditure looked to soar to £5 billion. Sir Kingsley Wood asked if it was feasible. Meanwhile Stalin's arsenal was growing. US Lend-Lease gave 60,000 aircraft and 45,000 tanks to Russia and Britain combined.

Nine months before Sarah's eyes got sore from scrutinising photos of Kiel, the Navy helped save Russia's Arctic ports. Operation GAUNTLET disabled mining equipment on Spitsbergen, stopping weather intelligence falling into enemy hands and preventing the islands becoming U-boat bases. In Iran the RAF maintained the flow of oil to Russia. Sarah's mother's Red Cross Aid To Russia Appeal paid for supplies to the value of £4 million (special football matches between England, Wales and Scotland raising £12,500). But the cry for a Second Front to ease pressure in the East could still be heard. 'Why help the menace that killed the Tsar?' some asked. The Churchills weren't stuck in the past: 'We were taught to respect our enemies,' was how Sarah put it. The Bolsheviks might have left an atmosphere of intrigue at Chequers (after

Molotov pulled a gun on the housekeeper when she came to tell him the blackout regulations) but Gil found them 'frightfully nice'. Packing pistol and bread in his suitcase, Molotov and his mob decamped to the White House and fared better. Asking FDR for a Second Front, he was given the OK. 'Tell Stalin a formation will happen within a year,' was the breezy message. Winston ignored a no-confidence vote from MPs and left for the First Moscow Conference (11–15 August 1942). Sarah heard about it on his return.

In the large garden of State Villa No. 7, raspberries grew in plenitude and the waft of pine from nearby woods was enough to awaken anyone from a vodka-induced slumber. Stalin's West Moscow home had an electric lift, dusky pink marble walls, shiny wood panelling and a kitchen with mod cons. That the dacha was bugged was no secret. For private matters, one took a stroll. Courtesies included Georgian wine, Satsivi (a dish of chicken and nuts dear to the Caucasus) and mountains of Beluga caviar on ice. Sarah recalled that Mrs Landemare had served a tiny amount at Downing Street the evening before his departure. They were down to the last tin from Max's supply from the previous year. He had told his secretary to 'get 25lb of caviar for Churchill and a jar of strawberry jam for me'. 'So that's why Papa was keen to go!' she thought. She was crying as he spoke of his emotions on landing after Parliament had been so rotten. He recounted how his eyes bore a glint when a little 16-year-old entered: 'So, you, too, have a redhead for a daughter!' he remarked through his interpreter. Mademoiselle Stalina had not seen her *Papochka* in three months. Told to travel from Kuybyshev Oblast to attend a guest, she put aside private issues she was having with her father. A copy of the *Illustrated London News* used for learning English had accidentally furnished her with the fact that her mother's death in 1932 was a suicide, yet sinister forces forbade mention of the truth. In London, Sarah's Papa described Moscow in his inimitable way:

> I found myself on Russian soil for the first time but it was a thrilling time in a Citadel defended by Siberian soldiers putting up a brave defence although there was no reason it might not fall. In the dacha an impregnable dugout was on hand if things worsted. The enemy obdurate in holding the gains of BARBAROSSA was merciless as it savaged through the Caucasus then BLUE extirpated the peasantry after the capture of 200,000 Red Army soldiers near Kharkov, a shameful act Stalin blamed on Commissar Khrushchev.

Stalin, a shoemaker's son, quickly felt patronised and lost his temper with Winston who calmly told the 'Gardener of Human Happiness' (as the dictator was called) that the North Africa victories and secret intelligence would benefit him. Translator Arthur Birse tried to keep in synch with the Russian's rages. 'It's not necessary,' said Winston, intuitively, 'I know what he said.' At a banquet on 14 August, Stalin's comment broke the ice: 'I do not understand the words, but by God, I like your spirit.' Yet, at the back of his mind Stalin reminded the PM of a character who tripped over his foot in a dance hall in Oxford Street back in the days when he was a young subaltern. It was the only occasion young Winston got knocked out.

On the last evening of Operation BRACELET Churchill was invited to Stalin's apartment in the Kremlin. Again, Winston encountered Svetlana and joked about his hair, once a shade of red. Waving his cigar over his bald pate, he said smiling: 'Look at me now!' He told her that his daughter was in the RAF. Svetlana later remembered how shy she had been, having never been at a meeting before; but her English was actually very good and one eyewitness said she put on an attentive performance, hovering like a 'little housekeeper'. Another remarked that, for such a young lady, she was most assured. She would ask her father about *Sarochka Oliver*, suggesting that an honour be bestowed on this noble lady.

'There is one thing you can say in defence of Molotov; he can drink,' Stalin said to Clark Kerr, ambassador to the Soviets. By 1 a.m., as Alexander Cadogan (Under-Secretary at the FO) recalled, many empty bottles surrounded the remains of a suckling pig and the PM was complaining of a headache. The party ended at 3 a.m.: just enough time to get to the aerodrome where Churchill put on his special oxygen mask allowing him to smoke his cigar. Paddington Station came alive in the dead of night on 16 August as the train chugged in. The floodlights went on and none were as excited as Diana and Sarah. 'I've never felt so refreshed,' Winston said. Respect for the *Vozhd* (Stalin) hastened Operation RUTTER on 19 August: a first stab at a Second Front. Mountbatten had been agitating to land in France. They could deploy 5,000 Canadian troops to Dieppe, Varengeville and Puys. Lack of secrecy, lack of intelligence, and changes in plan left the Dieppe Raid (as we now know it) a bitter failure. That's what you get for obliging Stalin.

The Katyusha launchers and the machines of Lend-Lease paid off with hundreds of thousands of the Wehrmacht obliterated at Stalingrad. The former weatherman of Tiflis was feted as a saviour and titled Marshal Stalin. Within a year of the Help Russia appeal, a remarkable change of attitude had come about. The notorious Stalin became Man of the Year in *Time*'s January 1943 edition. People stopped talking about the gulag, focusing instead on the bravery of the Russians. Under Roosevelt, Moscow got its first US ambassador, Joseph Davies. He wrote a book that was soon adapted for the screen as *Mission to Moscow*, with John Huston as the envoy and notably including the earliest depiction of Winston and Clementine as characters on film (Dudley Malone and Doris Lloyd playing them). All this came with FDR's support. The film presented Stalin as a man to do business with, ignoring his pact with Hitler. How FDR could warm to a leader who, a decade earlier, had let many of his countrymen starve and who had proved himself an expansionist, is hard to comprehend. Perhaps this man of the people appealed to the populist President. Perhaps the President partly dissembled in this in the cause of victory. The Communist International had been renounced but even if it hadn't, FDR wouldn't demonise the Soviets for encouraging socialism in surrounding countries. He bought the idea that they needed to protect their borders. Besides, Eastern Europe was sure to need American aid after the war. He was optimistic that Russia would progress along evolutionary constitutional lines. Henceforth, negotiations brought in a new phrase – 'The Big Three' – sounding like something coming to your cinema soon. US diplomat George Kennan, who knew the Baltic, loved Russia but loathed Marxism, was far more dubious and Harriman thought FDR should exercise caution. The Brits fell in with the idea that Stalin was heroic. Sarah hoped Britain's friendship with Russia would be to Poland's gain. Eden, whose direct dealings of Stalin had begun in 1935, knew the reverse was true. He gained first-hand knowledge of Stalin's wish to legitimise gains in Poland and the Baltic in December 1941. Russian requests for a secret protocol to keep the Soviet-German partition of 1939 turned the 30 July 1941 Sikorski–Maisky Agreement between the USSR and Poland on its head. Eden refused to negotiate.

The Nazis hoped to drive a wedge between Britain, Russia and the US. German radio claimed Poland was being abandoned to the Soviets and would be safer protected by Germany. Here was an excuse for Stalin to break off negotiations with the Polish Government in Exile (until then his ally). Calling them enemies could justify seizure of eastern Poland. On 15 April 1943 news came in about the discovery of a mass grave containing Polish Officers in a forest near Katyn in southern Russia. Nobody knew how many had been killed (10,000 was estimated) or when it happened. A Nazi source broadcast the news saying the atrocity had been committed by the Soviets in 1940 to deprive the Polish military of its lifeblood. The Soviets denied the accusations. They said the Nazis did it in 1941 during BARBAROSSA when Katyn was under German control. Sikorski and Victor Cazalet were certain the Russians were lying, having tried for ages to get answers. How could it be, Sikorski asked, that after April 1940 no letter or message got through to anyone connected with the dead? His ADC was among the men lost. Owen St Clair O'Malley (British ambassador to the Poles in Exile) concurred, sending, on 24 May, a report to Eden that Churchill had sight of. Eden concluded foul play. Dining with his wife and Noël Coward, Anthony said the Russian denials were abominable.

By the summer enough voices were (correctly) calling it a Soviet war crime for Churchill and even Sarah to take the rumour seriously. But to accuse a major ally in the thick of war puts one on a sticky wicket. Even Randolph, unbending in matters moral, didn't rattle the can. For the PM, coordinating Allied forces for the purpose of military gains took precedence. In April he told FDR that if the Russians took Berlin, they would see themselves as the main victors. He expected Stalin would make a play for the German capital and awaited a joint strategy on how to prevent the Red Army's thrust. He begged Eisenhower and SHAEF (Supreme Headquarters Allied Expeditionary Force) to understand that Berlin was essential for bargaining power. Meanwhile, he knew better than to provoke the Soviets and disturb the three-power summit. Raczyński, a diplomat who came with Sikorski to Downing Street, felt that, unlike Eden, Churchill stopped short of admitting the truth. Yet vital gains were all important for the PM, with Berlin the end game. Meanwhile, hell bent on bagging Europe's granary and securing *Lebensraum*, Hitler's ZITADELLE aimed to reverse German losses on the Eastern Front. His downfall was delay. When the British cracked the Wehrmacht's secret code this helped the Soviets in battles at Prokhorovka and Kharkov. Then the Sicily landings in July gave the Führer more pain. On 25 July *Il Duce* resigned. Sarah, Papa and Alan Brooke were at Chequers when this news broke.

WAAF Myra Murden sat at her desk to the right of Section Officer Oliver and bashed away with pride on her new American-supplied electric typewriter while 'K Section' measured the impact of Allied bombs. A handsome American officer was charming the girls, although Myra suspected his cute talk was a way of getting to speak to Sarah. Mrs Oliver's desk was sometimes vacant for long periods. Colleagues got used to it. At Plymouth on 11 November she waited to board HMS *Renown* with her father, Randolph, 'ABC' Cunningham (First Sea Lord), Desmond Morton, Alan Brooke, Moran, John Martin, Pug Ismay, Thompson, Miss Layton (the PM's typist) and Sawyers (his valet). Winant, who had made a hasty return from the States, was her concern. He had just had news that his son was alive, albeit in Colditz. Monty's forces had routed Rommel at El Alamein, so it was in this atmosphere of hope that Sarah's small part in the Conferences of Cairo, Tehran and Yalta (lasting one year four months) began. Her scribbles of 11 years earlier sounded prophetic:

> I'll hitch my thoughts to a star and my life to the Chariot of Time, And my dreams shall go forth near and far, to all and every clime.

The sentiment is reinforced by a remembrance later in life: 'A childhood's limitations steeled into devotion far beyond the ties of birth.' In 1943 she was a far cry from the white-robed ingénue pining for Romeo. Her part was a good one: sassy, international traveller attending world leader in time of war. She savoured every minute and the uncertainty made it exciting. When things were going well Papa compared the war to drinking a bottle of champagne every day. Now, despite Alamein, he couldn't enter into the spirit of things. A heavy cold lay siege to him and pneumonia was suspected. En route to Malta, a sea launch from HMS *Ulster* brought his special stores. Years later her captain would tell Sarah he was still waiting for his OBE for getting those twelve dozen bottles on board. Sarah crept off to write letters. Staying positive was a duty. She grabbed a blanket and sat on deck with Gil. An embarrassing WAAF story or self-mocking monologue might divert him from worries about his son. The next instalment of *My life as Aide-de-Camp* (ADC) covered her 'address to the Gibraltese' (rep training handy here) and with Papa sent to safety in a cable car, she took up arms and did a cracking job 'defending the Rock' helped by Barbary macaques. Responses never came back. The giant from New Hampshire didn't need words to make it known how valued her presence was. Dinner conversation turned to books. Gil, who was a slow reader, talked of *The Fallodon Papers* by Viscount Grey, liking the analysis of Wordsworth's *Prelude* and the part where Theodore Roosevelt compared English and American birdsong.

Malta was on short rations but the nosh they got at Valetta was scrumptious. At the Grandmaster's Palace, talk switched to Dr Moran's book *The Anatomy of Courage* about war's cost to our health and how labels like 'lack of moral fibre' are unfairly applied to shell shock victims. Old Charles, a veteran of the Somme, liked Winant, who spoke discerningly. As for the PM, Moran didn't believe he tolerated failure or downbeat people, recalling Churchill's line: psychology doesn't help soldiers. Gil kindly said that Winston couldn't help but be a man of action. The 'Ambass' got on with everyone, especially Randolph. Sarah made a point of telling Mummy this and described the Church of the Knights of St John and flying with Papa in a Dakota to see General Patton in Palermo. Bearing up among the boffins of Medmenham had given her confidence with senior officials although she gaffed on HMS *Renown* when making an address via the ship's RT. She ended her message inviting the boys to 'come and beat us up'. A RAF squadron took that as an order. Capt. Max Aitken halted it and had choice words. She wasn't in the doghouse long. A stealth of Mosquitoes made a flight over Etna, each wooden wonder carrying a VIP passenger. Sarah was in one, Gil in another, with Portal grinning behind his windscreen. Scourge of Göring it might be, but the Mossie was mortifying for Sarah.

The First Cairo Conference (codenamed SEXTANT) took place between 21 and 26 November 1943 with the Churchills installed in Richard and Maie Casey's home, Beit El Azrak: a blue and white tiled villa with a small fountain at its centre. The pièce de résistance was the 'Map Room', full of gadgets and allowing the PM to monitor fronts and fleets. Randolph's love of buzzers might originate from this control centre. Another diplomatic pair, Miles Killearn and his much loved socialite wife Jacqui, had Mrs Oliver and Thompson dine with them on the first evening. Jacqui pointed her in the direction of dry cleaners and beauty parlours. Since Sarah's father would yell 'No running repairs while in action' whenever he caught her applying lipstick or powder, Jacqui's uncurbed femininity was a treat. The heavily guarded Mena House near the Pyramids was the setting for the Conference of the Staffs. FDR was neck deep in guards when he arrived on 22 November. Churchill went to the residence of Kirk (US ambassador to Egypt) to pay the President a formal visit. ADCs weren't admitted and Sarah waited by the coat racks 'on guard'. It wasn't easy for a uniformed WAAF to look pristine in that most dusty of cities and she headed for the salon, only to be yanked from underneath the dryer to lunch with FDR, Hopkins et al. A revolting American concoction awaited them: fruit salad doused in salad cream. But there was fun to be had when Franklin accepted Winston's invitation to show him the Pyramids and Sphinx. Wearing civilian dress, the two leaders chatted whilst Sarah handed out sandwiches.

The US Chiefs of Staff asked the President about future occupation zones in a defeated Germany. He had his own ideas, pencilling them on a shop-bought map that went on to cause confusion when circulated. Despite EAC being Gil's area of planning, he never saw FDR's map although present in Cairo. FDR had come by air, as did Chinese Nationalist leader Chiang Kai-Shek and his wife, urgently in need of help given the Japanese onslaught. Eight months before Mrs Chiang had toured the US at Mrs Roosevelt's invitation and addressed both Houses of Congress. Educated in America at the finest schools, she was highly polished. The Chiangs promoted themselves as Christians but, acceptable as they seemed, some of America's China hands thought it more in the US's interest to include Communists (Mao's gang – then in distant Yunnan Province) in a potential Chinese government. The Generalissimo's wife wove a crooked path between the President and Churchill. The Chiangs wanted the British out of Hong Kong, Shanghai and Canton, and the Soviets to respect their Manchurian frontier. In return for FDR's help they would make China more democratic. The Chiangs were guests at Beit El Azrak on their first night and Elizabeth Layton and others were intrigued to see Churchill taking these black-clad figures on a tour of his Map Room. Winston regarded Chiang's wife as the best interpreter and Sarah found her 'very beautiful, exotic, sinister, a little phoney' while sympathising with the eye trouble she suffered from during the talks. The Mule committed a breach of etiquette, leaving the parcels Madame Chiang brought with an inspector and forgetting to present them to her father. One of them contained a silk dressing gown with blue and gold dragons. The PM's ADC sped off with Maie Casey to buy a precious relic as a return gift for China's first lady.

Sarah wasn't as lucky as Elliott Roosevelt, who got to see the Valley of the Kings, but shopping was squeezed into her six days with drivers ferrying her through Cairo's streets. 'Lord Moran is great fun,' she wrote after an excursion on 23 November. She was astonished that fruity Francis Stonon was now part of the PM's private office in Cairo. Last time she saw him he was disciplining a gaggle of squawking debutantes. She and Francis went to the Ghezira Sports Club and to department stores in Al-Azbakia to purchase a hot water bottle (essential item for wartime conferences). After depositing Moran minus shoes in a mosque, they headed for the spice and perfume bazaar, only to find it 'gaudy and trashy'. She wanted to plunge into a 'bath of Lysol' afterwards but settled on a splash of cologne. A cake worthy of a president was selected from Groppi's and there was time for an aperitif in its roof garden. Elliott had similar formal duties, deputising for FDR at the Chiangs' tea party on 24 November. He later said Madame Chiang had her hand on his knee, coaxing him to come to China where he'd be a rich man. Franklin called her 'opportunist' and thought back to his own meeting with her during her US visit when her allure caused him to position a card table between them to avoid being 'vamped'. At these conferences and on any public platform the Churchill family were a strong united front. Behind the scenes, Britain's leader could be at breaking point when unpleasant personal matters scraped the chalkboard, making the pressures of war seem like a mere bagatelle.

At the First Cairo Conference Anthony Eden resided at the Cairo Embassy. He needed to get PM approval before sending off telegrams and drove to Beit El Azrak late one evening. He heard raucous screams and shouts and witnessed Randolph, his father and Sarah in a terrible fray in the courtyard. Winston was berating his son for his misdeeds, Randolph retaliating using the vilest language. Most likely triggered by the Pamela business, it was ugly and deafening with members of the entourage taking cover in the darkness. Sarah was in the middle of her father and brother, tears streaming down her face. Anthony was disgusted at Randolph and, had the situation been different, might have been inclined to deliver a silencing blow on the mad cur. His suave bearing and intervention put an end to the mêlée. In the spring of 1941 Randolph had shown Anthony nothing but respect. All this was to change. Eden got what he needed but not before Winston's valedictory words about parenting: 'I hope that your Simon will never cause you the pain Randolph has caused me.'

The account (in one of Eden's notebooks) corresponds to the incident Randolph refers to in a 1952 letter to his father, looking back at his 'wayward conduct' and admitting he had been out of order. That the underlying issue was still unresolved troubled Randolph. Although the united front continued at public events, Churchill never again wanted him as right-hand man in private discussions. The Cairo showdown dented their relationship and made the war a miserable time for the *Chumbolly*. Thoroughly depressed, he wrote to Laura in 1943, referring to the PM as the bully and stubborn one. Laura could see how quarrels with his father truly got him down. It was tough for the young Churchills; bottling up their fiery spirits and acting like model officers and perfect children. They had just started feeling like individuals before the war but now, once again, were dim figures in Winston's shadow. Randolph used to start the arguments, but in later years the reverse was true. He was eager to state his point of view, not seeing anything wrong with disagreeing with the PM and others, even at inopportune moments. Later he realised how immature he was, although he knew it was the natural consequence of being Winston's son. Acts of injustice or wrongly meted out discipline stoked his ire and it was the same for Sarah. Both had a hitherto invisible, pent-up rage. Sarah had tested her father's devotion to the utmost already but when the war was on couldn't bear to upset him (although post war there would be new opportunities to stand her ground).

She was the perfect lady at the Roosevelt–Churchill luncheon and the Roosevelt Thanksgiving dinner party – the only woman to attend both. 'Let us make it a family affair,' said FDR when Winston, Sarah and Thompson arrived at Kirk Villa. In the large kitchen the guests sat around a long table. The President carved the turkey 'like a pro', filling a dish for the PM, then Sarah, Eden, Thompson, Moran, Leahy, Winant, Harriman, Hopkins, Hopkins Junior, General Watson (FDR's military aide) and finally his son-in-law and son. The party moved to a larger hall and about 20 guests joined. Waiters brought trays of food and a band from Camp Huckstep played dance music. Excitement invaded the atmosphere and all the men wanted to dance with Sarah. Good-natured gal that she was, she did her best to oblige, a lambent flame hot enough to cause hearts to palpitate. For an hour or so everyone forgot the war and Gil's gaze never left her. He mumbled something about asking her to dance but Eden, with his glow acquired from tennis at the *Ghezira* and Astaire-like rug cutting, swept her up, igniting other men's envy. Being the cynosure of all eyes is an experience many women treasure. Since leaving HMS *Renown* she had been separated from her '*Ambass*' and words were whispered across the formal atmosphere. The lack of women was absurd and a *pas d'armes* threatened to commence. Winston took the initiative by waltzing unashamedly with Pa Watson. Thoughts of tomorrow's timetable knocked the party on the head. Elizabeth Layton, regarded by Sarah as a head girl type, wasn't there.

The Map Room boys had whisked her off to sample a little of Cairo's nightlife. Sarah cherished the memory of *Terpsikhore*'s eve, a roomful of men competing for her attention.

They flew to Tehran at low altitude taking in a landscape of sepia terrain until a modern city came into view. Marshal Stalin hovered around Galeh Morgeh Airport wanting talks to begin right away. Some in the American delegation were insistent too. Winston was obliging but Sarah, knowing what a mistake it was for Papa not to rest, proved her worth as ADC by refusing. Talks could not start until the next day, she told them. She and Moran had their 'heads bitten off' and Gil came to their aid, giving one US official an earful. The secret police couldn't be more obvious, the majority seeming like idiots. Meeting in Tehran between 27 November and 2 December had been Stalin's choice and yet he warned of espionage being rife in the city. It prompted the PM's letter to the *Vozhd* requesting an impenetrable cordon around the conference area. Then, as soon as the Americans arrived, Stalin put everyone on alert owing to an assassination plot he had received intelligence about. Despite the threat level, nobody thought to protect the PM's convoy en route to its embassy. Stuck in roadblocks and exposed to passers-by, Churchill's presence was 'well out of the bag' with not one of 3,000 NKVD to be found. They reached Ferdowsi Avenue where turbanned Indian soldiers made them feel safe.

FDR dined at the American Legation and promised Winant that night that he would be made head of the future United Nations. Because of the assassination scare FDR chose to stay at the Russian, not the American Embassy. While Elliott says his father believed the plot, Harriman thought it fabricated (so the Marshal could be closer to FDR) and Russian records show that even prior to the Conference FDR knew his stay there was likely. At the Temple of the Soviets, his Filipino cooks could still turn out nosh the way he liked it. The downside was that he was bugged as no other American president has ever been bugged. Stalin's interpreter Valentin Berezhkov later admitted that at the day's close he would receive an English transcript of the American delegates' conversation.

Winston came to this austere Sparta on 28 November. FDR rejoiced in the promise he got from Uncle Joe to fight Japan. It would save diverting US forces to China. Iran had been 'neutral' until access to oil motivated the Allied invasion in September 1941. With Reza Shah's pro-Axis father deposed, Muluk Fawzia married the new Shah in a union of Sunni Arab and Shi'ite Persian. While Churchill was in the talks, one of Sarah's duties was to attend high tea at the Shah's Palace. The strikingly pretty cellophane-wrapped Queen Consort dispensed diplomatic niceties and introduced Churchill's daughter to her husband's twin sister Ashraf and to Princess Shams – more 'exotic

Hollywood creatures', as Sarah put it in a letter, criticising the 'unbelievably nouveau riche vulgarity' of these surroundings.

Sarah wrote less from Tehran, being on spy alert. Her radio appeals for the PRF hadn't gone unnoticed. Soviet intelligence knew Section Officer Oliver was wife to a naturalised American of Austrian birth. Even though Stalin had obtained Britain's promise that its secret service would refrain from covert activities in the USSR, he still suspected a cell of German-British agents in league with anti-Soviet Finns and Poles existed, believing this had prompted Hess's flight. Churchill's daughter was wary of this, but the bargaining that her father entered into the night before – that would result in Poland getting pushed west – was a surprise.

The handling of Poland at Tehran is considered egregious today, especially given the existing doubts about the Soviets' declared innocence over Katyn. The aim of the Tehran meeting was to coordinate military strategy, with frontier decisions secondary. Churchill went full speed ahead into the borders question, compromising the Poles in a late-night meeting on 28 November when he proposed that the country lose 40% of its eastern land, letting the Soviets keep their gains from the Nazi–Soviet Pact. Messing with the Polish borders wasn't necessary, although actions to crush East Prussia and eradicate the *Junker* class had been set in motion by Attlee's plan earlier in the year. The unexpressed idea of dismembering Germany had been hatched and this of course affected frontiers. FDR came into Tehran disinclined to change Germany's borders – not until the Nazis were defeated. Changing Poland's borders was dangerous but Churchill thought such a pay-off would be enough for Russia. He genuinely believed she deserved recompense for lives lost on the Eastern Front and asserted that Poland would benefit by losing the dismal Pripet Marshes in the East, gaining 'fruitful and developed land in the West'. His consistent view was that Poland would have been 'doomed to utter destruction at the hands of the Germans' so division at the Curzon Line was a reasonable compromise. Besides, Poland had been reconstituted 25 years earlier after barely existing politically for generations.

Familiar with the Polish cause, Sarah would ask why the Poles, who had resisted the Nazis so bravely, should lose land. Her father's psychological distance and ability to make sweeping decisions ignoring costs borne by ordinary people still astonished her, contrasting as it did with the normal behaviour of this highly emotional and empathetic being she knew and loved. His self-containment, she admitted, was a revelation but being with him was a wonder in itself, a privilege she hadn't enjoyed since she was a child. She was aware that Nazi saturation bombing was coming, though the form of the weapons had yet to be confirmed. Deals with troublesome allies were inevitable. Delays could have fatal consequences. In time she became aware that her Pa's 'philosophical wisdom, tolerance and compassion' was being stretched, writing: 'No one then knew the consequences of the decisions but the unaccustomed silence told me all.' Another comment he made – 'War is a game played with a smiling face' – was one he first used in 1916, having admired Shelley's observation: 'War is the statesman's game ... the lawyer's jest.' Terrible things were left unquestioned with that smile; and questioned about this 20 years later, Sarah would not elaborate.

In 1943 she wasn't short of words and Clementine, in letters to her husband, drew attention to Sarah's literary talent and the way she dealt with being the only woman at the Conference. If you included officers in the Soviet delegation, she wasn't the only woman. Zoya Zarubina controlled the cameramen on the steps of the Soviet Embassy vying for the best Big Three picture at 3.45 p.m. on 29 November. Chairs of separate design were carried on to the porch: Winston's chair somehow the lowest and most prone to wobbling. In film footage, except for her few minutes in the photo call, Sarah is scarce. Uncle Joe gives her a heavy and stiff handshake as the Americans smile. Eden and Churchill are not smiling.

*Were you really there? Did you really meet Stalin?* Sarah Churchill was asked years later. She always made light of it, doing her Russian Bear impression. Destiny had always followed closely on her heels. Like her mother, she played an unseen part, nannying a wartime leader. She was nearby when he was at his loneliest. It speaks volumes that she was in the group photo and not Randolph. Although starchily uniformed she looks vaguely human in a sea of grey. Millions who saw that image saw her as a patient daughter who might warm her Papa's slippers by the hearth in a tale from Russian literature (a vague comfort to those experiencing the general ghastliness). Sarah communicated hope at a cold and black time. Might it have been better if she hadn't been there? A symbol of youth and the freedoms of the western world, she was in some ways exploited. Her 'humanising' presence sculpted the false impression that all the players at the Conference were human. Uncle Joe essentially believed in government of the proletariat by dictatorship, believing liberty and democracy should be stamped on. Still, he was keen to give off a softer impression. Shaking Sarah's hand Joe indeed looks like a happy uncle in a world family portrait. This appealed to Roosevelt, a family man. An hour or so later she was standing at the back of the room thinking: 'You can't turn a bunch of gangsters into ballet dancers overnight.'

Pomp and circumstance were not lost on Stalin. Prior to the tripartite dinner on 29 November, as the Red Army Band played different national anthems, Churchill held up a gift from King George VI: the Sword of Stalingrad, commemorating the dead. It was made by silversmith Leslie Durbin (from RAF Medmenham) and came in a red scabbard with golden stars. He swung it around Stalin and passed it to him. For days John Martin had been its custodian, giving previews in his bedroom, and Sarah and Randolph naturally did a bit of knighting to kill time. In the ceremony the *Vozhd* was moved, despite almost letting it slip from its sheath to the ground. His voice was wavering as he opened it and kissed the metal. Elliott hadn't been invited to the Russian-hosted dinner but Stalin saw him loitering and insisted he sit down. The sly jokes the Russian favoured gathered pace: about mass killing, firing squads and retribution. Winston was affronted and stated indignantly that neither Parliament nor the British public would condone mass murder. He said he would rather be shot than see his country's honour sullied. FDR made a feathery comment about executing one less Nazi on the hit list than Joe's five-digit estimation and Elliott put his foot in it saying the US Army liked his host's total. Churchill left the room in disgust. Stalin went after him, pockmarked face in hangdog mode, claiming he had only been 'playing'. Winston re-joined the party like the Lone Ranger without Tonto. Sarah and Randolph weren't present and were tight-lipped at Ferdowsi Avenue.

How do you dodge the spies under the carpet and the spooks listening through pinholes? You spend the evenings silent in your quarters, next to a stoked coal fire with your hot water bottle. Winston's defensive manner stemmed from being excluded. Stalin and FDR hived off at a time Churchill was desperate for a private tête-à-tête over future plans to secure Berlin. The buttress keeping Winston and Franklin safe in each other's regard was dislodged. In his embassy quarters, the former retreated into a Dickens world. In *Oliver Twist* he saw the perfect doppelgänger of Uncle Joe in Bill Sikes.

At Teheran the Big Three's discussion wasn't three-cornered. It was a flaw that would impact future wartime conferences and lay the foundation for Russian domination in Eastern Europe for decades. The Marshal did his best work by listening and observing. He could see that Churchill thought this region important while FDR was far less interested in it (except as a place from which the Far East might be accessed by sea in his Japan strategy). Stalin made it seem he was doing them a favour to agree to the Curzon line and added Königsberg, Memel and parts of East Prussia as conditional to accepting the deal. He claimed Russia had no ice-free ports and badly needed these. George Kennan knew this wasn't true. The USSR was controlling the Baltic countries' ports. Churchill didn't want to make these concessions. In a private meeting between FDR and Stalin on 30 November FDR tried wriggling out of the Baltic question saying that he couldn't lose the votes of the millions of Balts in the US elections. He told Stalin he had to 'appear' as if he was opposed to the concessions (a signal that he didn't care if Stalin took them). His translator Chip Bohlen heard him joke that if the region saw occupation he wouldn't take the US into war defending it – manna from heaven for the all-seeing

Stalin. It put a chill up the spine when the British FO heard this from Kennan. FDR concurred with Churchill on the Curzon line. Badgered about restoring Poland's pre-war borders a few weeks later he said: 'I am sick and tired of these people – the 1941 frontiers are as just as any.' Britain alone couldn't present a force commensurate with the USSR in a future struggle. While Russia was an ally of convenience, its power had been built up (armed by Lend-Lease and bankrolled to the hilt by US dollars). When all is said and done in war, money and guns have the last word.

Earlier that day Gil enjoyed a private meeting with FDR in the morning and the Russian Embassy's gift shop was opened. While Sarah chose an ancient coin as a present for her father, Gil was mesmerised by a set of small, colourful cards telling the gruesome legend of King Zohak, who had a snake permanently on each shoulder. In this tale by Ferdowsi about timidity in the face of evil, these pets are fed daily on human brains. After losing six of his seven sons, a blacksmith finally does away with the King and those bloody snakes.

Like the Three Kings, FDR, Harriman and the Shah arrived at the British Embassy for Winston's birthday. The President came bearing a blue and white 13th-century Persian bowl, Harriman hand-tinted silks (again from the gift shop) whilst Reza Pahlavi brought fine claret. Leaving the Soviet Embassy for the first time, Stalin arrived wearing a light-coloured military tunic. In an elegant drawing room 15 chairs were positioned either side of a long rectangular table. Stalin was on Churchill's right with FDR on the other side. Six seats down from Stalin was Sarah, with Leahy and Admiral King (of the US Navy) either side. Across were Gil, Portal and General Marshall. Eden, Randolph and Elliott were to the other side of Gil.

'What do I do with them?' said Stalin, looking at the serried ranks of knives, forks and spoons. 'Just choose whichever piece of cutlery you feel most comfortable with,' advised Major Birse. Handed a cocktail, Joe's dumb stare turned to delight. On came soup, salmon, roast turkey and Persian cheese soufflé. A letter Randolph wrote to Laura Ward (now Mrs Eric Dudley) gives insight into the attitudes of the younger guests at the Conference and proves they had no cause to question the Russians or the deal-making process. Randolph sounds like a little boy describing the 'mountains of delicious stuff' and two types of caviar. While he sees through the ideology of the Soviets (reporting to Laura that in a battle with Western counterparts, Russian reps win hands down in the 'luxury lifestyle' stakes) the Randolphian sceptic in him has taken a rain check. He makes it clear instead how much he likes Uncle Joe. Excluded from the real meetings, he and Sarah were under the avuncular man's spell, never referring to him as a dictator. Sarah, who prided herself on being savvy about the direction of the war, wrote: 'Uncle Joe is a great man of that there can be no doubt.' The same faith or naïveté applied to the President.

At Winston's party the statecraft of glass in the air and speech counted. Sarah was proud to be the recipient of one of the first from FDR. In her letters he is her 'darling' and she even gushes: 'I love him.' She came up to the President to thank him, making a little speech. He told her he wanted to come over and would have, had he been able to get off his feet. Not to be outdone, Stalin appeared minutes later to toast glasses with her: a daunting experience as recalled years later. In her memoir she regrets that Randolph wasn't around. Yet he was present. 'He is trying,' she told her mother at the time, meaning her brother was being careful on account of his father. This contrasts with Moran's recollection of Randolph talking boisterously to Stalin. Perhaps it was her brother not being disgraceful she regretted. Joe was relaxed, his golden eyes gazing at people's navels. A huge cream cake came in, lit by candles, one for every year of the PM's life. A massive dollop slipped off the salver avoiding Stalin by inches, perching on the shoulder of Pavlov, the Marshal's interpreter. 'Missed the target!' quipped Peter Portal, at ease in home embassy territory. Performing to his guests, Winston joked about England becoming 'pinker' with the War Cabinet socialists. 'It is a sign of good health,' Joe interjected, impressing Sarah with his repartee. Eden later criticised Tehran and the other Conferences, believing these dinners did little for diplomacy and much for waistlines. The only 'atmosphere' detectable was when Brooke criticised the Red Army, provoking Joe's ire. Nothing was going to make the Ulsterman trust Stalin and if anyone could kick air out of the Big Three it was he.

The final day of the Conference saw the American and Russian disappear for talks with Molotov. The Marshal got his date for OVERLORD (the codename for the Second Front) with Ike chosen to lead it, not Brooke, as Churchill had hoped. FDR launched into a scheme to split Germany into five self-governing regions. This came as a shock to Churchill and a doom-laden mood returned: 'Restraints must be put on Germany's manufacturing capacity,' Stalin stipulated. For a buffer against invasion he got Königsberg and was even promised part of the surrendered Italian navy. The slogan 'Didn't he do well!' might have been coined for him. Had FDR stayed away from Tehran he might have been an invisible threat. Instead, this unmasked Wizard of Oz weakened the West's negotiating power. Leaving for the airport, Winston and Sarah were like paupers in an old yellow sedan with a tree trunk tied to the top as a disguise, as FDR's Liaison Officer recalled. They had no escort while FDR and Stalin left in grand style after the latter paid the Shah a visit. Anything was better than the nightmare that beset the Churchills on arriving. Flying back by Skymaster, Sarah felt elation. The in-flight turtle soup was delicious and the champagne plentiful. Papa had a malady and Moran heard him say: 'Something's got to be done about these bloody Russians.'

It felt good to be back in Cairo and the Second Cairo Conference (2–10 December) followed, with Churchill hoping the Turks would enter the war. FDR was pliable but unequivocal in his dislike of de Gaulle. The gardens of the British Embassy stretched to the Nile and seemed like Windsor Great Park under a scorching sun. Miles and Jacqui held a gathering and Sarah played with baby Jacquetta (later to become Lucian Freud's model and friend) and their tot, Victor. Many Egyptians were present including T. E. Lawrence's friend Ahmad Hassanayn. Dignitaries summoned Sarah for cocktails and ices at the Mohammed Ali Club eager to hear all. Gil and Eden had meetings in Tunis, then returned to London. Her Pa was out of sorts as he took leave of Cairo.

On 12 December they arrived at Ike's Carthage home, The White House, as guests. Getting Winston X-rayed, Moran saw his pneumonia and pleurisy worsening. It was a matter of life and death as they waited for Clementine. Sarah's presence made all the difference. Calm and loving, she tucked Papa into his mosquito net, read to him, amused him and kept things shipshape. Clementine arrived, sacked the cook and in the bosom of his family the snuffling Bulldog came through, listening to Randolph's diatribe about Gaullists purging ex-Vichy leaders (allegations others said were 'founded on some small foundation of fact – mostly bull').

A Christmas morning service was held in a Nissen hut while Winston held forth at the Villa in the dressing gown Madame Chiang gave him. A Marrakesh holiday lasting until 13 January was characterised by picnics, snake charmers and visits from friends. The Atlas Mountains cast their healing spell and Winston made a rope descent into a gorge while Sarah binned her airforce blues. Two weeks into 1944, a new uniform from Austin Reed arrived, worn at a huge party for Americans, WAAF cyphers, HMS *York* crew and VIPs, where Jack scored a hit with Clementine. Apart from Randolph, who remained in Africa assisting Monty's army, the Churchills took leave of Marrakesh and came home.

There is one occasion on which Sarah was lucky her fate had been acting and not journalism. She wasn't called upon to visit the ghastly mass grave at Katyn. That job fell to Kathy Harriman, one of two Americans in a press agency party. Her father organised a railroad car to southern Russia so an investigation could be made on 23 January. She and John Melby thought the methodical manner in which the killing was carried out suggested the Germans were responsible but with the proviso that what they were told by the Soviets wasn't satisfactory. While George Kennan thought the NKVD's efforts to cover up evidence was unmistakable and high-ranking Brits at the FO thought there was no way thousands could have passed from Soviet to German captivity, no further verdict was given for six years. There was no question of reversing Tehran and the matter was dropped. Wary of speaking out, the PM could only make the desolate comment: 'We should none of us ever speak a word about it.'

Oranges in bulk were shipped to Medmenham and Sarah's stories had everybody laughing. She talked about being 'twice the person' following her trip. Duncan brought her up-to-date with the latest findings. With mass-producible plywood wings, midget *Vergeltungswaffe 1* weapons, or V1s, were pilotless and jet-propelled, achieving speeds of 360 mph. Constance Babington-Smith was credited with spotting them. This intelligence arrived just in time for Britain to plan its defence. Locating the launch sites from the air was extremely hard despite a round-the-clock operation. Occasionally, buildings like skis in forest clearings storing V1s were identified, but photos of V1s in transit led PIs to the launch sites. A hundred were found, but the other weapon, the V2, was more worrying. MI6 revealed slave workers from concentration camps produced their liquid propellant. Shockingly, the British public was not yet aware of either weapon. Work took on a chilling context but even in the midst of this, the RAF and WAAF found time to laugh. Entertainment was valuable war work.

The ADC assisted her father on tightly scheduled meetings in British waters on board *The Rugged* with Ike and General Bradley on 23 March. Winston had been inspecting an all-American force in a parachute-landing demo. Crowding his jeep, men cheered and he said they would 'strike a blow for a cause greater than either of our two countries has ever fought for in bygone days'. They would soon get the opportunity of testifying their 'faith in all those inspiring phrases of the American Constitution'. He wished them the best of luck. Meanwhile, bombs fell on Monte Cassino where the Poles, under General Anders, attacked the heavily defended mountains, taking the brunt as the devastated monastery was encircled. Their families would soon be imprisoned behind Russian lines.

Pamela didn't come to Mrs Churchill's birthday. Visiting Cherkley, Bruce Lockhart wrote cattily how her son had met all the American generals. Admired by General J. B. Anderson (the quiet deputy of General Spaatz), her new passion was for Murrow and by the end of that year, she hoped Ed might divorce Janet and marry her. Little Winston's dad had been in Axis-held Yugoslavia since February with Tito. Letters home were friendly but he doesn't mince words in an exchange with the PM on 14 May about his turning a blind eye. Didn't they think to consider *his* position given his wife's philandering? Much later Sarah said that Randolph was bulldozing his way into war work he wasn't suited to. He got on well with Fitzroy Maclean, whom Sarah described as a 'tall athletic pimpernel'. Maclean tried to dissuade him from joining missions: 'Randolph really, you won't be able to keep your mouth shut for two minutes – you'll give it away.' Randolph would beg and promise to play the dumb idiot.

Then, after he placed limpet mines on ships in Algiers harbour, Fitzroy's predictions came true. Randolph realised he'd missed his exit and was alone in enemy territory. Prior to a rescue he spent hours with a mackintosh over his uniform unable to speak, weighing up the merits of pretending to be drunk. Another close escape was when the SS destroyed Tito's cave HQ on 25 May. Quality of life improved with a recipe book sent by his mother. Randolph had the cooks make kedgeree from tinned rations. Tom Mitford joined him and they made several trips to Italy.

Ike timed the D-Day landings on 6 June expertly, given the fact that weather and sea conditions could have made the operation a disaster on the wrong day. Swarming the beaches of *Utah*, *Omaha*, *Juno*, *Gold* and *Sword*, the 150,000 Allied Expeditionary Force troops were heroic, penetrating the mainland and paralysing sites in Cherbourg that gestated Hitler's weapons. It was just the beginning. There were hidden sites everywhere waiting to fire. Just one week after D-Day the Germans launched V1s and soon these were raining down over Britain. The refusal to warn people was appalling and the exodus from London no surprise. People were told to have faith in anti-aircraft guns and hope that pilotless aircraft might get tangled in barrage balloon wire. When Churchill gave a message to the Commons on 6 July he spoke only about V1s. Duncan chaired the Flying Bomb Counter-Measures Committee and sat on the secret Crossbow Committee chaired by the PM to monitor V2s. Espionage was crucial because these were manufactured in vast underground bunkers. Locations in the Pas-de-Calais had been identified, one of which, Bauvorhaben 21 (at Wizernes near Saint-Omer), has all the elements of Blofeld's volcano in the film *You Only Live Twice*.

Meanwhile, on 12 June, Randolph interviewed the Pope saying: 'I expect you know Evelyn Waugh. He's an R.C. too.' In the newly liberated city he ran up £200 in bills, then more at the Dorchester. He sought out Waugh. Did he fancy coming to Croatia and healing the Great Schism? Enlisting him was easy. On 10 July they met Tito and six days later began a fly-by-night to parachute over Croatia. They crash-landed in a cornfield trapped in the wreck of their Dakota with flames all around them. Very bravely, Randolph opened parts of the scorching fuselage to free colleagues. He emerged scalded and lame in both legs. Maclean was full of praise and Randie was later awarded an MBE. He and Waugh got to Topuska where partisans moved them to Bari and then Algiers.

Growing up, Sarah had always believed her brother was unpoetic and that was the basic difference in their personalities. Once, she was raving about dewdrops on a buttercup and he said: 'Sarah I don't really know, I honestly don't know that I quite see what you mean. Beauty for me lies in a woman's face. That's as far as I can go.' Yet the way he spoke of his near-death experience in Croatia, seeing 'flowers raining down from heaven', Sarah felt she was seeing a new side to her brother.

He shouted orders from his sickbed while Hitler yelled at his generals, whom he no longer trusted. White hot with rage, the Führer began making military decisions himself. It didn't help and 2 million Germans were slain. The Reds recaptured Minsk in early July while Mrs Churchill was visiting a WAAF exhibition at Harrods and the PM was making a trip to Normandy. When news reached Britain about Auschwitz, he joined the mass outcry. He stated his fear of communisation in May 1944, but FDR was lukewarm so he sought Ike's support for an Anglo-American presence in the Balkans to ensure stability post-war. Churchill wanted the Allies to proceed as far as possible into Germany to strengthen the British hand for later negotiations. Along with Cadogan, he requested that US Forces advance into Prague. Unfortunately, Ike didn't heed the call, stopping at the Elbe and telling the Czechs to get help from Russia to counter German attacks. This left the door open for that city's 'liberation' by Stalin's forces. The General acted on purely military grounds believing that favouring the objectives of Churchill was unfair to Russia. He then went back on the SHAEF plan to capture Berlin, allowing the Russians to race to the German capital.

Churchill cabled Stalin on 4 August informing him of an airdrop to aid the *Armia Krajowa* in their bitter fight to rid Warsaw of the Nazis. Polish flyers made the long-distance flight from southern Italy to Warsaw, dropping equipment and ammunition. On 12 August he asked Stalin again to aid the Poles but the *Vozhd*'s minuscule help, offered to appear obliging, was useless. Due to his neglect, 200,000 members of the *Armia Krajowa* were wiped out.

The V1 attacks peaked in July 1944 when Mary was a gunner girl in a mixed anti-aircraft battery. Taking a few days' leave, Sarah made Flying Bomb Alley her destination and stayed at Mary's Hastings digs. It was a joy to have a sister at hand. The Churchill girls attended a battery dance at the Queen's Hotel and Sarah caused a sensation on the dance floor during the calypso. Wearing a short skirt, she distinguished herself so well that one enthusiastic partner insisted on tossing her over his shoulder and later got a bollocking from one of the majors. That August at Chequers, around the time Paris was liberated, Randolph disgraced himself. Everyone knew he'd been through hell but they soon wished he'd go back there. Turning up unexpectedly as the PM sat with Freddy, Sarah and the Chiefs, he was loudly drunk, freely dipping into his lexicon of abuse. In a sisterly fury Sarah reprimanded him, scorning him for causing Papa so much stress. Her brother lost it and struck her – this time pushing toleration to the absolute limit.

Sarah never bore a grudge and sympathised with her brother. Looking back at the father-and-son relationship in the early days, she saw them as 'two lions in one cage', each polishing his technique of political attack on the other. Anger was natural yet Sarah pointed out: 'We can tear at each other but we do not tear down.' Randolph's hero was his Pa and he made sacrifices to please him. Banned from the house, depressed and guilty, he returned to Italy, relying on Waugh to prop him up. When they learned about the persecution of the clergy by Tito (whom the PM met in Naples that August) and wished to confront the dictator, Anthony Eden, keen to avoid a diplomatic embarrassment, pulled the rug out from under Randolph's feet, to the latter's disgust. The beast of Chequers then returned for duty with the SAS.

'I do hope you are being careful. What a hope!' wrote Diana to her father, concerned about the shadow on his lung. Winston and Clementine were at the Second Québec Conference (12–16 September) with Germany's future on the agenda. The PM was incensed at the Morgenthau Plan (a suspect proposal to wipe out Germany's industrial capacity, later dropped) although he signed it. At this stage of the war, the hand that fed could not be bitten. Every bit of the $6.5 billion FDR earmarked for Britain's post-war regeneration would be needed. Diana sent him newspaper cuttings from a survey Duncan produced that implied the VI threat was reduced. Duncan spoke too soon and just days after cries to make him Tory Party Chairman, Greater London was shaken by the first catastrophic V2. These mobile weapons could be transported to any flat piece of land for launching. The Blizna site was overrun in early September, while Tallboy bombs laid waste to other sites.

Britain was truly on a high alert when Mr and Mrs Churchill and Mary disembarked at Greenock on 26 September. An autumn euphoria took hold of Winston's children. Freddy turned up in Bari and he and Randie got shamefully drunk. Sinking gallons in the West End was Ann O'Neill. Her husband Shane had died in Tunisia. Guilt for her affair with Reuters correspondent and MI6 agent Ian Fleming showed, Ann's normally haughty exterior wearing thin. Just three months before, her lover vowed to make Jamaica his home after glimpsing Oracabessa Bay for the first time. Ann's misty-eyed supporters at the Dorchester included birthday gal Sarah Oliver, Mrs Randolph Hearst Jnr (one-time *Hot-cha girl* of the Ziegfeld Follies) and several American officers. Mary and Jock Colville stumbled upon this 'peculiar party' heading off to the newly opened Milroy Club to see Harry Roy. In his diary entry for 18 October Jock notes how drunk the party was, making him swiftly escort Mary home. The youngest Churchill was euphoric about standing for Parliament, fired up by Beaverbrook's career advice. Over at Chequers, meanwhile, the elation was high at the party Diana gave for Gil, Moppet Whyte and Uncle Jack.

Sarah was originally expected to accompany her parents to Canada but the demands of her unit put paid to this. She now needed respite from Medmenham's Army Section and each precious forty-eight was spent with family, at nightclubs or at The Ramblers. Her father couldn't attend her birthday at Chequers but was grateful to see her before he left to talk with the 'Old Bear' (as Sarah referred to Stalin). At the Second Moscow Conference (TOLSTOY), 7–19 October, Japan was on the agenda. The PM's priority was to salvage what he could of Poland, Greece and Yugoslavia. In the 1897 Siege of Malakand attacks were visible to the naked eye, but his new opponent relied on concealment. Stalin announced that there was no need for the London Poles to come back: a Polish cabinet existed with a Polish army to support them. Churchill knew this was a lie. The Lublin Poles were stooges with a Red Army unit masquerading under a Polish flag. The Poles had a perfectly good army. On 9 October, alone in Stalin's office, Churchill produced the 'naughty document' composed of percentages that split Russian and British influence in Eastern Europe. To his wife Winston wrote about his belief that the Russians wanted to work with the West. In practice he was playing 'sheriff' in a lawless town, given FDR's lack of interest; suggesting a 'dunces' game as a desperate move to protect Europe. Nations were being occupied on a scale never before countenanced, the Soviets claiming they were 'liberating' each time.

Sarah was now 30 and could be carefree in mentioning Gil to her family while never coming clean. In answer to her mother's question about bringing a man to her birthday bash, she asked, 'Do you think you could ask the Ambass? We could share him! And you know he will go for long walks with you.' A comment in this letter about Russia being 'women-minded' seems thoughtless. Miss Layton had been in the ogre's den with a Soviet general intrusively toasting her.

To everyone's mind, the cultural side of Russian life was thriving and her Papa was then enjoying a pleasant display of it. On 12 October 1944 a limousine pulled up outside the Bolshoi Ballet and the ecstatic applause of Churchill fans was so deafening it seemed suspect. He bowed to the Muscovites and took his seat in the Tsar's box. Stalin made sure that the limelight was all Churchill's. Ave and Kathy joined him. Recalling the pirouettes of his dancing daughter, his curiosity was aroused by the translated programme: a tale of respect shown by peasant girl Giselle to Duke Albrecht (whose safety is endangered by the vengeful Virgin Brides, all of whom have died before reaching their wedding day). No man is safe when these cocky teenagers rise up from the mist. But owing to the sacrifices of the peasant, the Duke survives, a new day dawns and all's happy in the Rhineland. 'Churchill might find his inner peasant?' hoped the organisers. In the interval, the PM and Eden convened in the restroom using sign language. This annoyed Stalin who brought it up, sarcastically saying how good the two of them were at washing their hands.

Stalin hoped to get the Straits of Bosphorus but didn't. Churchill received an assurance that the Soviets would stay out of Greece. On 16 October he hoped a Polish government could be made up from London Poles and Lublin Poles equally. If Joe agreed, the PM would agree to the new borders. Nothing came of this this and Winston left Moscow with 'personal regards' conveyed from Stalin as well as 'a handsome brooch, composed of the flags of Great Britain and the USSR' – a gift from Svetlana Stalin to Sarah Oliver. Beneath the flags Russian words were engraved on the theme of friendship. One can be terribly famous and not know it. Sarah's poster girl presence at Tehran had won a significant follower. Svetlana had much in common with Sarah, despite being ten years younger. Miss Stalin was married, had a flat and moved in the nearest thing Moscow had to a *beau monde*. Her first secret romance had been with an older Jewish man, a screenwriter for Russian films. Discovering his *Little Housekeeper* harboured this obsession Stalin imprisoned the fellow first in the *Lubyanka*, then in a Siberian prison camp. The Marshal forced his wayward daughter to study Modern History (the state-prescribed version): sheer agony. Just as Sarah loved her siblings, so too did Svetlana, although in her case, her family were victims of dictatorial whims, later imprisoned for being outspoken and forced to confess untruths.

Stopping at Naples prior to the last leg of his journey after TOLSTOY, Winston took Svetlana's gift out of its wrapping. Moran tells us the PM was cheered, thinking the Soviets were turning over a new leaf. Despite being President of the Royal College of Physicians, Moran relied on hunches. He was convinced the PM was carried away with this play on emotions, although a waking moment came when the PM chillingly observed that 'behind the horseman sits dull care'. In fact, Churchill had given up on Russia being a reliable ally after it failed to help the Warsaw Poles in August 1944. Writing a thank you for the 'Friendship Brooch', the FO was unsure how to address Stalin's daughter. They decided on 'Dear Miss Stalin' and Sarah was asked to compose it. Wearing the brooch as if it were a sign that nobility existed in the *Vozhd*, her Papa didn't tell her that facts were better than dreams. He did send her a birthday cheque to buy something special. She thanked him, promising not to use it for the gas bill. While Teutonic inhabitants of the eastern Reich feared punishing red angels and banishment to Siberian wastes, Churchill was rapped over the knuckles over his initiative to help the Greeks. FDR used Lend-Lease to blackmail the British into submission.

Back in Britain, Sarah's team, 'B6' – renowned for ingenious geological solutions – had the task of uncovering underground sites. Using the *Wild* machine they interpreted the rock strata below rocket sites while PIs assessed ground detail. This influenced decisions on air attacks to render sites unusable. Forty factories existed and hundreds of underground depots, built by slaves. Hitler's chief engineer Hans Kammler had even developed a nuclear programme. Sarah helped spot a plane being winched up a mountain and identified a shaved mountaintop as a runway. The work, alongside the Crossbow team, was of high strategic value, although Duncan was to change jobs on 21 November, becoming Minister of Works and Buildings. Between October and December 1944 'B6' was hard at it, but Sarah found time to produce a version of *Gaslight*. Her work gave her a sense of pride and relationships kept her grounded. She was fond of Bill O'Connor, Pleasant O'Neill, her Irish friend Jan Magee and her typist Miss Murden, whom she looked after when Myra had jaundice, arranging for her recovery at Dungavel Castle. Myra was curious how she could open such doors, aware that the Duke of Hamilton, its owner, had been the one Hess tried to contact. At times Sarah was cheesed off. A senior rebuked Grania and herself for not carrying gas masks. She liked the unorthodox ways of the 'Mad Men of Ham' but was bored with rules. She was relieved to take her mind off rocket factories when another conference spirited her off.

Sarah was in the PM's party lunching on 29 January 1945 with the White Rajah of Sarawak (whose daughter Didi had also 'married down'). They left Northolt on a C-54 Skymaster bound for Malta. Winston became hot in the head and freezing everywhere else. The line 'Sleep that knits up the raveled sleave of care' was appropriate for poor, very pink Papa. Aboard HQ – HMS *Orion* – Sawyers attended Winston. Sarah's bunk was so cramped that undressing and dressing was 'a feat unparalleled in the history of contortionists'. As soldier-like as the next man, she was inconspicuous while others 'collapsed into baths and shaving bowls'. The tour between 29 January and 18 February incorporated the Yalta Conference (MAGNET) to start proposals for peace. A letter Sarah sent her mother implies that she had mislaid Svetlana's all-important brooch. Sarah's sister had the precious item couriered and a *scandale diplomatique* was averted at the last moment: 'Diana has saved the day!' Sarah rejoiced with a 'Wow.'

While stopping at Malta she went on a walk with Eden and Cadogan. For some reason it ended up with them sprinting across a salvage heap, leaping over a stone wall, almost getting mown down by Ave Harriman (driving past at that moment in his car) and arriving at the wrong destination 'puce in the face'. After 'a cup of filthy tea in the NAAFI' they finally got back for dinner at the Governor's Palace where Portal did 'Houdini tricks with a piece of string'. They were getting reports about what to expect in Yalta incuding tales of 16 US Colonels housed in a small room. Back on the *Orion*, Sarah welcomed conversation that digressed from the war. She dived into the topic of palmistry, then they discoursed on the topic of hands as indicators of creativity. Moran mentioned Gorky's observation about Tolstoy's. Sarah was dying to know what the socialist realist author said but they changed tack.

'Are you flirting with my ambassador?' was her way of finishing a letter to Clementine: 'If so – desist for one moment and give him my love will you?'

On 2 February the USS *Quincy* arrived at Malta, dwarfing the *Orion* and producing FDR. Winston's party lunched with the President and his lovely but nervy daughter Anna Boettiger, before a fighter escort flew them across Turkey and the Black Sea to Saki near Simferopol, 80 miles from Yalta. Here were characters Sarah knew from Tehran: Molotov, Vyshinsky, Gusev and little Pavlov, the sweet interpreter. Next came a bumpy drive, taking them through land 'bleak as the soul in despair', testing her father's patience. His power to zap boredom was intact and Byron's *Don Juan*, with its hilariously contrived rhymes, proved a tonic. Seeing the conferences assume mock epic proportions, Sarah was astounded not only by Papa's delight in his fellow Harrovian's irreverent style but by his recall of 17 cantos. The torturous journey lasted until 7.45 p.m. Numb and sore, the Brits and Americans were given the first of many suppers of suckling pig and sweet champagne. Eden tried to talk to FDR but found him 'vague, loose and ineffective'. Winston spoke up, bluntly saying that the US failed to grasp how significant the Polish issue was. The British made their way to the Vorontsov Palace (aka the Alupka Chateau) while Roosevelt and the American delegation settled into the Livadia Palace where meetings and signings took place. The latter had once been summer residence to Tsar Nicholas II. Renovated for FDR's visit, it boasted an onsite barbers and a billiards room. So seriously did the Russians take hospitality that after someone asked for a lemon for a cocktail, a huge lemon tree (transplanted from Georgia) appeared next day in the conservatory. By contrast, Prince Vorontsov's former home had a sanitation problem. A US squad squirted DDT around everyone's beds to kills the bugs. The single concession was the double bed from a Moscow store purchased for the PM. He insisted that Sarah share his bathroom.

Kathy passed on gossip to Pamela about a funny thing that happened at the Livadia concerning two leaders and one toilet (or *John* as she called it). Marshal Stalin was making his way to the only restroom with a John that, unbeknownst to him, was occupied by Churchill. Some guys from the American Embassy, who thought it inadvisable to let both men in, whisked Stalin away miles down a long corridor to get him into the only other convenience. When the NKVD bodyguards discovered that Stalin was missing, a period of havoc ensued. 'Has Stalin been abducted?' they asked.

It was lovely having Anna and Kathy to pass long hours with and on 5 February they saw Sebastopol; a thriving city, so their guide insisted. It was a heap of rubble to any onlooker. In the only building left standing a lecture about the siege was given to the visitors. More Russian PR was spun during their trip to Chekhov's villa, preserved by the playwright's sister. Sarah seemed to dwell on one particular sight: of queues of Romanian prisoners waiting to take their pitiful share of food from a bucket. Late one night she talked about it with her father before he went to sleep. He said: 'Tonight the sun goes down on more suffering than ever before in this world.' She was aware that progress had stalled. Thirty years later she read through copies of her letters and said things about Yalta she couldn't say at the time, scrawling annotations in red pen. One was: 'I didn't know the details but I knew all was not well.' After hearing Papa's words she began to feel odd. The hulking crag of granite to the rear of the Vorontsov Palace made her claustrophobic.

Laughter returned when a banquet was held on 8 February 1945 on the attractive verandah of the Yusupov Palace. A newspaper cutting quotes one of the girls saying: 'We knew the Russians loved dancing but we didn't know until now, how much.' They met young Soviet officers and had the usual silly toasts, although as Sarah would tell her mother: 'Nothing can quite touch the Teheran birthday party ever.' As well as Uncle Joe there was Vyshinsky, Maisky, Gusev and Lavrentiy Beria, chief of the Soviet security apparatus. He would become feared in the post-Stalin leadership. Had the girls known about his secret drugging and raping, they would never have come. Something about the atmosphere jarred. A ride in a jeep and a long walk with Peter Portal to a waterfall the next day helped pick up Sarah's mood.

At Yalta most of the action involved men seated around a large round table. The President occupied a central position with his back to the marble fireplace where young Tsarevich Alexei and the Imperial Princesses once covered little packets of truffles with embers. Japan was fighting to the bitter end and FDR needed Stalin's help, despite Russia's expansionist designs. Enlisting Joe as one of 'Four Policemen' was another aim. The Marshal levelled $20 billion reparations at Germany. Churchill insisted that Russia collect it in kind, which led to the zone held by the Soviets being stripped of all raw materials. The Russians made sure it included a V2 factory (transplanting this back to Russia and seizing all personnel). They were hungry to benefit from German scientific developments. Churchill tried to secure a Danubian Confederation of States but Stalin opposed this. Least progress was made on Poland, despite Winston summoning the rival Polish governments to force free elections. Stalin got out of it by pretending he couldn't contact the Lublin Poles.

Seeing him reach for his pink pills, Sarah knew her father was fragile and even his relationship with FDR had taken a knock. When he left the President waiting one day, Anna complained to Sarah, referring to her father's busy schedule. As cold and crisp as a lettuce, Sarah defended Churchill's commitment. During a final look around Yalta, Anna and Sarah distributed chocolates to kids in the street and got told off by a Russian soldier exhibiting the usual brainwashed pride: 'There is no need to feed our children,' he said (Kathy translating). After this, the sound of hymns and smell of incense led them into a small Orthodox church. The atmosphere at Yalta felt Stygian.

The sight of prayer and ordinary people coping with their struggles brought Sarah back to sorrows on a human scale.

After march-pasts, drills and farewell tins of caviar, the US delegation left for Saki on 12 February. Churchill decided to visit Balaclava, given its Crimean War association. His daughter and Moran came along. The next day Winston had had enough. Settling into the Cunard liner SS *Franconia* Cadogan compared the atmosphere between Churchill and Eden to touring 'with Melba and Tetrazzini in one company'. Pug Ismay revealed that the crew got annoyed with Winston for ordering that the entire ship's heating be switched off because his room was too hot. Sarah's bridal suite cabin was divine. A hairdresser worked on her 'shaggy locks' and a stewardess was on hand with a Martini. Feeling elation that they had come through it all, she set to work on a letter to Mama, putting a positive spin on Russia knowing Clementine was travelling there with Miss Hamblin for her Red Cross award: 'He will take special care of you,' she reassured, referring to Uncle Joe like an old friend and joking how Papa's 'Cat' was joining his 'red kitten' in going Red. In fact, visiting Russia was dangerous; agitators were instructing people to no longer regard the US and British as allies. They were 'enemies' of the USSR now. A letter to Gil also pictured the Yalta Conference in an optimistic light. She brushed aside the inkling of truth she learned from Papa at the Vorontsov Palace.

The next part of the journey was by air. The Black Sea looked dull but a gorgeous sun emerged. On arrival in Athens, Sarah's Papa appeared with Anthony on the balcony of the Old Palace on 14 February while Sarah, Moran and Cadogan drove up to the Parthenon. Next day they were back at HQ, HMS *Aurora*. Boarding USS *Quincy*, also in Alexandria harbour, FDR greeted them for lunch wearing his Gatsby cap with a Québec Conference photo album for Winston. Randolph, whom they had seen the night before, joined them. He took after his father in the sense that 'tears flowed easily about the things he deeply cared about'. He was not his usual self having found out Tom Mitford had died in Burma. A C-54 Skymaster took them to Cairo where the Conference business was wrapped up. They received the horrible news that Lord Moyne, their lifelong friend and Britain's Middle Eastern affairs spokesman, had been murdered. Two militants would be hanged for this crime in March 1945, one accomplice being future PM Yitzhak Shamir. Moyne was killed for his opposition to mass Jewish immigration into Palestine. Britain's 1920 Mandate had safeguarded all inhabitants irrespective of race and religion when only 10% of Palestine's population was Jewish. Tens of thousands of Jews arrived year-on-year, waging war by population growth and terrorism: a realisation of a call by writer Michael Arlen in 1940 for a meek people to take vengeance. Sarah's mother and father were shaken and she was upset for Grania, Moyne's only daughter.

Gifts immeasurably more lavish than Svetlana's brooch were dispensed when the PM met Ibn Saud along with Emperor Haile Selassie, both of whom had earlier met FDR. After seeing the large holes in the decking of Saud's destroyer from roasting sixty sheep, Lampson got him to meet the PM at the *Fayoum* instead of Cairo. Saudi had been 'official' since 1932. How this Wahhabi leader rose to command this new country owed much to John Philby, father of future double agent Kim. Sarah could hardly believe what her father came back with: magnificent robes, diamond-hilted swords and massive diamonds and pearls. She and Papa had fun trying on the garments and jewels. There were many new tales to tell WAAFS and flyboys. Clementine was to receive her decoration in early April and her trepidation is plain when she asks Sarah to pray for her. In the 'ogre's den' she asked Maisky to justify the dispatch of Poles to labour camps, getting no real answer.

While there, Molotov told her that Roosevelt had died of a cerebral haemorrhage. The last V2 hit Britain on 27 March 1945, soon after the last V1, but 'Section B6' still had work to do. Two major underground complexes were found at Niedersachswerfen in August.

*Why didn't I see what was going on? Couldn't I have said something?* These are questions asked in the light of regret but Sarah didn't reproach herself for being innocent of what later became known. Her thoughts were clear: 'We were outnumbered but for my father not outwitted ... Dictators are dominated by themselves,' she opined, concluding that 'if Winston Churchill was dominated, it was only by the demands of England'. Years later she stated: 'I never had my life directed by thugs and crooks. Terrorists and assassins do not make the earth.' Something about Papa shielded her from evil, giving her *the force of light*. For his part he laughed at his rebel daughter when she said she liked to wear a general's badge (the one Alex had given her) and how she whisked it off when senior RAF officials came near. He smiled when she told him that at Yusupov Palace she had cleverly extracted things from Uncle Joe about his family: 'The daughter ... is now married and having a baby,' she reported. Of course she passed on her thanks to Miss Stalin. Winston had travelled far and long in the pursuit of Russian friendship; a goal that was beginning to seem like nothing more than a talisman. His daughter's sunny optimism meant so much to him. She sounded so proud saying: 'I wear the brooch on my uniform the whole time.'

# 10

# The Bell Tolls

Vic's final reconciliation request was declined, so a case for desertion went to the courts. Others believe in the permanence of escaping the nest but for Sarah, rediscovering her parents was the most significant thing that that had happened in those last four years. The feeling was mutual and Churchill at this time desired to build a house on the Chartwell Estate for this rufescent child whose company he loved. With Clementine away that Easter, they picnicked there, despairing at the theft of the last goldfish. The King and Queen led the mourners at FDR's Service at St Paul's on 17 April 1945 and Gil read the lesson. Churchill's tears fell during the Repose of the Soul, revealing the depth of his feeling for the friend who didn't falter when he was most alone. On 29 April came news of Mussolini's hanging and the next day, of Hitler's suicide. Reunited with John Junior, Gil proudly introduced him to Winston on 7 May. Simon Eden never returned and when his death was confirmed that June, Gil consoled his parents. Anthony's dog Nipper kept faith at Binderton, carrying out tasks for his master, even knowing which Penguin novel to fetch.

VE Day was a lonely one for the PM with his wife in Russia, busy with her tour that took her to Leningrad, Kursk and Winston's bedroom at the Vorontsov. After he made an address from the Health Ministry, Sarah, her sisters and Duncan mingled in the crowds as he stood on the balcony at Buckingham Palace. Winant's future was uncertain. Regarded as an 'FDR man' by many in the new Truman administration, he remained in limbo for months: still ambassador but awaiting a decision regarding his United Nations leadership. He presided over its related bodies: its operations for Relief and Rehabilitation (UNRRA) and its Economic and Social Council (ECOSOC), which supervised agencies prior to decisions on economic planning.

Back for Independence Day, Connie was alone at 3 Grosvenor Square. Her husband had been lent 7 Aldford Street by Winston's cousin Freddie

Guest. The Churchills' offer was a gesture to protect him, his private life a greater security risk at a time of change at the Embassy. Many of the town houses in the street are deceptively cottage-like. Gil's had a large entrance hall, drawing room, dining room, seven bedrooms, three bathrooms and a four-car garage. It was a minute from Sarah's apartment. When Clementine returned, Gil joined the family in drinking a champagne toast with the Gusevs in Kensington Palace Gardens.

The Great Coalition ended and the Opposition firmed up its attack. Lend-Lease came to an abrupt end and the task of addressing countless problems with a cashless treasury was more onerous than ever. The PM's promise to correct shortages – 'I am using any spare life and strength I have to see it is made good' – and the Four Year Plan guided by Lord Woolton failed to have an impact. Many thought Churchill had no handle on social issues, having been too caught up with warfare. With the General Election looming supporters rallied around but there was not enough time. Gil talked to Moran about Bevin's attacks and hoped Winston's doctor might influence him to change the mood of the electorate. None who saw the speech (due to be broadcast from Chequers on 4 June) could get him to drop its troublesome phrases. Foretelling a society devoid of free speech with people's work dictated by a socialist state, the language of the Old Man in his 'Gestapo Broadcast' was called paranoid. Yet anyone au fait with developments on the Continent understood why he said it. While the 'surrender agreement' signed by the US, Britain, Russia and France included (at Winant's insistence) a ban on 'dismemberment', Germany was nevertheless partitioneded quickly in the summer of 1945 with four controlled areas and Berlin a fifth zone. The freedom of citizens in the Russian zones was questionable. Writing to her father on 5 June to report the effects of his speech on RAF colleagues, Sarah told him clearly his words wouldn't 'turn' Labour supporters since nobody feared totalitarianism. All the government had to do, she advised, was adopt the bits of socialism that affected people's lives. These were things like 'common sharing' of milk and meat that the majority of people had seen in the war. She pointed out that people didn't get his Four Year Plan and that he had to do far more about housing, or pass the socialists the 'strongest card'. Duncan knew this too. Criticised for not fulfilling promises to sort out Tulse Hill's blitzed Arlingford Road, he got flak from residents. A few hours later, a squad of workmen arrived and stayed Saturday and Sunday repairing the houses. The *Sunday Mirror* pinned an accusation of vote hustling on him, knowing how desperate he was to keep Norwood. He and Diana would travel to Hull to open pre-fab houses at Hopewell Road.

On the campaign trail cheers turned to heckling at Walthamstow Stadium on 3 July. Virginia Cowles caught up with Sarah and Mr Churchill for beer and sandwiches in the private room of a pub. Polling day was 5 July with the result delayed until 27 July. On the Continent, meanwhile, monumental efforts were needed to clear aside rubble, spies and collaborators. Before the Potsdam Conference Sarah told her father her colleagues had been 'shattered' by an idiotic decision relating to aerial surveys. She urged him to meet with Kendall. The extent of the bombing in Europe would not be made public until November when *Time* published the United States Strategic Bombing Survey for Europe. At Potsdam new Secretary of State James Byrnes was wary of offending Stalin and accepted Stalin's promises that trade would continue freely east and west of occupied Germany. The US stood back as Berlin (to quote Winston's secretary Joy Hunter) was left 'absolutely flat'. At least the PM had a tour of the Summer Palace of Frederick the Great. Returning to Britain, he waited in the Map Room at the Annexe, with Sarah, Max and other friends. The BBC announced the Labour landslide. Brendan, Randolph and Duncan lost seats. The family's last weekend at Chequers began on 27 July. Colville, now Private Secretary to Attlee, admired Churchill's lack of self-pity and for caring about the new government. After drafting a statement about the atomic bomb, Winston sat down for dinner. Fifteen guests including Gil were gathered in evening dress, acting as if nothing had happened. With their Jeroboam of champagne it seemed like old times.

Who could staunch the flow of memories or silence the echoes of great speeches? Sarah and Gil returned to London and kept the discussion alive with Sarah giving complete speeches in the style of her father. A friend recalled how effortlessly she could reel off word-perfect renditions ten years later: utterly brilliant, if they hadn't ended with Sarah passing out. That same evening she wrote Mama a letter saying that without her help she wouldn't have learned the key to overcoming defeat – finding humour in it – and used the words of St Ignatius – 'To give and not to count the cost' – to describe their years of duty. Based for a while at the Sandyses' flat at Westminster Gardens, her parents were Vic's neighbours. It's testimony to Winston's high regard for him that Vic acquired many Churchill paintings (sold on his death). Things picked up for the ex-PM with a £20K offer from Henry Luce for articles, but according to Moran, he was troubled with depression. It wasn't just about losing his post. It was coming to terms with what Uncle Joe got away with and technology's impact on the scale of destruction as at Hiroshima. Truman made the decision to bomb after Japan refused to surrender. A second bomb fell on Nagasaki on 9 August taking the number killed to something like 200,000.

Returning to Britain on 14 July to work for UNRRA, Maurine found Gil's seat at the Embassy empty. He was somewhere in the country: a mysterious place she was aware of but had never been invited to. On his return he obliged her with a tour of Aldford Street and dinners at the Connaught and Cavendish

Clementine holding Sarah at Lullenden Farm in 1915.

*Top:* Diana and Randolph visit their father's constituency, Dundee, in April 1922 during a time of dissatisfaction with Lloyd George's leadership.

*Above:* Chartwell Manor.

The Churchills with their Mitford cousins at Asthall, 1923. Back: Diana Mitford, Diana Churchill, Lady Redesdale, Pamela, Tom; Front: Randolph Churchill, Deborah, Unity, Jessica, Sarah Churchill.

The Bonham Carters' visit to Chartwell in 1927. Diana stands with Lady Violet behind the bench with Peregrine seated and Sarah on the lawn beside the dog.

The former Chancellor of the Exchequer Winston Churchill waves to his followers as he leaves his polling station in Epping during the October 1931 election.

*Above left:* Diana Churchill went from debutante to actress at RADA in the autumn of 1930.

*Above right:* Randolph's candidacy in the Wavertree election in 1935 threatens to split the vote. He campaigns against the Democratic Constitution for India and calls for stronger air defence.

*Above left:* Sarah Churchill seated between her parents at Cranbourne Manor, the home of her father's friend Bobbety, in 1932.

*Above right:* Diana Churchill and new husband Duncan Sandys in 1935.

*Left:* Vic Oliver, Aristocrat of Comedy (photo by Murray Korman), with second wife Margot Crangle (*inset*). As the vaudeville act *Oliver & Crangle* they toured the length and breadth of America between 1925 and 1934.

*Above:* Clementine visits Manchester where her 'chorus girl' daughter is performing in C. B. Cochran's *Follow the Sun* at the Opera House. *Inset:* Sarah's digs in Ackers Street.

*Above left:* Vic and Sarah at Ealing Studios on the set of their first film, *Who's Your Lady Friend*.

*Above right:* Just married, Vic Oliver and Sarah Churchill face the press on their return to Britain in late December 1936.

*Right:* April 1939: Churchill has his Eye on Youth. Speaking at a City of London recruiting centre for the Territorial Army.

September 1938: Vic, Sarah, Judy Campbell, Heron Carvic and others from the touring production of *Idiot's Delight*.

*Above left:* 1932 caricature by Lisl Weil showing the unique stage presence of Reichsgräfin Triangi in one of her popular stage concerts in Vienna.

*Above right:* A photo of Vic's aunt Beatrice.

March 1940: Soon-to-be PM Mr Churchill.

Anti-British Nazi propaganda from late 1939 entitled 'Churchill's noble kinsfolk', mocking the Premier's Jewish in-laws through his daughter's marriage.

Publicising London Zoo's Adopt an Animal scheme in September 1940, Sarah, Vic and Phyllis Luckett pose with lion cubs Jane and June.

London, early 1990s, Phyllis Flax (*née* Luckett) and Lady Soames get nostalgic about Vic, Sarah and the war years.

*Top:* Hopeful about America's entry into the war, Vic meets General Wade Hayes, leader of the American Home Guard in London.

*Above:* Sarah's scrapbook cutting of the Polish Relief Fund Concert on 2 June 1941. Second from the right is Borenius, whose secret mission weeks before was to cut a deal with Germany.

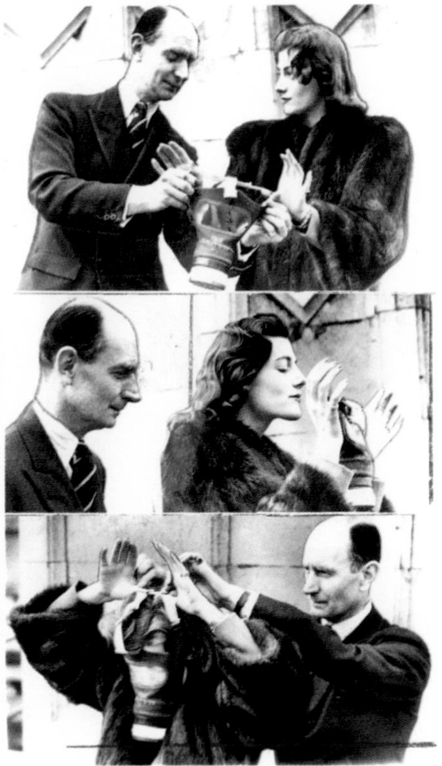

Sarah Churchill in a publicity campaign to educate the public as to the best way to put on a gas mask. Wg Cdr Hodsoll (Inspector General of the Civil Defence Services) provides expert assistance.

IN NOEL COWARD COMEDY

Vic Oliver as Karl Sandys and Sarah Churchill as Louise Charteris in a scene from "We Were Dancing," one of the Noel Coward comedies in "To-night at Seven" at the Glasgow King's.

Cutting from Sarah's scrapbook of the Olivers in Noël Coward's playlet *We Were Dancing*, February 1941.

Sarah, Vic and John Paddy Carstairs on the set of *He Found a Star* in April 1941.

October 1941: Vic Oliver, the star attraction of *Get a Load of This* at the London Hippodrome, is an abandoned husband.

Independence Day 1941: Cutting from Sarah's scrapbook showing her warm greeting by Ambassador John G. Winant and his wife Constance at the American Society's luncheon.

Churchill inspecting bomb damage in Bristol in April 1941. Behind him are Winant, Clementine and Detective Thompson.

*AMERICAN AMBASSADOR WITH WASHINGTON VILLAGE MINERS*

Mr. Winant, the American Ambassador, who submitted himself to "off-the-record" questioning after he had addressed 300 Durham miners on Saturday. With him are men from the village of Washington, home of some of George Washington's ancestors. Mr. Will Lawther, President of the Mineworkers' Federation, is second from the left.—DAILY TELEGRAPH picture.

TURKISH VIEW
ON WAR TREND

"MAY BE NEARING

*Above left:* June 1942: The magnetism of Ambassador Winant. In Washington, Co. Durham, his speech averts a miners' strike.

*Above right:* The third woman in Gil Winant's life: his loyal friend and colleague Maurine Mulliner.

October 1942: 'Halloween revue' from Squadron Leader Ted Wood's photo album. Seen in the loud checked sweater, next to Charlotte Bonham Carter, Woody had the secondary duty of being RAF Medmenham's Entertainments Officer. Wearing peasant costume, Sarah is in the front, fifth from the right.

*Above left:* Sarah with colleagues in 'B6', the section specializing in the study of underground facilities (from the '*Chalk House with Tudor Chimneys*' album produced mid-1945 by the Central Intelligence Unit).

*Above right:* The hours occupied in photographic intelligence duties at Danesfield House take a toll: Sarah in spectacles in early 1945 (prior to gaining a Defence Medal to wear on her 'battle dress').

*Left:* Celebrating Churchill's birthday at Chequers in November 1941. Back: Peregrine, Jack; Middle: Pamela, Sarah, Duncan; Front: Clementine holding Rufus the dog, Winston and Diana.

*Above left:* Winston Churchill at the Teheran Conference. Stalin shakes hands with Sarah Churchill while Roosevelt, Winston Churchill, Molotov, Harriman and Anthony Eden look on.

*Above right:* February 1945: The calming presence of Air Chief Marshal Sir Charles Portal outside the Vorontsov Palace during the Yalta Conference.

*Right:* February 1945: Sarah Churchill, Anna Boettiger and Kathy Harriman photographed by Sergeant Robert Hopkins (Harry Hopkins' son) at the Livadia Palace, February 1945.

*Above left:* February 1945: John G. Winant, President Franklin D. Roosevelt, Secretary of State Edward Stettinius and Harry Hopkins on USS *Quincy CA-71* in the Mediterranean Sea.

*Above right:* A welcome friend at the Yalta Conference: Roosevelt's daughter Anna with Sarah.

*Above left:* Four months after the war Sarah made two films in Rome, living there for fourteen months. Seen here with friends Valerie Hayes and Captain Peter Moore.

*Above right:* Late 1946: Sarah's director and friend Mario Soldati and her leading man Vittorio Gassman on the set of *Daniele Cortis.*

*Above inset:* Sarah as Elena.

*Left:* A new presence on the American stage: Sarah Churchill in *The Philadelphia Story* with the young Pat Crowley at Connecticut's Westport Country Playhouse in August 1949.

Antony Beauchamp in his uniform for the Royal Leicestershire Regiment.

A study of Sarah Churchill by Tony Beauchamp's mother, Vivienne.

*Top left:* Antony Beauchamp (front row, left) with his brother Clive as pageboys at a family wedding.

*Above left:* Vivienne and Ernest Entwistle in their Hamilton Mews studio, late 1940s.

*Top right:* Antony with Jean Duff at Franchise Manor, East Sussex, in 1939.

*Above right:* Antony in 1938 with friend Robin Duff in Campania, Italy.

St Simon's Island, Georgia, October 1949. Antony Beauchamp and Sarah Churchill mark their engagement with a set of photos.

*Right:* Sarah Churchill with her friend Rupert Allen and attorney at Malibu Courthouse in January 1958.

*Below:* Julia Lockwood as Wendy, Sarah Churchill as Peter with the Lost Boys in *Peter Pan*, Scala Theatre, December 1958.

*Above left:* Photo by Ken Walker of Sarah in June 1961 in costume for Sadie Thompson for a performance of Somerset Maugham's *Rain*.

*Above right:* Photo by Robert Pitt in May 1961 of Sarah as Ganymede and Fenella Fielding as Phoebe in *As You Like It*.

*Above left:* April 1962: Sarah Churchill and Lord Audley announce their marriage.

*Above right:* Sarah Churchill at the funeral of Sir Winston Churchill on 30 January 1965.

Sarah Churchill in Rome with artist Lobo Nocho in 1964.

*Above left:* June 1966: Sarah with her PA Delphine Clues on a Mediterranean cruise following the publication of her book of poems, *The Empty Spaces*.

*Above right:* Hugh Hastings and Sarah Churchill take *A Matter of Choice*, their cabaret-style show, to the Mickery Theatre, Amsterdam, in November 1966.

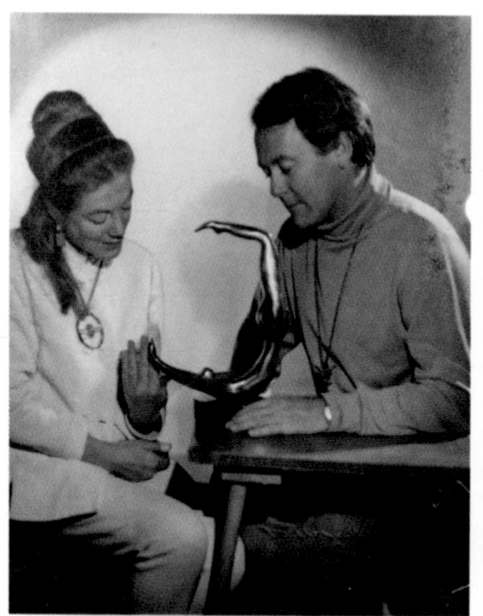

*Above left:* Sarah with sculptor Colin Webster-Watson. Photo by Vivienne.
*Above right:* With Colin's portrait head, *Queen of the Shells*.

Sarah with artist Curtis Hooper at Chartwell in 1978.

(where they met the legendary Rosa Lewis who claimed Mr Winant's good influence showed itself on Winston Churchill). Maurine felt she disappointed Gil by not bearing the hoped-for message from President Truman to say he could lead the UN. With Attlee and the King he met 'Haberdasher Harry' on 2 August when the USS *Philadelphia* was at anchor, afterwards referring to the meeting as 'snafu and all'. When colleagues John Corson and Janine Perrett got engaged, Gil was generous as ever, paying for rings and the reception. Over cocktails on 7 September with economist Thomas Blaisdell he seemed lively, but two days later Maurine and her friends encountered him on Park Lane looking lonesome. He took them all out to dinner and the evening ended on a high. Orol said how glad she was they had found him just then, rescuing him from one of his terrible lows.

Alexander of Tunis had come up with the idea for Winston to holiday on the shores of Lake Como, organising a Dakota to transport his party (including Miss Layton and two officers) to Milan and a motor to get them to Moltrasio where ABC Cunningham would join them. Sarah was asked to look after him although getting leave now Papa wasn't Premier was hard and she had to resort to a doctor's note. Winant's eagerness to liaise on her behalf came as no surprise to Moran, but he was rather forgotten during the Mule's Italian pèlerinage. Clementine invited Gil to Chartwell to make up for that. Winston and his daughter waltzed to the *Blue Danube* and during those 17 days were never apart. He wore his white suit and sombrero while making studies of the lake. The glorious melting sunsets produced thoughtful discussions over supper about chivalry in war or heated debates concerning paintings at Villa Le Rose. 'Ladies' feet look best emerging from long gowns,' Sarah's father insisted. Tanned, glowing and composed, Sarah flew home with Elizabeth while her Pa extended his holiday, staying in another villa near Genoa.

All across the land servicemen traded in uniforms for clothing coupons and WAAF Smith became Miss Smith. 'Torn by personal and business problems', Gil gave Maurine a timid kiss before departing for Washington to meet with the State Department and get X-rayed. On 22 October he returned with his son. The gatherings with Attlee and co. weren't the same as those spent with the Churchill clan. He drafted a set of topics he felt Truman should discuss with the Labour Party. The Randolph Churchills were to divorce soon and Winant was obliging to Pam, agreeing to chair Herbert Morrison's talk, *The Case for Socialisation*, on 6 November at the soon-to-close Churchill Club. He looked deathly pale at a Thanksgiving Service at Westminster on 22 November. Britain after the war wasn't known for its vivid blues and golds and the ex-PM's pursuit of colour took him to Marrakesh where he sought Sarah's opinion of 'The Gathering Storm'. 'Too many acronyms,' she told him.

Sarah's *decree nisi* came on 25 October and she was demobbed a month later. Her priority was to return to the stage. Bill Duncalfe had written a great part for her in *Squaring the Triangle* about a near marriage breakdown redeemed by a happy ending. He played the neglectful husband with soft-spoken Bob Roberts the other corner of the triangle. The latter had been a radio announcer in America and later played a small part in *A Matter of Life and Death*. Pauline Growse, Pamela Hayes, Enid Phillips and Bill Franklin were the other players and following rehearsals (some at Sarah's flat) they opened at Henley's Playhouse on 13 December for a week, proceeds going to the RAF Benevolent Fund. Hundreds of playgoers were unable to get tickets and police controlled the crowds outside. Clementine came and with her Gil, Randolph, Mary, Diana, Duncan, Villiers and several friends. A critic talked about the play's witty dialogue and how the audience awaited every entrance Sarah made.

A New Year bash at Margaret Biddle's saw Gil in a 'vile mood'. He had taken to drinking at lunchtime, something he never used to do. When Bevin and others said they weren't supporting his UN chairmanship, he felt let down by Labour. As if on purpose Sarah disappeared again with her parents to the US and Cuba, but Clementine's affection for Gil was constant. Five years into their relationship she invited him to call her Clemmie when she wrote from Miami. From 23 January to 16 February 1946 he was in London, attending the first session of ECOSOC. Both Maurine and Beatrice Eden (who found him at Aldford Street at a low ebb) knew he had suicidal thoughts. A year-and-a-half earlier, Maurine had been certain that Gil's pathway to the presidency required him to sacrifice personal happiness. Now, she wished for the opposite, believing he was better off making a change. If he could just face facts about his marriage, finances and job, he might find a way of dealing with his depression.

Winston gave a press conference in the Hotel Nacional. He was revisiting scenes of his youth at the invitation of the Cuban government (and was practically buried in cigars). Speaking at the University of Miami, he showed gratitude for their role in training RAF recruits during the war. He received an honorary degree at a ceremony at the Orange Bowl Stadium before a stop at Casa Alva in Manalapan (Consuelo Balsan's Florida mansion) for swimming and peace. At Washington he built on his rapport with Harry Truman before meeting Randolph at Union Station. The family headed for Missouri where Churchill gave a speech entitled *The Sinews of Strength* at Fulton's Westminster College on 5 March. Harriman and others knew only too well that Stalin was having his demands met too frequently. With the Bulldog removed from power, standing up to Stalin seemed a remote possibility. In Fulton, Winston made the acquaintance of J. C. Hall, the Nebraskan greeting card king and sponsor of radio shows. Gil saw the Churchills in New York, standing in for new Under-Secretary of State Dean Acheson at the dinner following the Winston Churchill Address on 15 March. Winston called for Anglo-US relations to be characterised by more harmony and referred to the UN Charter. Free elections and people's rights to 'mingle freely with one another' mattered to him and he criticised Russia's forced control of the waterways of central Europe and her meddling in Persia and the Straits. Sarah restored some of Gil's calmness in New York. She also wrote a 'Thank You from a Former ADC' to her Papa on 1 April and tried to pay for her holiday expenses, receiving a note from him refusing to allow it.

As Gil swapped ambassadorship for roles at ECOSOC and UNESCO, Sarah's new mini-sitcom *The Young Sullivans* (by Bill Duncalfe) began and ran for fourteen weeks as part of the BBC's *Monday Night at Eight*. Aldford Street was full of farewell gifts and emotional letters. Dinners in Gil's honour ranged from the informal (with the Churchills on 12 April) to the grand, at Lancaster House on 23 April. Two days later Maurine witnessed Gil exploding with rage after Connie made a small putdown about the tone he had used with one of the generals. These situations were increasing. One guy at the Embassy suffered a torrent of undeserved abuse and Gil lost it with a taxi driver in New York. The Winants said goodbye to Queen Mary at Marlborough House on 3 May and left Bournemouth's Hurn Airport. Reporters heard him contrast walking into the eye of the storm on his arrival in 1941 and the spring sunshine of his return.

Rivington Winant had seen little of his father, having been on service in the Pacific. The Winants returned to life at 510 Park Avenue. On 1 July they came to Washington for the Roosevelt Memorial Speech before Congress, staying at a hotel the night before. When Maurine saw them next day she noticed how happy and even intimate Gil and Connie were. At FDR's memorial a baritone from the Met Opera performed and Winant read the eulogy stating that Franklin 'dared to see the facts, to face them and to act'.

After a short homecoming, Gil returned to Britain on 12 July. The horrid weather couldn't dampen his love for London and small things lifted his heart. Orol Mears was minding house at Aldford Street and Sarah was around. Gil had his memoirs to write, hence the two-month stay. Making some independent money was the reason he was doing it. He was otherwise a reluctant writer. In the right company, the ex-Governor could tell a good story but putting it down on paper was another matter. That September Sarah wrote to Clementine about the murky realm she was trapped in, comparing herself to Penelope. It suggests that even if the death knell to their passion had been tolled with new suitors appearing in the aftermath, she was still Gil's 'alternative wife'. Her tone is that of someone unhappily accepting this role. Her question about whether a 'three-volume tome' might be more fitting for his book appears to be a cry of frustration. She'll support Gil in his endeavours – 'though I do not tear up the pages' – she adds playfully. The report to Mama ends with a dry and haughty note about how 'it's nice to have something to look forward to in old age'. Though a minute away, she was communicating most of her feedback to Winant by letter. She wasn't exactly steering him towards the lighter things in life. She still couldn't socialise with him. He wasn't at the party she held in her flat: a send-off for Grania, who was going to South America. The gang from Medmenham and Uncle Jack (the only other Churchill) stayed until 1.30 a.m. enjoying cocktails, hotpot and sardines-en-croute. Sarah had just recovered from a bout of nettle rash and wasn't the only one. Bill Duncalfe had a breakout over large areas of his skin. In a letter to her mother, the first thing Sarah mentions is Bill having the same problem. They were in a romance.

Eighteen months earlier Gil had told Clemmie that he dreamed of marrying Sarah and she considered them compatible, even with their disparity in ages and difficult issues to surmount. She now sensed that her daughter regarded him as a friend. There is scant evidence to suggest Gil was going to make his dream a reality. For a start, he was never free, having let true love pass him by. There is no evidence that Sarah entertained the idea of marrying him. Had he been free two years before, she might have followed her heart to the altar. While they could have married eventually, she was inclined to write off this love affair. She refers to it six months later in an extraordinary letter to her father, weighing up the gains and losses of putting a career before marriage and children. She admits that she was the one who ended it. Returning to acting after a hiatus, she claimed her job was incompatible with a real marriage. She admitted she was selfish, controlling the reins, crossing over into what was traditionally a man's space and even pursuing 'glory'. In this letter she refers to a 'cage of circumstance, even affection' which hemmed her in. She needed to take flight, just as she had from Vic. For years she and Gil had been locked into a shadowy union that couldn't declare itself. She had moved on. It wasn't her fault he was depressed. He was the only one who could solve his problems.

A comment Connie made a few years later (recorded in Maurine's diary) is worth considering. This was that Gil had never seriously wanted a divorce because if he did, his credit would be stopped and he would descend into bankruptcy. With debts of $750,000, he had to think where he would be without his wife. His sense of duty to the thousands who believed in him meant that any decision regarding his private affairs was forever suspended. Despite this, when he returned to the US in the second week of September 1946 he might have come closer to divorce, given the bitter arguments at home. At this juncture it seems to have dawned on him that he had overlooked the third woman in his life. Attending another session of ECOSOC in New York on 12 September he took Maurine to lunch at the Roosevelt Hotel on East 45th Street where he complained bitterly to staff after finding that the lobby's décor, which had once projected a comforting old-world atmosphere, had undergone modernisation. He asked Maurine to read chapters from *Letter from Grosvenor Square* and also Sarah's letters with their feedback. Something clicked and this unexpected acknowledgement and the doom it conveyed proved too much in Miss Mulliner's case. Her feelings for Gil were profound and the next day she attempted suicide. Gil knew something was up. Not being able to get hold of her, he and Connie rushed to her apartment. They were just in time to get an ambulance. This episode is the only time Maurine refers to Sarah in her diary. Two years later she records a conversation with Gil's wife in which the subject of her attempted suicide came up. Not yet having seen the intimate letters from Sarah to Gil and thus unaware of the bigger picture, Mrs Winant expresses regret for regarding Maurine as Gil's 'girlfriend'. It is ironic that Connie was pointing at the wrong girl while the right girl had extricated herself.

Back in Park Lane, when Sarah penned her letter to Clementine she mentioned a drama an Italian company was filming. In July its producer Salvo D'Angelo had seen her photo in a magazine and contacted her, but Sarah laughed at the idea. The actress Maggi Johnston (much younger wife of Sarah's agent Al Parker) saw Salvo and said she would persuade her friend to take it. Sarah made a test and sent it to Mario Soldati, director at Universalia Films. The offer had a lot going for it. Top of the list was the budget: the Vatican was backing it. The downside was the film's distribution was aimed at the Mediterranean and Latin America. Well, if it was lousy, she told Clementine, nobody had to see it unless they went to the pictures in Brazil. The ease with which Sarah carried out intelligence checks suggests help from Gil. She sent the script (adapted from Fogazzaro's novel) to Marie Ozanne, who knew about 19th-century literature. 'Take it!' Marie said. After all, Eleonora Duse had wanted it for the stage, only to be turned down. *Daniele Cortis* concerns a love affair between a married noblewoman and her idealistic cousin Daniele who has returned from studying abroad and seeks election to the senate. Sarah plays Elena whose faith is tested by her senator husband's fraudulent activities. His jealousies, infidelity and violent threats require forbearance. She comes close to running away with childhood sweetheart Daniele. Fogazzaro's tale is modern enough to look with sympathy at adulterous feelings. The ending is austere with Elena's husband forgiven and marriage vows adhered to. The settings Soldati proposed to shoot in included Lake Lugano, the Alps, fin de siècle Rome and the villas of Vicenza. For someone used to shaky sets, this had the makings of a spectacular picture. If only her vetting had been as officious when it came to *Sinfonia Fatale*, the film she was doing in tandem (for the Scalera Company, made with American money and directed by Victor Stoloff).

She set off for Rome on 15 September, checking into Hotel Grande Albergo (later the Plaza) on Via del Corso. Valerie Hayes (daughter of a Barclays CEO) would be her PA and language coach. Valerie's fiancé Captain Moore was ex-PWE and had known Winston in the war. Representing London Films in Italy, he surpassed everyone in savoir-faire. Years later he was to get into serious trouble faking the work of his business partner Salvador Dalí. Other friends like Battle of Britain hero Whitney Straight, then establishing an Anglo-Italian airline, were a godsend, ferrying Sarah's letters back and forth. Her health check diagnosed a floating kidney, nephritis and cystitis. She injured herself on set picking up a heavy brass pot then a bad chill put her out of action for a week. Sarah was now painfully thin but as she pointed out, 'thinness is never bad photographically'.

The ECOSOC session completed and Gil visited Maurine at Blythewood Sanatorium in Connecticut. Soon, she would return to the SSB and a long and eventful career. A month later Gil was in London for more punishment with the book. Hearing Sarah wasn't well, he ordered things she might need, enclosed a letter and sent them via Whitney Straight. He called her in Rome saying he would come out. Sarah later said his trip lasted five minutes. In fact, he was there a few days. Mary was also coming to Rome to check on her. Sarah had heard about her sister's admirer Captain Soames (a Coldstream Guards Officer and military attaché at the British Embassy in Paris). Mary and Christopher arrived on 23 October bringing food and wine before sightseeing with Soldati whilst Sarah dined with Gil.

He tried to keep faith that December with the principles that Winston Churchill believed inviolable. When the Soviets refused to grant free navigation of the Danube, Gil recommended a conference in Vienna but got little backing in ECOSOC and resigned. For someone who had spent years fighting for basic freedoms, the refugee crisis and attitude of Russia were agonising. An exile from Grosvenor Square, he was broken inside and drinking heavily, as Jock Colville witnessed when Gil invited him to Aldford Street. Colville was burdened with FO work and by 4 a.m. was begging for his bed. Finally Jock ignored Gil's cry of 'Don't leave me.' Despite the pride he had in serving the Court of St James's, Winant neglected his memoir, preferring to read Ruskin's *Our Fathers Have Told Us*. St Jerome features in that historical travelogue and Gil must have identified with the hermit who strikes his breast with a stone. He sent Mary a copy for Christmas.

In Vicenza Sarah had the best room in the hotel. The silver trees and mountains topped with snow reminded her of Persia. Gil troubled her. She told her parents that he knew too well the 'dark secrets of human unhappiness'. The upbeat film crew was a blessing. Soldati's perfectionism meant creating an artificial Alpine springtime by sweeping snow aside and attaching fake leaves to the trees. The finished film shows his trouble was worth it. Every day on set this Groucho Marx-lookalike borrowed a hat from anyone nearby. He got creative with lighting using masses of tiny lights instead of arc lights for reflections on water, or broken pieces of mirror in huge saucer-shaped aluminium dishes. Sarah and Mario become life-long friends. She later gave Mario a copy of her children's stories for his granddaughter Chiara. Soldati found a spiral staircase perfect for a scene between 'Elena' and her husband. They only had a limited time and noticing strange items behind screens, Sarah realised the villa he had found was a brothel. Sad for the sex workers, she dedicated a poem, *The Weary Heart*, to them. Graham Greene, who worked with Soldati soon after *Daniele Cortis*, admired the Italian's lack of formality. When his play *The Living Room* toured in 1953, he and Soldati drank black velvets and got into fights. Vittorio Gassman, the 'Italian Olivier', in his fifth film, was a sensitive Daniele and Gino Cervi played Elena's husband. Soldati's team moved north, settling into another hotel on Lake Gardone.

*Sinfonia Fatale* was a contrast. As Iris, the flirty and comically frivolous artist's muse, Sarah initially played against type. She went along with it until realising the folly. She argued with Scalera, wanting to change how Iris came across. She complained about her hair being taken up several shades, making her a dead-ringer for one of Chartwell's cats. The scenes with the offending hair colour and hairstyle are the worst but weren't re-shot. Hence, they contrast with the 'natural' Iris in the latter scenes. Her co-star was Douglass Montgomery; he was badly used too. He and Sarah share a very warm and humorous scene near the end. Marina Berti is the star of *Sinfonia Fatale* and her naturalness saves the film.

Eden and the Redesdales were among the guests for Mary's wedding on 11 February 1947. Sarah flew in and met a drowsily happy Gil. Randolph couldn't attend being on a lecture tour of the US. Travelling by car, he was caught doing 80 mph. He conducted his own defence but was fined $50. He wrote to his father, admitting mistakes that had come from over-confidence and regretting the law career he had passed up in the 1930s. He still had parliamentary hopes. He kept up with events in Pamela's life. When she went to the London Clinic in March, her ex-in-laws were solicitous. He and Pam attempted to get back together but after a weekend of mishaps settled on being friends. On her flight to Italy Sarah wrote to Villiers. She spoke of the help she had given the ex-'Ambass'. His decline was so noticeable now. With a mixture of guilt and vanity she says what a 'bitter time' it was 'to see this great spirit despairing and failing because of me'. Villiers criticised her sentiment, eliciting

Sarah's response: 'I'm feminine, imperfect and vain, unreliable, changeable, inconsistent but never *indifferent*.' Villiers wrote back saying she was *exactly* this. She telegrammed that she was 'very hurt'.

This muse shaking off a master believed further opportunities might present themselves in Italy and she lent her London apartment to Al and Maggi. Taking a year's lease on an attic flat above Peter and Valerie's in Palazzo Buonaparte she became truly Roman. Before this, on 6 March, she wrote a long letter to her Pa rekindling their conversation en route to Yalta. She quotes from *Don Juan*: 'Love is of man's life a part – T'is woman's whole existence,' but admits her nature had been to go against this. The victims were Vic and Gil.

The wonderful thing about having Winston Churchill for a father is that in letters one can give vent to one's noblest philippics, ask sublime philosophical questions, admit *hubris* and make literary references. Returning to Winant (not referring to him by name, although Winston was clear who she meant) she speaks of a burning issue: the exchange of marital happiness for freedom. Yet the marital happiness she was exchanging was a fantasy. Besides, freedom, in her case, celluloid glory (if it exists), had already been chosen. She tells Papa she will feel a 'goose' if no success comes of the venture, given the happiness she has passed up. She claims her work has made her sensitive to the human heart.

The not-so-wonderful thing about having Winston Churchill for one's father becomes apparent when discussing human frailty. Conversation seldom involved him giving personal views about other people, whoever they were. Outsiders were surprised by his complete disinterest in psychology. His family, of course, had long learned to work around this. Sarah could only be direct with her father to a point and out of respect never put him on the spot. She relied on Clementine to delicately brief him on any sensitive matter. Yet, she was desperate for her father's advice and wades through poetic language as she puts her point across. Without 'naming' Winant, her former lover, she admits how much had passed, how he had gone downhill after she prised herself out of their tricky relationship. How do you deal, therefore, with casualties that fall about you? It was a decent enough question for a soldier, except that emotional arguments were not his forte. She settles on an un-feminist cry that her freedom was at 'someone else's expense'. She then admits that while she ought to have been with Gil at his lowest point, she was seeking personal success. In later years, Sarah is droll, looking back on this exchange. She tells us how her father got the biggest 'epic' ever written, after simply asking her: 'When will you be back home?'

A few days later, almost in tears, she was writing madly to Villiers. It had nothing to do with forgoing marital happiness and everything with how she looked in those terrible scenes in *Sinfonia Fatale*. She also mentions her disappointment in Bill Duncalfe (a failed experiment). She refers to her mission to help Gil with his book, wanting to repay the Ambass for being there in the 'darkest and worst of all days' when she was trapped with Vic. Sarah's genuine love for Winant shows itself here. She returned to London on 20 March and gave him more assistance, later telling her father how Gil spoke a lot about him. Gil wasn't at her side at a dinner party given by cousin Johnny (then married to Mary Cookson). Johnny, Pebin and Clarissa had recently lost their father and there was talk about Winston's tearful reaction and demands regarding which hymns should be sung at Jack's funeral. Jim Lees-Milne, whom Diana had liked years before, was present. Now secretary of the National Trust, he was charming as ever. In his diary he remarked that Sarah didn't take after her father's side of the family and found her 'prettier than her sister'. Clementine's family intrigued him: only ten days later Jim was peeling off gossip from Lady Ilchester about the Churchills and Mitfords.

Sarah and Diana accompanied their parents to Paris, arriving at Le Bouget on 10 May with Papa giving his 'V' sign. At Les Invalides PM Ramadier presented him with the French Military Medal. Churchill's opinion of the USSR had completely changed from that expressed to the Commons in early 1945. He no longer believed in Russia's 'wish to live in honourable friendship and equality'. Privately, he supported a nuclear strike against them while the US still had the upper hand. He said this to Styles Bridges (Winant's successor as New Hampshire Governor). Since his Zurich speech the previous year, a United Europe Committee had grown up and Duncan leapt into it, aiming to increase European cooperation and trying to enlist Noël Coward in the movement. The Churchill Cup, engraved both with Winston's signature and lines from speeches, was a Vic Oliver initiative. Vic had a reunion with Lilly. Now running a fashion accessories business, she stayed with Phyllis at Nelson House, Dolphin Square. That February she headed for Paris where the *New Look* was all the rage.

On 11 June Winston was at Mary's cottage in Brighton with Sarah and Maggi Johnston. He was recovering from a hernia operation. There had been a terrible fire at Korda's Rome office in which several people were killed. Peter and Valerie got out at the last minute, the former jumping from a window. *Sinfonia Fatale* came out that month and surprisingly won a prize at the Lugano Festival. Her father was anxious to see *Daniele Cortis* and Korda arranged a special viewing with Sarah present to explain the plot. She then went to the Brussels Film Festival on 27 June to attend this film's premiere. Vic was following his ex-wife's career and sent Winston and Clementine a cutting that talked about her dignified and commanding performance. While *Daniele Cortis* was highly acclaimed abroad, British exhibitors felt it was 'undesirable and un-commercial' with its long passionate discussions and Catholic message of sacrifice. Sarah talked to Villiers about drowning herself in 'self-criticism and several glasses of gin!' As well as proving she had a face for the cinema, the film conveys her empathy, poignancy and humour. Her lonely visage reflects in the black window of a train carriage when Elena and her conscience travel by night. In an interview she admitted: 'This is the best role I have had.' It's easy to see why Václav Vích won the *Nastro d'Argento* in 1947 for best photography. The costumes are beautifully understated, something no Hollywood film could have achieved. Italian films took greater risks in camera angles and lighting arrangements. Sarah has emotion in every limb, poetry in gesture and earthiness in manner. Her love for Gil made this possible. A Roman writer said her performance was so warm and vital 'it seems impossible that she is English'. The most glowing review argued that Sarah's performance justifies the 'universal rule that the biggest stars are still immigrants'. It asks if Sarah Churchill could be the 'Garbo of Europe'. The glorious music was by Giovanni 'Nino' Rota, later winner of the Academy Award for *The Godfather Part II* as well as enriching works by Fellini and Visconti. One day, when the neglected *Daniele Cortis* receives critical recognition, people might be inclined to say that Sarah got one over Garbo. Sadly, the film can be hard to obtain. Sarah's father intervened in order to alert Sarah about a colour test for *Bonnie Prince Charlie*. She was later put up for *A Sort of Traitors* based on the Balchin novel, but stage work would often get in the way of films.

Gil had made progress with his book and Maurine saw him on his return to the US. It was Valentine's Day 1947 and she came to his hotel in DC where they lunched. Gil took out a platinum watch and gave it to her as a gift. He was travelling back to Britain on the *Queen Elizabeth* on 7 July with Connie to attend John Corson's wedding. Seeing Gil with his wife seems to have prompted Sarah's poem *Love in Hyde Park*. It's about seeing unashamed couples entwined in the grass and subtly points to an affair just a stone's throw away but one condemned to the shade. She devoted it to Mario Soldati. Sarah arranged an interview for him with Evelyn Waugh who stupidly wrote him off as not Catholic enough. Mario's new proposal was a life of Cardinal Newman for the big screen.

A tiny rustic scene – a wall relief on the outer wall of Gil's old home – made Sarah think of him as the running herald who bears a hopeful message. He was in Concord and it was Miss Mulliner he was running to. Maurine called and suggested he put Orol on the phone. Gil's housekeeper couldn't tell her the problem, with Gil standing by. He also spoke to Sarah long-distance suggesting he was going to end it all. He craved company, asking for things that were impossible with her so far away. From Rome, she talked him out of killing himself at least once. He made no mention of his financial situation. He only talked of punishment. Connie had taken control of the finances.

The notes Bellush made after his interview with Maurine tell us that Connie experienced his suicide threats. Gil argued with her and in one violent scene 'put a pistol in his throat and threatened to shoot' if she didn't do what he wanted. His housekeeper finally talked him out of doing something awful. He saw sense and the urge subsided, but anything can happen in such a moment.

Since meeting Sarah at Johnny's, Jim Lees-Milne had kept in touch and hoped to see her during his study visit to Rome. He observed Sarah walking past the Teatro di Marcello, commenting on her 'translucent as alabaster' skin and the galleon-like thrusting movement of her walk that was not inelegant. Why she was 'breasting the storms of life', he didn't know. At her most relaxed in cafes, tucking into turkey in bacon garnished with cheese and washing it down with red wine, she intrigued him. She had never bothered to see St Peter's or the Pantheon. She lived in the present and cared little for a past that wasn't her own. Jim saw as much of her as he could. Her door opened, revealing her tiny two-room apartment under the eaves. She picked him up, driving confidently through the city before dropping him off. Out strolling he noticed how indifferent she was to the stir she caused in the menfolk. He wrote of her 'Botticelli hair' in similar vein to earlier writings about dream girls like Diana Mitford. Both he and Sarah were outsiders to the hunting and shooting world. He feared she might, one day, be a victim of somebody's manipulation.

The subject of combat and weaponry often leaves women cold. Judging by the frequency in which bullets were inlaid in objects in Gil's home such as bookends, cigarettes lighters, tables and ornaments, Maurine, in her diary, asks herself if these indicated an unhealthy obsession. At different times of Gil's life, bullets left a haunting legacy. As well as fighting in the skies in the Great War he shot a sniper in the woods – an eerie episode he never forgot. His second youngest brother Cornelius, whose military career was tumultuous, was reported as dying from a fall in New York in 1928. Maurine had heard that he had been shot in a speakeasy, although this was never admitted. Gil had employed a detective to find the killer but when he was found, he let the man go free, perhaps to avoid publicity.

Everything glowed in autumn. One of the chandeliers at Palazzo Buonaparte became a harvest moon while the Bow Hills of Concord blazed in russets, bright greens and yellows as November fell upon New Hampshire. The colours would find Gil indoors and lead him outside from Pleasant Street towards St Paul's Campus where he had inspired pupils. His secretary Eileen Mason was staying at Concord and had sent the completed *Letter From Grosvenor Square* for publication. The book opens in the form of a letter with the ambassador in London, telling a friend in the US he's leaving the Embassy soon. It was important that the book's title and opening read like this: frozen in time. The publishers had printed and sent a copy to Concord's post office for collection on Monday 3 November. The 58-year-old Winant didn't go out that day but remained in his large house. Mrs Winant was not at home. She only lived there half the year. Gil had made a reservation to fly to see her the next day with a copy of the book. Since making that reservation, he had entered the tunnel that today is called cognitive constriction. Eileen was clearing up in the office and Orol was downstairs (having collected Mr Winant's untouched dinner tray). He never made it out to the post office and spent the day in his dressing gown. The hills were coloured blue under dark grey. Night fell in John Junior's old bedroom as Gil kneeled by a desk, trying the long number again, elbows on a chair. He didn't know it was early morning there. He got through. She tried to reason with him. He drew the automatic up to his right temple, his fingers closing forcibly on the trigger. There is a wrong and a right time to do it and this was the right time. He died after an hour.

'I will pay my debts tomorrow' was something Winston was once overheard saying to the director of a Paris casino. Gil thought along the same lines. When it came to paying he was periodically in trouble. Spending money on others incurred the costs. For this reason, his most humble associates came to his aid. Orol Mears had produced her savings to deter his debt collectors but his wife would help no more. He had, she pointed out, benefitted from the sale of his mother's New York house but had spent the proceeds. After Winant's death, it became public that he had bequeathed sums to his personal staff. Isaac King, Gil's last chauffeur, was left $5,000 and later admitted: 'The poor man had no money, there were no bequeaths. In fact he owed us all for back wages. But we all loved him and never would have left him.' His probate record in England later revealed a paltry £322. In fact, an oil well Gil owned in Texas was still a viable source of wealth. Maurine believed that had he been alerted to this it might have staved off the crisis, saving his life. The next day Governor Charles Dale broadcast the news. In England Eden collected Gil's son, taking him to his home. On 5 November a New England paper gave the time of death as 7.45 p.m. adding dramatic details such as the fact that two souvenir pistols were involved. The first failed to discharge and he had to reach for another. That day a service was held miles away at St Paul's, Boston. England's King and Queen sent condolences, as did Attlee, Bevin and Eden. Thinking of the generation who had gone through the war, Anthony talked about the difficulty for future historians to properly assess the work of one 'whose steadfastness was unshakeable'.

Jim Lees-Milne called at 55 Park Lane on 7 November. Sarah was ready but he was shocked to see her so thin and wan. She explained that for three nights in succession she hadn't slept but wouldn't give the reason. The two went to the Curzon cinema in Mayfair to see the Italian film *To Live in Peace*.

Sarah would have laughed through the tears in one scene with the idiotic townspeople prematurely believing the war was over. Its comment on the futility of war would have struck a chord. Jim insisted that she stay at his top-floor flat at 20 Thurloe Square. One minute she was falling asleep, the next chattering away. She couldn't rest. On Armistice Day Sarah wrote to both her parents with thoughts about Gil: a man who believed in the 'goodness of the human race' and whose strength had been expended in serving the needs of others. If he had kept back just a little for himself, she felt, 'An ounce would have stopped him.' Guilt set in. He might have been twice her age when they indulged in their secret love affair but he was innocent. She had claimed a place in the private life of someone who spent most of his time in solid service to mankind. She hadn't stayed the course and was ignorant of the financial pressures he had faced. Gil's memorial service at St Paul's Cathedral in London on 19 November brought it home. She didn't believe she deserved to go and turned to her father, asking him 'what place or right' she had 'to mingle any more in any remaining affairs of his'. She had been cruel ending the affair. She later expressed guilt for Gil's 'agony and the part I played in it'. Winston had initially resisted going, but a grieving Clementine resorted to begging and sternly pointing out that his absence 'would strike a chill in the hearts of all his friends'. Both joined their daughter and mourners in saying farewell to John G. Winant.

He was a married man. There was nothing more to say. She once mentioned something Winant had said to her. His words explained something of their secret relationship: 'It's all part of a soldier's business to have known great things and be content with silence.' Years passed and even with close friends she would bottle up and avoid talking about the nature of this relationship. It was strictly off-limits. Then, if she got very drunk, she would subvert her rule and admit the *final horror*. When the older Sarah produced her 'candid' autobiography she omitted to talk about Gil. He was someone from long ago: just another person from a time she was very young. Yet, she wrote more poems with him in mind than anyone else, channelling feelings of bitter frustration and cynicism (*And Yet*), regret and love (*Of Love and War*) and desolation (*Sometimes at Night*). Had Gil not died, Sarah would have remained his friend for life. He became part of her complex thoughts about the war. Her short poem *Reappraisal* was written much later – a refusal to sentimentalise the Second World War with the speaker watching a ghost ship sailing away from the harbour after cutting the cord – happy to lose those spirits and remain on terra firma. The funeral pyre receives the 'fruitless desire' of her relationship with Gil. She bids farewell to it, disbelieving of its value. After all, 'The world that was ours is a world that is ours no more.' In the hollowness of peacetime she was free of her *cage of affection*. The day after

Gil's service she was at Janet Attlee's wedding at Ellesborough Church in her bold hat and stripy ribbons.

Randolph's lecture tour took him to Australia and New Zealand where his opinions met with controversy. He went on to Washington and on 6 February 1948, on *Meet the Press*, took on aggressive journalists. He explained that he wasn't against all forms of socialism, saying that parts of the US's infrastructure were run by state authorities. The British were giving Attlee a chance. He said it was possible for Jews and Arabs to co-exist so long as the Jews didn't bring in too many people. Randie was particularly good when they asked if in exchange for the Marshall Plan, the holdings of European investors in American enterprises should be liquidated. He told them that the Plan was to put Europe on its feet. Leaving people in a state of beggary was myopic. He pointed out that British businessmen liquidated four to five billion dollars' worth of assets in Lend-Lease to afford aircraft and ammunition long before the US came into the war. The loss of his country's gold and foreign currency reserves funded America's surge into economic boom. He rubbished a story about Winston being drunk when he gave the Fulton speech.

Sarah continued to see Jim, cooking for him on the evening of 7 December after they went see Chaplin's *Monsieur Verdoux*. Three days later she accompanied her Pa to Marrakesh: a place for resting, painting, writing and ignoring critics. Viridian oil paint and a copy of *Letter from Grosvenor Square* were among Winston's Christmas stocking gifts from Sarah. She wanted to know if he could help her get its frontispiece portrait substituted. The image of Gil wasn't to her liking. Thanks to culinary wizard Joseph Genarro, the food at la Mamounia was exceptional and local friends including Thami El Glaoui saw to it that each night there was an entertainment held in honour of Winston and Sarah. Villiers David, who owned a property in Agadir, was passing through. He called to see Sarah and was introduced to Churchill, evincing a reaction that might be termed biologically dry. Seeing Villiers shockingly judged at face value and for being a Jew, Sarah went on to give Papa a verbal thrashing, writing chillingly soon after: 'If you love me, do not tear and destroy the people I care for.' She pointed out that he had passed up the opportunity to talk to someone genuinely knowledgeable about painting. Such an angry episode was nonetheless followed by a remarkable demonstration of Winston's love for Sarah.

She took off from Marrakesh on a plane bound for Lisbon via Casablanca on a night beset by heavy storms. Churchill was so fraught he could think of nothing but his beloved Mule and conacted every embassy and consulate south of Paris. Many tears were shed when he got her on the phone finally in Lisbon. What had provoked Winston particularly was when *News Review* journalists linked his daughter and Villiers romantically. He didn't mean the things he said. That storm in a teacup was silly, given that Sarah was reported saying in that same paper: 'It's a change for them to get me *engaged* to one of my friends. Usually it's to someone I don't even know.' One who had fallen for her was Jim Lees-Milne, then fretting about how he could he marry on his current salary.

Connie was part incredulous, part bitter. She struggled to come to terms with Gil's action. Too often he had made threats he hadn't acted upon. She sought out a reluctant Maurine to help her sort out Gil's papers. His Girl Friday later wrote of the trial it had been listening to Connie between August and October 1948, but she was determined to help preserve her ex-boss's paperwork. When Mrs Winant sold Pleasant Street to the State Government, Orol remained with her, anxious about her seeing the batch of 'London letters' that her working-class brother had hitherto stored in his home. These were the personal letters Sarah had sent Gil. Initially, Connie didn't think getting them mailed over was worth the expense, but after giving consent for Gil's papers to be stored at the Roosevelt Library, she decided to retrieve them. They arrived on 14 October and Orol was frantic. Connie had already burned letters and seeing now the position Sarah had in Gil's life, more letters saw the same fate. What remained was archived. Suicide was considered a sin and it took 20 years for permission to be given for Gil to be re-interred in the consecrated cemetery of St Paul's School. In 1953 Connie married scientist Captain Marion Eppley, the widowed husband of her sister. For years he ran a Research Foundation producing scientific precision instruments. They lived in Newport, Rhode Island, and later Long Island, where a Joseph Wright portrait of George Washington hung on the wall.

Sarah kept her Park Lane residence close by Gil's old home until the end of 1949. Visualised in her poem *Of Love and War*, the left-behind lover gazes up at the window of what was once a 'celestial portal'. One must overcome guilt by looking upon one's joy and derring-do with the warmth it deserves. She kept in touch with Fred, Gil's youngest brother, and others in the family. Two months later she was within 80 miles of Concord.

11

# He Took Me for Life

According to Stanley Lief, guru at Champney's, hot baths followed by icy cold ones got rid of nettle rash. In February 1948 in between dismal fruit dinners, Sarah and Diana trekked through snow to the cinema. The name Borenius came up when Villiers called, mentioning a book by Von Hassell, who tried to overthrow Hitler. Diana was on burglar alert and broke her regime to return home while Sarah, anxious to look her best for her new play, *The Barretts of Wimpole Street*, stayed to the bitter end. Alec Clunes and Maggi Johnston played the lovers united by poetry. Neat whisky on the palate – an old-fashioned remedy 'Papa would approve of' – was employed when Sarah's wisdom teeth suddenly caused her agony. Thanks to that 'delicious anaesthesia', rehearsals were fun. She played Henrietta, the sister whose gaiety won't be stifled by an unhappy home although 'Mr Barrett' was hardly tyrannical given Tom Walls' ironic playing. In her dressing room Sarah got busy with her own *Pursuit of Love*: writing down family anecdotes both funny and extraordinary. She tried getting others to do the same. The debate in Winston's studio between her brother and father must be preserved, she argued. Papa declined, then surprised her, producing an account that Randolph said he 'couldn't have bettered'.

Her adoration of Villiers, then minding her flat, was unusual. Longing for 12 uninterrupted hours with him: 'Champagne, caviar (to hell with Russia), six hours for me to taste and then if there is anything left of you six hours for you to talk,' was a typical flourish. 'I should cover myself in perfume and jewels and occasionally flutter my eyelids,' she swooned, laughing about how bad he was at fitting into surroundings: 'I can step out of concrete and chromium but you do not look right doing so.' That he liked boys didn't matter. He was discreet but she knew about his adventures in the tenderloin districts of Fez and Tangiers and even tried to help fix him up with a certain

Marcus at the BBC. They intertwined their thoughts and non-physical love under a private canopy. The 'crush' was enough to make Winston jealous. He scoffed at his daughter's insistence that they were friends, referring to Villiers as her 'true husband'. When *Barretts* came to the Garrick, critics were lukewarm. Sarah's Henrietta was spirited, although the Victorian hoops and girlish skips weren't in her line. They played to full houses. Winston and Clementine attended on 21 May.

That month saw a chance reacquaintance with Antony Beauchamp, the photographer she had met eight years earlier. Within months of meeting her in 1940, Antony joined the army. His commanding officer recommended him for Sandhurst and a commission. He scraped through and surprised Cecil Beaton by revealing that Sandhurst hadn't been harsh. Bribing his sergeant major with whisky, he would slip off to luxury hotels like Great Fosters, where most of his time was spent. In May 1941 he joined the Royal Leicestershire Regiment, its battalions serving in India, Burma and the Far East. The army made use of infantrymen with photographic skills but someone high up, either Louis Mountbatten or Robin Duff, a lightning rod of the arts and trailblazing BBC correspondent, furthered his career. In 1940, after Antony sketched Lady Mountbatten for *Tatler*, commissions kept coming. His 'Crayon and Camera' composites, contrasting views of a celebrity, were highly praised. His becoming 'Official War Artist to the 14th Army in Burma' was a strange leap and he said he little deserved it. Antony knew all the Fleet Street and BBC correspondents. In 1942 he was part of a large party at Humayun's Tomb in Delhi. His Burma colleagues included Stuart Emeny, Martin Moore, Randolph's friend Alaric Jacob and John Deane Potter. In February 1943, he joined these four on a three-day trek tailing the 14th through the jungle to the western banks of the Chindwin River (a 200-mile journey) before returning by foot to India. Few of the men they followed returned from conflict. They endured Japanese snipers, intense mental strain and exposure to a catalogue of disease. A 'Forgotten Army', they took their name from the Chind-te (heraldic griffin-like figures guarding Burmese temples). Even Antony and his pals had it tough, isolated without guides. Beauchamp luckily had a revolver to see off a ferocious wild boar.

The first floor of 23 Hertford Street had been his studio and home since 1946. Framed images lined the hallway: familiar faces of debs Sarah knew before the war. She sighed on seeing his study of Leslie Howard. Antony had been brought up in artists' studios. His mother worked just round the corner. Despite churning out 'glamour' stuff to pay the bills, he was striving to find the perfect technique and model. He wasn't doing badly despite competition from Sterling Henry Nahum, 12 years his senior and always with a classier address. Baron (as he was known) had a love of laughter and a passion for sports. Through contacts in the ballet world Mountbatten became Baron's client in 1935 and soon he and Lady M were personal friends. The Dukes and Duchesses of Kent and Gloucester, and even the King and Queen, wanted to be photographed by Baron. Antony, whose contacts were already excellent, craved similar patronage. The two photographers were rivals but great friends. Both were refreshingly undeferential in attitude, all the while masters of illusion; keen to perpetuate social distinctions in a market powered by snobbery.

He couldn't believe that the woman at the Dorchester was the same rigid sitter who came to his Cleveland Row studio. Her eyes had humour and womanly sympathy. He knew then that marrying her was only a matter of time. Sarah liked his directness: 'I needed Antony's forceful, vital, uncomplicated approach,' was how she put it, to 'challenge me back into the fight.'

'Come to Chartwell to meet my parents,' she asked him. Her Papa would be interested to hear of his dealings with General Wingate. This was 13 June, the day after the play closed, so last minute that Antony hadn't time to go to the barber. He attempted a selfie trim and cut so much off he had to retouch a bald patch with charcoal. He met Winston while he was feeding his carp, using weird sounds to attract them and rejoicing as they raced towards him. Antony showed interest in the waterfalls and Tilden's improvements (his brother Clive was an architect so he knew about such matters). Next day Sarah told Villiers she was changing the pattern of her life. Having reverted to the diffident person of old, it was time to snap out of that. Here was a guy who was real and she wasn't going to hide her natural impulses even if this 'new compulsion to walk with truth' was sure to invite age-old confrontations. She felt motherly towards Beauchamp. Why shouldn't he have a key to her flat? Villiers could hardly fail to notice the lover who, as Sarah put it, 'completed the liberation of [her] soul'. She placated her RAF friend by saying that it was *he* who began this process.

Sarah took Jeff, her lady's maid of ten years, to Lyme Regis where she was making a film. Norman Wooland, the lead in *All Over the Town*, knew about printing having once designed posters. He played demobbed RAF fighter Nat Hearn, reclaiming his old job as a journalist at *The Clarion* only to see free speech as ever stifled and the palms of local big shots greased to keep the paper afloat. Nat is sympathetic to socialist Britain, believing that housing and town development require public consultation. He desires a more even society and considers emigration. His wish to modernise places him firmly in the Britain of 1949. A woman, Sally Thorpe, has been doing his job very well. Sally's gripe isn't about playing second fiddle to a man. She knows she's clever and won't be patronised. She just hates a town where hypocrisy is rife. She stands up to employers and defends ex-WAAFs displaying signs of liberation. Nat falls in love with her and exposes a corrupt housing plan and risks the paper's survival. Sally was perfect for Sarah: mischievous, intelligent, daring and a gal you would depend on in a crisis. Thrilled to be in Lyme despite her responsibility as dresser, Jeff was sent out with coupons to get 'off the peg' frocks from Horrocks, the Preston cotton firm, for Sally's outfits. Sarah and Jeff were at the Langmoor and at the close of each day the cast met up and traded stories about interesting townspeople and played a match against a local team at Oxton cricket ground. The rest of the film was made at Pinewood. Filming the tense crisis at the printing works, Sarah's line, 'Isn't there anything we can do?' caused a laugh when a large arc lamp on the set belched and fizzled out making a pathetic moaning sound.

The great Beauchamp debate continued and the cynical Villiers poked a needle in her balloon. In early July Sarah questioned herself but asked where do you get if you never take a chance? 'We cannot buy the future any more than free oneself completely from the past.' Antony's proposal prompted this. She was giddy and disbelieving. He was thirty, energetic and exciting. 'You must have done something very bad to be landed with me,' was her line, the door swinging between self-deprecation and dangerous vanity. One letter has her stirred into rebellion: 'To think I would not face the "ire" of my family.' She was happy for him to flip that door off its hinges. Clementine showed no inkling of Sarah's dilemma, writing on 19 July to tell her about a fancy dress ball at the American Embassy where Eden twirled her round the dance floor. Princess Margaret danced a cancan with four friends, and Prince Philip and Princess Elizabeth made a surprising pair: he a waiter and she, a 'Nippy' from Lyons Corner House.

Matters of the heart, from the time of Diana Witherby (now literary critic on *Horizon*) to Gil, had never come easy for Sarah and she reveals her essential loneliness: 'People do not know how much they take of me when I become their friend ... my heart is like a harbour when the tide is out, when they leave me; it becomes an empty space.' 'Professor Beauchamp' supplanted Villiers as Sarah's editorial consultant. When the Westminster press privately printed a slim edition of *The Empty Spaces* in 1948 Antony 'reviewed' it, scrawling annotations against mawkish lines and making no bones about what wasn't good. He gives marks out of ten for each with rude comments. Sarah's flowery *Who Can Say* scored nil points. *Leave Me My Grief* incurred a two-point penalty because of a repeating word. Another poem, *Song,* was trashed with 'Oh come off it!' plastered over the page in pencil. His interpretation of *My Heart's A Secret Place* (about Gil) is interesting and the poem scored nine. He picks up on the fact that Sarah and her lover have a different outlook. Antony's comment, 'You are obviously about to give the wretch the TREATMENT,' must have made her chuckle. He gives her *ACW2 To Pilot Officer* ten points and says 'It's the ruddy blinking tops for me.'

After he left her building she watched him from her window, checking to see if he would look up and wave – as if it proved affection. When he disappeared without a glance, she produced *Lullaby* – about love being in the eye of the foolish beholder. Still, she rushed to do things for him. No sooner had her father met Beauchamp, Sarah was begging his consent to have the photographer make studies of his hands (for a magazine feature – Antony's idea). Sarah's effusive letter to her Pa has mules' hooves doodled at the bottom. It was a vain hope. Liaising with siblings over arrangements for her parent's fortieth, she got permission for Antony to rifle through albums to illustrate a commemorative sketch. Sarah saw her parents before they left to stay with the Windsors at Château de la Croë, then fell into secretive ways, taking a small flat with Antony on Brighton's seafront.

Randolph had met June Osborne through his literary friends and they married at Caxton Hall on 2 November, his three sisters cheering him with Brian (June's brother), Eleanor and Major Morris-Keating (June's relative) at the Savoy reception. The couple went to Biarritz, then moved into 12 Catherine Place. Randolph was writing for *The Evening News* and June shared in the care of young Winston. The boy had left Gibbs' School for Institut Le Rosey with Pamela beginning a life in Paris. In 1948 Duncan Sandys continued his European Unity campaign at Gstaad, Montreux and The Hague. He and Diana went to New York and Washington in June and met Truman. That November, he stood as Conservative candidate for Streatham.

On 30 November Sarah was on TV's *Designed for Women* giving tips on quick and exciting supper dishes and in early December hobnobbed with local Conservative societies. She hoped Papa would lunch at 'Mule's stable' and she and Diana arranged to take Mama to a revue on 8 December featuring pal Diana J. Churchill at the Lyric, Hammersmith. Winston came to the 'stable' and Clementine convened for evening cocktails. Antony Beauchamp was present at both. Jim Lees-Milne, invited to the theatre night, described him as a 'dark gigolo with a scar', adding in his diary that he assumed Beauchamp would marry Sarah. Jim thought Mrs Churchill unchanged since his early visits to Chartwell (still disapproving, 'as though she feared to touch or swallow dirt'). Sarah was her father's companion that Christmas at Monte Carlo's Hotel de Paris. Allowed to bring a friend, she opted for Antony and no opinions were expressed. Seeing his former ADC in thrall made Winston behave atrociously. She and Antony or 'Tony' (as she now called him) kept escaping to Villefranche to enjoy its old harbour and restaurants. Sarah couldn't believe the 'point blank rudeness and unkindness', prompting her most sarcastic letter to Papa to date. Tony, she stated, had been invited. Why insult him when he could easily have privately told her he disliked him? While he wounded this 'young man of considerable dignity and spirit', if he thought it would change the way she felt, he was mistaken. 'Am I not a human being?' she asked, ending with the excellent 'But I see now how right I have been to build a life for myself and arm myself with four good *hoofs* and a crusty carapace, for the slings and arrows of family life are sharp indeed.' Sarah won the day and the 'Great Man' in his white linen suit stood up when Tony came to the table. Mule and her beau could accompany him to Eden Roc, where he painted. Tony's knowing an old hand at roulette helped. This was Prince Radziwill, then living in sumptuous exile. Tony got Winston to try the Radziwill system and the chips started to stack up. Mr C insisted he join a gathering given by the Duke and Duchess of Windsor. The Duke was taken with Tony and they discussed photography. Sarah briefed her Papa not to give information about Beauchamp to them if asked. It might compromise him, she said, adding: 'No one knows better than you how to say nothing.' What the withheld information was is unclear.

Sarah rehearsed a play by Roland Pertwee due to open in Cardiff, before going on to Wimbledon and the Q Theatre. Set in the antiques world, *House of the Sand* has Sarah's character standing up to a blackmailer. Fellow actors were Kenneth Kent, David Peel, Helen Haye and Hugh Hastings. Winston and Clementine saw it in April 1949 and people threw their hats in the air and patted Churchill on the back. *All Over the Town*, meanwhile, was released to good reviews and part of J. Arthur Rank's strategy was to send Sarah to the US and Canada for openings in Rank cinemas. Her film and tour would be promoted by a good magazine story. Walter Graebner, chief of the London bureau of *Time* and *Life* and liaising with Winston over the serialization of his memoirs, had visited Sarah in Lyme. Keen to help Tony, Sarah persuaded *Life* to use him as its cover photographer. Tony obliged with an eye-grabbing stroboscopic image.

Just a couple of weeks later, at the opening of *Sauce Tartare* at Cambridge Theatre, he asked about the girl 'with the eyes', thinking she'd do for a Marshall and Snelgrove department store shoot. When Audrey Hepburn turned up at Hertford Street with her short hairstyle, leggings and absence of vanity, Tony emptied the room of its gilded furniture to emphasise her unadorned, gamine presence. Audrey couldn't afford his rates but Tony told her not to worry, even recommending an agent. She never forgot his kindness and the images became iconic.

A more expensive kind of beauty in a full-length fur, Sarah had made four personal appearances in Canada by the time she wrote to Papa on 3 May 1949. Their letters reveal her tour had a 'Conference' quality, replete with strategic meetings benefitting Winston. Sarah was to give Alexander of Tunis a formal 'salute' at Government House, Ottawa, to meet Bernie and courier a painting to J. C. Hall, now favourable terms had been discussed about rights to reproduce

Winston's paintings on greetings cards. Fanny Holtzman, attorney to big names from Hollywood and Broadway, boasted five million pre-orders. She was Hall's go-between. In exchange, Sarah asked Winston to write some lines about his earlier career as a journalist for use at Toronto's Press Ball and she insisted that the name *Mrs Oliver* be dropped from all future official gatherings. How different it would have been, had she taken Vic's advice and gone to Hollywood ten years before. She was no longer a starlet. Still, regrets were few. Because of Papa she had walked with destiny and he was investing in her career.

On the day she saw Alex, *Life* magazine with its Beauchamp cover hit the bookstalls and made her a celebrity. The machine of fame produced an offer for her to play *Tracy Lord* in a stage revival of *The Philadelphia Story*. Her heroine Gertrude Lawrence (whom she met through Miss Holtzman) encouraged her to play the strong-willed divorcee set to marry again. Sarah hastily said farewell to close friends like Villiers (whom she had been championing at the BBC).

Life was quieter for Clementine, even if the work on 28 Hyde Park Gate, meetings for the National Hostels Committee, chairmanship of the Trust and panic about her husband returning to the political fray were hardly stress-free. She was happy for her daughter. Unfortunately, Sarah's film had been subjected to the super-tax rate. Her Italian earnings were spent and she owed £2,000 in tax dating back to 1946. She tried ignoring it, but prior to leaving in late August, told Tony. Intent on pursuing her, he was arranging his own travel to the States.

On 11 September, without telling Sarah, Tony wrote a long letter to Mrs Churchill forwarding demands from the taxman he had picked up from Sarah's flat, saying he feared the press would blow this up given the chance. He acknowledges she barely knew him but goes on to voice many opinions. He was rather forcing a reaction, which is something few dared. It's a repetitive letter with the tone of someone currying favour. His tone veers towards the chauvinistic when he assumes expertise about the shelf life of actresses and comments on Sarah's limitations. He even confronts Clementine about the communication problem preventing Sarah from coming clean to her and Winston about her financial woes. Where he goes wrong is sounding rather like a controlling husband.

Clementine acted immediately, getting Bracken's advice on the tax and writing to her daughter in Pennsylvania, telling her that the Trust would bail her out. Randolph's debts were a greater concern and she was already settling £8,000 of these. She invited Tony over for a lunch with Mr C in a gesture that echoed her first response to Vic Oliver. It seemed friendly but it was like the spider charming the fly. She must have known that a marriage to Beauchamp was coming. Sarah had written on 29 August saying she was near to taking the plunge and would confirm the when and where. On 3 September Sarah wrote the same to her father. When Tony visited he was shaking with nerves. He later told his young cousin Henry Sandon about asking the Great Man for his daughter's hand. 'How did they ever come round?' he was asked. 'It was the quality of the photographs that did it,' Tony revealed, which implies that if there was one way to impress Winston, it was artistic skill.

Rank executive Jock Lawrence and his wife Mary let Sarah make 910 Fifth Avenue her home. Jock, who had met the Churchills while working at Ike's London HQ, got her an agent, Howard Hoyt, and soon Sarah was heard exchanging banter on air on popular shows like *Tex and Jinx*. One weekend at Princeton's Drama Festival she watched actors at McCarter Theatre, and joined in the straw-hat drama lying limpid in the arms of playwright and summer circuit champion Harold J. Kennedy in a scene directed by Tallulah Bankhead. At Cannon Green behind Nassau Hall she saw the 1840 firearm that great-grandfather Leonard Jerome rescued after the Battle of Princeton. As it was the university Gil dropped out of, she had a friendly ghost for company.

Phillip Barry's high society comedy had revived Kate Hepburn's career in 1939. Her 'Tracy Lord' was impossible to beat, but Sarah gave her all in the Theatre Guild's revival. Jeffrey Lynn, who had tested for Ashley Wilkes in *Gone with the Wind*, was the raffish first husband who disrupts Tracy's wedding plans. He was a joy to work with, as were Alex Clark and Frances Tannehill (married stalwarts of the American stage). At one point Kate's brother Dick was in the cast. Sarah writes to Tony from Wellesley College, after the show began in New England. 'Who was he flirting with?' she jokes and brags that Jock will get him prominent clients. Yet after a 'deluge of unbearable letters', with Tony fixated by 'intrigues' perpetrated by Al Parker and Maggi, she's weary of his scolds. He has to calm down. All she wanted was for them to lie together on a beach somewhere, where Tony 'could get brown and fat'.

There was another *Philadelphia Story* doing the circuits with Diana Barrymore (tragic daughter of John). At Fayetteville NY Summer Stock Theatre that June, Pat Crowley was Dinah alongside Miss Barrymore. Her agent got her into the second *Philadelphia Story* with Sarah Churchill opening the last week of August 1949 at Connecticut's Westport Country Playhouse. Pat recalls:

> We ran for a week and one evening Richard Rodgers and his family came and we were told he loved it. Miss Churchill was a dream to work with – perfect in the role, friendly and gracious to one and all. So that started my working in 'the business.' What a start – what a summer for a 14-year-old kid from a coal mining town in Pennsylvania!

A reporter from the *Westport Herald* noted Sarah's British reserve. He described her voice as 'closely resembling a monotone pitched over a high C' and lacking the histrionics of Papa Churchill. Nevertheless, he praised her 'magnificent acting ability' and mentioned that Jeffrey Lynn played his part Hollywoodian fashion, 'hogging the camera whenever chance permits (and sometimes when it doesn't)'. He had much praise for Pat Crowley who went on to appear in almost every popular 1950s and 1960s TV show, from *The Twilight Zone* to *The Man from U.N.C.L.E.*, then guesting in *Dynasty*, *Frasier* and *Friends*. Touring was tough and Sarah worried about flagging. Yet, she felt no difficulty, regarding her work as 'the only serenity I have ever known'. Between playing the Casino, Newport and Maryland's Olney Theatre on 27 September, this wandering player met Gil's younger brother Fred. New England looked verdant even in a drought, and the sheer racket made by the tree frogs and crickets was memorable. When Harry Truman and his daughter Margaret came to the Olney's benefit performance it was a boost.

Tony arrived in the States completely shattered. He saw the play the same evening. Five days before, he had written to Clementine seeking her blessing. He said he wanted a family. Quite sweetly he told her that any drawback to being a few years her daughter's junior was more than compensated by the strength he drew from her. Not looking well, Tony travelled in the retinue of this busy actress as the company went on to Atlanta. Jeffrey Lynn's friends suggested he go to Sea Island (on the Georgia coast) for some rest.

In her next letter to her parents Sarah apologised for the tax business and confirmed her wish to marry. She gushed at the prospect of a home with Antony. The light and dark Mule treading in opposite directions illustrating her letter seemed an unconscious recognition of her contrary nature. Tony carried a heart-shaped diamond ring and right away knew Sea Island was the place to solemnize their 'double harness'. Its owners Mr and Mrs Alfred Jones conveniently offered a room overlooking the Atlantic for the reception and Sarah took a week's holiday. They pulled it off in two days: announcing their engagement, posing for photos at Fort Frederica on St Simon's Island and marrying on 17 October 1949. A Scotswoman transformed Sarah's green and pink cocktail dress into a bridal gown and Mr and Mrs Harned of 'The Cloisters' provided a cake and stocked the fridge of their honeymoon bungalow with champagne. A telegram dictated via phone the next day didn't reach Mr and Mrs C and they learned of the wedding when the story broke in the press. Her parents sent a short telegram with a wish for their happiness but no personal letter. A chunk of Sarah's 'honeymoon' time was spent begging forgiveness for the hold-up, which wasn't her fault. In one of her ignored letters she speaks of founding a Beauchamp line to supply the baby boom. Mary and Christopher (known as 'the Chimp') had two tiny tots and June was expecting. But motherhood is work and her request for Jeff to come to help keep her clothes tidy doesn't shout out parent mentality.

Arriving in New York, the newlyweds were given a breakfast at The Colony with Tallulah offering graphic advice about ways to keep a man. They moved into a hotel on Madison and Tony was quick to get commissions. Mary and June wrote, making her homesick. Jim Lees-Milne hadn't forgotten Sarah and when he went to Chartwell that November where Johnny was mounting his slate frieze in the loggia, the writer had a nostalgic look around and learned how Johnny liked Duncan but hadn't hit it off with Christopher. The estrangement between Clementine and Sarah lasted two months. Nobody thought that the hurt from 1936 could once again rise up. Tony wrote to Mrs C, boldly asking if the marriage was to her distaste. He begged her to write, alerting her to the fact Sarah was over-working by speaking at functions as well as acting. A parcel of toys for the young Churchills and nylons for mums accompanied the letter. Clementine replied, saying he was mistaken and added a kind word about his being there for her daughter. Sarah got a 'Please forgive me.' She had been 'numb', she explained, when the story broke. After passing through Virginia and stocking up on *anahist* (Quaker medicine for colds), the play bombed in the industrial heartlands of Ohio, Missouri and Kansas. When they didn't see full houses, Sarah halved her salary. The cast loved her, hating the Guild management. After seeing Tony in Chicago on 14 January 1950 she missed her train and went into a panic. Against the odds, she got to Seattle for a successful week.

While 28 January saw four Conservative MPs adopted as candidates for the seats of Woodford, Devonport, Streatham and Bedford – Winston, Randolph, Duncan and Christopher – Sarah was so homesick that even socialist Britain seemed attractive. Tony went to Hollywood on a *Life* assignment and after a hard day's graft at the Beverly Hills Hotel headed for San Francisco to join Sarah. Missing her family got too much and she made a lightning visit to Britain, then she was back for a few loved-up days with Tony at Mark Hopkins Hotel on Nob Hill. Onto its revolving restaurant floor one evening arrived Lillie Messenger, who had seen Sarah's play and was keen to represent her. MGM wanted her for a supporting part in a movie, *Royal Wedding*, as Fred Astaire's English love interest. Moira Shearer was unavailable. Sarah couldn't believe it. She had never done a musical on screen and her dancing hadn't been put under scrutiny for years and now the studio with the best of everything was beckoning.

The setting had been shifted to London at the time Princess Elizabeth married Prince Philip, the producers battling to incorporate newsreel footage of the actual wedding in Westminster Abbey. This was refused and MGM couldn't use the coach the real royal couple used and had to re-title the film in

England. Unable to exploit the Windsor name, the studio tried the Churchill one instead. Miss Holtzman, who negotiated Fred's RKO contracts, got on to Winston regarding MGM's request. An emphatic 'no' came back. Hiring Sarah may at first have hedged on this. A memo to executives from Frank Whitbeck (in charge of the film's trailer) reveals how the name was everything: 'Photogenically I don't think that she would be that attractive unless people knew that she was Winston Churchill's daughter.' It was just a 'pale little part' but the chance to be a 'bright celluloid Sarah in Technicolor' isn't one you turn down, especially if Astaire is in the picture.

In early March the Beauchamps returned to Britain for Easter for just over a week. At a large dinner at 28 Hyde Park Gate, Tony was taken into the bosom of the family, Mr C assuming his natural role as Sarah's father. They saw 189 Ebury Street, the home that would be theirs and also Vivienne and Ernest Entwistle, with whom Sarah was on intimate terms. Prior to Christmas 1949, Mr and Mrs Churchill paid a visit to 20th Century Studios at 7 Hamilton Mews – the pretty photographic portrait studio created in a war-damaged building (after Mrs Entwistle took out a lease in 1943). It was a real mews and Mayfair still had a village feel. Vivienne had a crystal voice, a maternal air and apple cheeks and as she led Winston and his wife inside, gave the impression she had just been baking cakes. Forthright as ever, Churchill asked 'Well – what expression do you want? Shall we have a smile?' Vivienne rushed behind her camera and noticed that his smile was the barest twitching of the lips. His sitting lasted ten minutes only, but hers was the only photographic studio he ever visited. Vivienne was also the only woman who took his portrait. Churchill liked the results, using them in his 1951 election campaign. He spread the word about her. Quickly there was a queue of political VIPs hoping to follow in his footsteps, including Eden, who apparently blinked a lot when he came to her studio.

Vivienne learnt her profession at the Electroplate Company, Willesden, as an apprentice artist in photography, alternating shifts at the Fancy Dress Studios at Oxford Street and Tottenham Court Road with her younger sisters. People wandered in, found a costume (highlander dress was a favourite) and posed against a hand-painted backdrop. She was taught a range of skills including fashion drawing at an art school in Caversham Road, St Pancras. Ernest Entwistle, who ran it with Valda (who had studied under Millais), married his pupil and closed the school. Whereas Ernest's family lived for a while at The Three Crowns, Stoke Newington, Vivienne's family, the Mellishes, was distinguished. She and her siblings worked for a living but their cousins gave off an air of breeding; the legacy of great-grandfather Henry Mellish, who composed *Drink to me Only with Thine Eyes*. After fighting in the Peninsular War as ADC to Wellington, he reached the rank of Colonel, became terribly rich, married the widow of the Earl of Lansdowne then lost everything through gambling. His descendants holidayed on the Riviera while Vivienne's father taught violin and sold sheet music. As Tony's cousin Henry amusingly puts it, 'The upwardly mobile Mellishes were South of France, South of England, while the rest of us were merely *Sarf of London*.' The siblings (Vivienne was the fourth of eleven) were accomplished on piano and in her glorious soprano, Vivienne sang at Wigmore Hall.

Ernest married her and they went into business together only for the Great War to begin and send him into the RAF for two years before injuries discharged him. Vivienne's first child, Betty, died an infant. Clive followed, then Tony on 17 April 1918. A later child died in infancy. They shared 30 Abbey Gardens with *Encyclopædia Britannica* editor Sir John Keltie. Its huge basement was a playground for Clive and Tony and was still a place of adventure in 1933 when Vivienne's nephew Henry stayed with his cousins. Tony left grammar school in 1933 before he was fifteen. Sarah once said he ran away, but his mother insisted he came away with 'excellent' in every subject. Around this time he stayed with Henry's family. His uncle ran a restaurant in Brewer Street with a sideline in training dogs for the cinema. Newport Buildings, off Shaftesbury Ave, where they lived, was a second home for young Entwistle. He loved Soho with its races and creeds happily co-existing. Henry's father's connections might be how seventeen-year-old Tony came to be in a film with Hughie Green, then the highest-earning child star in Britain. That was *Midshipman Easy* made at Ealing and on location at Weymouth. Billed as Antony Roger, he's Master Viglis, an out-and-out bully who threatens to make Easy's life a misery. Viglis mooches and growls, his unruly forelock of black curls springing into his eyes. With brows as black as Gil Winant's, Tony is lithe and physical, jumping across a table to attack one of the boys.

He never felt comfortable with the name 'Entwistle' even though it never did his brother Clive any harm. When furnishers Arundel Clarke set a challenge in 1938 to design 'England's most ideal week-end cottage', Clive and his partner le Corbusier won the prize, their creation on show to the public at Olympia. By 1940 Clive had gone into industrial design. As Sir Frank Whittle's assistant he helped create the turbo-jet engine. He also moved in a circle of artists and painters. One day with Augustus John and critic John Davenport he met a tall, highly sexed blonde, the widow of Horace de Vere Cole (Neville Chamberlain's brother-in-law) now married to Sir Mortimer Wheeler. Clive couldn't resist Mavis, sending her intimate poems. Her husband was away a lot and Porch House (at Potterne, Wiltshire) became a love shack until Wheeler discovered her with the young man in his underpants. Citing Clive as co-respondent he divorced Mavis in July 1942 and she dumped her toyboy soon after. That didn't stop Vivienne listing Mavis as one of the ten most beautiful women. Just after the war, working for UNESCO, Clive remarried and had two children.

Mr and Mrs Churchill learned that Tony's mother followed her son into 'society' photography. Her son's study of Vivien Leigh, capturing her strange mix of the delicate and the barbaric, was extraordinary. Looks and sociability made Antony Roger a hit with the smart sets.

Didi (also known as *Princess Pearl*) and Marguerite Strickland dazzled at the Mayfair Hotel and the Florida. They came to Antony's attic or to 20 Orchard Street, where, from 1939, his parents operated. Tony obliged as 'escort' for the evening. His looks were his business card. Jean Duff was barely 18 when she met Tony. She got a lot of attention from men and had a job back then at Harrods on the make-up counter. Perhaps it was getting make-up for his models that first drew Antony into the orbit of the Duffs, a Scots family of ancient origins. Her brother Robin had just graduated from Trinity College Cambridge. There, he acted in the Arts Theatre production of *Hamlet*. By 1937 Robin could list the leading lights of the ballet amongst his friends. Ashton, Constant Lambert and other luminaries signed his programmes. He knew beautiful people from the film world like Merle Oberon and was close to dancers like Wendy Toye, proudly fixing their portraits into his photograph albums. Some of them sat for Beauchamp. Antony was like a star falling from the sky with joy exploding all around him. Jean adored him and he liked her (although most people said they were like brother and sister). Robin has an ancestral line dating back a thousand years but was entirely without snobbery. Three years older than Entwistle, he was a great influence and liked him perhaps more than he admitted. Duff had just been hired as a BBC announcer and took Tony on a trip to southern Italy in September 1938. They stayed in Naples, hiring an automobile to Vesuvius, Pompeii and the Phlegraean fields. They floated inside Palinuro's underground cathedrals getting bathed in natural blue light, then took the boat to the Aeolian Islands with Tony stripped to the waist in skimpy shorts.

They were best friends and in the period 1938–43 Tony was always with Robin's family. In September 1939 at Franchise Manor in Burwash, East Sussex (a farm managed by Robin's solicitor father Douglas Garden Duff and his wife Margaret) he was listed as a photographer. Robin's grandfather was General Sir Beauchamp Duff who had reorganised the Indian Army and was once Lord Kitchener's right-hand man. Photographs in Robin's album show Tony with the Duffs making bonfires and at other times, sitting serenely on the lawn with Jean, now his 'secretary'. Tony might also have been instructing schoolchildren staying at Franchise in photography. Just before the outbreak of war Robin made a mad dash across Europe by car with Marina, Duchess of Kent and the Yugoslavian royals. He had spent some months as tutor to the sons of Prince Paul (later considered a traitor by Churchill for signing a pact with the Nazis). Robin's broadcasting network was vast and he counted Mountbatten, Churchill and the press barons among his associates. His voice was well known on the air at the time and he got to grips with new technological developments such as midget recorders for front-line reporting.

Tony, meanwhile, posed Jean in a boat moored by a lake at Franchise in a portrait that bears the precision and innate drama that Beauchamp would later be renowned for. In this night fantasy she looks flawless in her frothy white dress. Jean's granddaughter believes that the family had means at their disposal to help Tony get a real start in the photography business. The Duffs arranged for Tony to have a room and studio bordering St James's Palace, bang up against Beaverbrook's home, Stornoway House. Robin was a *Daily Express* correspondent while Tony was among the 20 resident in the building. Here, personalities like David Niven and Leslie Howard numbered among his sitters. Tony oozed charm as he adjusted his lens while less equanimous office mates scurried around him, knowing how precarious their survival was. Robin was on the ground providing commentaries while burnt-out buildings were dynamited. He shared cigarettes with men from the army sent in to tidy up the damage. Tony was given stills work on *The Lamp Still Burns* and he and Robin hobnobbed with the stars at the cast party.

When he changed his name to 'Beauchamp' it was a sincere tribute to Robin's family who had been so kind. It was a more aristocratic-sounding name and his target clients were the sort to opt for a 'Beauchamp' over an 'Entwistle'. He naïvely assumed Mrs Churchill would see where he was coming from. Part of the essence of Tony's character was surmounting barriers and even being someone else. Sarah understood the need to transcend one's circumstances to make a genuine difference. Her father conceded that the Entwistles knew a lot about art. At Hamilton Mews in 1949, he was thrilled to see Vivienne's miniature of Tony, saying how he would love to be able to paint like that. That Christmas he was touched to receive one she had produced of Clementine.

At Culver City on 19 May 1950 Sarah's first day under contract began with producer Arthur Freed introducing her to Astaire. Her 'little gnome' was hard to talk to until they got on to the subject of thoroughbreds. Unused to Hollywood traffic, Sarah was late for the press but in the next few months grabbed the headlines. Matt Busby's Wonder Boys were in town as part of their US tour and beat LA 7-1. Before they played Mexico's Atlas FC on 4 June 1950, Sarah appeared with the teams and kicked off before a crowd of 15,000.

She was keen to escape the Beverly Hills Hotel if a house was available. Old friends Ben and Bebe offered them their Santa Monica beach house complete with Rudy Valentino's swords, old-world antiques, a semi-alcoholic caretaker and a modest rent. They were lucky to get it, so Sarah's unkind descriptions of the 'ghastly' marble 'sarcophagi' baths and over-the-top cedarwood dressing closet designed for pondering 'which diamante evening gown you will wear tonight' were a little cruel. Here, the Beauchamp marriage was fulfilling and at its apex.

Clementine sent news of Randolph. Failing to get a seat at Devonport and seeing Labour get in, he returned to the Oxford Union to counter a motion that 'This House regrets the influence of the USA as dominant power among the democratic nations.' Seventeen years after 'King and Country' Randolph still saw that Oxford generation as a disgrace. He gave his old opponent C. E. M. Joad – now the BBC's *Brains Trust* anchorman – a public dressing down, believing this 'third-rate Socrates' wished to lure a new generation along the wrong path. This caused uproar and Robin Day, who was chairing, had to overcome the jeers and restore order. Carrying an introduction to General MacArthur, Randolph then plunged into reporting from Korea where the North had invaded the South. Many correspondents had been killed but nothing could deter him and soon he was wounded in action. Sarah's mother, meanwhile, needed hairnets in pale grey or white (impossible to find in Britain). Sarah sent dozens, getting the size and colour wrong. The Beauchamps had problems getting staff. Eventually, Billy Rose Simpson joined them. Her cooking left a lot to be desired, but Sarah loved how she sang as she did the laundry. Ocean Front's rooftop *terraza* and telephone cables stretching to the beach were to her taste too.

*Royal Wedding* was about the characters Tom and Ellen Bowen – brother and sister stage-partners appearing in London where each finds romance. Judy Garland accepted the role of Ellen when June Allyson found she was pregnant, but then director Charles Walters withdrew. He didn't want to put up with Judy's problems. Vincente Minnelli stepped in to help his wife even though the Minnellis' psychiatrists thought it inadvisable. She tried out a song with Fred. In Sarah's reports, Fred was concerned, whispering to her about Miss G: 'She is so unreliable.' On 10 June the cast attended Judy's birthday party but soon after she was told she was being replaced. In the midst of this 'terrific crisis' Sarah had a session with stills photographer Clarence Bull and polished steps with Nico and Pierre Charisse – brothers of Cyd. Designer Helen Ross did her dress fittings. When she and Fred were in wardrobe, he apologised for being without his toupee, saying to her: 'It makes me two inches taller.' Ex-dancer Stanley Donen then came in to direct. They were lucky to grab Jane Powell for the part of Ellen. Jane wasn't primarily a dancer but handled the scenes brilliantly and had a lovely, clear soprano voice.

Fred cared about his dance partners, wanting them to do something they liked as it made the scene look great. Sarah's choice was an eye-catching solo, so the film wasn't affected by her lack of chemistry with Fred. The number *You're All the World to Me* worked, having Fred reign solo in the most memorable scene. The idea of Sarah Churchill as his 'great love' was a theme to play on. Holding her photo, he dances on the walls and ceiling (achieved by putting the 'hotel room' inside a rotating 'squirrel cage' with a cameraman harnessed on). The story of Tom and Ellen mirrored his own life with Adele. They became the toast of Broadway in 1917. Jane Powell captured Adele's spontaneity and the number *How Could You Believe Me* was a throwback to the *Whichness of the Whatness* number in 1922's *For Goodness Sake*. The scene when they slip back and forth dancing aboard the liner really happened to Fred and Adele at sea in 1923. The character played by British-born Peter Lawford was based on Lord Charles Cavendish, son of the Duke of Devonshire, who married Adele in 1932. Peter, who later married Joe Kennedy's daughter Patricia, was seen canoodling during production with a young actress he had known since 1947.

Marilyn Monroe got to know the Beauchamps who were warmed by her belief in true love, loyalty to agent Johnny Hyde and her ability to immerse herself in character. She surprised them with her love of Bartók and the soft German accent she adopted (channeled from mentor Natasha Lytess). She opened up to them about her mother's illness and her early struggles. There were times she seemed sad and shy; but Marilyn could be an exhibitionist, a mood reflected in the clothes she wore. Tony was excited at the thought of capturing this and his most famous session with Marilyn was the yellow bikini shoot in November 1950. When Marilyn removed her mackintosh to reveal her startling bikini, Sarah estimated it must have taken all of three minutes to knit. Marilyn was carefree, running along Santa Monica beach doing cartwheels, handstands and crawling in the sand while Tony pursued her with his camera. Shoot over, Marilyn put the coat back on and instantly became a quiet non-entity. From 1951 to 1956 the pictures appeared on bookstalls in small format mags like *Pageant*, *Focus*, *Male Point of View*, *Cheesecake*, *Eye* and *Follies*. Sarah and Vic's friend Hugh French became Monroe's manager and Tony's memoir suggests that their cocktail party in late September was partly to aid Marilyn's promotion and to thank film colony friends. Guests included Van Johnson, Sally Cooper (daughter of Gladys), Charles Laughton, Elsa Lanchester and Anne Crawford (a friend of the Churchills who would join Sarah's father on holiday in Venice the following year). Zsa Zsa Gabor and her third husband George Sanders also came. Jealous about the courtesy Sanders was paying his *All About Eve* co-star, Zsa Zsa bawled, 'I will not stay in ze room wis her!' and stormed off upstairs with her mother Jolie.

While Tony created sultry images of the hottest female stars (claiming Ethel Barrymore impressed him the most) and photographed Chaplin with his family, reporters concocted a feud between Sarah and Deborah Kerr, with

Tony apparently forbidden from photographing Miss Kerr because of her Labour sympathies. It's true that Sarah viewed the socialist voter with little sympathy. So did Villiers, whose book *Pleasure as Usual* was a satire about an aristocrat plagued by taxation. When Sarah fantasised about surrendering herself to the socialist state in a letter to Clementine, it was as 'an incompetent idiot unable to earn my living'.

The Beauchamps posed in their Hillman Minx, schlepped at the Coconut Grove, met with Anne Crawford, singer Tony Martin (Cyd Charisse's husband) and veteran producer Hal Roach. They dazzled with the A listers at the Beverly Hills Hotel's Crystal Room. They were a dream team and Tony made her look beautiful. Everyone fell for him, even L. B. Mayer, who convinced him to do screen tests. Beauchamp was initially cast for the film version of Kipling's *Soldiers Three* with Stewart Granger. He returned to California in mid-January 1951 to photograph Garbo, her only colour session. The Beauchamps entered Garbo's dream world of imaginary balls with people dressed as Pierrots. In her garden at night, she dispensed Moscow mules in copper mugs at a table lit by a single candle. She teased Tony when he returned with a mind to shoot, keeping him on a string. She 'wouldn't say yes and wouldn't say no', conceding at the eleventh hour. Clementine reported the visit of L. B. and Mrs Mayer to Hyde Park Gate, which may have been a return favour for Sarah's film role. The seven-year contract Sarah mentions in her memoir (that they didn't mind her jettisoning) doesn't seem plausible. Released on 8 March, *Royal Wedding* played five weeks at New York's Radio City Music Hall and was a massive success. An all-plastic Christmas village lit their Hotel Salisbury apartment. Re-writes were required for her new play *Gramercy Ghost* (about a spook soldier helping a woman choose the right husband) and she and Tony took an elegant house at East 61st Street for ten months. The play opened in Delaware on 16 March 1951.

In Boston Ed Cashman had a proposal for her from J. C. Hall. She was flattered that he wanted her for the TV show he was sponsoring but uneasy about being asked to exploit her family's connections in political interviews. She put her hoof down and Hall allowed her to interview show folk instead and let Tony come onboard. He would be seen photographing the celebrity, then viewers were whisked to the darkroom to see the photo develop. Episodes of *Hallmark Presents Sarah Churchill* had taped fifteen-minute interviews with Sam Goldwyn, Helen Hayes and Alan Lerner among the notables. Sarah's steady gaze and arresting voice suited the small screen. She telecast a scene from *Gramercy Ghost*, did *Sweet Sorrow* for CBS's Lux Video and turns for singer James Melton on *Ford Theatre*. Charles Z. Wick, a former songwriter who went on to represent Peggy Lee and Benny Goodman, sold Melton to Ford Dealers of America and secured Sarah. A force in star bookings, he saw a great future for her on TV and didn't give up on the prospect of exploiting her connections.

Churchill paid for Diana to fly out and return by boat and Mule made sure she was taken to the smartest clubs. Diana and Tony hit it off. Sarah's play saw full houses at the Morosco Theatre. Jewell Baxter, who did PR for Alice Faye and others, became Sarah's publicity manager and friend. Sarah met up with Bernard Bellush, the University of Columbia professor nominated by Winant's friends (including Belle Roosevelt) to collect material for his life story. Laying on the charm, she deprived Bellush of personal recollections, passing him on to Portal and Eden, sending each a note. She suggested he see her mother, knowing this was unlikely given the series of difficult operations she was having. When the play closed on 21 June, American Actor's Equity made a fuss about her alien status, forbidding her from touring in New England. Established actors were exempt from these rules but Equity, rather insultingly, didn't consider her to be of this calibre. Sarah said it didn't matter as she planned to leave for England that July.

Travelling alone, her time in London was fleeting. She was soon staying with the Lawrences in Paris. Back in the US, the Beauchamps stayed with the Franchots who ran the Little Theatre, Niagara Falls, where Sarah took the play. She got round Equity by crossing the Canadian border daily. Tony was so tanned that a border guard said: 'I didn't know he was Sarah Churchill's husband. He looked kind of foreign to me.'

12

# Cold War, Warm Heart

It was time Churchill's daughter explained the British electoral process to Americans, thought J. C. Hall. Her country was a loyal ally, sending troops to support the defence of South Korea. For all its economic problems, it was on the brink of change. Just short of his 77th year, Winston might be PM again with an election called for 25 October 1951.

Sarah stood on Westminster Bridge in a voluminous yellow swing coat, mic at the ready, while Tony fussed with her hair. Ken Tynan and other reporters flocked to ask if she would help her father, brother and in-laws in their campaigns. Would she vote? 'You bet!' came the reply in posh Americanese. As pigeons sabotaged the programme in Trafalgar Square, Sarah and Tony talked to floating voters, then with their large entourage went into pubs. A committed socialist in Roehampton's King's Head said he'd be the first to offer Winston hospitality: 'Don't think we don't like your old man, we love him.' Later in the recording, Sarah exchanged jollities with ambassador's daughter Sharman Douglas (It Girl and friend of Princess Margaret). Ed Murrow featured in this *Sarah Churchill Show*. Outside Buckingham Palace he questioned her about her Pa. For contrast, she took viewers to London's Theatreland. Wandering past the Adelphi, she remembered *Follow the Sun* before calling on Gielgud at Drury Lane. Viewers got a flash of Ebury Street, Sarah waxing lyrical about her new home.

With Winston Senior, young Winston and June, the Beauchamps travelled to Devonport where Randolph was standing against Labour's Michael Foot. On the journey to Chartwell, the Beauchamps commandeered a train carriage as a set. Winston refused to be filmed but Randolph let Tony seat him by the window as he spoke about the withdrawal from Trieste in 1945 and Tito's resistance to Soviet infiltration in 1948. A pilot documentary could be pitched to the US using Randolph's recordings and film material. On election night,

Sarah and Tony spoke from the CBS platform at Nelson's Column, getting the crowd's reactions. In his memoir Tony tells us his wife's bouncing and jumping was apt to upset the cameras. A true professional, he didn't care for Churchillian high jinks. The embarrassing dances happened each time the Conservatives scored a victory. Bizarrely, Vic Oliver was in the same mood, dancing a jig in the wings of Derby's Hippodrome at that moment with 'Girlfriend of Song' Sylvia Campbell. Ever the pro, Vic changed one of his gags from 'Mr Gaitskill keeps you broke,' to 'Mr Butler'. The Tories had a small majority and chairman Lord Woolton had to accept it. When Sarah interviewed him for CBS, her style of putting a subject at ease was ahead of its time.

Tony's pal sent him a copy of Robert Fabian's true tales of crime, stimulating the idea for a TV drama. Inspired by NBC Radio's *Dragnet* he wanted to be true to these Scotland Yard narratives, right down to forensics and investigative strategies. He met with Fabian and produced a pilot. His 'first-person' camera technique didn't feature the Inspector but Peter Sellers, just getting *The Goon Show* on air, impersonated Fabian's accent with the Chamber of Horrors as a setting. Tony was certain that he could interest a US sponsor, relying on Charles Wick's help.

With Aneurin Bevan attacking Truman's 'sinister' policy in Far East matters, the Beauchamps listened to Winston at the Commons that November before returning to New York. Sarah represented her father at a dinner for General Alexander at the Waldorf and was at New York Harbour to welcome Churchill and his now rather peeved 'Crown Prince', Eden. When the 'GM' met Truman in Washington on 5 January 1952, lack of unity was a pressing issue. As he addressed Congress she witnessed Papa move that 'taut, wary audience'. He resided at the British Embassy, Sarah and Tony at Blair House, guests of Margaret Truman, now a great friend. Secretary of State Dean Acheson gave Churchill a dinner at Larz Anderson House after the Society of the Cincinnati awarded him the 'Eagle Insignia'. Sarah was a strong presence, entertaining everyone with her wartime stories, but when Acheson made a joke about the cavalry charge at the crushing British victory at Omdurman being stupid, she took it as an affront. (Churchilll had ridden with the 21st Lancers.) Next day Acheson got the *treatment*. Sarah arranged for Clive Entwistle to be invited to a party at Bernie's and rejoiced in the fact that Tony was fully accepted. At the time of the King's death, spasms in the PM's cerebral artery left him with temporary speech problems. Sarah's next letters were frantic, but her father seemed to recover.

To compensate for those unimaginative *Hallmark* dramas she got 'literary' in a semi-staged act at Kleinhans Music Hall, Buffalo, reading the letters of Ellen Terry and Bernard Shaw. Her collaborator was her Poets' Theatre pal

Edward Thommen and she had future performances in London in mind. She and Tony still had use of the apartment overlooking the Park at 910 Fifth Avenue, where Sarah's parakeet would fly about or settle on one's wrist. Determined to learn Italian prior to a forthcoming summer holiday with Mama, they bought a Linguaphone that would be switched on in the morning whilst Sarah pin-curled her hair and Antony shaved. The result, as Sarah told Clementine, 'My hair is straight and Antony half-bearded – so far not much Italian!' Nightlife was fun. The Village Vanguard at Seventh Avenue South in Greenwich Village offered folk music, beat poetry and jazz by Thelonious Monk. One night Sarah ran into Hughie Green, whose British career had gone awry since 1948's *Opportunity Knocks* was prematurely dropped from BBC radio. Believing a conspiracy against him was behind this, Hughie took the Corporation to court. An exile from the entertainment establishment, the ex-pilot went back to flying and selling surplus Dakotas. Hughie was astonished to find that Tony, whom he knew from *Midshipman Easy*, was married to Sarah. Green was gaining insight into American TV, noting trends like interaction between host and public. He was a regular at the Beauchamps' home. Sarah put herself out to help him, encouraging him to meet Soames. He recommended lawyers who looked at his claim against the BBC. Having access to Soames and Duncan, Hughie later tried to further a scheme to increase Britain's share of the transatlantic flight trade.

Closely following political debates, Tony sent his father-in-law news cuttings about the reaction to him Stateside. He praised his response to attacks by Herbert Morrison and for taking active steps to nail lies. He sent his love to Mr and Mrs Churchill. Sarah attended a plaque unveiling at 426 Henry Street Brooklyn, where Grannie Jennie was born, then took a short holiday with Tony to Bermuda. In the lucrative field of magazine photography, Tony's name was hot and his portraits (including those of emerging actresses Julie Harris and Janice Rule) ranged from the natural to the heavily artificial. His obsession with setting never ceased to amaze and his publicity for Sarah's *Queen Nefertiti*, a forthcoming *Hall of Fame* drama, shows the influence of fashion photography pioneer George Hoyningen-Huene. One study in *McCall's* of Truman's daughter as Queen Bess prompted Clementine's approbation: 'Papa and I think Antony's lookalikes most remarkable and clever. What an inventive creature he is!' Tony also worked on the film that began with Randolph talking on the train. Beauchamp created a full-page ad for *Outside USA* with a large image of Randolph: 'Celebrated Journalist and Political figure', someone forever onto a good story with his interviews with Italian Premier de Gasperi and Togliatti ('the most dangerous Communist outside the Iron Curtain'). Any interested network was to get in touch via Charles Wick. When a rough cut was screened for Randolph, he thought the editing and commentary 'first rate', recommended good lawyers and sent his love to Antony. Sarah told Winston how TV might be a great medium for her brother's 'warm human quality and fine mind'. She hoped that Randolph might get a break in the business. Sadly, this went no further.

Tony genuinely wanted Churchill to benefit from the world's most powerful medium. He boasted that by providing the best lighting and camerawork he could achieve the 'utmost audience'. He spoke of leaders frightened by the technology and how poor presentation affected Eisenhower (now a candidate for the presidency). He praised his father-in-law as a peacetime PM standing 'head and shoulders above contemporary statesmen ... England needs you now more desperately than it ever did.' He highlighted Britain's contribution to historical 'advancement' and how no nation is more modest, which made it all the more galling when New York hacks referred to it as a second-rate power. 'I beg you to wake them up with unassailable facts and figures that will penetrate the fog of baseball and political conventions,' he entreated. He made suggestions to the PM about reviving the Empire. He suggests sending people to the Dominions to cultivate the world's 'backward areas'. America's failure to aid Britain's economy was, he argued, similar to Chamberlain's actions at the time of Munich. If only the US could get a good verbal spanking for not hastening Britain's recovery. Winston should look his best doing this. Sarah's Pa was interested in the TV idea, but he didn't feel confronting America about the issues Tony cited was wise, though he was glad to hear his opinions. Frustratingly, he let the BBC (not Antony Beauchamp Productions) televise him live that October during his speech at the tenth anniversary of Alamein at London's vast Empress Hall.

When their Pan Am flight to London touched down in early July Sarah told the press they would spend three days there before a holiday in Italy. Her zebra silk gloves were noted when the Beauchamps gave a luncheon at 10 Downing Street for Miss Truman (dubbed 'America's Princess Margaret' by the US press) and joined Doug Fairbanks at another bash. Clementine had begun sightseeing prior to Sarah and Tony's arrival in Italy. On the Appian Way she felt cured of fatigue and, meeting the Beauchamps in Naples, they headed for Capri for a stilted meeting with Mussolini's daughter, Edda Ciano. Winston's wife had expressed sadness on hearing about Eva Peron's painful end but had been against meeting Edda. It was Sarah who persuaded her, believing Edda deserved sympathy. A more joyful occasion was calling on Gracie Fields. They saw the Collodi Gardens near Monte Catini and swam in a velvet sea. Tony got on very well with his mother-in-law as they walked in the steps of Emperor Tiberius. Sarah's mother saved her disapproving note for the 'ancient decadence' that involved feasting, killing enemies, then more feasting between visits to the (apocryphal) vomitorium.

When Sarah's cousin Clarissa was married on 14 August 1952, well-wishers gathered outside Caxton Hall and cheers were heard when bride and groom Anthony Eden returned to Downing Street. Few smiled in the formal photo taken in the Pillared Drawing Room although there are signs of a twinkle in the faces of Duncan and Johnny. The Old Man hated bright lights and Tony stood close by as if to guard him. Randolph wasn't allowed near in case he spoiled the day. Sitting on a divan, Clementine looks relaxed and Sarah is plump and glowing. At last Ebury Street's owners were in residence but only for three months because *Hallmark* lured away its mistress. Sarah welcomed Anthony Montague Browne as a new Private Secretary before Churchill journeyed to La Capponcina and then Balmoral, informing the Queen about the testing of Britain's first atomic device and asking the Queen Mother to resume her role in national life. On his return he arrived at Ebury Street for dinner with Clementine bearing roses in an antique cachepot.

At 1952's Scarborough Conference her father's campaign to recruit young Conservatives continued with his talk of sturdy, jaunty and unconquerable lions. Randolph was upset that Soames accompanied him. He wrote a long, emotional letter complaining that not once since Devonport had his father wanted him by his side. Didn't that say to the world that he was a disappointment? He referred to the Cairo indiscretion years before, accusing his father of not understanding its 'psychological background' with Eden capitalising on it. Driven crazy by the family never being open and instead uttering 'platitudes' had caused resentment on Sarah's part when Vic was a banned subject. Winston never capitulated over any question of guilt regarding the Pamela business. He obliged Sarah, who asked if he might fix it so she and Tony could be present at the Coronation and opening of Parliament. Afflicted by a bad cold while staying with Tony's friends, she told her mother about wanting her husband to 'cut his ties completely in London' because if not, she would leave for New York earlier than planned. Some vexation is detectable but Sarah didn't take the early flight and was with Tony at the première of Chaplin's *Limelight* at Leicester Square. *The Sunday Graphic* said that with all Sarah's TV work in America, she was achieving more in the interests of Anglo-American goodwill than countless diplomats. Quizzed about her Chelsea home she flicked her auburn hair off her eyes and modestly pointed out: 'It's at the Pimlico end.'

Tony was still pursuing Winston for a telefilm, enlightening him about tricks of the trade like make-up. Greeting her Daddy off the *Queen Mary*, Sarah took him to Jennie's birthplace on 7 January 1953 before dinner with the Windsors, Clare Boothe Luce and Belle Baruch. Help from Truman's administration to let Britain recover prestige was non-existent. Gone were her oil reserves and the privileges of the Anglo-Iranian Oil Company (following its nationalisation by

Iranian PM Mossadeq). While US measures to contain Communism received active British support, Britain's position in Egypt following the 'revolution' led by Neguib and Nasser didn't get theirs. As always, the US balked at British imperialism. Sarah recalled her Pa being ticklishly diplomatic at a dinner in the White House's East Room with members of Truman's outgoing team:

> Truman kept looking at the Great Seal of the United States – a gilded image displayed on the wall above a mirror. Father asked him 'Why do you keep looking at it?' 'The reason is,' Truman said slowly, 'when I look at the eagle I see arrows at its feet when I wish there were only laurels.' Truman wondered if the set of thirteen arrows at one of the eagle's feet didn't give a good message and suggested it might be better were it redesigned with less conflicting symbols. Winston's practical answer to Truman was 'Couldn't you put a hinge on it?'

When Eisenhower's presidency began there were hopes it might be to Britain's advantage and when Stalin died in March many, like Secretary Dulles, talked about the chances of peace increasing. In Jamaica Noël Coward was Winston's host. Sarah, her mother, Colville, Mary and Christopher followed via Bermuda. Tony had returned to Britain because his father was unwell. He made use of Ebury Street, storyboarding his police series while Sarah became a coast-to-coaster using Charles Wick's penthouse at 40 Central Park South (next to the St Moritz Hotel) as a stopping point to LA, her travel fatigue requiring a shot of sustenance. She was doing something right, getting nominated for a prime-time Emmy for Best Actress on 5 February.

At the end of March she wrote to her father to say how moved she was reading his speech about Queen Mary. As one queen died another was born when Sarah enacted Queen Elizabeth I's ascendance before making history in *Hamlet*, the longest TV drama, made at a cost of $180,000. Shown on 26 April, it starred Maurice Evans, Ruth Chatterton and Joseph Schildkraut. Sarah intoned the words 'Shakespeare Belongs to the Ages' in her opening and was an effective albeit 1950s vintage Ophelia. The audience was calculated at 16,000,000 and Al McCleery sent the Great Man a copy. Soon after he received his Order of the Garter from the new Queen, Sarah came home to appear in one of Tony's true crime films.

Her husband had received finance from mail-order millionaire sponsor Isaac Wolfson. Hughie was busy so, for Fabian, he opted for Sandhurst-trained Bruce Seton. Outdoor photography was a feature of this pioneering TV series. Women were often victims, as in *The Golden Peacock* where a dancer is killed and in *The Deadly Pocket Handkerchief* where a thief chloroforms and robs them, although *Nell Gwynn's Tear* showed women could be disingenuous. One episode told the story of the shooting of Alec de Antiquis, the motorcyclist who put his machine in the path of Charlotte Street jewel robbers in 1947. Ian Whittaker, who had been at RADA with Roger Moore, was in *Murder in Soho,* cast as a lawless 'Ted' and he recalls how well known Beauchamp was. The *Daily Mirror* created a 'Not Here Please' campaign, wishing to forget that black day in Soho. Some stories were not violent and even had poets as thieves, such as *Robbery in the Museum. The Executioner* was chilling: a murderer kills people in their bathtubs. Many touches made *Fabian of the Yard* unique. At the end of each episode Seton's image faded and viewers saw the real Robert Fabian who delivered a brief homily concerning the crime depicted.

Sarah felt that if any sin merited a homily it was her husband's. She states that the first cracks in the Beauchamp marriage appeared at this time, adding dramatically that acting in Antony's film filled her with dread. The marriage, she says, existed *on paper only* and that they saw each other to save face. This isn't true because letters reveal that she and Tony didn't give up. She had caught him out being naughty in London the previous autumn, but it wasn't enough to destroy her faith. She certainly disapproved of the 'pre-shooting party' for the cast and crew held in March 1953 at Ebury Street. He hired a quintet of jazz musicians and laid on a good spread. People she barely knew got to see their home and Sarah hated that. In early May in Berkeley Square, they were on good-humoured terms during working hours, shooting *The Actress and The Kidnap Plot.* One scene had Sarah (tormented by threats to kidnap her son) sheltering in the square's summerhouse. Tony acted out how the terrified character ought to look seeing a villain face to face. Hardly her idea of a great actor, his gestures made her crack up. Eve Perrick, The *Express*'s smart-set follower, was watching. Tony bluntly shouted to Sarah that the airport had called to say her flight was cancelled and that she wouldn't get back in time for her next TV *Hallmark*. Everyone saw Sarah's face drop as Tony cried out: 'Roll 'em!' This unethical trick worked and it lifts the lid on a welter of frustrations. They had once talked of 'equality' but he hadn't expected her to work in America to his exclusion. He hated the place now and was finding she wasn't subject to his authority. She wasn't near ready to begin that line of Beauchamps, while he found himself tagged 'Sarah's husband'. He felt unwanted and wondered where the motivation was to remain faithful.

Sarah knew Beauchamp's family well. Vivienne's photography business was flourishing. As she chatted from behind her ancient plate camera, her sitters were so at ease they didn't realise the shot had been taken. There was never any 'watch the birdie' stuff. Ever since Winston's knighthood the Entwistles had been offering to photograph him. Ernest raved about Vivienne's colour process, saying she could bring her equipment to Downing Street, but the

PM's Private Office was reluctant and refused her a commission. Her portraits nevertheless adorned the staircase wall at Downing Street.

Of Tony's good friends, there were some Sarah distrusted. While the Beauchamps dined with Baron at Les Ambassadeurs, her relationship with the older photographer wasn't warm. Baron mentions her fleetingly in his book, merely recalling having to hang his head low after Sarah snapped at him for his innocent remark about her father's *last term* of office. Mrs B and Baron tolerated each other. Tony had a male network of friendships solidified a decade before they met. Gossip floated around – mainly ancient history relating to Tony's life before they married – like his association with the Thursday Club, the all-male drinking society that met at Wheeler's in Soho. Baron started it in July 1946 with friends like Arthur Christiansen, Sean Fielding and illustrator Antony Wysard. Ex-dancer turned restaurateur Bernard Walsh served oysters (excluded from rationing) prising them open at frightening speeds. Not all the gossip was true. Recent writers have seen the club as a hub for louche extra-marital activities, even though evidence is limited. Sarah was too far above it for it to matter.

Baron started his club while cultivating friendships with David Mountbatten (the Marquis of Milford Haven), Prince Philip and Mike Parker (Philip's Private Secretary), offering them annual outings and a meeting place where speeches were banned and risqué jokes welcomed. At his unpretentious flat at 2b Brick Street they felt at ease. It seems unlikely that Tony would have had much to look after as club 'record keeper' (a role he's alleged to have had). Not repeating what was said was assumed and keeping compromising material wasn't sporting. A Fleet Street editor's fraternity, most of the denizens were much older, but the Thursday Club later attracted actors like James Robertson Justice and Peter Ustinov. The younger Thursdaying crowd looked up to Baron as part wise man, part stooge. *The Sketch*'s Jack Broome was a regular, so *Broome boys* Tony and Vasco 'Latin' Lazzolo came to keep in with the boss. The contacts were good and it was a way of getting pictures published. Tony photographed Milford Haven when the latter was Philip's best man. David could rely on Tony's discretion and the two were friends, but Tony wasn't part of the Prince's circle. When he came to Wheelers, he seems to have been a victim of the older men's jokes. The *Daily Mirror* on 7 May 1946 featured a strange letter to the editor from 'Anthony Beauchamp, Hertford Street' asking for an explanation as to why a ring suspended on a strand of human hair should swing back and forth in a straight line over a male stomach and in a circular fashion over a female's. The sender refers to the ring as 'wedding or otherwise'. This was two months before the Thursday Club's inception and was from a prankster. The event that prompted it is lost in the mists of time, although the *Mirror* admitted Beauchamp's test revealed how hen's eggs hatch and addressed him as 'laddie'. Someone alleging Antony was responsible for an unspecified pregnancy seemed to have been behind it. His involvement in the club was slight and by the 1950s non-existent, as he was forging a career in the US alongside his wife.

Occasionally tales surfaced about others Tony knew in the art world. Vasco, who sketched fresh-faced girls for the Aero ads, was a good friend. Baron cultivated a friendship with Pietro Annigoni and Tony admired his work. His own pen sketch of Dr Stephen Ward has an engraving quality and dates from 1947 when Ward had consulting rooms at Cavendish Square. Beauchamp had met him earlier (possibly in India but most likely through Vasco, who had met the osteopath on an art course in 1945). Ward's draughtsmanship was esteemed and his company exhilarating. He enlivened supper parties, could introduce you to Danny Kaye and other big names, and was seen arm-in-arm at premières with models or actresses. The Churchill family came to like this 'second' Dr Ward (the first being their GP at Chartwell). Tony recommended him to Diana when Duncan needed treatment. Sarah thought him convivial but was never his client. Rich and influential people endorsed him and some had suspicions. Stephen's Cinderella moment came when he secured Bill Astor as a friend in 1950, although Bill's brother David sensed Ward liked having people on strings. Outside the clinic, Stephen was a Bohemian with a hatred of humbug. His tales of Soho folk running the gamut of sexual persuasions were titillating. On the way up he craved respectability enough to wed Patricia Baines in 1947. His wife discovered, over several farcical episodes, his peculiar fondness for meeting up with working girls. Unlike other men of his class, Stephen helped them and genuinely cared about them. Later on, few had anything bad to say about him. Ultimately, when he was at the centre of the Profumo scandal, Ward told his agent Pelham Pound to sell his possessions to raise money to assist these young women. A representative of the Royal Household bought all the artworks connected to the royal family when they were exhibited at a Museum Street gallery. Whereas Tony and Baron photographed pretty girls and Vasco painted or sculpted them, Stephen loved their company. Whether they were on the make or dreamy innocents anxious to experience life was immaterial. Some took risks, were available and got exploited. He didn't see it as prostitution and he was never a moralist.

Tony never begrudged the osteopath coralling a set of rich friends or his liberal lifestyle. He didn't behave like him though. Ward admired Beauchamp not just for marrying his way into Britain's elite but for his easy-going attitude. In a short unpublished autobiography (like the pictures, bought up by an agent and unlikely to see the light of day now), Stephen praised Tony because 'He knew no barriers of class in his relationships with men and women. He took friends from all walks of life.' He was the embodiment of the suave character he wanted to be himself. Model Vicki Martin was an effervescent Eliza, and Ward, her Higgins. They lived together as friends. He was trying to help her get a rich boyfriend, engineering her meeting with the Harrow- and Cambridge-educated Maharajah of Cooch-Behar of the State of Bengal. She might have married Cooch-Behar had she not died in a car crash in January 1955.

'London: scene of excitement, glamour, dreams made true' – Tony, in his own way, sustained this illusion for the ordinary Cinderella in the street. He transformed attractive women into stars, like Cheshire teenager Norma Sykes (pin-up girl Sabrina). Yet there was nothing about Tony that was louche. He was the opposite. Throughout his life he was sensitive to women. His mother's influence is important and Vivienne's philosophy was to make a subject look as good as possible, perferably beautiful. No woman was ever photographed looking stark or unfeminine by an Entwistle or Beauchamp and none was humiliated. Though busy with *Fabian*, his studies of Pier Angeli and Yvonne de Carlo made the covers of *Picture Post* and *Illustrated*. A very 'Antony Beauchamp moment' occurs in his *Fabian* episode *Bombs in Piccadilly*, when his female character transforms from inconspicuous policewoman into glamour girl. The actress is Ann Hanslip, who had a tiny part in the Diana Dors picture *Lady Godiva Rides Again*. Many actresses from *Godiva* have uncanny links to *Fabian of the Yard*. Tony's protégée Dana Wynter went to Hollywood and won the lead in *Invasion of the Body Snatchers* and had a long career. Gina Egan was another, and so was Vicki's flat-mate, the tragic Ruth Ellis.

Rich boys and ostentation bored Sarah and she was excluded from areas of Tony's life. She had met Robin Duff during the war but for almost the entire period Tony wooed, married and lost her, Robin was in India as chief advisor and foreign liaison to the Maharaja of Bundi (who attended the wedding of Princess Elizabeth and Prince Philip). Duff's sister Jean, now married with a daughter, lived for a while in India as part of the Maharaja's exclusive set. After Independence the Mountbattens went tiger hunting with Jean and Robin's crowd in Rajasthan. When Tony next saw Robin, the latter had inherited Meldrum House near Aberdeen, a historic residence that had played host to Bonnie Prince Charlie. Robin began transforming it into a stunning hotel and himself into a master chef. One link in the chain of mystery, scandal and rumour is that Profumo and Christine Keeler apparently later enjoyed the last Laird of Meldrum's hospitality.

While stress was causing Tony to become less social, the Duffs were loyal to him. Through Robin, Tony got to know others in India's glittering elite such as Cooch-Behar's sister Gayatri Devi and her husband Jai (Man Singh II – the last ruling Maharaja of Jaipur). Tony was a frequent guest at Jai's home in Ascot. Seriously rich, the couple had £2,000 worth of jewels stolen in May 1953. None of this smart set was introduced to his wife. While Sarah knew 'man about town' David Metcalfe (a godson of the Duke of Windsor) she wasn't, unlike Vivien Leigh and Margot Fonteyn, invited to the parties in his flat in Motcomb Street usually attended by Tony and Baron. Sarah accepted that her husband transformed girls into stars and didn't keep him on a tight rein. Her implicit trust is astounding.

Some of her friends believe that Tony was the husband she loved the most. When they argued she vented her spleen. The trouble in 1953 did not originate from a tomcatting incident. It wasn't louche. The liaison was always subtle: a friendship she hadn't been party to and couldn't control. It was sad and hurtful when infidelities emerged, particularly with close friends she had up until then trusted. One of Tony's flings she never knew about was Margaret Alsworthy, Sarah's friend from the London stage, who later married Guy Rolfe. After Sarah's death, Margaret admitted she had once had a one-night stand with Tony.

Another concern was her husband's unpredictable behaviour. In Hollywood they used to go to Alla Nazimova's *Garden of Allah* hotel to enjoy its shabby chic and cannabis-tinged atmosphere, beloved of screenwriters like John Farrow. One day, Tony stripped off and dived into Nazimova's pool, then suddenly lay still. Sarah panicked seeing him underwater. Jumping in, she caught him doing something weird – playing at being dead. It was enough to prompt a serious talk. She suggested he get help but he declined. Another time he told her he almost drove his car over the edge of a cliff.

Sarah had migrated to the home of Lillie Messenger. Originally from West Virginia, Lillie had married the nephew of Empress Elizabeth of Austria, Alexis Thurn-Taxis – now a director at Universal and Columbia. Sarah did a few *Hallmarks* then made a trip to London. Tony met her at the airport and they beamed through the car window for the *Mirror* before they took their seats by the Abbey door for the Coronation on 2 June. A few days later the Beauchamps had tea with Princess Margaret at Blenheim. The Marlboroughs had 1,300 guests including British and European royals, Prince Akihito of Japan, Queen Salote of Tonga, Commonwealth leaders and the Australian cricket team. Bad weather forced everyone to abandon the lawn and shelter inside tea tents. A party for Winston followed with Lady Churchill, Mary, Christopher and Randolph. Tony still hoped to get footage of his father-in-law. Ignorant of the rift, Clementine came for cocktails at Ebury Street and complimented Tony on the garden. Sarah left for LA yet within a week flew back, this time in worrying circumstances. At Downing Street on 23 June the PM was lively one minute and slumped in his chair the next. A stroke left his left side almost paralysed. Mary met Sarah at the airport but she found Tony was at the PM's bedside at Chartwell. Christopher took the helm in government matters. Thankfully, a miraculous improvement was evident in a week. That August Sarah took off, without Tony, to Spain and Majorca before returning to the US. She was wondering if it was time for a permanent return to England.

Friends were surprised that Randolph could settle in the country. The Trust had bought him Stour House (on the site of Constable's birthplace). He was in the chair at a Foyle's Luncheon at the Dorchester on 10 September and said things about the 'pornographic' nature of some sections of the British press. He wasn't attacking the girlie magazines but *The Sunday Pictorial*, *Mirror*, *Sketch*, *Empire News* and *Sunday Dispatch*. Their sales, he argued, were not from selling news and commentary but from crime, sex and inaccurate stories. He alluded to the way Princess Margaret's potential marriage had been discussed. Randolph the stirrer-upper and verbal scourge was back, but the papers ignored him and when he published his ideas in pamphlet form, stockists refused to take it. Questioning if free speech was alive, he spoke to Manchester Publishing Association on 7 October, questioning the 'Hands off the Press' cries and whimpers about censorship if anyone criticised it. He urged them to welcome criticism and not to be so defensive. He reproached *The Times*, under the modernising Sir William Haley (whom he would lampoon as *Silly Billy*) and referred to Lord Rothermere's crime merchants. He praised 'good' papers like *The Manchester Guardian*, *Telegraph*, *Scotsman* and *Yorkshire Post*. With complete lack of fear Randolph carried on this argument on radio and TV. Winston, meanwhile, was going to agonising lengths to conceal signs of his stroke ahead of his recovery. Sarah later said how she 'died with pride' seeing footage of him at Margate. Being an expensive employee given her travel, she hoped *Hallmark* would end her contract, but this didn't happen.

From the Beverly Hills home Lillie Messenger found her, Sarah wrote to Mama in October, saying she was relieved to distance herself from Tony: 'I was so sure I could make him happy,' she sighed. A letter to Winston implored him to be measured in his recovery as well as asking him to 'accept the truce' between herself and Antony without working himself into a torrent of hate. She told her parents she believed her marriage was a rope that must be slowly unwound. Her mother suggested that Beauchamp move out, allowing her to live alone at Ebury Street. She had underestimated her Pa's admiration for Tony who, along with his letters, regularly sent him witty gifts like angelfish cigar lighters. From France on 30 October Tony makes much of Churchill's peacemaker role and anticipates a Russo-British entente. Where America was concerned, he begged Churchill for once not to care about being so 'vulgar' as to blow Britain's trumpet, but to point out that Britain had split the atom and invented radar, the jet, television and penicillin. Clive's influence is detectable in Tony's desire for Winston to attribute these achievements publicly. Yet, while son-in-law and PM were united in lamenting the decline of the once-dynamic British Empire, 'cool Britannia' wasn't the latter's style and Winston didn't attempt the independent talk with Russia Tony hoped for, preferring to stay within the old Big Three set-up. Sadly, when Churchill met President Eisenhower in Bermuda on 4 December, hopes for closer solidarity were frustrated and nothing was achieved.

In charge of the Anglo-Australian programme of atomic development, Duncan Sandys flew to Adelaide in late August 1953 to inspect the Woomera Rocket Range as a prelude to a series of guided weapon tests. His love of air travel had not waned since the time he and Fuller flew a light aircraft under Tower Bridge. His job required helicopter-hopping between sites like Sellafield, Windermere and Risley Warrington. He was trying to get the Iron and Steel Bill through against bitter opposition. The previous year his wife had accompanied him to Trostre Works in South Wales. Diana never faltered even after walking miles around such enormous works. She enjoyed talking to people and thrived on new experiences.

For the Churchill siblings, letters were plentiful. Words flowed beautifully although Diana didn't sublimate energy into literary endeavours. She was a loyal older sister and even Winston's fish had nothing to fear from the Gold Cream Kitten. At Chartwell, a fungal disease affected the Golden Orfe. The finny tribe had to be netted, lifted by hand from the top pond, administered with potash and deposited in the middle pond. Several members of staff and professionals from Regent's Park Zoo flinched at the slimy task. Diana arrived and to the amazement of Edmund Murray (newly assigned as Winston's bodyguard) suddenly tucked her skirt into her bloomers and stepped in to help.

She could get on her hobby horse about religion. She showed less restraint than her siblings in getting emotional. Only her father attempted to interrupt her when her voice became higher in pitch. Sarah thought he was best at releasing Diana's tension. He didn't always succeed. On his 79th birthday she launched into *Happy Birthday to You*, forcing everyone to sing, unaware that he bloody hated it. Sarah saw the Sandys children quickly growing up and said: 'I feel sometimes there is a void in her life she doesn't know how to fill.' Diana's help at home didn't lighten the load. She missed Duncan when he was away. Emotional problems affected her when distractions were few, prompting a stay at Crichton Royal, Dumfries. Putting his Housing Repairs and Rents Act aside, Duncan visited his wife with Clementine. Sarah anxiously wrote to her mother, hoping the treatment had been a success. By 6 April 1954, Diana was back at Chartwell, drinking brandy with her father in his velvet boiler suit, Duncan confronting him about his pronouncements on MP's salaries.

Moran observed that Duncan sometimes took comments the PM made out of restlessness at face value. Christopher was better at knowing which ideas were serious.

For Sarah, it was time to try again with Tony and in May they were at Chequers. Tony took her to Paris for a week and they spent time with Clive's family and called on Pamela Churchill. Gianni Agnelli (heir to the Fiat fortune) was looking after Pam handsomely and was a friendly uncle to her son. Escorting Clive's daughter Aladine to England and taking her to Trooping of the Colour, Sarah became motherly. The Beauchamps gave a dinner in the little girl's honour, inviting Aladine and some young friends to Ebury Street with Diana's daughter Celia in charge of them. Clementine, Diana and Sylvia were present along with actresses Edana Romney and Cicely Courtneidge (with whom Sarah was appearing on radio). David Metcalfe was there and Clementine met Baron for the first time and was asked to pass on a copy of *Baron at the Ballet* to Winston.

Sarah reassured Mama that things were 'going so much better' despite the ups and downs. She still thought Tony a brilliant person and felt positive: 'We have an interesting life with so many opportunities – we know it's silly to waste it.' Given that most British homes didn't possess a television, Tony decided to give people a taste of *Fabian of the Yard* presenting three episodes (including Sarah's) as a portmanteau film in cinemas. Re-editing meant that for the last few days of Sarah's holiday he was getting it ready for Charles Wick. Nerves were frayed and Clementine witnessed a terrible row at Ebury Street. An explanation followed – one that gave little hope: 'I am deeply distressed that you have to witness these disturbances ... I know what I am doing – forgive me, if I cannot always explain everything.'

Billy Graham, two months into his *Crusade to London*, diverted Clementine's attentions. Deeply troubled by the 'great decay in belief', Winston met the evangelist on 27 May 1954. They discussed how anti-communist measures were allied to spiritual salvation. When he and Eden were in Washington that June, he asked how many communists were in the US and was told 25,000. Securing Eisenhower's support over Egypt had brought them there. Eden was doubtful they would get it and they didn't. The splintering Beauchamp marriage affected the Entwistles, who holidayed with Diana and her children. Sarah and Tony appeared united when they came to the Cambridge Theatre in October to see Judy Campbell. When he suggested talking to Churchill about their problems Sarah asked him not to. Disobeying her, her Pa got a long letter requesting a private talk. He was given one that December. He defended himself against accusations that he didn't contribute to Ebury Street and said he wanted to save the marriage. If certain changes were made they might look forward to a full and good life. Only with Winston's assistance was there any hope: 'You have an overwhelming influence upon her and I can do nothing if you too stand against me,' he said gravely. This small fragment might be the truest thing ever written about her:

> Sarah is not being made to suffer at anyone's hands except her own. She has an incredibly obstinate streak to her nature which is terribly exhausting and which causes unnecessary unhappiness for both of us.

The pressing issue that only the Great Man could solve might have been Sarah's drinking or its underlying causes. Yet her parents were never inclined to discuss it. As a Winston worshipper, Tony had been the ideal partner for a daughter whose father came first. He appears to have been calling for more 'openness' and less face-saving. She needed to trust her husband and marriage as an emotional shelter. Tony is funny, challenging the family's apparently established view that he was a two-headed monster: 'I am one-headed!' he protested. He could at least feel relieved when *Fabian* began transmission on 13 November. He encouraged his wife in her career, backing a proposal for her to play Gertrude Lawrence in a screen biopic. Gertie's former rep, Fanny Holtzman, was negotiating this as well as touting a version of Sarah's life story to run in *Reader's Digest*. She called on Winston who, grateful for his greeting card royalties, was pleased to see her. Sarah was writing to Alec Wilder ('the Wizard'). She told the composer on 27 November she was certain the film would happen and chattered in beat poet free flow, applying thick paint to descriptions and begging him to come to Chequers. Fanny couldn't set up the Gertie film because *Hallmark* thought it interrupted her career. Robert Wise later developed *Star* with Julie Andrews.

At the official ceremony for the PM's 80th birthday Sarah hid behind Randolph and June as they walked to Westminster Hall with an excited Winston Junior and Arabella. Before members of both houses, Winston was at times visibly weeping but gave a cracking speech saying it was the nation, not he, that possessed the *lion's heart*. He even imitated the lion's roar. When Bevan and Jennie Lee first rallied to get him a present, the PM was touched, but when he saw the Graham Sutherland painting (after giving five sittings) he couldn't have been more underwhelmed and believed it was an insult. Some time after, it was burnt in the back garden of Grace Hamblin's brother's home. (A *Private Eye* cartoon of the conflagration was tagged with 'I don't know much about art, but I know I like a good fire.')

Sarah found another way to avoid Tony, by being a showbiz presence at Bedford's Conservative Christmas Fair on 2 December. Soames observed how he had tried so hard to get Sarah to come down to one of these functions in the past but she has been 'busy flying round the world'. Sarah praised the couple with the 'drive, faith and capacity to serve'. Charles Wick, who had earlier visited Hyde Park Gate, arrived at Chartwell. Winston and his wife liked him, as Wick bragged later in an interview. Tony avoided him but was present when Miss Holtzman came – the last time he attended a Churchill gathering. He and Sarah saw her off at the airport in early December 1954.

Chequers was the clan's next destination and the grandchildren longed for the arrival of Father Christmas (a role assigned to Duncan) and to open the presents wrapped by Winston's former secretary Mrs Hill. Neither Sarah nor her 'Wizard' was there. With a bad respiratory condition, she was self-isolating at 86 Vincent Square with Diana's Mrs Johnson to tend her. In her room overlooking the rooftops, silhouettes danced across the wall in a 'battle' between chimney pots and church spires. She heard distant noises including the tears of Julian (leaving soon for army training). She didn't set foot in Ebury Street. Tony's friend Audrey Hepburn called by with husband Mel Ferrer and dragged him off to the country to pose her on trees and take part in snowball fights. Writing to the Wizard in January 1955, Sarah spoke of a literary undertaking but this was merely reading from a book by Elizabeth Borton de Treviño on radio's *Home for the Day* after Fanny Craddock had declaimed on dishes in season.

While the film press praised *Fabian of the Yard*'s realism, Scotland Yard didn't want to be associated with it. The real Robert Fabian was making vast sums from speaking tours and TV game shows in the US and it probably rankled. TV histories list 39 *Fabians*, but Tony's involvement was limited to ten. After this his name vanished and 'This has been a Charles Wick Telefilm Production' is seen in the credits. Tony didn't possess rights and Wick could legally edge him out. The look of the series became more American and was rechristened *Patrol Car* with fast Humber Hawks shooting through London streets, and a voice-over commenting on London landmarks for the benefit of US viewers. Beauchamp never recouped his investment and Wick passed distribution to CBS-TV film sales. Agent became enemy, with Wick thereafter re-revising the origins of *Fabian*:

> Churchill introduced me to Fabian of Scotland Yard, the legendary detective, head of Scotland Yard. So I put this television series together. Sold it around the world – first in Australia. Then I converted a factory outside of London into a motion picture studio ... I became very friendly with the Churchill family.

The worst rows between Tony and Sarah were about her keeping Wick on as agent. He won some wifely loyalty as she aligned herself with another agent in the firm. He never sought help as regards his mood swings and she wouldn't keep 'dry'. It was a 'painful marriage'. Sarah arranged for Jeff and her secretary Priscilla Norman to store her furniture from Ebury Street. In New York, Brackett, whom Sarah described as 'a sort of Villiers', had a key to her room at Wick's. He lent it to Alec who brought musicians Jackie Cain and Roy Kral there for rehearsals. The parakeet flew around whilst Alec sat at the spinet with the huge photo of Winston above him. Roy would exclaim: 'Alec Wilder and Winston Churchill in the same room!' Sarah chose the St Mortitz Hotel as an intermittent home.

The real Churchill faced Defence Minister Harold Macmillan – the latter telling him plainly it was time to go. Having thought he had secured Britain a bomb veto in a secret Churchill-Roosevelt agreement (in which the right to prohibit the US from using the bomb existed) he blamed Attlee's government for surrendering it with the McMahon Act. Attlee's lot had had little choice with the US threatening to withhold Marshall Aid if they said no. Churchill hated the lack of consultation and the stockpiling of weapons on British soil. In 1954 a decision was made that Britain develop its own hydrogen bomb and the PM gave his last major speech on 1 March 1955 about the threat of nuclear holocaust. He mentioned his 'Fifty Years Hence' article in the *Strand Magazine* in December 1931. He wanted phased disarmament. 'We shall by a process of sublime irony have reached a stage in this story where safety will be the sturdy child of terror and survival the twin brother of annihilation' sounds optimistic and deathly in the same breath.

By coincidence, America's Civil Defence Committee asked Sarah to come out to Yucca Flat to witness an atomic blast. During the first half of 1955 a dozen tests took place. Thinking it worthwhile to report to her father, she came to that million-dollar village with mannequin residents. After a suspenseful lead-up the test was called off owing to bad weather and for once mushroom clouds weren't glimpsed sixty miles away in Las Vegas. The atmosphere of the Pantages Theatre at the Academy Awards had more explosive appeal, as did the fanciful *Samarkand* and the *Plains of Tartary*. At the Morosco Theatre she saw a Jacques Deval drama with Louis Jourdan as magician Sourab Kayam. She hoped to do the play herself and take it to London. Papa had seen a similar thing on stage as a boy.

Alec Wilder laughed, talked rapidly, swore in an old-fashioned Mark Twain way, drank 16 Martinis in one session and scribbled verse on cigarette packets and menus. With his music championed by Sinatra and Mitch Miller, the Wizard rehearsed *The Long Way*, an opera about a girl and a gangster with the face of her father. The theme of magic and adventure entranced Sarah and she was hooked on this tall, slim man with grizzled hair whose professorial air reminded her of Gil. Alec influenced Sarah, who was writing 'less sentimental' poetry. At this time she read her work at a California poetry event in a stadium before 7,000 people.

Clementine's birthday coincided with a leaving party. Eden's new government was taking over on 26 May in the midst of rail strikes. Duncan was still Housing Minister, working on slum demolition, while Christopher was at the Air Ministry. On VE Day Copenhagen paid tribute to Winston with a bust by Oscar Nemon in Churchillparken. Diana came to unveil it but afterwards took issue with the model. Sarah asked her if it had been 'planted by Graham Sutherland'. Before returning to the US she urged her father to visit the Guildhall to see the Nemon there, thinking it the best of the lot – so good, she predicted, the Queen was sure to be jealous. He did so and was thrilled. Diana was with her parents when the City elders unveiled it at a ceremony on 21 June.

Sarah had not had news from Tony, who now lived at Flat 1, 30 Hyde Park Gardens, a classy street to the north-west of the Park. It was a very pink first-floor flat, apart from a splash of mustard or blue on the carpets with the usual Regency furniture and gold-tasselled curtains. There, he played jazz records late into the night. He attended the first night of *Kismet* at the Stoll Theatre starring Doretta Morrow, a musical Marilyn Monroe. He had always loved ladies who could sing. The audience stood up at curtain call. Tony was smitten with Doretta, whose voice was like cut crystal. Just like Sarah, he was haunted by missed opportunities.

Sarah had been delving into her own inner consciousness, but concern for her older sister made her snap out of it. Diana had relapsed and doctors in Britain were considering electroshock therapy. Sarah was panic-struck believing this was morally wrong, potentially leaving people inert. In Chicago she sought advice and reported to her mother on 1 September that US doctors now prescribed powerful sedatives instead. She asked why Diana wasn't tested for an underactive thyroid gland. But just a month later (the day she flew back to Britain) her notebook reveals that Diana was having the much-feared treatment. Knowing Clementine was deeply affected by something Diana had said in the throes of an argument, Sarah scribbled the line: 'The Truth is not one-sided.' Winston was staying at La Capponcina between September and November, writing and painting. Emery Reves had just bought Chanel's old home, La Pausa and to Clementine's horror, Winston was considering a property near Roquebrune-Cap-Martin. She joined her husband in late October, cautiously dining with Emery and his Texan girlfriend Wendy at St Pol Restaurant. Sarah joined the 'conference' on 7 October. She believed Marrakesh far more suited to both her parents' needs.

Flying back with Mama to see Diana, Mule was ultra-suspicious of medics. Wildly articulate as ever, she writes that putting someone through a terrifying ordeal when they've committed no crime is never justified, no matter how inconvenient their distress or even violence is. She writes in her notebook about Ralph Blum, who was sincere about healing what disturbs the soul. He was a strong influence, helping her get through many issues in the mid-1950s. She makes an interesting comment about 'A. M. B.' (Anthony Montague Browne) who had come to the Riviera with his wife Nonie. Remarkably, A. M. B. confided in Sarah about his balancing act between wife and mistress. The Mule records that her advice was to 'have his mistress or plenty of them [but to be] nice to his wife now and again'. At this, she discloses, 'he shot me a glance – remembering something of my story perhaps'. Could she tolerate such an arrangement? She next leaps into a passage about the weakness of men, calling them 'a bunch of weak-kneed tadpoles'. Montagu Browne, later a cherished friend, is summed up here as 'not a very strong character but more brain than most'. It was still a time of turning a blind eye and keeping things private. Archbishop Welby is Montagu Browne's son, born in January 1956, three months after this exchange.

Sporting a shorter hairstyle Sarah made a return trip to the South of France where she met up with Maggi, also there on holiday. She wrote to Clementine on 9 November about Diana who had come too. Still on sedatives with an average of three hours' energy before fading, care had to be taken with conversation and any newspapers with insensitive coverage of any subject connected with religion. These set Diana on a downward spiral. Diana couldn't wait to meet Wendy whom she had heard so much about. They invited aviatrix Jean Batten who had been world-famous two decades earlier. It did Diana good to see someone her age surviving (even if Jean was barely robust). Intolerant of anyone 'giving up', Winston insisted Miss Batten find new horizons. To her mother, Sarah wrote that in the long term Diana should be occupied with a cause. The time she had watched her sister wake up humiliated as it dawned on her why she was in hospital broke Sarah's heart. 'While I am alive,' she determined, 'she will never be abandoned.' Her loyalty ran deep, no matter what impracticalities her transatlantic lifestyle posed.

It was time for Mule to leave for New York before heading west. Pamela had been spending more time in America and had recently undergone a biopsy at New York Hospital. Her wealthy friends invited her to country estates to aid recuperation and because of this, Sarah had Winston Junior stay with her at the St Moritz and her nephew's visit proved a happy distraction. Pamela wrote to Clementine saying how lovely it was to see Sarah and how kind she was to her son. Sarah was booked for a week at Phoenix's Sombrero Playhouse for another *No Time for Comedy*. A local reporter caught up with her and she spoke about how TV drama devoured scripts and talent. Wilder may have been in Phoenix, given the lines about him in her notebook: 'I feel about A as I feel about G – it is the same sort of feeling ... It is something to have my eyes uplifted again [by] proud and manly and lonely mountain peaks of men.' Sarah feels a need to correct herself, pointing out that Gil was never detached. The composer made himself remote. According to his biographer, Wilder was resistant to her overtures, barely taking notice of her when she attended his rehearsals. Sarah admits that meetings could be 'distressing' but she was resilient, unrealistically vouching: 'I can not and will not abandon the hope,' which seems a throwback to the time she was the wishful partner entering into the affair with Gil. Her lonely mind drifted between time and place. She found herself thinking of Rome where Gil visited her. Then her mind travelled to the fearful dark house in Boston where Ralph comforted her in her terror.

Tony, she reveals in her notebook, wasn't interested in reconciliation and would divorce her if she admitted to being the 'guilty party'. His audacious request to keep her furniture was the last straw. She hadn't set out to commit crimes against marriage. Circumstances had altered her moral compass but personality had to be accounted for: 'I'm not unfaithful but I'm independent,' she would later say, adding: 'I guess that's hard for a man.' On *The Jack Benny Show* on 29 January 1956, Benny asked Sarah what Churchill thought about his act when he last played London. 'Never has so much been sacrificed for so little,' was her reply. Randolph also appeared before blindfolded panellists on *What's My Line?* on 5 February. There's a shot of good humour and a line in a Brooklyn accent but Randolph wasn't at ease on US TV. He was better suited to dispensing satirical *Child's Guides* for *Punch* or peddling mild insults in tiny free-flowing articles in *The Spectator*. He was quick to sue when *The People* called him a 'paid hack' (winning £5,000 in damages) and quick to apologise when his own use of the phrase got him in hot water. His previous week's coverage in Washington hadn't done Eden many favours.

The success of the PM's new marriage was annoying enough, but discovering that his father had aided Eden's path to power by shielding him from scandal was deeply resented. Randolph had found out about Eden's affair with Dorothy Furey. It happened light years before (when her scheming politician husband pushed her into Eden's arms). Hearing about it in June 1955 Randolph got on his high horse about crimes against marriage. Churchill had intervened to stop Anthony being cited during the couple's divorce, while failing to intervene when his son's marriage to Pamela was at stake. This rankled. He longed for Anthony to trip up but the former PM-in-waiting had been a popular MP even with Labour colleagues. Randolph focused his ire instead on the Press Council's whitewashing of the 'yellow press'. In March, the Egypt situation caused Eden to lose his composure. Randolph was tickled pink.

# 13

# The Unwanted Illusionist

Appearing by Royal Command and gracing *The Max Miller TV Show* on 3 February 1956, Doretta Morrow was the star of the moment. Before her return to America, Tony's TV film about her was to feature her farewell performance. Trust a dispute between the Musician's Union and BBC to throw a spanner in the works. Love-struck, he wanted to know if the recently divorced Brooklyn-born singer would have him if he were free. She went to Rome, returning to London on 5 March, but it was Pippin, her poodle, she really cared about. Another love goddess was in Britain. Tony saw Marilyn at Terry Rattigan's house in Wick Lane, Englefield Green.

Sarah's TV appearances were thinning out but she was often on CBS radio. On a short Easter break at *La Pausa* she offered consolation to Diana, whose marriage was unravelling. As Sarah climbed into her plane she was annoyed when asked why her husband hadn't come to see her off. In the US too, gossip mongers speculated on her marriage. In *Portrait of London*, she visits the zoo, Petticoat Lane and Buckingham Palace and a 'Mr Roger' permits her a glimpse into a gentleman's club. Beauchamp might have been helping her with her CBS broadcast. With an American twang she explains the naming of 'Big Ben,' recalling Ed Murrow's wartime broadcasts.

Like Tony, Marilyn, Clementine and Randolph, she saw the crisis unfold. Britain had already offered to remove troops from Suez, where they had remained since Nasser's takeover in 1952 and had, like America, pledged millions to build the Aswan Dam. When Nasser's arms deals with the USSR came to light the US pulled out of the dam. Foreign secretary Selwyn Lloyd did the same. Nobody expected Nasser to seize Suez. Sarah returned to New York, appalled at the lack of authority that let Nasser break international law.

On a break from rehearsals at Sacramento's Eagle Theatre, a local reporter said Miss Churchill was easy to talk to, smoked but never carried cigarettes and looked forward to a time when clothes might be made of paper and need no caring for. Could we conclude that cooking didn't interest her? 'Don't get me wrong,' she interjected, 'I really am an expert with a can opener.' Singing wasn't a strength either, but she found a 'cunning way' to put over a song at The Music Circus, when *The King and I* opened on 13 August. She later said performing there was unbearable but critics thought her Anna charming. Flown to San Francisco in a DC3 care of General Sarnoff, she joined Randolph at the Republican Convention at Cow Palace (where Ike and Vice President Richard Nixon were re-nominated as candidates). Sarah asked her brother about dramatising their father's only novel, *Savrola – A Tale of the Revolution in Laurania*. Winston was less excited at the prospect. When the creative team met him at La Pausa on 23 October, a meeting McCleery described as the 'peak of his life', Churchill found fault with the script. On 4 November, before the US went to the polls, Sarah's voice rose to peaks of emotion in Dickens's chilling tale *The Signalman*. Immediately after her radio drama, the fireside manner returned as she told Americans to use that 'precious franchise' – the vote.

What to do about Egypt was on everyone's mind. A Suez Committee was in place but Duncan (who was pro-military action) and others were not kept informed. Confronted by Sandys on 22 August 1956, Eden admitted they were in talks with the French but, owing to security, couldn't reveal what the committee's wider objectives were. At the Party Conference Sandys demanded that Eden force Nasser to stick to the 15-Nation Plan or else fight. Randolph, meanwhile, interviewed Antony Head, Britain's War Minister and Duncan's nemesis, about the current state of the army, finding that only by calling up reservists could the army outside Germany be brought to war strength. Days later, Eden went ahead with the Protocol of Sèvres with France and Israel, agreeing military action to topple Nasser. The man Winant said had the most integrity and was above dodgy secret treaties had acted without consulting Parliament.

Everything went wrong, with the US refusing to support the invasion and Saudi Arabia supporting Nasser, ceasing oil shipments to Britain and France. British troops landed at Port Said and advanced several miles along the canal. Randolph used his contacts from Israeli Intelligence and provided exhilarating exclusives to British newspapers. His excitement came to an end at the end of November when America's threat to damage the British financial system forced Eden to accept a ceasefire. On Christmas Eve the British and French began a humiliating withdrawal whilst Israel refused to return Gaza to Egypt. Eden tendered his resignation in January 1957. In an exclusive for *The Standard* Randolph predicted that Macmillan would succeed him. British ships would now be forced to pay a toll to Egypt for use of the canal. Nothing could lessen the horror felt by patriotic Brits who recalled the Middle East in the glory of Empire. A new order began, with the US increasing its own influence in the region.

Sarah cast herself as Lucille in *Savrola*, asking Lamont Johnson to be the hero. Lamont said later he had a job keeping her sober. For all the 'huge affections' it was a 'touchy relationship'. The Churchill adaptation for US TV went out live in colour on 15 November just before things went belly-up over Suez. Sarah's parents telegrammed their 'Love and blessings for *Lucille*'. The kindest among the next day's notices called it 'an interesting experiment' while the rest spoke of viewers yawning their heads off. It wasn't TV fodder and in the wake of Randolph's bungling performance on *The $64,000 Question,* columnists found fault. Sarah wasn't swayed, swiftly pointing out that *Savrola*, with its focus on repression and rebellion, was relevant to current events. One could substitute Poland or Hungary for *Laurania*. She was right. Russia had just invaded Budapest, making good use of the distraction of Suez: 2,500 Hungarians lost their lives, far exceeding the number of Egyptians killed.

No sooner were the costumes for *Savrola* hung up, than rehearsals were in progress for a new stage presentation due to open on 25 November. Sarah didn't have to travel far to the Pasadena Playhouse. *Tonight in Samarkand* was a dream made real for a girl still obsessed by the exotic circus tales her Papa had once read to her. Barbara Vajda was directing. Austrian-born Helmut Dantine, with looks, ability and a long connection to the Playhouse, co-starred. In a provocative costume Sarah played Nericia, a tiger-trainer more in love with her vicious cats than with any man. And yet three desired her: a juggler; a rich man; and Sourab, who foresees her death. Critics called Sarah an 'actress of stature' bringing 'fire-power to her role' and unanimously welcomed this haunting, engrossing play.

Tony was as good as forgotten, although for the blockbuster *War and Peace*, filmed in 1955, Audrey Hepburn insisted on bringing him in as her stills photographer. Dantine and Soldati were both involved in the film and Sarah heard much about it. Tony's infidelities weren't the reason why the Beauchamp marriage failed. It was more about escaping his control, just as it had been with Vic. Sarah speaks of Tony's cold sweats, death wishes and depression. Seeing General Slim (who had led the Forgotten Army in Burma) at a party in 1953, he flinched and sped off, leaving his wife to make conversation. It was Slim, Sarah tells us, who suggested getting him checked out for malaria owing to his experience following the Chindits. South African cricket ace Aubrey Faulkner saw active service in the Middle East in the Great War. What happened to him serves as a warning to anyone in denial after contracting malaria. While outwardly happy, Faulkner battled with periods of depression and gassed himself aged 48. Tony refused to seek treatment at the Hospital for Tropical Diseases. By enlightening readers about this in her 1981 memoir, it conveniently shifted the focus from her. She might have been settling a score; branding him unstable and suffering from a disease. Her notebook at the time reveals how aware she was of her own health failings. She acknowledges her problem with drink with its severe lows after highs, and blackouts on the worst occasions. She was aware it was time to get help. She spent Christmas in LA with Helmut, with whom she was romantically involved. Niki Dantine, a young actress who had just made her debut in *The Power and the Prize*, would become Helmut's wife. She knew Helmut had cared deeply for Sarah:

> I came out to California and met Helmut. One of the first friends to whom he introduced me was Sarah and we spent many evenings together. Sarah was so open and friendly to me and was one of those rare women actually happy that a man she had cared for had found his special love. Helmut and I were married in 1958 and spent almost a year in Europe.

In early 1957 Sarah felt she had reached the end of the line. She went to London, seeing her mother and falling out with Al Parker over his handling of her affairs. While Clementine helped find her a studio flat, Sarah's writings include an unusually stark rumination over her mother's true attitude. She writes: 'One feels she doesn't expect me to succeed and that everything is one's fault.' Randolph's fight with the press continued and he would later publish his speeches and transcription of a libel case in *What I Said about the Press,* which WH Smith, Rymans and Harrods refused to stock. Soon, he appeared on one of the best episodes of ITV's *Youth Wants to Know* and found fans among the new generation. He used the BBC's *At Home with Randolph Churchill* in 1957 to plug the book (available from his company Country Bumpkins Ltd). Viewers saw Stour's book-lined library and saw an ancient ash tree (blocking Randolph's view of the nearby Abbey) getting felled. He left *The Standard* after his friend Charles Wintour's departure, switching to US magazines like *Esquire.* One article said America needed a king. In mid-March Tina Onassis accompanied Sarah to Nice, introducing her to Winston's new friend Aristotle. Emery's partner Wendy greeted Sarah at the airport in furs and dripping in jewels, but Tina was the quintessence of continental chic.

On 29 March Sarah was reunited with Constance Babington Smith and in May her portrait by Vivienne was on the front cover of *TV Times* advertising her role in *Armchair Theatre*. In *The Heiress* she was Catherine Sloper, crushed when her lover fails to turn up for their elopement and now heartless: 'Of course I am cruel,' she says, 'I have been taught by masters.' All the British critics now praised Sarah. Bernard Levin talked of her 'freezing fire'. On 18 May she returned with Winston to La Pausa. His adoration both for that villa and its châtelaine was a subject of gossip for Pamela and Noël Coward, the latter wondering if repressed desires were flowering in old age. It was his sixth visit that year. At Chartwell, Sarah introduced Ralph Blum (then studying Russian and visiting ancient antiquities) to the family. Winston was keen to meet him and Ralph later recalled how surprised he was by Churchill's short stature. Sarah came to Prof's funeral on 9 July and welcomed Emery and Wendy to Chartwell.

Jane Vane Tempest Stewart was a petite blonde, running a boutique with Philip Pound selling custom-made furniture. Jane admits: 'It was doing pretty badly to be fair. Only Lord Snowden was kind enough to buy a piece.' One day in early 1956 a friend, Davina Portman, told her: 'There's a lovely man you *must* meet – you would be able to cheer him up. Why don't you have a go?' Antony was the charming man in need of saving. Jane heeded this rallying call. It did Beauchamp good to have her to socialise with. They talked about friends in common and places they had been to. Jane had been one of the six Maids of Honour selected to attend Her Majesty at the Coronation. She would have been perfect material for a Beauchamp portrait, but he wasn't doing much creative work then and had been spending much time alone. She hoped to lure him back out into the world. Tony's connection to the Churchill family was sometimes discussed and Jane got the impression that Antony felt disappointed, having hoped his work in America would have resulted in greater recognition. He could be easy to talk to, down-to-earth, witty and fun and Jane remembers how he came alive when they went to fashionable restaurants and parties. It did him good having a young lady on his arm. While handsome with a darkish skin that made his blue-green leopard's eyes all the more striking, their having an affair was out of the question. For a start she had a boyfriend. Married albeit estranged from his wife, Tony behaved like the perfect gentleman. It was obvious he was painfully in love with someone else. This was the cause, Jane believes, of his gloom. At 30 Hyde Park Gardens, Jane saw images of Sarah on the wall but what stood out most was the Doretta Morrow obsession. Photographs of her were everywhere.

> He was madly in love with her and I remember being bored hearing him play *Stranger in Paradise* over and over again. He had all her records. She had divorced and while Antony might in time have been free, she had unexpectedly gone back to America. She never got in touch and can't have felt the same. She wasn't very nice to him.

Jane soon found that dragging him up from his stony depths was hard. The time she recalls Antony at his happiest was when they went to a big party at the Maharajah of Jaipur's. The two of them sped off in his black Jaguar to Saint Hill Manor near East Grinstead. Generally, Antony could not let go of his consuming obsession with Doretta. Just when Jane thought his spirits were lifting he slipped back again and the man who had spent the evening laughing and telling anecdotes disappeared. She made more efforts to get him to socialise. There were one or two astonishing mood swings and looking back Jane wonders if the modern term bipolar might be applicable to her friend. She recognises an imbalance and feels Tony's grip was disintegrating.

Viewing figures were piling up for *Patrol Car* in US cities like Detroit, Salt Lake City and Syracuse. It was the highest-rated film series on Milwaukee television, yet Tony received nothing by way of return and had £6,000 of debts. He felt cheated by Wick, who claimed Tony owed him money. In the middle of August 1957 Wick's solicitors were proceeding with a suit against him. Antony was up against it, but not once did he mention these issues to Jane. Wick was to go on to become Director of the US Information Agency and close advisor to President Reagan.

Baron had died in September 1956, the Thursday Club dying with him. Just round the corner from Wheelers was Dean Street's Colony Club, where Diana Melly, or Diana Ashe as she was then, worked periodically. Her boss, Muriel Belcher, required her to fascinate punters as they forked over their Bohemian dough at the bar. Things had happened to Diana at an impossibly young age, such as becoming a chorus girl in a London Cabaret, marrying, having a child and leaving her husband. She remembered how polished and gentlemanly Tony Beauchamp was – not that it made him hard to speak to. She can't recall exactly where it was she met him but just knew that Tony would never have set foot in Muriel's and would have hated that place. By 1957 Diana had found happiness with man-about-town Michael Alexander, one-time PoW who faked being Field Marshal Alex's nephew to escape death and who was now doing well as a writer. While not controlling, Michael could be jealous. Diana knew Tony through the group and she and Jane were friends. She can't recall any specific conversation with Tony, just that whenever they talked it was light-hearted and fun. She knew he had a passion for the singer of *Kismet* but wasn't exposed to his depressive side as Jane was. She wonders why she didn't talk more to Tony to elicit facts about his life during the time they spent together. He never spoke about his career, or the Churchills. She didn't know him a long time. It was brief – about two months or so. He didn't take her out, although he might have wanted to. Her boyfriend tended to throw a strop when she mentioned visiting Tony's flat. Diana admits with a note of candour that she was curious about Beauchamp. Any young, needy woman would have been. She adds:

> He was sophisticated. I wasn't. Not then. Everyone in that circle seemed upper class. Tony was too, but perhaps it was more a question of sophistication where he was concerned. There was nothing deep or complicated about our relationship.

She said it wouldn't surprise her if Tony had fathered a child. His appetites might have been red-blooded, promiscuous even, but not in any bad way. At his home she honestly felt safe, not threatened. He was sweet and kind with nice manners and didn't pressure her to go to bed with him. He was curious about her. Diana doesn't remember much about Tony's flat, possibly because he did make some kind of amorous advance, which wasn't repelled – a point Diana is a little coy about. Still, she wasn't single and about to let go. She loved Michael despite the attraction to Tony. There was only one occasion where she used the word 'alarming' in reference to his behaviour: something that only became apparent to her years later. She came invited to his place one day and unexpectedly a pretty young half-Indian woman was present. After fixing each with a drink Tony suddenly announced he had to leave for a short time on an errand. The woman then surprised Diana by making a couple of advances, repelled instantly by the young Englishwoman who waited Beauchamp's return. Thinking back to that fleeting moment, Diana thinks it had to be a set-up for a threesome. She forgot about it after. Generally, she looks back fondly on her life with Michael Alexander. She had a wonderful circle of friends and parties just sprang up every other night. The group constituted the earliest Chelsea Set of the 1950s, though the name stuck to similar groups in the 1960s. Her crowd went to coffee bars and parties that frequently had costume themes. Tony Beauchamp wasn't the biggest partygoer, but he turned up with a bottle of gin at a late night bash in a top-floor flat in Harrington Road at 11 p.m. on Saturday 17 August. About eight people were there and one male guest insulted Tony saying a number of things, one being that he was a 'common little man'. When the evening was reported in the press, Michael Alexander told *The Mirror* that the attack was cruel and hurtful, given what Tony was going through. Beauchamp stood there, taking it. While Michael didn't name the man doing the insulting, he caddishly divulged to *Mirror* readers that Beauchamp was in financial troubles, was soon to enter divorce proceedings and that a woman was alleging that he had fathered her child. Hardly the work of a loyal friend; he probably saw Tony as a rival.

Nobody understood feminine beauty more than Tony and women avidly read the articles he penned for magazines like *Woman's Own* that acted as advance advertising for his memoir, *Focus on Fame*, to which he was adding finishing touches. One might ask why a 39-year-old needs to write an autobiography. One might also ask why he needed so much medication. An hour after the Harrington Road party, on what was now Sunday, he rang up a sleepy Diana Ashe and begged her to come over to cheer him up, telling her how depressed he was. He called again later, saying he was going to finish it all with a heavy dose of tablets. She didn't go, making an excuse. Years later, Diana said that she regretted not going. She was at Michael's home and her boyfriend's words were: 'If you go, don't come back.' He meant it.

It was 4 a.m. when Jane Rayne awoke to the ring of the telephone. She picked up the receiver and recognised the very low and sad voice. Antony had never called her at this time. She listened sympathetically and before she could try to say something helpful, he told her he had just taken 42 sleeping pills. She began to plead with him. Seconds later, the line went dead. Thinking about it 60 years later, Jane believes Antony died when he was on the phone. Before rushing off from Maunsel Street to his apartment, she called the police, giving her name and contact details. This, she thinks, was her biggest mistake: letting the police know that Beauchamp had called her at this late hour. It turned a tragic event into a headline story. Jane had never asked to get in the papers. She didn't know him that well when all things were considered. All she wanted to do was help him. For a while she endured press intrusion and unkind things were said about her. Diana mentioned to someone the next day she too had had a late call from Tony, so the press were on to her as well. The two young women suffered for their friendship but had been shining beacons during his last few months.

Tony was found in a bedroom to the rear of his apartment, lying in bed in trousers and shirt, his right hand holding the telephone handset, with a long letter to his mother beside him. The man who had made the Beauchamp name illustrious had died the year Tony came into the world. Robin Duff's grandfather had suffered for the military debacle when British troops went to protect the oil fields of Mesopotamia from the Turks. Unable to live with the shame, Duff had taken a similar overdose of Veronal. Such is the dangerous power of fame.

Sarah didn't go to the mortuary or inquest. Those unfortunate tasks fell to Jane, who also joined Vivienne in giving evidence on 21 August at the coroner's court. The public were at first refused admission to the inquest, causing some criticism. Sarah's sister made a short statement about the distress caused by the news. On 23 August there was a chance for mourners to pay respects at Putney Vale Crematorium. Tony's wife, guarded by her loyal sister, sat in the front row having left a tribute of red roses and pink carnations and a note simply saying 'Sarah'. Clive came with his parents and a few of the Entwistle family's artistic friends like the Arthur Ferriers, writer Sigmund Miller and Tony's friend David Metcalfe. Within the throng of black cars two small, pretty heads could be seen: Diana Ashe, starkly and endearingly honest; and Jane Rayne, quietly self-possessed. Sarah gave Jane a hug and seemed to understand exactly what the younger woman had meant to Tony, and how she had helped. During the service Sarah made a speech about the husband she had been so far apart from. She finished by saying that 'Somehow they couldn't make a go of it.'

Diana Ashe was still in shock. She kept crying. Michael came with her to the funeral service. Diana didn't speak to Sarah but found that the Entwistle family, whom she had never met before, seemed to know exactly who she was. Vivienne asked if she could take her photo. Diana was a model at the time and it would not have been an unusual request – only that it was being asked by a mother at her son's funeral. Diana wondered if having a photograph of a girl Tony had spoken of assuaged Vivienne's grief. That said, she also recalls Vivienne stating that 'The only woman her son loved was Sarah.' The other thing that took her aback was getting a call from Clive soon after the service. He said that there was an item belonging to Tony that he thought she might like. She expected it might be something like an ashtray. Diana came to where he was living and there was no such item. What she got was Clive making a pass at her. She was appalled that he could attempt to do this so soon after Tony's death and felt very angry. Perhaps this was his way of mourning – to be close to someone Tony had felt close to. Listening to her in 2018 the feeling of what it is like being so young and vulnerable to hurt comes across. Soon Diana was at Michael's side en route to Afghanistan.

Lord Beaverbrook lent *La Cappocina* to the Churchills and on the morning of 7 September Clementine fetched Rhoda Birley for lunch. Her son Mark was married to Jane's sister Annabel. They must have been trying to make sense of Tony's death. Vivienne was dear to Sarah and they cooperated in closing his affairs. Sarah took over debts owed to Wick telling Tony's mother that she was sure her son had scored a 'moral victory' in his battles with the big bosses. How much she paid isn't known but the net value of Tony's estate was nil. In a heartfelt letter to Vivienne, she admitted she had been aware of his fears and the lonely path he trod:

> But his pride would not let anyone help him – and I understand so well for I am proud too and when I am frightened I want to run away from my friends so that they shouldn't see my panic.

Sarah moved to a cottage raised on stilts with the mighty roar of the ocean beneath her window. In the evening it was a womb-like capsule with distant breakers regular as a heartbeat. At the Sombrero Playhouse she resurrected a playlet from the Coward cycle that had been part of her life with Vic. She wasn't the whimsy socialite this time but the virulent Mrs Pepper. She chose this cathartic role for a single benefit: to raise money for the Arizona Boy's Ranch and Arizona Girl's Ranch, organisations based in Maricopa to serve young people with mild mental and emotional health issues and special education needs. At Malibu she produced gouaches of the bay. She was so proud of them that when Wendy Reves returned to Europe, Sarah asked if she might take them to her parents, whose opinion mattered. Clementine and Winston thought them 'captivating'. Sarah's health issues were such that she became a victim of carelessness. Living a cut-off life without a protector, she could cope for a limited time only. Her painting, poetry, laughter and silent grieving came to an end after she got into a tussle, lost it and was publicly disgraced.

## 14

# Neverland and After

Wendy came up with all kinds of ideas to amuse Winston, enlisting Sarah in each delicious diversion. When Winston bid everyone goodnight and his chair was carried up the grand staircase at La Pausa the chorus girls outdid each other with high kicks. The Old Man waved as he ascended like the Pope giving a benediction. This was the therapy she needed. The trappings of fame had been a horror. When they were little, Papa would console them saying: 'We are all in this adventure together!' Now Sarah couldn't help but say: 'I too, my darling, am every step of the way with you in this little set-back.' His health concerned her more, her diet being a source of mirth: 'I don't mind the carrot tops! What Mule does?' It was Wendy who chose the clinic and who boosted her confidence saying how stunning she would be when her teeth were made over. 'Poor old Wendy Girl,' she declared, 'will look like a real ole' bag' in comparison. Clementine helped with money and requested that medical staff report to her following their assessment. Instead of being an in-patient at the Bircher-Benner Clinic, it was cheaper taking a room at the Dolder Waldhaus for 'rest.' Dr D. Leichti, her woman doctor, was ten minutes away. Wendy could pass news from her parents and anticipate Sarah's next visit, when it would be mood music time once more. Diana visited via Monte Carlo's Hôtel de Paris on 20 March 1958 and Mary days later. Field Marshal Montgomery and others sent messages of support.

Sarah didn't stay too long. Niki and Helmut were riding on the tide of opportunities in Europe where motion pictures were still more important than TV and she wished to enquire about openings. At the end of May she was expected to represent her father in Israel and would go on to Rome. Busy schedules had been her lifeblood and it was the same for her brother, who regarded being on the move as a correspondent as a 'shot in the arm'. In May he was reporting from Algiers. 'Never waste a day' was Papa's mantra and they were hard-wired to lead manic lives, with alchemy substituted for time from infancy to adulthood. When did they breathe, read and produce lorryloads of letters? Manic behaviour was thought to be a cause of Sarah's distress and over-drinking. In correspondence with Lady Churchill Dr Leichti confirmed that while recent events in her personal life were upsetting, depression had been affecting her for some time. In her view, psychological assistance was needed and she asked Dr Meerwein to help. Sarah reluctantly underwent a few weeks of analytical probing and if the psychobabble caused her to recognise a behavioural fault, it isn't obvious. Meerwein referred to her drinking as a chaotic 'protest' against 'an order forced on her by the demands of public life with little consideration for her personal emotional needs'. He spoke of her having occupied a high position for a long time. When she got drunk it was a way of throwing off these demands. He hypothesised that it was an unconscious attempt to force a reaction from her parents and compel them to demonstrate affection. Because her misdoings caused reproach, a new cycle of 'rejection-protest' began. Anxiety made her neurotic, affecting her relationships and career. The quest for success was compensation for the affection she craved. While the report says that Sarah had seen psychiatrists before and had a negative view of them, Meerwein recommended she try again. The Mule had done enough probing and took off on her travels. Niki found it amazing that Sarah suddenly came to stay: 'She was concerned that I would be lonely by myself in Venice and flew down to stay with me for a whole week. I find that a remarkable gesture of friendship, don't you!'

She arrived after her stint in Haifa, checking into Rome's Gritti Palace Hotel. The press dived on her, not stopping until the controversial star had given them a photo. Sarah still thought about going back to America and Wendy's mother Blanche had offered to outfox the paparazzi by meeting her at the airport. She chose instead to remain in London for the foreseeable future, moving in July 1958 into 7 Randolph Mews, a party to end that peaceful month. Her mother was pleased to have her back. Sarah joked about not having spotted Edgware Road's ladies on the prowl yet and mentions neighbours like playwright Christopher Fry, historian Patrick Balfour 'and I am told – lots of longhair intellectuals! ... I had better put some bookshelves up.' Clementine preferred London's shady characters to the Riviera's idle jet-setters and when she told Sarah a story from Anthony Montague Browne (AMB) it gave her daughter a laugh. It was about Winston emerging from a spot of roulette in the casino at Monaco's Sporting Club that June. Frank Sinatra was in the main building, rehearsing a concert. Seeing Churchill, he came running out, grabbing the Old Man's hand and gushing. Hating strangers touching him Winston asked who the man was. He was none the wiser when told. Sarah had no objections to the Riviera or to being a guest of Princess Grace, who she knew from Hollywood. There were a few grumbles when Winston was left waiting for Rainier to arrive.

Had she attended a dinner in September given by Daisy Fellowes, she would have renewed her acquaintance with Garbo (then meeting Winston for the first time). Pamela Churchill talks of the touching scene of Winston, in total innocence, slipping his hand beneath Greta's dress to test if she was cold. Finding that long English thermals were doing their job he was reassured. He was on Onassis's yacht, *The Christina*, with GG before seeing Sarah at *La Capponcina* on 11 September for a golden wedding anniversary party. At Chartwell, Randolph organised the Avenue of Roses. By now a gardening enthusiast, he loved spraying machines and faced with an invasion of plantains on the lawn, masterminded Operation PLANTAIN, with neighbourhood kids invited to pull them up – £5 given to whoever finds the longest root. Arabella was on measuring duties and Lady Astor, nagging adversary of Randolph's youth, handed out prizes.

In October Sarah was back in rep. Critics picked holes in Rattigan's plays but crowds flocked to Worthing's Connaught Theatre to see *Variations on a Theme* with Sarah a major draw. Dressed to the nines, she was a socialite in love with a bisexual ballet boy. *For He's a Jolly Good Fellow* greeted Sir Winston as he took his seat. His party watched the pas de deux entrée by Gerald Flood and Susannah York and later Sarah introduced him to the cast as local VIPs looked on admiringly.

Her next champion in the theatre was Patrick Desmond, whose bad teeth were permanently clamped around a cigar. He offered her the long-dreamed-of role of Peter Pan at London's Scala Theatre. She would star alongside John Justin as Captain Hook and 16-year-old Julia Lockwood as Wendy. Writing to her Daddy to tell him how unforgettable his Connaught appearance had been, Sarah elaborated on her work pattern, describing *Peter Pan* as 'just what the doctor ordered ... the days I don't film, I rehearse *Peter* and I have also a TV appearance next week. Life is spinning again.'

The film was *Serious Charge* – a story of lies smearing reputation. A vicar is falsely accused of homosexuality. The mere suggestion of this topic had long made getting a film censor's approval difficult but post-Wolfenden Report, filmmaker Mickey Delamar was able to make progress, albeit only slightly. Seeing the rough cut, the censors ordered re-shooting so words like 'creeps and fairies' were removed. Delamar was fighting for category 'A' but it was deemed 'X' nevertheless. *Serious Charge* is largely Anthony Quayle's picture. His Howard Philips has the authority required to take on a town's juvenile delinquency problem. Delamar thought it best to arrange boxing lessons for the actor, given the run-ins with the kids Howard endures, but the ex-SOE guard (ADC to General Liddel in Gibraltar at the time Sikorski's aircraft crashed) didn't need them. We see Sarah early on when her character, Hester, gets off a scooter. Director Terence Young (soon to direct James Bond films) spent a few late nights riding pillion around Stevenage as the ex-WAAF became scooter lady once more, but otherwise Hester is un-hip, unloved and detached from the gum-chewing nymphets at the youth club she's a patron of. Cliff Richard steals the scene singing *Ain't No Turning Back* as the kids go into a wild jive that stiff-upper-lip Howard isn't happy about. Sarah was a wistful onlooker. Having been a dancer, she took great interest while Andrew Ray – as bad guy Larry Thompson – mastered the rock'n'roll steps. Liliane Brousse, married to Delamar, played the maid that Howard can't fail to notice. Her skirts fly high as she dances gymnastically, shaking her hair Bardot-fashion.

Sadly, Howard doesn't notice Hester and even his mother barely clicks that this non-entity is in love with her son. Sarah's performance is beautifully controlled and her scenes with Quayle touchingly natural. Given that the main thread of the film hinges on the emotions and actions of this repressed ex-vicar's daughter, this was a fantastic part. As Howard's spurned admirer she bares her vulnerabilities, then everything she believes in comes crashing down. She knows in her heart that lies are behind the calumny. The dramatic climax (not in the original play) was added specially for Sarah. Hester proves she isn't stuffy and as the condemned man's saviour, she's extraordinary. Legendary cameraman Georges Périnal ensured she looked amazing in this entirely unpredicted scene. To a reporter, she said: 'I feel we brought the girl to life today.' It was a new actress they were seeing – someone physical, wild, totally alive. Those short moments on screen show she could outperform Liz Taylor or any feisty actress. As Howard's mother changes her attitude to Hester, everybody watching feels the same about Sarah. It's a terrible injustice that what should have been a new beginning should be her last film. It wasn't released until 14 May 1959, distributed by Eros Films – the Wardour Street Company that had handled Tony's independent films.

Reporter Roy Nash discovered a down-to-earth girl who disliked spiders and dripping taps when Sarah gave her longest press interview to date. At a flat at Hyde Park Street, where Lorraine Merritt was helping find the best way to display Churchill's paintings, Nash compares the red plush of the furniture and curtains to a theatre's interior and speaks of the blazing 'rufescence' of Sarah's hair, her magnolia skin, the greyhound elegance of her bone structure, her transatlantic accent and enigmatic green eyes. In front of a roaring fire, Sarah got on to the topic of not revealing too much. Artists, she mused, leave a permanent record of who they are in paint, but it isn't the same for actors who so often are merely the characters they bring to life. Who the actors are can't seep through with the character as a shield. There's a blessing in that if you're shy, she argued, with a perceptible Churchill growl. She admitted:

'I didn't become an actress to find myself. To lose myself was what I wanted.' Sarah chatted about being stage-struck. It's better to be so, she stated. Nothing was worse for her than cynicism. What actor can seriously say that he isn't in the business to create magic? Perhaps thinking negatively of psychotherapists, she told Nash that too much emphasis was being put on self-criticism. Most important of all is that you *do* things.

The Scala Theatre, off Charlotte Street, was an unprofitable theatre but each Christmas and New Year had a unique role presenting *Peter Pan*. Returns took the form of smiles on children's faces and the gratitude of staff at nearby Great Ormond Street Hospital benefitting from the royalties of Barrie's play. Over the years talented actresses gave their services, causing Peter's look to vary from boyish elf to curvaceous Principal Boy. Julia Lockwood knows the *Peter Pan* era better than anyone. Five consecutive years of her life were devoted to it. It was the best thing she had ever done. Two years running she played Wendy alongside her mother, Margaret Lockwood, and now Sarah had the lead. Patrick Desmond directed the previous year's production and Julia recalls:

> Patrick had *Peter Pan* in his soul. He was sensitive to the things that children respond to and could see things through the mind of a child. He loved Sarah.

Julia adored her and is reminded of her unusual magnetism: 'Everything was fascinating about her,' she says. People young and old were anxious to see the play when it opened on 23 December. Edmund Murray took his wife and three kids. He didn't say he was coming but Sarah spotted him and sent a message insisting they come backstage during the interval. Young children are always sensitive to the smell of a theatre as much as to its sights. Sarah showed them the magical fairy costumes. A nostalgic Noël Coward came on Boxing Day, recalling his own time in the play in 1912. Glamorous Wendy Reves came and forever more had visions of Peter flying through the window at La Pausa. When Winston came on 30 December, the Scala opened its Royal Gateway specially so he could walk into the dress circle avoiding the stairs. He acknowledged the standing ovation with a flourish of his cigar and a wave of the pale pink muff Lady Churchill had placed on his lap. The party of 15 accompanying him included Sylvia, June, Mary and Christopher and grandchildren so plentiful they were on a rota system for sitting next to Grandpa. 'Do you believe in Fairies?' Peter shouted, receiving a deafening 'Yes'. Sarah was boyish and sincere and when she said 'To die would be an awfully big adventure' the critics thought her credible. She had the kids totally on her side. Introduced to the cast, Winston told Jane Welsh, Mrs Darling, how proud he was of Sarah.

Reporters were desperate to discover what he thought about *Peter Pan* and Angus Macleod (in charge of the annual performance) explained that it was the first time he had seen the play. He remarked that, old as he was, he wasn't too old to take pleasure in it. The tradition was no better exemplified than by the presence of 80-year-old Lionel Gadsden, a mainstay of the Scala production since 1913 and now among the pirates. Julia, nicknamed *Toots* back then, recalls the team spirit. The cast and crew, including Kirby's Flying Ballet (who brought their wire-flying equipment to every provincial theatre as well as the Scala) were sociable, many heading off to a local Charlotte Street tavern after the show.

At the end of January Sarah sent an impressionistic study of Sir W and one called 'Bedroom' to the Actors as Painters exhibition at the RWC Gallery in Conduit Street (joining works by Spike Milligan, Ralph Richardson, Peter Finch, and Bea Lillie). The following month her Papa had his own exhibition at the Royal Academy. Randolph didn't paint but loved a woman who did. Natalie Bevan came into his life after June began divorce proceedings. A muse to Gertler and Augustus John in her youth, Natalie and her husband collected art and lived at Boxted. While loyal to the PM, Randolph caused Macmillan embarrassment. After a private talk with him, he told the press that Britain would support the US against China and the Soviets during the Taiwan Strait Crisis. It was questionable that the 'special relationship' could work in Britain's favour with Ike urging the British to join the Common Market to avoid being left out in the cold by a United States of Europe. That April, Duncan Sandys looked to a future when Britain wasn't dependent on America in space research. He was dismayed at the prospect of a brain drain of British talent to America.

Another type of brain drain was about to happen. Sarah remained sober throughout her time at the Scala despite the tempting pubs nearby. She had trained herself to be 'good' whilst in London. It was only when the three-month provincial tour began in February that she succumbed. Staying in hotels while Julia and others were in digs, Sarah began to flip from sober to drunk and at times raged and swore. It would be nice to think a lawless ethos in certain scenes in *Peter Pan* averted people's attention. What shrewd audience members made of the distortions to some of the lines like: 'Youth and Joy – a fucking omelette' replacing 'Who and what art thou' is anyone's guess. The next day she came in full of remorse: Meerwein's annoying protest and rejection theory rising from a crushed corner of her mind. Unclear about the form her behaviour had taken, she feared how people regarded her. She admitted she had a problem. Something about her tears, earnestness and determination not to let it happen again made them forgive her. Her comment about life 'spinning' says it all. She never could be idle. Performances went swimmingly and then, without warning, she would add an ironic twist to the 'Boy Who Wouldn't Grow Up' theme.

Barrie's *The Little White Bird* had first introduced Peter and later works developed the setting of Neverland and his fellow Lost Boys. One scene in the stage version has Wendy climbing a rope to a high summit, gliding across the stage and getting hit by a Lost Boy's arrow fired on nasty Tinkerbell's orders. Heedless of Wendy's plaintive cries, the boys mistake her for a great white bird and poor Wendy falls to the ground. Sarah ran in from the wings one time with a cry of 'Get the fucking white bird' leaving everyone dumbfounded. That day she had been stomping around and bashing into the set. Those who understood Sarah's illness could tell that she was far from herself. She had a constant drive to prove herself, yet a demon disrupted what she most sought to justify. Theatregoer forbearance and a tenner slipped into a hand to silence a provincial press protected actress and producer from censure.

Business was great in Southampton and Cardiff. Julia and Patrick were protective throughout the tour. Julia admits that they thought they could help her and influence her to take a cure. They didn't know at the time that only professional care or cold turkey treatment stood any real chance. She had reached a point when those around her needed to be on constant alert. Once, she was in a bad way half an hour before the curtain went up and there was no way she could go on. Her floating understudy was absent owing to illness. Julia, who knew every line in the play, volunteered to go on as Peter with another member of the cast standing in as Wendy. Julia was in costume and the scene began with Peter's entrance by the window. As soon as the hero was off stage, commotion was heard. Sarah appeared and insisted she was going on. It didn't matter that the children would be confused to see an entirely different Peter. She was truly dreadful that night. For a while it looked as if they would be taking the whole production down owing to outside pressures. Lady Churchill phoned up Margaret Lockwood and put the suggestion to her that she ask her daughter to leave the cast. If so, she would do the same, exerting pressure to get Sarah out of the show. Margaret, anxious her daughter was under Sarah's spell, asked if she would like to leave, but Julia adamantly said no. Julia has never regretted this decision and her mother and Lady C had to accept it. Julia believes that had she not become an actress she would have been a historian. Her colleague and best friend easily could have been one:

> Sarah was entirely unique – like nobody else I could name. She was ethereal like someone from another world. She was one of the most intelligent women I had ever met – and taught me lots of things about life, history and current affairs. She discoursed on things that left me dumbstruck. She knew about every subject and sometimes made a joke about a topic that went over

my head. Patrick knew what she was referring to. She said several times she wished she had had children.

Nobody wanted to sacrifice the art and the magic of *Peter Pan*. In terms of worse-for-wear behaviour, Sarah's misdeeds are mild by today's standards. Being a liability on the road is a far more serious matter. Her car insurance premiums and annual compulsory excess of £3,000 prove this. In her 1981 memoir Sarah writes about being called before a judge in Liverpool and being treated badly by the men ushering her into the courtroom. Julia was sent by Patrick to pay the necessary fine that day, 3 May 1959, and Sarah, as usual, was apologetic. Julia knew how traumatic it was for her friend to be arraigned in court: 'She was very private and didn't like the Press. She lived in fear of them – even back then, when they were relatively mild.'

Finally, there was no choice but for Angus, Patrick, Julia and stage manager Pip Flood-Murphy to keep Sarah out of trouble. They forced her to sleep in the theatre in Liverpool. Each night they came up to the room containing one of the cots from the nursery set (small but better than nothing). Patrick and Julia did their best for their leading lady, bringing her anything she needed and taking her for walks on the roof to ensure she took exercise. They did this willingly, never once resenting it.

Winston was then aboard *The Christina* along with his talkative white budgerigar Toby, a gift from Montgomery who bred them. Diana was present with her daughter Celia. Thinking of missed opportunities made Sarah keen to play mother to Julia. From the onset of their relationship they called each other 'AD' and 'AM' with Julia the Adopted Daughter and Sarah her Adopted Mother. A postcard from AD survives sent that July from Antibes. Julia had been trying to produce art like her friend: 'Just typical *Toots* type painting.' She mentions she had 'made great friends with The Carousel, the strange boy girl troupe'. She promises to tell Sarah more next time she sees her. Sarah would soon be maternal not just towards Julia but to one whose potential for notoriety exceeded everyone's and whose chance of survival seemed fragile. A new Tony entered Sarah's life: Liverpool-born Toni April, artiste at the nightspot Julia referred to (an offshoot of the Paris Carousel – the brainchild of Jewish pied-noir Marcel Oudjman). Like other transsexuals, Toni struggled with an impossible fate, eventually making a decent living on the club scene where *Get Me to the Church on Time* featured in her repertoire.

Toni was Julia's friend before she entered Sarah's life. In fact it was all down to Julia's little sister Ginny that the chance meeting happened. Ginny wasn't yet ten years old. Rupert Leon had requested that his elder daughter come to Juan after *Peter Pan* finished that May (and before Julia's play for the Jersey season began). She could help with Ginny's education. Ginny's innocent, friendly nature made her strike up conversations with languorous sunseekers on Juan's beaches. She befriended the gang from Le Carousel. There was nothing unusual about Toni, Les Lee, Coccinelle, Annabelle and Bambi. These warm-hearted individuals took to this perfectly natural child. Julia came to the beach to fetch Ginny and this is how she got to know Toni – better known as April Ashley. Ginny and Julia saw gentlemen bowled over by these impossibly tall glamazons and then someone would whisper a word in the ear of a love-struck young man, who would say: 'Can't be true. Surely they're girls.' Julia had introduced April to her mother and couldn't wait for her AM to meet her.

Later that summer Sarah awaited a move to the seventh floor of a corner block, Hawkins House, facing the Thames. Dolphin Square had Neverland associations. Margaret Lockwood had a flat there, now occupied by Julia. Sarah's original 'Adopted Daughter' Phyllis Luckett had lived in the neighbouring block. Phyllis was then living in America with her husband and children, Peter and Wendy – that's how serious Phyllis, like Sarah, was about the Barrie play. Now in Palm Springs, Vic's protégée was getting parts in television, dodging the still prevalent casting couch (turning down a great part in *Father Knows Best* on account of its producer). Her son thinks his mother saw Sarah again in LA. Phyllis Flax had a long career turning up in *Wonder Woman*, *Dallas*, *NYPD Blues* and later, *ER*. Peter could never resist joking about his mum's obsession with *Peter Pan*. When he married his wife Pam he would tell his mother: 'You know I planned this: Now you have Peter, Pam and Wendy!'

Sarah, alas, had little time to enjoy her London home because she had committed herself to another play and tour. It's a strange irony that *The Rise and Fall of Sir Anthony Eden* and *The Night Life of a Virile Potato* took off at the same time. The first was a book by Randolph and the second a play with Sarah in the lead. His Eden biography was fact-based, scathing about Anthony's speeches and sneeringly admiring that in finding no friends at the top, the former PM nevertheless felt at home. Randolph congratulated himself for predicting that Eden would become unstuck. It wasn't all anti-Eden. He praised his diplomacy in Indo-China that secured a ceasefire and the fact that Eden knew much Shakespeare by heart. Yet he said what nobody else would say and the book was thought unkind. To give him credit, he tried to stop his book being used for political purposes by Labour, pursuing a court case but losing it. Randolph's attempt to be a politician and journalist failed. Conservative Central Office blamed him for meddling and when he considered standing that October, as MP for Bournemouth East and Christchurch, he didn't stand a chance. He told Robin Day on ITV's *Southern Affairs* programme: 'I think I know a great deal more about politics than at least half the Conservative MPs.'

Julia Lockwood remembered the time Sarah took a week off and came to the south of France. Her kid sister had heard so much about her that when Sarah got to the station, Ginny ran all the way up the platform and into her arms. Sarah instantly made her the AGD (Adopted Grand-daughter). Winston was staying at the Hôtel de Paris and Sarah invited Julia and Ginny to join them for luncheon. This was early January 1960 and Clementine was not present. Winston specifically asked that Ginny sit one side with Julia the other side. Being rather old, it wasn't always easy to know what he said. The miraculous thing was that Ginny's child's ear understood everything Winston said when nobody in his entourage had a clue. Julia found that she was asking Ginny to translate each comment Winston made. He was ushered upstairs but insisted that the two girls be brought to see him before they left to say goodbye. In Winston's suite Julia found it touching to see the elderly ex-PM so animated in Ginny's presence, which made him speak more. Julia tried to communicate but found she was saying 'Pardon Sir?' too many times. Ginny happily translated every utterance. Originally lying down, Winston took to his feet and led them to the terrace to show them the view. His closeness to nature made Ginny perfectly receptive. Without her, Julia would not have enjoyed the following description: 'Watch very carefully when you see the sun coming down. Watch as the mountain opens up and swallows it.'

Worried about Churchill being affected by her occasional noisy, tearful behaviour, Murray and A. M. B. struck on an idea to spirit Sarah off to a cabaret bar, sober her up by ordering a hefty meal and tiring her by several turns on the dance floor. It worked and Sarah quietened down and was great when they returned to the hotel. Julia says that Sarah and her father shared a kind of *naughtiness*. Winston would sometimes call her 'My Baby'. Parting he would say to her: Now My Baby, you will be good, won't you?

*Night Life of a Virile Potato* was one more play with a dreadful name. Charles Hamblett, home again after documenting California movers and shakers, got mileage out of the title in his article *The Sex Life of a Virile Cabbage* – about L. Ron Hubbard's interest in hortipsychosis. A controversial figure in the US, the Scientologist had purchased Saint Hill Manor (where Tony took Lady Rayne) as his new HQ. Gloria Russell, a busker turned private detective and 'angry young woman' with a fondness for farce, was responsible for *Virile Potato*. Perhaps a Stephen Ward character inspired her philandering gynaecologist. In this Mayfair world, mistress and wife both fall pregnant. Sarah was Lisa – the wife – and Geoffrey Chater was the doctor. Geoffrey remembers:

> Miss Russell's script was light hearted and not aimed at anything deeper and this is why Sarah chose it. Her performance was up to the mark. She was a

> 'fellow pro' and an enjoyable person to tread the boards with. It was tough with the world making comparisons between her and her Dad.

The critics loathed the play, especially lines like 'Don't be a moaner Lisa.' Original music was by Eric Spear, best known for the theme to *Coronation Street*. On 10 February 1960 Sarah appeared on BBC TV show *Wednesday Magazine,* ending up beaten up by the interviewer who focused on negative press responses and probed into her personal life. Was she rebelling against her aristocratic circumstances? Sarah was so defensive it made uncomfortable viewing. Shortly after, she reneged on her rule about staying sober in London and had to be ejected from a pub, resulting in an appearance at Marylebone Crown Court. A fine was paid and a lawyer found with softeners proffered, like: 'Alone at that hour she became a little frightened.' At his beautiful home overlooking Green Park, Villiers introduced Sarah to Annabel – his blue-eyed Siamese who was never allowed out the door. He could see that none of her detractors considered the fate of one whose anger had been stymied by nannies and pretty much everyone since. Yet, he was stony-faced as she harped on about being 'punished', denying her role in initiating outbursts. He kept silent as she blustered and finally she left for La Pausa where Wendy would sympathise. At Robert Viale's restaurant, Le Pirate, overlooking Menton, they sent Winston a telegram signed 'Your Two Geisha Girls'.

Back in 1957 the Sandys marriage was in the news after Diana made a brief statement about their separation. She moved to 58 Chester Row, where Winston's paintings brightened the walls while Duncan worked on a White Paper proposing unpopular changes to the RAF, radically ending the use of fighter aircraft in favour of missile technology. Such a deterrent meant a reduction in garrisons in the Colonies, West Germany and the UK. Conscription was being phased out alongside a rationalisation of military industries. Field Marshal Templer couldn't stomach it and turned on the Defence Minister, pulling him out of his chair by his lapels. It mattered to Diana that Duncan continued to see her Papa at The Other Club and she asked if they might meet privately instead. She tried to be a brave *battle cruiser* but three years on, couldn't face another stormy sea. In March 1960 Randolph informed his father she had been admitted to the Royal Northern Hospital. Duncan by then had begun divorce proceedings. He and Humphrey Trevelyan (ambassador to Egypt) were guests at 48 Upper Grosvenor Street, the home of Margaret, Duchess of Argyll, witnessing her jealous husband turning up unannounced and drunk.

Randolph invited confrontation, flying to South Africa in the wake of the Sharpesville Massacre and speaking out about Apartheid in a way few others dared. The nomination of John F. Kennedy at the Democratic Convention in

LA in July was something he thought boded well. Randolph had remained close to Kay Halle, who opened doors to JFK, Jackie and Bobby, and he knew them well. Having accused MP Gerald Nabarro of slander, he came away from court £1,500 the richer. Litigation never fatigued him. Discoursing on consumer protection on a TV programme in April 1960, he seemed to lose the plot with unrelated diatribes ranging from debased newspapers to cigarette brands and Diana Dors (who had received £35,000 for stories about her private life). 'I don't understand what happened,' a BBC spokesman said, 'he was perfectly all right when he got to the studio.' At a ball celebrating the wedding of Princess Margaret and Armstrong-Jones on 4 May, Noël Coward consoled Lady Churchill. Alcohol had played a part in her brother's despair and Sarah's struggle tormented her. Writing to Sarah, she merely said that Mr Coward sent his love and was complimentary about her acting.

Julia Lockwood had played Peter for the 1959 season and would do the same for 1960. She was a generous friend to April Ashley, fully accepting her at a time when there was no sympathy for transexuals. Julia had already introduced her to Sarah. They met at the Hôtel Le Bristol. April had returned to Rue du Colisée and was trying to make money. Sarah flew to Paris and they went to Boulevard Saint-Germain to drink a bottle of red wine. April wished she could take a plane to lunch and have the entrée that comes from having an icon for a father. No life could contrast more with the less-than-wholesome one she knew. Sarah's clean-spun Englishness sent April into the clouds and she latched on immediately, dazzled by the Churchill name and all that came with it.

Julia was quite cross at April because her own relationship with Sarah was so special. She agreed that April could possess the status Adopted Friend but was unhappy about her being an AD too. Sarah was pleased to find herself the object of adulation. Toots had invited April to use a room at her Dolphin Square flat, moving her vast collection of dolls off the bed in her honour. Soon, April was competing for Sarah's affection. Three days before April left for Casablanca to undergo sex reassignment surgery, Sarah was due to appear in *Dear Brutus* for the Pitlochry Festival. She had acted in this Barrie play as a 14-year-old in Broadstairs. She hated playing a man back then and wondered how April was getting on. Stopping at a pub en route to Kirriemuir on 9 May, she remembered how Barrie had drawn his title from Shakespeare: 'The fault, dear Brutus, is not in our stars but in ourselves that we are underlings.' Time and sustenance got the better of her and she didn't reach her destination. The wife of the festival director had to stand in. Tail between legs, Mule retraced her journey south by car.

Vic conferred with judges and the winner in white lace claimed her throne surrounded by maidens. 'When I was Santa Claus, they didn't make me give a speech!' he lamented. He told them how the Peel Pageant (on the Isle of Man) wasn't *just* a beauty contest but a chance for today's young lady to develop good taste in clothes and to learn to be gracious and vivacious. The day before he had asked his secretary who the composer of the song played on her turntable might be – the one with the line 'Tomorrow may rain, so I'll follow the sun!' Looking at the acetate disk, Gladys told him it was by The Quarrymen.

No other British star was as cultured as Vic Oliver. The previous month he had conducted Donizetti's *La Favorita* at the Scala and remembering Dickie, asked about that boy who never grew up. Meanwhile, at Croydon's Pembroke Theatre, Sarah was due on as Eliza: a woman who sheds the dominant man who moulded her into an image, then failed to be a true life-giver. The *Aristocrat of Comedy* might have made an interesting Mr Higgins, she mused. Ellen Pollock, who had known Shaw personally, directed *Pygmalion* with Amazonian energy. Sarah had first met the sunbathing addict in 1937 and Ellen and her artist husband, the hugely entertaining James Proudfoot, were loyal friends. Going pure cockney, Churchill's daughter astonished everyone. Looked after on a flight to New York by Nancy Oakes in October that year, Sarah was glad to see Alec Wilder, whose opera about a boy's dream was the basis of a film, *The Sand Castle*. She struck up a friendship with Elizabeth Seal, the star of *Irma La Douce,* the 1963 American romantic comedy.

At Sarah's poky flat – not somewhere you expected to find a great lady – David Burke auditioned for Orlando in Ellen's *As You Like It*. The play has Rosalind, Sarah's character, passing herself off as Ganymede, a young man. David disagrees with a critic's comment that 'principal boy archness' was detectable in her playing. He insists it was sensitive acting and remarks that nobody had, until then, exploited the 'brave boyish quality' that genuinely existed in her:

> Sarah was very natural playing Shakespeare's truth-seeker. In real life she seemed very shy and reserved. I was told that she would like to rehearse our scenes privately. With only a two-week run at the Pembroke, rehearsal schedules were tight. We worked a lot. She made sure a drink was ready for me before I left.

David says that Sarah's background and name were never highlighted and that during the run she was just one of the team. There was a wrestling scene, a device used to show where Orlando stands socially (brutal sports being his lot, rather than gentle pursuits). With no wooden floor to take the impact, David got beaten up every night. Sarah insisted on him being examined by an osteopath in case he had sustained a serious injury. First and foremost, Sarah was 'kind and courteous' David recalls, adding that she seemed older and responsible for everyone's welfare. It's moving to witness David not only reciting lines word-perfect after sixty years but singing the song Rosalind sang the day they performed in Sir Winston's presence. Sarah sat strumming a lute to words she penned, a tribute to a great actor and role model central to her life, to whom she still needed to prove herself:

> Some days in the forest, the trees are so bare. Those are the days that I'll know you're not there. Though I lose you, I'll hold you to the dream, so green were the rushes that border the stream.

Fenella Fielding had just scored a great success with *Valmouth* and *Pieces of Eight* with Kenneth Williams. She remembers the uncertainty about the part she would play. With Ellen worrying Sarah might be overshadowed, Fenella opted for Phoebe, the shepherdess in love with Ganymede:

> I didn't want to seem like I was sticking out for a leading role in my first Shakespeare – I could imagine them saying 'Who the fuck does she think she is, walking into a Shakespeare and playing the lead? Has she ever done it before?'

Much newsprint was devoted to whether the Bard would have approved of Fenella's injection of burlesque and Phoebe's Bernard Miles vocals, but critics admitted she conferred distinction on the character. Fenella, who had a lasting friendship with Sarah, remembers the play fondly:

> Sarah was lovely. She was charm itself. These productions were so underfunded you were lucky that they didn't ask you to pay for your own costumes. Sarah supplied hers for her scenes in the forest after she had run away from court.

As Ganymede, Sarah looked like Peter Pan. When she climbed up on a tree stump a critic thought she was about to be strapped into a flying mechanism. Fenella says the Pembroke Theatre-in-the-Round was accessed via aisles. There was one special entrance she recalls:

> Sarah was as nervous as hell. She didn't know if her father would come or not. Then he did arrive. He came because she was his daughter and, of course, he adored her. She didn't know how he would act. He came in through the main entrance to one side of a swathe of seats. Before he sat down he bowed

> to the four sides of room to those seated in each area. He acted beautifully. I was introduced to him afterwards.

Winston was fresh from a month-long cruise on *The Christina* and had made his last visit to the US. His entrance at the Pembroke had so much grace, it was copied. A few days later Fenella recalls that Laurence Olivier came with a gay man who used to put on revues. Both were inconspicuously dressed and few recognised them. She adds: 'To my absolute horror they did the same thing, bowing to all four sides of the audience and then sitting down.'

Sarah's company, Jerome Stage and Screen Ltd, dealt with the tax implications of her transatlantic career and aimed to find theatres where they could present decent plays with new writers, one of which was James Liggatt. He wrote *Divorce on Tuesday* years before he was casting director on *A Clockwork Orange* and *The Shining*. Sarah didn't intend always to take the lead, but she agreed to be Sadie Thompson in Maugham's *Rain* at Bristol Hippodrome beginning 29 May 1961 followed by a short tour. Costume-wise, this was a departure for Sarah, but she wore her sluttish outfit like a lady and looked terrific. A young actress from RADA, Christine Ozanne, who had flat-shared with 'Tiger Lily' from *Peter Pan*, was assigned 'trough duties' simulating the downpour. Sarah, Christine remembers, treated everyone with equal grace. Too often, lead players were lofty. Her drinking was only quietly mentioned and intruded on their work just the once. She suffered a short lapse at the end of one performance. Perhaps the audience thought it was a dramatic crescendo:

> We heard the thunderous bang of a door slam shut, which made no sense. All eyes looked to the stage entrance and there was Sarah, draped in black – standing with her arms outstretched. Her eyes seemed dead as if she was temporarily without her senses.

Prior to the next tour date, they travelled to Brighton where they had digs. Sarah tangled with the law on 3 June outside The Elephant and Castle in London Road. She jostled with the landlord, who tried to get her into a taxi and might have coshed a policeman (if one report can be believed). Because of this, on the morning *Rain* opened in Eastbourne, Sarah, in tartan coat and sunglasses and accompanied by Patrick, appeared in court. She was warned she would deal with worse than a fine if she persisted with this. She completed the Eastbourne show. In London Sarah had a 'court' of young folk, most of them adventurous and creative – not always loyal. They were savvy enough to scram the minute they got wind the police were coming. Sarah had reached the stage where a small amount of alcohol made her unsteady. She shouldn't have been in these pubs without a protector. Things were beginning to close in on her in the summer of 1961. Dolphin Square Ltd, perhaps vindictively, took against the resident at 708 Hawkins House, raising an injunction to restrict her from leaving bottles in the 'common parts' (and from allegedly throwing them from the windows). Then she 'offended' again, flying into a rage against authority. Carted off to prison, her only comfort was the vague feeling she was reliving her father's experience donkey's years ago: captured by Boers and condemned to serve time in Pretoria.

It took a while for Sarah to grasp that this was indeed reality. She went into Holloway on 15 July for nine days. She talks in her memoir about being denied letters but finding bouquets and packs of cigarettes in abundance. The latter became bartering tools. It was only after she was discharged and designated an informal patient at the Maudsley and NHS Hospital in Denmark Hill (where she would receive psychotherapy) that she could correspond with friends. During a confinement that wasn't long but was certainly anguished, Sarah drew strength from Julia and Ginny, a photo of the sisters being the 'only thing that comforted this old battered heart of mine'. A single letter from Sarah to AD makes this fact plain. Many similar letters originally existed. Julia shared them with a member of Sarah's family after her death, thinking they might bring comfort. When she asked for them back, she received an offhand explanation that they'd been disposed of, which hurt her a lot at the time. Julia could never forget her friend's description of the unique sensation of hearing 'Sarah' whispered down corridors by fellow prisoners.

Sarah told Julia things about her life she would never tell another. They had always shared things. There were things she seemed extremely hesitant to talk about, dismissing them as taboo. Then, when she had had a drink and felt a great need to explain, she talked fluidly for hours about the subject deemed off limits. A great listener, Julia was aware that Winant's death had left her with an eternal sense of guilt. She never spoke, however, about Vic Oliver, which was odd. She should have been proud of the time she lost her hang-ups, yet she cringed at that memory. She was still burying the old Sarah. In her letter to AD, she describes aspects of her imprisonment, adopting a breathy, galloping pace, making everything matter-of-fact. Perhaps the most extraordinary episode illustrative of a certain *je ne sais quoi* held dear by Julia and Sarah, is the time the magic of theatre crept inside 'those dreary walls'. Sarah refers to 'that something that you and I know about', and how it 'was there in living quantity'. As if some Pentecostal conversion was in the air, queues of young women flocked to her cell. Some had attempted murder, some were prostitutes and one was a serial lorry thief. Sarah mentions the 'masses of stories about sex', the tragic lesbians, that 'they wouldn't believe I wasn't butch', with one candid inmate attesting that Sarah was lusted after and if she were in on a long sentence, she would *go for her* herself. As she writes, Sarah never dwells on anything dark or unhappy.

Alan Gordon, a Maudsley doctor, became Sarah's friend. She would go on to attend his gatherings at 15 Nevern Mansions and co-own with him a number of greyhounds. One of them, Bellfire Susy, scored a hat-trick at Wimbledon. When she met the magistrate, former RAF Squadron Leader Anthony Plowman, she took Alan's advice about keeping silent in court. Designated suitable for the Maudsley, she was initially put in a private room and afterwards a public ward with a pass issued. She had to attend every day. Sarah told Julia she liked it there, especially the art studio, where patients could paint and sculpt. She mentions Maggi Johnson and Patrick Desmond. She suspects the former hoped she would suffer worse punishments, while the latter observed this 'musical comedy' gleefully. Her true feelings are not easy to gauge. You can't get more of a wake-up call than Holloway Prison – but Sarah comes across as someone in denial. 'Today's verdict was what I wanted – a complete bill of good health,' she tells Julia. She talks of an 'ugly picture that was building up' but that she was now free. The *monkey on one's back* connotation didn't apply to her. She then talks excitedly of the future and ends the letter with: 'Give Ginny a great gin-soaked hug.' Sarah has to be admired for her unflagging surety and determination. She was like her father in that respect.

15

# My Darling

April Ashley was a sensation in her yellow bikini, riding horseback along the beach at sunset. If you're turning heads, do so when European royalty is in town or head for Torremolinos where posh boys from the Chelsea set hang out. She brought style and élan to the Jacaranda, a Marbella haunt owned by Arthur Corbett, first son of a former Governor General of Tasmania. The two met in November 1960. Married but beset by troubles, Corbett latched onto her, much to the consternation of his family. April's attitude to her admirer was lukewarm but after being outed as a transsexual by the *Sunday People* in November 1961 and beginning a short reign as Britain's foremost celebrity freak complete with tawdry club act, choices were limited and selling her story to *The News of the World* was a fair deal. Here, the weather was better and the clientele gawping at her was at least sophisticated. She knew everyone from the Marqués de Villaverde to Ava Gardner. When her 'AM' arrived, the Jacaranda came alive. Sarah grabbed a partner and after shots of cucaracha, broke Arthur's rules by jumping on the tables, rivalling April's dance with flicks, kicks, twists and a few lifts. Orange blossom was thrown, but Arthur stood scowling. He returned from Málaga with fitters and changed the Jacaranda's tabletops from wood to glass.

Despite being 'discovered' by rich visitors, Marbella was a quiet resort. On good terms with her 'huntin' shootin' psychiatrist', no objection was raised to Sarah going abroad and devoting time to her writing. Money wired to Gibraltar via the family solicitor enabled her to move from the Golf Hotel to Villa Santa Cecilia and she bought a car, adopted a dog and persuaded Katie Jones, her help from Hyde Park Street, to come out (flying with her since Katie had never flown). Squat, working class and calmly cunning, Julia describes this 'real sweetheart' as an unusual case of someone who morphed from charlady into 'one of the gang'. Her husband didn't object. His wife's support let him look after their daughter Barbara who, to use the unkind terminology of the day, was a 'deaf-mute'.

Sarah made Marbella her base but was restless. She returned to Rome in spring 1962 and saw Soldati. At a British Embassy gathering for newly settled English-speakers she met Colin Webster-Watson, then teaching English at Ciampino Military Airport. A former choreographer and admirer of Rodin, he led her onto the floor when the band struck up. Fluid movements excited Colin and characterised the figurative sculpture he was creating in his spare time. He longed to see this ethereal creature again. Never short of admirers, Sarah promised to keep in touch and hotfooted it back to Spain. Then she met someone at a party whom she felt she had known forever. The smiling redhead stood six foot three, but Lord Audley had to go about in a wheelchair or on sticks because of a car accident. A stroke had worsened his condition and swimming aided recovery. Sarah recognised him from the Martini adverts that featured the fine tracery glasses that he designed and marketed. The ads made much of his Norman ancestry. Like her, he was a poet with a love of theatre.

He was a year older. His mother died when he was nine, but he was close to his aunt and sister Lois. Under the name Henry Jesson he began a career as an actor. In 1937 at the old Westminster Theatre alongside Anthony Quayle he was Fortinbras and the following year went to America with Leighton Rollins. During the war he organised welfare in India. Before inheriting his title, his connection to the Audley-Stanleys and the Earls of Derby was distant. There were nine barons in the family, but it was not the richest. Henry married an older woman in 1952 who divorced him six years later. A Catholic and humanitarian, he contributed to the work of the Lords over open prisons.

Sarah fussed around him as she had once fussed over Papa. She got him to wear a white linen suit. The poodle puppy she gave him was a 'Rufus I' throwback and she insisted he enter Villa Santa Cecilia a second time when Katie began each day, so she could 'announce' him. This boosted his ego. Corbett said that Sarah and Henry cut him dead at a Costa del Sol party and referred to them afterwards as part of the 'British snob world'; yet the two were distancing themselves from glitzy circles. Under thatched beach umbrellas they lunched on sweet wine and ajoblanco. Abandoning the wheelchair, Henry towered over her and she shone by his side. Julia was certain that he was prepared to love Sarah unconditionally: 'He was a truly gentle and kind man – and a good husband to her – the first. One time he called me from Spain. Sarah had gone missing on the beach – but luckily she was found.'

The chill that followed her last whirlwind wedding was still biting, so in announcing that she was marrying Henry, it was paramount that Sarah's parents feel assured that they were the first to be informed. Sounding chronically guilty, she asked how one with a life so marked by disaster could dare expect happiness. At Chartwell, a dinner was held for Henry, who afterwards thanked Sir Winston and Lady Churchill, saying he loved Sarah for 'her beauty, sorrows and instinctive goodness' and that the prospect of supporting her in her work gave him sheer joy. Sarah visited his flat and he showed her Farm Street Church and the little seahorse fountain in Mount Street Gardens where he sat and wrote. Leaving Winston a set of engraved brandy glasses, they left for Gibraltar where the Audley marriage was blessed in the Rock Hotel on 26 April 1962. Diana was matron of honour and Sarah a chic bride in a Breton hat. Inspired by a Churchill Marrakesh painting, their honeymoon included a stop at Hotel Mamounia despite its lack of swimming facilities for Henry. Her husband wrote to Clementine about Sarah's 'non-stop enthusiasm' for the old haunts like Villa Taylor – a US HQ in wartime. Then it was back to Marbella via Casablanca, Mogador, Tangiers and Fez.

Duncan was Secretary of State for the Commonwealth and concerned with migrants. Five days before Sarah became Lady Audley he remarried and Marie-Claire became a glamorous figure by his side as he travelled the world. Navigating the path sensitively, Randolph remained Duncan's friend while his sister changed her name back to Diana Churchill. She was joyful over Sarah's good fortune. Having attended a course on household design, she was mad about Marbella with its farmhouses transformed into state-of-the-art residences. Julia Lockwood recalls that Sarah got on best with her elder sister, whose scatty, eccentric nature was a pleasant contrast to her own. Diana forgave Sarah's failings. She was lovely to Julia and other friends and close at hand at Middlesex Hospital on 29 June after an RAF Comet flew Winston home when he broke a thigh bone at Hôtel de Paris. From early 1962 she worked for the Samaritans. Nobody knew who she was. She was just Mrs Spencer, or Diana. Back in 1953, when Chad Varah was first incumbent at St Stephen Walbrook, the suicide of a girl who had no one to talk to moved him to start a confidential listening service. Diana felt she could offer spiritual aid and joined Reverend Chad five days a week. He thought her decision was transformational. Doing something worthwhile made her feel appreciated.

Everyone wondered how JFK, the new President, would surmount difficulties lying ahead with Russian leader Khrushchev making trouble. Winston expressed gratitude for the present the Audleys sent him: 'With Cuba as it is at present it is v diff to get Havana cigars and ones as good as these are a rarity.' He was promptly sent another box. The Audleys moved to Villa Aurora, further outside Marbella, approached through a tunnel of trees with eleven doors needing to be locked and unlocked. An outhouse, known as the Cell (where the Mediterranean could be seen from a small window), was created for Henry to write in. Sarah told Pebin's wife Yvonne how her 'creaky old bones' benefited from the climate. Besides, she was 'always a bit "fraught" in England'. They longed for visitors, hoping it might be possible for Mama to stay at a comfortable hotel nearby.

Sarah's happiness with Henry was such that when Randolph suggested a reunion with Jenny Nicholson, she agreed. Now a *Spectator* journalist, Jenny was living in Little Venice, married to Patrick Crosse (a high-flyer at Reuters). Randolph, who kept up with all his old friends including Tilly, Adele Astaire and Virginia Cowles, was watching a story unfold and even though the identities of those concerned – a minister, his popsy and a society osteopath – were not revealed, it was obvious who they were. On 21 March 1963, the day 'James Montesi', 'Gaye Funloving' and 'Dr Spook' featured in *Private Eye* with 'Bolokhov' substituted for Eugene Ivanov (naval attaché at the Soviet Embassy), Labour MPs began asking questions. Things blew up when a West Indian was arrested for firing shots outside Stephen Ward's flat. Ward never betrayed his titled friends but blabbermouth girls in his circle did. Confronting rumours about his extramarital doings, Minister of War John Profumo denied any 'impropriety whatever' with Christine Keeler – the girl, half his age, he'd met through Ward the previous year. Downing Street described the matter as closed.

Patrick Desmond came and encouraged Henry to finish *From This Hill*, a play he had started years before. Patrick had a week's booking at the Ashcroft in Croydon lined up. A hillside becomes a microcosm of the world in Henry's text, but the play hadn't undergone proper examination. In early March 1963 the Audleys came to London, staying with Diana and friends in Chelsea. The Catholic Stage Guild helped with rehearsals. When it opened there was praise for Sarah as the character who attempts to shoot her lover. However, the turgid verse led critics to write it off as a wasted evening. The Audleys held an after-show party for Clementine and talk was about Randolph's defence of Profumo on *That Was the Week That Was*. Bernard Levin kept interrupting him, spoiling the entertainment and causing a columnist to brand Levin *Bore of the Week*.

In early May, Lady Audley received another court summons and she and Henry retreated to Marbella. While they were away Arthur Corbett (now divorced) married April in Gibraltar. 'Oh, Sweetheart!' Sarah cried, almost choking on her champagne. While marvelling at her friend's pluck, she knew that no more precarious union had ever been forged in the history of nuptials. April had helped make Arthur's club a success. How many times had she given her fans what they wanted, spinning deliriously on the dance floor, the tassels of her dress liable to make whipped cream of anyone. Now she wanted something in return. It was plain that she wasn't in love and Sarah sympathised with Corbett, telling April what a monstrously cynical attempt at advancement it was, while secretly admiring her. In Marbella and Torremolinos, April was drifting among the hipsters, ever willing to seek out admirers, especially rich ones.

Randolph was horrified as story after story blasted the Establishment for its double standards, lies and corruption. Personal friends were being victimised. Margaret, Duchess of Argyll was one. Her husband set out to ruin her reputation in the divorce courts. Lord Wheatley gave his verdict that May, considering the Duchess depraved and unnatural. A Polaroid (taken in the 1950s but assumed to be from a recent orgy) was purposely stolen from her home and produced in court by a barrister. Her husband had also had detectives follow her. 'Who was the identity of the man in the photo with the "Dirty Duchess?"' the papers speculated. Randolph asked if we had saved the freedoms of the world for this. Profumo resigned after admitting he had lied to the Commons and Randolph watched as Ward's girls profited like brazen Cinderellas from the pornographic industry he vehemently opposed. *The News of the World* had 'Christine's Confessions – the girl rocking the Government' on the front page, for which Keeler received £23,000. Stephen Ward was arrested on 8 June for being a pimp. Public censure about trafficking followed and people wondered if the Tories were protecting a call-girl racket. Randolph maintained his silence while crusaders talked of the 'clear flame of socialism' burning out 'the nest of fleas' and how the 'iron broom of proletarian rule will sweep aside this human refuse'. The veil that covered the darker side of aristocratic excess had slipped with the old codes of discretion and secrecy questioned.

Randolph could be moralistic about the press but he never judged others for their private sexual adventures. He couldn't give a toss about the moral proletariat and its calls for transparency but saw that deference was sliding and accepted the social revolution begrudgingly. On 19 June Profumo and his wife Valerie returned to their Regent's Park home. Randolph was with them and declined to speak to reporters. He didn't believe for a moment that Profumo would be so careless as to reveal state secrets (although Jonathan Haslam alleges that security arrangements were so slack in Profumo's home that Ivanov could photograph sensitive documents lying about in the minister's study). Back in 1940, Jack had played his part in history, courageously voting against Chamberlain in favour of Churchill. Randolph never forgot it.

Ward's trial began in July before a hostile judge and a viper heading the prosecution. Tony's old friend Vasco Lazzolo was one of the few who bravely gave evidence on Ward's behalf, despite threats that if he did so, pornography would be planted leading to his arrest. Vasco had to leave the country. Randolph offered the besieged Profumos his home as a hideout. Strict instructions were given to staff for Operation SANCTUARY. 'We will not stand any rot!' he declared, impressing Martin Gilbert, one of his research assistants. Randolph left the couple to enjoy Stour, inviting himself on a cruise aboard *The Christina*. His father's toleration of Pamela's seductions made him angry once more. Many were seeing a side of Stephen Ward they hadn't expected, but not everyone was up in arms. Sarah had heard rumours about Ward's lifestyle, but the idea of the osteopath being seized horrified her. She had undergone the same humiliation. Diana had liked the doctor. Valerie, whom they had known for decades, was the true victim. The Audleys followed the coverage at 11 Mount Street, but Sarah could take no more and on 20 June they drove through the summer mist to Dover.

After reaching the Midi-Pyrenees they passed elegant Bayonne taking the sea road to Biarritz with thoughts of the Old Man as they passed the Casino. In Madrid, everything got cheaper. Their car took them way down south and it was only when they reached Nevada (in Grenada) that it broke down. They got help and found somewhere pleasant to stay, although Sarah had to do without a hairdresser. Henry badly needed rest. He seemed well enough on 3 July but that evening, when Sarah was in the other room, he died, seemingly of heart failure. He was 49. In that town off the beaten track Sarah was thrown in a panic. The hotel staff did their best, but language was a barrier. When the doctor came he was an unsympathetic type and Sarah had to beg him to allow her to spend a little time with Henry's body. Her husband's face turned black on account of cerebral haemorrhage, the real cause of death. Their beautiful future together was denied. She thought he would outlive her.

Diana rushed to her side and was able to liaise with the Consul and organise a burial at the British Naval Cemetery in Málaga. Sarah swore that Henry 'died in the arms of God' leaving a profound 'legacy of love'. At Chartwell she thanked Mummy and Diana for looking after Henry's sister Lois (Mrs John MacNamee) at events held in his memory. Her Mama felt crushed by the unsettled lives of her elder daughters. Mary, thank heavens, had stability. Clementine had been a tower of strength for so long, but by September couldn't cope. Back in Marbella, Sarah wrote mournful poems and worried for her mother and sister.

Religion was part of Diana's life. She carried a missal the day she married John Bailey and prayer got her through life's challenges. Those lavender-scented City churches, refuges from the greed, one-upmanship and scandal practised on their doorsteps, had significance. Diana respected pillars of society like politicians, governors, civil servants, vicars and doctors. She trusted the professional judgment of GPs as she dealt with insomnia and anxiety. When other solutions failed she could rely on sleeping pills, even though it was a dangerous dependence. Helping others deal with the strain of life, she could forget her own medical 'history'. At one time a chatterbox, she now excelled in the role of listener. A woman called Maud Lindsay, who felt she could no longer carry on, called into the Samaritan's office one day. Diana told her that she had lived through many troubles too and gave up her afternoon to listen to her over coffee at the art nouveau Kardomah Café on Cheapside. Diana explained that putting one's trust in God would help. Maud came away uplifted by this angel with red-gold hair and cream complexion. Diana's colleagues heard her on the phone pleading sweetly with callers, telling them that 'suicide was never justifiable'. But what a craze for overdoses there had been of late. One only had to think of Tony, of Marilyn and Dr Ward.

To Sarah, Diana claimed she had never been a fighter or rebel, unlike the Chumbolly and Mule, preferring to hide from trouble, sticking her head under her pillow. She wasn't being fair on herself because she wouldn't have been at the Samaritans if that were the case: and who else could have sorted out the crisis of Henry's death? Having loved Duncan, she never got over the breakdown of her marriage. Their last years together had been rocky and he had soldiered on. His dependence on sticks (the result of injuries) had brought on Dupuytren's contracture, requiring an operation on his right hand. His main concern was Kenya threatening to withdraw from the Commonwealth unless the government acceded to constitutional demands. Duncan had seen the transition of African states from Empire to Commonwealth and tried to secure overflying and staging rights in these countries. With Alan Lennox-Boyd he worked on many issues. Family ties meant he was always around. Diana might not have been robust, but she seemed better. She could forgive people, although sometimes it was hard to determine if one was 'in' or 'out' with her. Sarah's proclivity for falling foul of authority at least meant there was a job to do in picking up pieces, carefully walking through aftermaths. The Mule didn't wallow in depression as a consequence. Diana laughed at Sarah's suggestion that this approach might be a way of combatting the blues. She would rather rely on a GP willing to receive calls in the early hours. Sarah's latest mishap was driving into a wall – causing two workmen to run for their lives – the Málaga court apparently recommending her immediate deportation.

It was a terrible shock to everyone when Diana took her own life on 20 October, aged 54. Those closest to her took the brunt and would forever deal with the hurt that comes from an action defying adequate explanation. Had she come off the sleeping pills, the nightmare might have been averted, but in 1963 these were prescribed far more freely than they are today. Her son thought that she had been happier in the last 18 months. When she called Dr Macrae on the morning of her death she was in a rational frame of mind. But the pathologist discovered she had ingested the equivalent of 17 sleeping capsules and a third of a bottle of spirits. Mary had the unenviable task of communicating what had happened to her parents and siblings.

A service was held on 31 October at St Stephen's Walbrook. A mountain of condolence letters included those from Ernest and Vivienne, Sunny and Tina, Harold Warren, Hugh French, Spyros Skouras and Josephine Baker (whom Diana had known many moons before). Randolph was drinking heavily and smoking eighty cigarettes a day, but found a distraction from grief in early November, staying with Tina and Alfred Beit at Blessington. He even spoke well at Trinity College, Dublin, opposing the motion 'that young men should be angry'.

Given what had just happened, one might think it a reckless decision for Sarah to transplant herself to a Chicago theatre, but she had a contract to honour for *Glad Tidings* (about a man coming into contact with a former girlfriend and finding out he's a dad). Too vulnerable to stay in a hotel on her New York over-night, Sarah took an apartment, but found herself answering questions from an idiotic porter who hadn't heard of Diana and thought she was the one who died. 'Just pick up the luggage, please,' Sarah said bluntly. 'Spooks don't carry bags.' It was unbearable to be grieving and performing comedy. While a newspaper report says Sarah withdrew, she says in her 1981 memoir that she completed it. Her time in Chicago coincided with JFK's assassination. Returning by boat that Christmas, Bingo served as a distraction.

She was numb to the reality that her sister had gone, reaching for the telephone to call her. Taking her notebook one day, her hand trembled as she scratched the line: 'Amber and Porcelain were your pain, the eyes a questioning to the soul.' She remembered precious summers, but even these had painful moments. Long ago she witnessed her sister looking bereft when cousins Diana and Tom and a disloyal Randolph cruelly ran off and hid. Sarah's heart sank to see Diana C pathetically searching for her playmates, singing 'Yes we have no bananas' while they sniggered in their hiding places. Years later Diana Mosley regretted the way they had treated her during these get-togethers. Sarah hadn't been included in the games but understood the pain of rejection.

There had been times when it was just herself and Diana: two girls breathlessly rushing around the Flower Room desperate to get a closer look at two butterflies that had entered their private domain at Hosey Rigge. The Gold Cream sister threatened to break glass singing in the shrillest voice, while Sarah diplomatically applauded her saccharin ballads, even handing Diana a bouquet. A loud banging interrupted them. It was Giles and Esmond – the sprogs of Aunt Nellie, aged seven and five. Those two couldn't wait for holidays, when they could escape 15 Pimlico Road. In they came, crashing into Sarah's realm and while they participated in every game, they weren't wholeheartedly welcomed.

In 1964 Sarah turned to the arts, or more exactly to Colin, the New Zealander she had met in Rome. Teaching at an orphanage in Alberobello in the early 1960s he had given children clay, getting them to work relying only on imagination. He was gaining a foothold in the art world. Longing to start life anew in Italy, Sarah couldn't wait to see his studio nestled beside Monte Mario, in the northwest of Rome; but she couldn't leave yet because the stage was beckoning.

Barbara Vajda from the Pasadena Playhouse gave the OK for Sarah and Ellen to stage her husband's *Fata Morgana*: a Hungarian rhapsody about an isolated but virile young student, George (David Hemmings), whose glamorous aunt Mathilde (Sarah) sweeps in and relieves him of his virginity. George's love-struck disarray worsens when his family and Mathilde's husband appear. Rehearsals for *Fata Morgana* began in March 1964, the cast ascending the creaky stairs of The Roebuck pub near Sloane Square. Hemmings had been a boy soprano in Britten's *Turn of the Screw* and was a rising star. Edina Ronay, soon to become an It Girl and fashion designer, played George's sister and Christine Ozanne played the daughter of a man-hater. Tony Singleton and Anthony Marlowe also featured. Christine recalls the camaraderie from day one and Ellen's skill in guiding the actors. She remembers David being lovely to work with on and off the set. He could make people's watches disappear, being an expert in magic tricks. Sarah arrived with a tall, elegant lady whom she introduced as her PA, Jane Spencer. Downstairs was an American-themed bar where the stools faced a line of angled mirrors and your reflection had a habit of cascading without warning. Later that day, as Jane tested Sarah on her lines, Christine and Tony, perched at the other end of the bar, were transfixed by her uncanny image and voice. They weren't left in suspense for long. Sarah's PA suddenly got up and faced the entire company: 'I'm not Jane Spencer,' she boldly testified, 'I'm April Ashley.' The name was still glamorously infamous. Everyone cheered. When she entered The Roebuck, April (now separated from Corbett) had whispered to Edina not to blow her cover. A few nights before, Edina met her at The Pickwick Club, marvelling at the huge pearls at her neck. April's presence benefitted Ellen Pollock and she was like their lead's minder.

While Sarah had reached the point when even a glass of water could bring on erratic behaviour, there was no cause for worry and the play ran at the Ashcroft between 16 and 25 April. At a cast dinner, Sarah enchanted everyone with stories and it was a bonus when Sir Winston and Lady Churchill attended the last matinee. It wasn't such a good idea giving them front-row seats with the stage so high, but when Winston was ready to meet everyone, the stage was lowered for his chair to be wheeled on and then raised. Sarah had a large glass of brandy waiting for him. A year or so previously Christine had been in the crime play *Distinguished Gathering* with Vic Oliver as Felix Montague. She had mentioned it to Sarah already and couldn't believe it when she saw a flyer saying Vic was due at the Fairfield Halls (next door to the Ashcroft) that evening to conduct the BCO in *Night at the Opera*. Rushing to tell Sarah, she noticed her hesitation: 'Have you seen him?' asked Sarah in a strange, hushed voice. Christine thinks there would have been limited time for them to meet after the show, given the effort it took to see off her parents. Vic was aware that Sarah's play was finishing and hadn't planned to intrude on her party, yet Sarah made time for him, entering her parallel universe and becoming *Mary Rose* again. Christine was waiting in the bar and a familiar Austrian drawl was suddenly heard on the other side of the half-moon counter. Vic came over beaming and told her he had to shake her hand. He was so grateful to her for instigating his reunion with Sarah. What they actually said to each other isn't known, but Vic looked ecstatically happy. Tony Singleton and Christine became great friends with April. They took jobs at a Villiers Street marketing company and brought April into the office where she had a job which she kept long after they had gone.

Eight days after Winston Jnr and Minnie d'Erlanger married on 15 June, Sarah was forbidden from boarding a plane, resulting in an angry confrontation. Defending April might have triggered Sarah's harsh words to airport staff. Forced to appear in court at Uxbridge the prosecutor told her she had behaved disgracefully. Sarah made it to Rome and re-entered Colin's life. Via Durazzo was the studio he loved most and Sarah painted its orange door, sun-bleached floorboards and terrace shaded by a scarlet pohutukawa. At this time they had a relationship that was physical and caring.

In his unpublished memoir the sculptor describes a frightening moment. Sarah was in the bath with one toe up the faucet, attempting to cut her toenails with his hedge clippers. Colin found something more suitable and offered to give her the pedicure, straddling the bath with his back to her. They were chatting away but he realised she had stopped talking. Looking around he saw that her head was under the water. Aghast that he might have drowned his 'lovely Sarah' he 'whipped her up and gave her mouth to mouth'. Soon enough her eyes opened, fixing into a deadpan glare. 'Have you finished dear?' she said.

While Colin's life had purpose, the same couldn't be said for Sarah's six-month Roman interlude or for that matter, April's, unless you could say going full gallop *cavallo e carrozza* down the streets like a bejewelled Ben Hur before cooling down Anita Ekberg-style at the Fontana di Trevi is purposeful. She obviously needed a complete contrast from her photocopying job.

Sarah was exorcising the ghost of her formal self. She speaks of talking to uninhibited Italians, linking arms with ragamuffins on the street at night and trusting the kindness of strangers. Friends among the *proletariato* are all very well, but it was the Hilton bar she was propping up overnight (even though it wasn't far from Hotel Sistina where she resided). It meant a call to April next day for a change of clothes. Red-faced in their steam baths and each armed with a Bloody Mary, they planned the next evening's onslaught. April talks about them dodging the paparazzi; something Sarah didn't achieve after nights out with dishy actor Mauro del Vecchio. The press didn't seem to catch on to Colin. She was frequently at his studio. He was then creating beautiful, biomorphic animal and figurative sculptures in bronze. Lorraine Merritt visited and they headed to Capri.

News came that Vic Oliver had died aged 68 in his dressing room at the Brian Brooke Theatre, Johannesburg. His doctors had advised him against going, owing to a blood clot in his leg. For two months he had been the star of *Distinguished Gathering* and was about to make his second entrance on 15 August when a call boy discovered him.

With Stephen Ward damned as 'utterly immoral', Keeler punished with a stay in Holloway and Denning finding no link between MPs and sex scandals, Macmillan departed. Harold Wilson had a majority of four and promised to deliver Britain into a modern age. The Empire-loving Max Beaverbrook had died and Britain's newspapers were embracing entry into the European Common Market. Sarah was enjoying life. The night after TV viewers watched *Ninety Years On* (written by Rattigan and narrated by Coward) Sarah came back to Hyde Park Gate for brandy toasts, champagne and oysters. Every inch the lady of the theatre, one gift she carried for Papa was *The Mocking Bird*, painted by a new artist friend of hers. Fate marks certain people out like Tony, April and Colin, sending them on journeys. Sarah was a Thursday's Child herself (though born on a Tuesday or Wednesday, nobody knew).

Another Thursday's Child had travelled to Europe as a protest against how blacks were treated in the US. He had been outstanding at art as a young man and in the war was with the Canadian tank corps, transferring to the American 386 Division before participating in the Normandy Landings. Life gathered speed for 'Lobo' (as the Pennsylvanian became known in the 1950s). This lonesome wolf reinvented himself as a singer while studying at the Beaux Arts. New York had once been the home of jazz but constraints caused an exodus of black musicians to Paris where they were recognised for their talent.

Annie Ross, then performing in clubs and recording music, moved in the same jazz circles. She says that people involved in jazz were of a certain ilk. The nature of the music was that you built up an empathy with musicians and trusted them. This way you turned in a great performance. Annie's pals included Kenny Clarke (known as *Klook*) and Don Byas, a Sax player from New York as well as French performers like the bass player Pierre Michelot. She shared a large apartment with Klook and a few others, including Lobo, for about year. Annie sighs thinking about Paris back then and can't recall a time and place that equals it. Nobody had money, but restaurants were cheap. They went out after a gig but didn't stray far from the 7-ième. Here was The Mars, an intimate club owned by a French lady and her American husband. These were peaceful places, Annie remembers. There weren't problems and the audiences were small. She would sing sometimes solo, sometimes with Lobo:

> Yes, I knew Lobo well. He was a fine person. Sound! He wasn't the kind you might worry about. He wasn't louche or difficult – just a great person to be around. I forget how he went out of my life. It was so long ago. How did Lobo sing? He was 'OK'. He typically sang in a modern jazz way. Did he know Duke Ellington? As well as anyone knew Duke Ellington.

She remembers the time she and Lobo did the first Paris-to-London broadcast for the BBC. They did numbers like *Baby It's Cold Outside*. Jazz was new on TV and they had a hell of a time with the broadcasting people on the English side who made a fuss about a black man and a white woman giving such an 'unselfconscious display' to British viewers. They just didn't 'get' what everyone loved about the Paris jazz scene. Annie's vocals were distinctive and she teamed up with Dave Lambert and Jon Hendricks to form one of the most innovative groups of the era. She recorded *Twisted* – a song about a woman outfoxing her analyst. It might have been written about Sarah Churchill. By late 1964, Lobo was predominantly working as an artist in Rome.

Sarah trusted his judgment and liked his original way of seeing things. She could really talk to him and began to use the one-room flat on Via del Corso Lo had decorated with his psychedelic paintings. She hit it off with his poodle, Lady Cha-Ba-Dah. By then Annie had left Paris, escaped Lenny Bruce and New York, married and started Annie's Room in Covent Garden. Sarah and Lo were frequent visitors and good friends. In her Roman circle there were other artists in Sarah's life and at one party she met Roloff Beny, a Canadian based on the Lungotevere. He had recently been commissioned to illustrate Rose Macaulay's book edited by Constance Babington-Smith about buildings of the classical era. Sarah's gang were cooking on a campfire near the Via Appia Antica one day and Roloff took shots of her through the flames. She got a shock when he sent her a large bill for the images. Colin recalls that Sarah seldom lived within her means. That Christmas Colin had an idea to buy presents for the orphans he had taught some years before. He and Sarah took a little car through the fairy-tale landscape of Puglia, only to be turned away by an over-officious nun, reducing Sarah to floods of tears. She told her Mama that *Mocking Bird* was by Lobo Nocho, whom she was arranging an exhibition for. Lobo's art was being used on greeting cards, she divulged.

'Sarah was always looking for the right person,' Julia Lockwood recalls, although her boyfriends after Henry's death never lasted. She believes that the lone wolf was a *great love*. Unfortunately, Julia didn't like Lobo, his goatee beard or his existential jive-talk. Neither did April, who got *the treatment* from Sarah for sending reports about her African-American boyfriend via June to the Churchills. Sarah admitted it wasn't an easy relationship, but it helped bring her back to life.

On 10 January, while holding Clementine's hand Winston drifted into a coma after a massive stroke. Sarah came next day from Rome and saw silent crowds keeping vigil outside Hyde Park Gate. Churchill seemed a little more alert between midnight and 2 a.m. and everyone wondered if it was a throwback to the time he would work productively late at night. One time when Sarah was with him at a late hour he slowly lifted two fingers into the shape of a 'V' then raised his hand towards his face before appearing to exhale. She ran downstairs to fetch a cigar and placed it between his fingers so he might sense it. Suddenly he opened his eyes and shook it violently out of his hand. 'I think he preferred the imaginary cigar,' Sarah told a friend some years later. She whispered regrets at having hurt him, Mama and others over the years. On a cold winter morning on 24 January 1965, Papa took his last breath and those present sank to their knees.

Sarah told David Burke a story that happened soon after. She didn't have a hat suitable for the funeral. She went to Harrods' millinery department but didn't have any luck finding the right one. Then, in the mirror, she caught sight of a lady wearing the exact hat she wanted. She was just about to come tearing over to ask where she could get one when the lady turned round. It was the Queen.

The funeral was on 30 January, a numbingly cold Saturday. To the chimes of Big Ben they left Westminster Hall where the embalmed body of Sir Winston Churchill had been resting in its coffin on a catafalque. Long planned by the Earl Marshal of England, Operation HOPE NOT, the greatest non-royal state funeral since the Duke of Wellington's, began. The hearse progressed through the centre of London. The family followed the coffin in horse-drawn carriages, glancing at the half a million people lining the streets. At St Paul's the great and the good led by Her Majesty, the Duke of Edinburgh and other royals awaited them. Ike, Alexander of Tunis, Viscounts Portal and Slim, de Gaulle, Pug Ismay, Bob Menzies, Attlee, the Mountbattens, Eden and Macmillan were all present. The male members of the family did the two-mile walk by foot up Ludgate Hill, then everyone stood on the cathedral steps immobile until pall-bearers had carried the coffin inside. The Churchills were told there was no need to bow and curtsey to the royals. The service began with *Battle Hymn of the Republic* with Ike's tribute televised. The Grenadiers carried Winston's casket onto a ceremonial vessel, MV *Havengore*, for the journey by river to Waterloo Station. Sarah didn't see her father's body taken down the Thames. According to John Pearson, Lady Churchill left instructions with attendants that Sarah was not to be allowed on the special train for taking passengers to witness Churchill's interment at Bladon Churchyard. Her daughter went back to Hyde Park Gardens with Julia Lockwood. They watched the coverage on television. Julia remembers that Sarah had a beautiful ceremonial copy of the order of service. All of a sudden she saw her take the programme and open the window. Julia rushed to her crying out 'Don't do that!' but it was too late. Sarah had let it fly into the wind outside.

# 16

# One's Own Way

Before Chartwell opened its doors to the visiting public a luncheon was held in June 1965 honouring the original donors with Sarah, Mary and Randolph a united Churchill front. The family valued discretion but sometimes, when the diaries of close friends were posthumously published, truthful opinions came to light. Noël Coward, who liked all the Churchills, had known Sarah the longest. Recording a dinner with her, Noël talks of her paper-like fragility and his sense that she was sinking. He saw her again for drinks at the dreadful apartment she had taken at 36 Halsey Street, Cadogan Square, his hostess's incense burning. Sarah was hoping he would see Lobo's impressive qualities but he went on to describe Lo as a 'coloured abstract painter with a very abstract talent'. Coward felt her lifestyle was below her class and dignity. Over dinner Sarah expounded on the benefits of independence and defying others' objections. Having atoned for her youthful rebellion, she was at it again as if she hadn't got it out of her system. Sore about her punishment at the funeral, she talked about the shortcomings of having Lady Churchill as a mother. This was unwise, with Noël now close to Clementine. Lobo remained silent, appearing to agree with everything Sarah said while 'The Master' sat tight-lipped throughout the soliloquy. His conclusion was that 'self-indulgence and lack of discipline seldom add up to happiness'. He felt Sarah was to blame.

Yet Clementine could at times be odd: inexplicably cool and not lowering her guard. Her high moral code caused Wendy Reves, an ex-dancer, to believe her profession ever tainted her in Lady Churchill's eyes. Years later Wendy spoke of comments Lady C made about Sarah's fingernails, so emblematic of carelessness and disavowal. These were pristine when she was Vic's wife. Sarah's comment to Noël is her only reference to Mama's superciliousness. Emotions after the funeral were the reason. Nowhere else does she share a criticism of her parents.

With her childhood wrapped in Chartwell legend, her family was keen for her to produce a memoir (while works of a more serious nature fell to Randolph and Mary). She was ready to finalise a book of poems for Leslie Frewin, an ex-film industry gatecrasher to the publishing world. She had a children's story in the pipeline and recruited a new secretary, Delphine Clues from Adelaide. David Burke thought her rather 'butch' and liable to trade on the relationship. Delphine remained her friend for life. Lady Audley had been booked to interview cinema legends like King Vidor for a TV company in Rome. Taking leave of Lobo, Lady Cha-Ba-Dah and the incense sticks, the *free spirit* had an excuse to see Colin.

A fashion show at the Dorchester featured slim-fitting tartan trousers for young girls. 'With it' boys got their outfits from Carnaby Street. Among the older Britons haunted by bombs, some railed against the government and Churchill, even if he had seen the country through. On 19 September Sarah, her mother and siblings gathered in Westminster Abbey when the Queen unveiled a Churchill memorial. Sarah sought to raise money for the Churchill Memorial Trust and was involved with the Tall Ships Youth Trust and the National Youth Theatre.

At Stour in January 1966 Randolph was happy with the snowdrops but concerned that no daffodils were in evidence. At a time when the Labour Party's relationship with many of the newspapers was deteriorating he was a behind-the-scenes advisor to journalists in a modern-day Kit Kat Club. Clive Irving (on *The Express* and later *The Sunday Times*) and Denis Hamilton held him in great esteem, valuing each thunderous response he was sure to make. He had a loyal secretary in Barbara Twigg, who organised gourmet dinners to which country bumpkins and newspaper proprietors were invited. The dining table at East Bergholt seemed like the last great political high table in England, their host transmogrified into a grandee from a different century. Miss Twigg also had the knack for making Stour radiators warm and was an expert with Randolph's new-fangled piece of kit: the telex. Passages for his father's biography were delivered verbally in between breaks for eggnog, Randolph making about six telephone calls per hour and shouting orders to researchers. In March 1966 he exhibited his father's paintings at The Minories in Colchester, inviting Lady Churchill to the opening.

So that she would never go hungry again, Laurence Olivier paid 'Scarlett's' rent for 54 Eaton Square and Baroness Audley moved into number 53. Vivien Leigh could little afford a Roloff Beny or other works at the galleries her neighbour took her to. Sarah's home was over two storeys and in her small garden, Hum-Hum, her French Boston bulldog, could yelp and scurry under the cherry blossom and sometimes dig up posh Eaton Square Gardens. 'For once, it's not me they're making complaints about,'

Sarah told friends. In June 1966 *The Empty Spaces* appeared in bookshops containing 63 poems. *The Telegraph*'s Kenneth Rose found Sarah's style somewhere in between Betjeman's satire and Eliot's stringency. On *Woman's Hour* Sarah advised that people make out what they will from the poems. She demurred from mentioning Vic and nobody had any clue that *My Heart's a Secret Place* told of her tragic, secret love affair. They say poetry never sells but 40,000 copies sold in Britain and 80,000 in the US. Sarah treated herself and friends to a Mediterranean cruise aboard a hired yacht, *The Thomana*. She sent David Burke a ticket in the post knowing he didn't have much money. David liked Sarah immensely but felt he wouldn't fit in with her Hooray Henry friends. He got out of it by inventing a conflicting commitment with the BBC. He would later regret it. He was touched that Sarah thought of asking him.

Scheduling an exhibition in London of Lobo's abstract paintings was a promotional tactic since Lo had designed the cover for *The Empty Spaces*. Mary bought a £50 picture and Charles Hamblett wrote about the couple for a magazine featuring monochromes by Terry Donovan and David Bailey of the Beatles and Stones. Hamblett had his finger on the pulse and charted the rock'n'roll era in Britain. He 'got' it, writing the first book on the Beatles in 1964 and documenting the youthful groundswell in *Generation X*. In *London Life* Charles talks about Sarah's direct vision: enough to make pompous folk uneasy. She was, he insisted, no snob, being used to poets, actors and even conmen (he mentions Peter O'Toole and Lobo at this point). He had seen her first in her Cambridge Rep days (when he attended the New Anatomy School) but today she was hip and existential; a Dylanesque creature in command of the men in her life, agelessly desirable and surprising in her desires. 'A witty bellhop will as much engage her as a port-wine duke,' he opines, mentioning her Churchillian disregard for bores. While a massive photo shows Lobo holding up his paintings for Sarah, the article coyly refers to them as friends. Charles's daughter recalls how he liked people good with repartee and how his affinity with Sarah made sense. He was earmarked to help with her memoir. A draft interview exists between 'CH' and 'SC', although it wasn't used in *Thread in the Tapestry*, which is Sarah's work.

When it came to fortitude nobody came near Lady Churchill, but everyone worried about her, even her rebel daughter. Lady C had downscaled, taking a five-bed flat. While walking alone in Hyde Park in October 1966, she broke her shoulder falling after being hit by a football. The boys brought her flowers. A few weeks later Sarah invited David Burke for lunch. He recalls the two little au pair girls who looked after Sarah's Mama at 7 Prince's Gate. Lady Churchill was kind and gracious but the mishap affected her mobility. David felt like a mouse between these two great ladies. One snippet of conversation lodged in David's memory and with his actor's gift for recall he sounds out Lady Churchill's words – the last line having a slightly indignant intonation:

> Lady Churchill: Oh, Christopher's going to Jordan next week.
> Sarah: Who's he staying with?
> Lady Churchill: The King.

When Robin Day asked Randolph to comment on mistakes made by Sir Winston, he was told that the first part of the biography related to his Pa as a little boy (a 'damned obstinate' one) but admitted that there would be issues to address later. On 27 October Sarah, Mary, Winston Junior, Minnie and 17-year-old Arabella joined him at a Foyles Luncheon to launch Volume One. Sarah didn't carry it in her castaway luggage on *Desert Island Discs* in November. The epic *My Early Life* sufficed. One of her records was a Gertrude Lawrence song about the physician who suffered 'wild ecstatics when I showed him my lymphatics' and she must have been thinking of the time Papa forbade her from seeing Vic with the speech of Prospero in *The Tempest* warning Ferdinand not to break Miranda's virgin-knot. Her father, who once found succour in a paintbox, emboldened her. In the absence of film and TV offers, for her it was poetry. Self-help meant 'digging into yourself without recrimination'.

She had a cabaret show in mind, allowing her to read verse, parts of old letters and recall family anecdotes. It was a way of remembering Papa. Nursery rhymes, limericks and even tombstone inscriptions would find their way into *A Matter of Choice*. Drawing upon Variety (having had the best tutors), she worked on scripts, but despite her penetrating Edith Sitwell-like voice, she lacked the warmth to carry off such a pure form of entertainment single-handedly. She needed a compère and someone to contribute material. Hugh Hastings was a past master of avant-garde comedy. He had done all kinds of jobs down under before coming to England in 1936. Hugh later told colleagues he was kicked out of Australia for being gay. He survived the Dieppe Raid and his Navy experience went into *Seagulls Over Sorrento,* which he staged following his appearance with Sarah at the Q. Its peppery dialogue and all-male cast shocked, but its long run earned £50,000. Norman Coburn, familiar to *Home and Away* fans, remembers him as a friend and party animal:

> I was 15 when I first met Hugh. He cast me in a play he had written, *Blood Orange*, about his childhood in some Aussie backwater – very odd for those days and for an Australian play. I did other productions with him but it was this that started my career. He loved theatre – actors et al.

When Norman moved to London in 1957 he lived for a while at the playwright's Chelsea home and acted alongside Hugh and Michael Gaunt in *Seagulls* in 1960. Despite being multi-talented and handsome, Hugh's career was waning by the time of *A Matter of Choice* and his fortune largely lost. 'I did him a lot of good too because he was on his uppers playing in pubs' was how Sarah put it later, sounding very like Mrs Pepper.

She and manager Hubert Woodward needed finance too and got it from American actress Gilda Dahlberg. That wasn't an easy relationship either and Sarah called this grande dame, whose legendary jewellery was stored in bank vaults, '5'4"of gold lamé steel-lined'. Ellen Pollock choreographed Sarah in black tights portraying Portia, Juliet, Viola and Lady Macbeth in a scene later panned by critics. Ellen also helped the Mule in a mime, tapping her feet to music on a park bench. Hugh sang, provided arpeggios to the words of Coleridge and clowned with his braces at the piano. Vivienne did publicity photos, some showing Sarah in the black and white Carnaby Street clobber she wore in the show. Lobo was supposed to add psychedelic art for backdrops but didn't. On 15 September *A Matter of Choice* was at the Library Theatre, St Peter's Square, Manchester, then was well received at Brighouse, one of the northern clubs.

Sarah opened an exhibition of Lobo's paintings in Manchester, coinciding with a bomb scare that day. She and Hastings played Liverpool's Everyman before opening at The Arts Theatre on 24 September, but London critics didn't quite get Sarah's public storyteller persona and weren't moved by this 'Kaleidoscope of Music, Drama, Comedy, Poetry, Colour and Movement'. While Dietrich or Coward could carry such a thing, it was a 'curiosity' with Sarah and Hugh.

The Continent, however, embraced the avant-garde – especially the Mickery Theatre, an experimental theatre founded by Ritsaert ten Cate on his farm in Loenersloot, near Amsterdam. Hans Keule booked *A Matter of Choice* for seven evenings starting on 18 November to include a Dutch TV recording and a radio broadcast. The expenses would cover six members of Sarah and Hugh's staff and a company manager to direct the stage and lighting. It was Michael Gaunt's first experience of directing a star name. He hadn't seen the production at the Arts and they neglected to give him a prompt copy or lighting plot, but he was able to re-stage it and take responsibility for the travel, welfare, safety and security of all members of the team. Michael was invited by Hubert to Eaton Square to meet Sarah and Patrick Desmond. Working with the daughter of Sir Winston Churchill was a deep privilege and she was delightful despite her formidable air. A few days later he was by her side flying to Amsterdam Airport. Sarah and Hugh's staff included PAs Katie and Doreen Evans and stage managers Penny Charteris and Pauline Dake. Lobo was in

Amsterdam too, although he had no role in the production. Aware that Lo and Sarah were together even if they did little to demonstrate it, Michael recalls his passivity and deadpan face. Lobo didn't seem at ease. They were actually putting up a front, having clashed badly at the exhibition. She genuinely loved him and splitting up after two years was tough. She hadn't tried to make him something he wasn't. Who could change a lone wolf's nature? There had just been a 'situation domestic' that Sarah admits she contributed to. Lo had been violent and she mentions suffering a 'disfigurement' but calling off the police, preferring no charges. It seems serious, but the details are lost.

Hugh Hastings had also 'taken a lot of knocks'. Michael remembers Hugh's roguish spirit, his voice that bore traces of an Aussie accent and how he sang in a Jack Buchanan way, making the show part old-fashioned, part avant-garde. Everyone stayed at De Nederlanden, a hotel-restaurant on a peaceful canal to the south of the city. During rehearsals in the bar, guests witnessed something like a scene from *Private Lives*. This was Sarah and Hugh rowing histrionically. It would have been quite awful had it not been so funny. Nevertheless, Hugh supported his leading lady 'making her sound and look good when she was performing'. Sarah wasn't a singer but managed a fair rendering of the 1940 classic *A Nightingale Sang in Berkeley Square* and used a melodic speaking voice for other songs. (Hugh later made occasional appearances as Private Hastings in *Dad's Army*.)

Michael made sure each scene had individuality and confirms that 'Sarah only drank after the show and was perfectly cooperative, taking direction well.' One night the cast and crew drove to the nightclub where the radio broadcast was to take place. Lobo wasn't around then. Michael recalls Sarah crying as he sat with her on the stairs. He instinctively put his arm around her shoulder. She told him sweetly that there had been three men she loved, all gone now: her father, Vic and Antony. She didn't mention Henry for some reason. As the evening drew on the hits of 1966 blared from loudspeakers and Sarah kicked off her shoes and bounded around like an elf, grabbing people in a childlike way. Hours later she was still at it. Hugh was in a vacant state at the bar and was no disciplinarian. Michael wanted to leave in case the press came. He thought Sarah liable to do something daft, ending up at the mercy of some unscrupulous photographer. He wanted to protect her. Several times he tried to explain, catching her as she flitted between tables: 'Sarah, we must go home now.' He then got the shock of his life. The woman who hours earlier had been so gentle looked like one possessed. A sea change came over her. Her eyes were black and inhuman and she was pressing her nose against his. Her 'FUCK OFF' sent the unworldly Devonshire boy reeling. He knew nothing about Sarah's run-ins with authority. The catchphrase 'Lady Disorderly' had yet to be substituted for Lady Audley by her detractors.

Winston Churchill had been Michael's hero and he was proud of having met Lady Churchill in 1959. Sarah's actions shattered the spun glass image he had of women of her class. Next day *Madame* was charm itself with no memory of the night's behaviour. It was a wake-up call and with Katie fond of a drink too, the dangers were many. All went well at the TV studio at Hilversum, but 'On the night of the last performance a large party of Sarah's friends, mostly "Sloane Street types", arrived and some checked themselves into De Nederlanden. They were there when everyone was ready to leave.'

Lobo and Hugh had gone, Sarah, Katie and a few others remained. Michael's brief was to return Sarah to London. Flights had been purchased but no cash was left to cover mishaps. Getting her to the airport tormented Michael. Those at the bar had no consciousness of time. He pressed Sarah and got only resistance. Missing the flight looked like a reality. Michael was on the phone at reception when he heard a deafening sound. Cries of excitement could be heard from the gin-soaked party. Motorbikes had arrived en masse: Hell's Angels, a leather-clad army filling up the hotel's courtyard. Frustrated in attempts to reason with the airport, Michael came running into the bar asking 'Where's Sarah?' A lugubrious voice told him she was outside. He hurried out in time to find Sarah climbing onto the back of a bike, shakily holding onto its indifferent owner. Michael made a plea to Penny and one or two others to help while Sarah insisted on staying put, cursing the naysayers. They prised her off and carried her inside. She got so hysterical Michael had to summon a doctor. He arrived and gave Sarah a mild sedative. Michael hoped to God a ferry might provide passage home. He asked Rosita, a Portuguese friend with a car, if she might take them to the Hook of Holland. Sarah refused to get into the car and the doctor was called a second time, with another sedative given. Not that it worked:

> I had no resources for hotels so it was essential to get a crossing. Sarah would not have been allowed to board a plane. The young Portuguese woman was an absolute brick to take us to the port and on to London. It was a challenging drive in pouring rain with the route uncertain. I think we 'secured' rather than kidnapped her. We didn't know how the crisis might end. In terms of how I acted then I would do the same now with the benefit of increased life experience and a credit card!

Miraculously, a ferry was waiting and Michael asked to see the purser. The official appeared and heard about the need to guarantee safe return of Sir Winston's daughter. No questions were asked. Not trusting Katie, Michael asked Rosita to remain with Sarah in the cabin. Through Kent and London the complaints were colourful. Michael followed her up the stairs of her Eaton Square home, lugging her suitcases. A while passed before his summons. A glower flickered over her face as she sat in bed speaking to him like an old friend after a long absence. Departing, he never heard from her again. He looked quite the worse for wear. Asked by an actor friend he bumped into in Charing Cross Road what he'd been doing, he explained he had returned from re-staging *A Matter of Choice* with Sarah Churchill in Holland. His friend gave an 'Ah!' and offered to buy him lunch. Operation ELF had been a trial, but Michael feels fortunate to have had the opportunity to work with Sarah.

Sarah later said she lost money on *A Matter of Choice*. This might have been because she waived her fee. Lobo went to Canada to mount an exhibition and Sarah's letter to him reveals why she was broke. She talks about Rosita – the daughter of Big Audrey – whose curious name brings to mind the friend Sarah made in Holloway. Audrey's girl was short of cash and without Sarah's generosity would not have been able to afford De Nederlanden. Katie's daughter seldom got to go on holiday and Sarah adds: 'I took Katie's Barbara, also Rosita. I suppose it was mad money-wise – but I love to do things for the young – it was wonderful to see Barbara cope and blossom and she had a letter from a young waiter there!! All I got was the bill!!' She needed to earn a regular sum to keep Katie and Doreen and was 'at square one' job-wise following quarrels with Hugh. She mentions asking Annie Ross to help find her a new accompanist and mentions things in the pipeline, such as a play Hamblett had written for her. With all the twists and turns of her career she predicts she will soon be 'turning up in opera'.

Sarah wanted Lobo in her life but at a distance. They were better apart, she judges, joking about their 'open relationship' and mentioning an upcoming visit to New York when, if Lobo isn't 'entangled' with someone else, they might meet. She was due to appear on Johnny Carson's *Tonight Show* (broadcast 1 February 1967) to publicise *Thread in the Tapestry*.

Having been out of favour the day of her father's funeral, the slow march of *Hope Not* was a way of framing a lifetime in her memoir. People were hungry to know more about her father and on BBC1's *24 Hours* on 12 June she spoke to Michael Parkinson about the 1945 election and Papa's surprise at being turfed out of No.10. There was an old music hall number about getting the sack from the Hotel Metropole and the Claridges doorman didn't expect the ex-PM to be so adroit in performing it. Sarah's Winston impression was a touching treat for viewers. She went on to read from her book in places like Wembley's synagogue and at a poetry review with Irish writer Ulick O'Connor. When the country lost Earl Attlee that October, a TV obituary featured footage from *Aircraft Firefighting at Naval Air Stations* with Sarah speaking the lines of 'the bombers'.

Sarah's name and sell-out memoir meant she was a busy chat show guest on US and Canadian TV and radio that September and October. She talked about *The Prince with Many Castles*, illustrated in pen and ink and muted colours by Eric Critchley who later worked on Michael Jackson's *Billie Jean* video. It contained *The Ivory Tower*, *The Boy Who Made Magic*, and the title story. In each story she presents deep ideas in the lightest way. A novel, *The Wife* – about an English girl's journey from the ages of 18 to 38 – was intriguing but never saw the light. She had been considering a work focused on the off-duty Winston Churchill, who quoted poetry, Schopenhauer and Macauley, sang music hall songs and made quirky comments. As a concept, nothing better would reveal his witty, humane and compassionate nature. Writing from Alan Gordon's pad, Sarah asked Randolph's permission, promising it wouldn't detract from the biography and suggesting it could be deferred until his book was fully complete. He vetoed the proposal.

July 1967 saw the death of Vivien Leigh. Within a few months, Laurence Olivier was the centre of a controversy. He and Ken Tynan wanted the National Theatre to produce German playwright Rolf Hochhuth's play *Soldiers* that tarnished Winston's war record by saying he and Lindemann hatched a plot to cause the death of Sikorski. The Old Vic board turned it down and Olivier planned to produce it. It wasn't just the family that was upset. An international outcry found its spokesman in Guy Bolton (one-time musical comedy king). He sent Lady Audley his view that 'A blow struck against Churchill is a blow struck against England.' Eisenhower, he assured her, would issue a statement quashing the conspiracy theory. Bolton added that the Cazalet family believed a fault in the plane's design caused the crash. Sarah looked for guidance after Bernard Levin proposed a TV debate between Hochhuth and the Churchills. Randolph advised her not to get involved, citing the playwright's low profile, but she didn't do as he advised, issuing two statements. In one she questioned the sources. Wasn't it strange that all the evidence was locked up in a Swiss bank that only Hochhuth could access? The whole thing died a death when a jury discredited the playwright.

Randolph no longer visited the battlefield but Winston Junior was a journalist, so he received dispatches at East Bergholt. Arabella, who had modelled clothes to raise money for the NSPCC, had found her niche in organising events and handling publicity. In May 1968 Randolph was embroiled in the struggle to recover the letter lost from Sarah's flat in the 1940s, negotiating with a New York auction house. He spoke to Sarah on the phone about that 'bloody letter'. On 6 June, he died in his sleep. Everyone felt the loss of that former *enfant terrible* whose confidence was so limitless it seemed pure insolence. He never told a lie, was loyal to his friends and courteous to strangers. He had enemies but had just as many friends. In latter years the 'dear Beast' had mellowed. Aunt Sasa comforted his children, telling them how truly inspirational they were. In September she was in Eire with Ulick and a statue of Christ face down in a garden inspired a poem. The 'heroic concept of man's predicament' summed up her brother, to whom she dedicated her next volume.

In the autumn of 1968 Sarah visited Tony's mother and listened to Hutch on the turntable as Pussy-Wooss, the cat in residence, trod nonchalantly through the clutter. Ernest had died in 1963. Aged 81, Vivienne still painted miniatures and her photography business was thriving. She came up from Brighton three days a week to 16 Adam and Eve Mews and sitters loved her for instinctively concealing faults and even changing their shape. This figures, since *Alice in Wonderland* had been her favourite book too. She also placed people's hands in a shot, believing these said much about a sitter's individuality. For Sarah's 1968 session, Vivienne made the most of her Grecian-style floor-length white dress and white trouser suit. Sarah arrived with a tall, floppy-haired, fashionably dressed young man, not so good-looking with his large teeth, but transformed into a continental Casanova by the shutter of Vivienne's plate camera.

This was Liverpudlian jazz pianist Dennis Wiley. Sarah's outfits were for a new one-woman show playing 26 venues in South Africa over a four-week period. At a time when Equity barred members from performing there unless they gave multi-racial performances, she told the press it was entirely apolitical and made no comment on Apartheid. Ten years later she stressed how she and Katie nevertheless got into scrapes, with the sound of Katie's Welsh accent apparently getting them out of trouble. Sarah once said of her housekeeper that she could 'talk a glass eye to sleep'. Formed by Peter Bankoff (who had recently brought The Byrds to South Africa) and Andrew Ray (Sarah's *Serious Charge* pal who was married to a Rhodesian-born actress), Raybank Productions initiated the tour. Andrew's boyish charm and original compèring gave *An Evening with Sarah Churchill* a contemporary edge. Sarah's radio play for South African audiences (Giles Cooper's *All the Way*) would dovetail with her visit.

A rock star rebel arrived on 22 January 1969, but the next day the Churchill groupie was lost in paterfamilias dreams seeing the original settings of *My Early Life*. She visited the building in Van der Walt Street, Pretoria, from which her father escaped in the Boer War. How she had loved this story as an eight-year-old! Evenings saw her edgy alter ego dressed for a party in a white Pierre Cardin outfit with jockey cap and white leather boots: 'They're made for women to relax in,' she said of the fashions, adding: 'I follow in my own time.' She skirted over Randolph's death, saying that a don at Oxford, Martin Gilbert, would complete the biography. A Pretoria cabaret was Sarah's first port of call. *The Poetry of Pop* traced the development of song through five decades with costume changes for each number. The debutante at the Savoy left the stage and she was spinning two pistols for *Anything You Can Do*. There was *One for My Baby (And One More for the Road)* and *Those Were the Days*. Peregrine and his wife were in the first-night audience and Winston Junior, covering the situation in Biafra, caught up with Sarah later. Images of starving children were shocking the world as the region tried to break from Nigeria only to face a blockade. Arabella organised a ball at Madame Tussauds raising £2,000 for Biafra and Sarah wrote to *The Times* a year later, criticising Wilson's ministry for backing Nigeria: protecting British investments in Nigerian oil, pretending all the while it had to because of African instability.

In Johannesburg changes in her song sequence were far from seamless and a critic called her troupe 'slap-happy, careless and very amateur', while conceding the poignancy of *One More for the Road*. The second half was quieter, Sarah reading from children's stories, poems and letters. They headed for The Casa Mia, beloved of overseas actors, then played the Brian Brooke before it was on to Cape Town. She was praised for her sense of fun: disarming theatregoers, moving gracefully through her songs and ad-libbing. All notices slammed the 'pistol scene', but Sarah won with *The Ivory Tower* and by lifting the curtain on the private life of the Churchills. She was noted for the feathery touch to her comedy and her timing – even if she did arrive late to a do held in her honour by Joburg's mayoress. She had to fetch her make-up, heedlessly left in the theatre.

At Port Elizabeth's Opera House on 11 February she got immense laughs for her story about Papa ticking off Americans over security: 'We shan't falter, alter or palter between Malta and Yalta' were his words. Critics said she seemed vulnerable when she got to the last line of *A Nightingale Sang* – 'I was there' – which, from her, had undeniable force. It was fitting that the day she arrived she met up with Elizabeth Layton, whom she had last seen on the journey back from Como in 1945. Married to Frans Nel, an officer in Prince Alfred's Guard, Elizabeth told reporters how she regarded Churchill's daughter in the old days: 'I was devoted to her and would have done anything to serve her.' VIPs and a candlelit lawn awaited Sarah at the consular residence. The *Rand Daily Mail* considered that she did not 'offer hearers the blood or the sweat, but the tears are there'. There was a trip to Victoria Falls before TV work in Rhodesia and a row with officials in Salisbury.

When Sarah, Dennis and Co. took *An Evening with Sarah Churchill* to the Teatro dei Satiri in Rome that April, she partied with Colin Webster-Watson, who joked about Roloff swiping every important female off him, whether rich patron or even his secretary. The actress Carroll Baker, then living in Rome and soon to embark on an affair with a rich Italian, was true to him, buying several pieces. Attractive to women and men, Colin was focused on selling and his extravert side helped. Those gathered witnessed his Apache Dance, or saw him strip off for an improvisimente. Sarah gave him a plug, talking about his *Poseidon and the Mermaid* that she had given Jackie Onassis on her marriage the previous October and recommending him to London galleries.

In need of money herself, she parted with her Pa's *Barges on the Seine*, which fetched £5,500. Was it to buy the $11,000 Maserati for her new boyfriend – an Italian half her age? This and the other gifts for Renzo Renzi (a former waiter from Pesaro) such as the 54 suits and allowance for his mother were fabrications. A story explaining why 'Italian men make better lovers' emphasised what a cradle-snatcher Sarah was and another said that she drank whisky and vodka, no ice, during sizzling weekends at the Grand Hotel, Rimini. The press saw to it that Dennis Wiley was transformed into 'Renzi', the young stud Sarah had met at a gallery. Journalists were looking for opportunities to deride her. She fought each battle and won a defamation suit the following year.

She had a publishing deadline for more poems, so in April 1969 rented Stanbury Manor near Bude for three months, apparently haunted by a man gored to death. It's unlikely Sarah braved the apparition alone. Emerging on 3 June, she drove to Cambridge, picking up Constance Babington Smith from Little St Mary's Lane for a lunch hosted by the master of Churchill College with Medmenham colleagues. September saw Sarah shuddering at headlines claiming that T. E. Lawrence enjoyed being birched. The legend-busting brought her father's words to mind: 'People think what they like, object to what they like and imagine what they like ... the answer doesn't matter.' When *The Unwanted Statue*, containing over 50 poems, came out that November, a columnist tackled Sarah on the subject of loneliness. Her response made him conclude that she was stronger than one might suspect. Her philosophy was to get to grips with it and be happy alone. 'Try creating a little world for yourself,' she advised. That December, donning a short blonde wig, she and Jewell went to The Camelot at 73rd Street where a set meal included all the bubbly you could manage. On the lookout for a new pianist, Idris Evans proved to be the cat's whiskers having tinkled in the US, Canada, the Far East and the USSR.

Deeply affected by the Biafran famine, Sarah could joke about diplomacy performed by crusty Brits. The story concerned a meeting with African leaders on a barge on the Niger. The Lord speaking for the Queen and Prime Minister stood up to thank his hosts, stating: 'Gentlemen, as we leave the land of the Niger…' mispronouncing the last word to gasps of embarrassment. This story might have come from Duncan, sacked from the Tory Shadow Cabinet but active as a backbench MP. He had visited Nigeria in 1968 questioning if it could ever be democratic. Arabella, meanwhile, was raising money for Africa with her charity shows. Held at Chelsea Town Hall or Club Dell' Aretusa she wasn't far from the small studio Sarah had for painting and writing. Her ex-RAF friend 'Twinkie' (Conrad Nockolds) also painted in this hidden courtyard accessed from 5 Kensington Church Street. He ran Aero Stills Ltd that used cameras attached to hydrogen balloons controlled by a bicycle wheel. First used in the war, the system presaged the drone. Hugh Oloff de Wet was Church Street artist resident. The former agent, cruelly treated by the Gestapo for six years, now swapped stories about Nureyev and other sitters at The Catherine Wheel pub with other hearty drinkers.

In March 1970 Sarah saw her former AD at 'AD8'. April Ashley part-ran the restaurant at 8 Egerton Gardens Mews. She had tried four years earlier to get maintenance out of Corbett but he had the marriage annulled with the judge deciding that she wasn't a woman. The closeness with Sarah had gone but they were together in August 1972 at Arabella's wedding in Kensington, with April in Circassian slave get-up walking a few respectful paces behind her former mentor. Idris, meanwhile, brought a little international pizzazz to East Grinstead when *An Evening with Sarah Churchill* came to the Adeline Genee Theatre that October and Sarah got news about a certain someone in New York: 'Lo is well and flitting about' was how Jewell put it.

Sarah slipped over to the States in February 1970 for *The Dick Cavett Show* and *David Frost Show*, then on to Rome for a 'working holiday' at Colin's new studio at Vicolo Della Penitenza, Trastevere. She found writing in that ménagerie difficult given the budgerigars overhead and the distracting acrobatics of Kink the kinkajou. Colin began a sculpture of her and threw a party, inviting models, writers and actors. In his memoir he says little of Sarah's attempts to work, talking of her 'drinking steadily', one night going into 'full binge'. So desperate was she to booze, he locked her in the apartment and smashed the bottles in a sink, getting a 'torrent of abusive language'. Eventually she 'screamed her last scream' and went to sleep. Next day she was as sweet as can be:

'Good Morning Darling. Was I very naughty last night?'

'Naughty? Yes Darling. I would say definitely naughty.'

Why did she drink? Was it to do with being the daughter of That Man? Colin asked. Her parents seemed like a force, flinging her up from where she was pitched with a magician and landing her in a lonely place expecting her to hide her anxiety. She assured him there had never been anything unhappy on that score. It had just been an adventure and she was pushing her creativity for all to see: 'I'm alive. I'm here to have fun and all the rest is nonsense,' was her take. Her impressive contacts brought business to artists and sheltered the oddball. She kept pace and much of the time appeared quiet. She owned up to wrongdoings relating to her drinking and accepted that close friends and family bore the burden. Her Daddy had gone and her Mama was old now. All the same, she seemed girded for the next rebellion. It's true she sometimes came close to the self-destruct mark but she reverted to sober and Colin and others saw the strength of her optimism.

17

# Smile of La Gioconda

Schlock horror came to The Place, Kings Cross, in 1971 when Sarah assembled a cast for a series of short plays, including one by Hamblett. *Grand Guignol* harked back to the blood and gore so beloved of cousin Esmond. Rescued by Sarah from a low patch, Charles was put into Idev Productions with Idris and Hubert and for a while ended up house-sitting and putting up with Sarah's 'perpetual croak'. He accidentally preserved Sarah's shopping list from October that year, which lists rice, pepper, salad, whisky, Winalot, chicken, angostura, gin, vodka, wine, hot dogs and rolls. Almost all Sarah's female friends had husbands. Julia's friend was a true daughter of the aristocracy, as protective of her friends in the privileged upper crust as she was of those at the Bohemian end of the spectrum:

> She invited me to parties that were staggeringly elite and full of aristocrats with double-barrelled names. Sarah would, in this setting, be incredibly ladylike and totally unlike the way we saw her in other situations. She was really living in two worlds entirely and somehow managed these transitions with no apparent effort. There were also the smaller more intimate gatherings – letting her hair down and dancing and singing. That was a very real Sarah but a total contrast.

She enjoyed her social standing but at the same time didn't want to be placed under scrutiny. Her friend Niki stresses Sarah's dislike of the press:

> Sarah was actually a very private person and because of her family, could never have the privacy for which she longed. She was talented, smart and generous. Her fame and that of her family, I think, kept her from being able to share that talent as much as she wanted to. In those days, the paparazzi

> were not as powerful as they are now, but it was still enough to torture Sarah! For her, relief came in the form of alcohol.

Having goofed in grand style, her reputation preceded her and a little reinforcement helped one hold one's own. She hadn't appreciated men like Tony or Lobo attempting to control her. Colin hadn't run off at the first sight of trouble, but he had been laying down the law recently. Sometimes he came to stay. He adored 'Hum Hum' and added touches to her garden. There is a remarkable story in his memoir relating to one visit. Sarah appeared by his bedside saying: 'Darling we're going to have lunch with Mama.' She was dressed – which given the early hour, was unusual. She ran him a bath and implored:

> 'Darling, I wish you would get up. We're having lunch with Mama. I soaked in the bath but in she came: 'Oh Darling, please hurry up. We're having lunch with Mama.' I casually decided what to wear. She rushed in: 'Please hurry. We're having lunch with Mama.' I said: 'I hear you darling, but it's only 8.30!' At 9am she announced 'A car is waiting. Hurry! We're having lunch with Mama.' A limousine had indeed been outside for an hour. I'm baffled as to why she kept repeating the sentence. I thought, well, I know where Lady Churchill lives. It isn't far. As we left London I asked: 'Darling, where exactly are we going?' She replied: 'I've told you, we're having lunch with Mama.' I assumed we were going to Chartwell but soon I realised this was the opposite direction. Then the airport loomed ahead. The car took us straight in – no questions asked.
>
> We climbed into a jet. Well, that's interesting, I thought – a private plane to fly to Chartwell! Champagne was brought immediately. As we flew over the Channel I yelled: 'Where on earth are we going?' Calmly, she repeated her famous line 'To have lunch with Mama'. We landed at de Gaulle, cleared the steps and someone said: 'Lady Audley, we have been waiting for you.' I was on French soil with no passport, no identification, nothing. Our limo pulled up in front of the Ritz. One of Sarah's sayings had been: 'Darling, no matter where in the world you are and you don't know where to go, just tell the driver, *Take me to the Ritz!* And here we were, with the doorman saying 'Your suite is ready.' I asked: 'Darling, where are we actually going?' She replied dryly: 'I told you darling, we're having lunch with Mama.' The waiter rolled a trolley into our room with champagne, salmon and caviar. 'Is this lunch?' I asked, 'Is Mama coming here?' Sarah replied, 'No. I told you we're having lunch with Mama. We had a little drink and a bite and then someone called to say a car was waiting. It pulled up into the circular drive at the British Embassy.

Sarah's sister Mary was married to Christopher Soames – the British Ambassador to Paris. Mary greeted us and then led us to Mama, a very grand lady. She was somewhat hard of hearing so they put Lady Churchill on my right. Sarah sat opposite me. Christopher sat to my left at the head of the table and faced Mary at the other end. In between sat Johnny Churchill, Sarah's cousin, on my left. He was a brilliant pianist and the spitting image of a young Winston Churchill. Lunch with Mama began.

The waiter came around and Mary asked: 'Johnny would you have a drink with us dear?' 'No, I've given up drinking Mary.' Was his reply. Everyone glanced at each other and said 'Well, that's nice.' I found this very British and so polite. When the waiter returned Johnny said 'I'll just have a wee drop.' Wine was poured and Johnny tipped his elbow to fill up the glass. Not a word was said. Everyone was cordial and terribly British. Halfway through, Johnny disappeared under the table. He went swish without a word. Nobody said anything. Two waiters pulled the chair back quietly, lifted Johnny up and supported him out of the room with his feet inches off the ground. Still not a word! I looked at Sarah and she smiled politely at me. I understood. You just don't discuss things like that.

Before dessert, Christopher stood up and said 'I would like you to raise your glasses. I would like to welcome into our family one of the nicest men Sarah has brought into our circle. Colin, we welcome you.' I realised that this was an engagement party. Sarah never said anything to me about it. She kicked me under the table. Her face spoke volumes as if to say 'Don't ruin it.' I said how honoured and happy I was. Suddenly I heard music and asked: 'Who's playing the piano?' Sarah said: 'It's Johnny.' A short time earlier he had passed out. Now he was playing brilliantly. Such was Johnny Churchill. I liked him immensely.

Colin's story continues in London when Sarah takes him to Vivienne's studio. 'So you're Sarah's young man,' was how the terribly English Mrs Entwistle greeted him. No sooner had he said 'I guess I am,' than the retort came: 'Well, I hope you have better luck than my son.' Vivienne not only talks about her son's suicide, but also is eager to take their 'engagement' photograph. While Sarah was changing, her ex-mother-in-law apparently snapped: 'She's drunk. I can tell straight away,' worrying if the vacant look in Sarah's eyes will ruin the photo. Colin never mentions that he had placed his bronze, an *underwater ballet,* in the centre of the portrait. Bringing his work to the studio suggests that the shoot's purpose was more about publicizing the sculpture than celebrating their engagement. Sarah certainly looks out of sorts in the picture though.

Wonderful as Colin's memoir is, you find yourself questioning his relationship with Sarah, when he wrote it and why. They spent 15 years on and off together followed by a bitter-sweet estrangement and another decade passed before he wrote his book. With the passage of time you would think he would be more sympathetic, but Colin's 'tell it plain' style is authentic, being the natural entertainer he was and perhaps it shines light on a relationship that was far from inhibited. He says he is surprised that Sarah discussed their future with her family, but surely it's natural she would. He expresses hopes for a marriage yet while friends congratulated them following the announcement, life stayed the same. He refers to his love for Sarah, but his anger comes across too. He seldom conveys the emotional connection between them, even though it ran deep for her.

Sarah found it hard to hook the New Zealander, but support came from comrades at her studio. Twinkie's niece Olivia, who often saw her uncle, remembers how Hugh de Wet had an adjoining studio with a still in the kitchen for producing neat spirit. Olivia's fiancé Robert found Hugh's attempt to appear Bohemian far too *obvious*. Quite a few of them were trying to look like the young Ezra Pound, but his goatee seemed 'affected'. On 22 May 1970 a newspaper story ran about Sarah and Hugh's decision to marry. This might have been a manoeuvre designed to make Colin jealous and provoke him into action. Secret agent Hugh was an expert at such tactical manoeuvres. The story vanishes in a few days. No duels over ladies were fought and Colin stayed in Rome, going to Joburg for a while and living largely on credit. The truth is, drunk or sober, Sarah took love very seriously and could be obsessive about it.

Sarah was back in Holland in autumn 1971 appearing with TV legend Willem Duys. The next year she and Idris joined forces with Hugh in *Here & Now* in Ebbw Vale with items like *Moments with Sir Noël Coward* and *Brush Up Your Shakespeare* either side of Sarah's poetry. The downside was the Welsh pubs being dry on Sundays. After Sarah did *The Secret of the World* in Tokyo, Fuji Telecasting wrote to tell her how understanding between their two countries had improved as a result. A week in Australia followed and arriving home she heard of a film about her Pa's early life with Dickie Attenborough directing and Carl Foreman producing. Mama, Johnny, Winston, Minnie and Sarah attended *Young Winston*'s Leicester Square première on 20 July 1972 and were thrilled with it.

While she had an income through the trust, her earnings barely covered her expenses. Lady Churchill would step in, writing: 'I hear you are in difficulties' and send a painting, jewellery or a cheque. Sarah would say how 'overwhelmed' she was by Mama's kindness. She struggled to keep her studio and Twinkie's niece recalls how the Kensington crowd often paid her rent. Olivia was extremely admiring of Sarah's poetry, even if the faded beauty with the youthful spirit was a little offhand. She witnessed her 'horrible' mood swings once or twice and wondered if she drank either to free herself from a psychological state or if anxieties relating to her career (one that isn't kind to ageing women) might be a cause. Colin was someone she wanted to be with. He had a distinctive voice and his friends believe he could easily have been an actor. He dubbed voices on several movies. Claude (Coco) Eriksen and her husband first met the sculptor during his early days in Rome and were among his closest friends. He was godfather to one of their kids and Claude calls him 'the pillar of our family'. They met Sarah for the first time at Via Durazza:

> We met her many times with Colin: first in Rome. She was a darling. Every time she came we saw her. She had been so sad about Henry Audley who died in her arms. She had really loved him too.

Colin and Sarah might have been intimate at the onset, but the dynamics of their relationship are difficult to pin down. Colin's memoir resounds with stories of famous friends and women he loved and bedded, but he applies the phrase 'Eternal Virgin' to Sarah. He wanted her to be freer with regard to sex. He was bisexual and it wasn't a secret to friends, although he never goes into this in his book. His niece believes he may not have wanted his legacy as an artist to be clouded by it. His was the first generation that could freely experiment with no threat of imprisonment. One of life's great explorers in matters emotional and sexual, Colin was fascinated by the animal side to people's natures, his art going some way to express this. Having no illusions about him, Sarah was prepared to have him at all costs. Claude recalls Sarah saying that Clementine hoped he would marry her. *Lunch with Mama* might have been a gesture to assuage her mother's anguish that she be left single. Yet, asked if they were lovers, Claude says: 'I don't think they were lovers but they loved each other.'

A musical stood the greatest chance of attracting an audience and Sarah's ambition was to base one on work she'd authored. For *The Boy Who Made Magic* in mid-1972 she enlisted Angelo Badalamenti (or Bedale as he was then) for music, and Nashville-based Frank Stanton for lyrics. James Liggatt helped turn the book into dialogue. 'Jan Fable' is the youngest sibling while 'Mirabelle', like Diana, is so radiant growing up that walking beside her was like 'having the sun with you'. Peter is the brother in the middle (Randolph) while Winston is Mr Fable: so busy with operations in the woods and so immersed in the struggles of life, he forgets the ages of his children. Wonderful as it sounds, the musical was a slow burner and Sarah didn't devote enough time to it. To interpret the songs she got Elizabeth Seal to liaise with Andy in America. Elizabeth remembers various attempts to produce *Boy Who Made Magic* including an off-Broadway try-out. The project was shelved several times. The music was nice but required collaboration to get it into a reasonable shape. When work resumed, she remembers the lunches and parties, some attended by Lady Soames and Edward Heath:

> Idris Evans was something of a uniting force. He lived with his Mama and would throw these big lunch parties at their home in Bedford Square that were a draw for actors in musical theatre. The atmosphere was down-to-earth and good-humoured and each time there was Mama's Anglo-Welsh dishes served up for those who were hungry.

Leonard Parkin, ITV's *News at Ten* frontman, came to Chartwell that summer to make *Place in the Country* with Lady Soames and Lady Audley recalling their early life. Sarah mimics her father: 'Dogs look up to man. Cats look down on man. Pigs accept him as one of their own.' Christopher had been excellent at the embassy. An advocate for entry to the Common Market, he was the first vice-president of the European Commission under Ortoli. Colin believed Sarah was a little jealous of Mary, recalling times she called her 'Goody Two Shoes'. The TV work provided income for *Boy Who Made Magic*, one of many projects Sarah pursued with energy. In 1972 there was a scheme to sell engraved plates featuring images of Sir Winston that Johnny had designed, employing the New Jersey-based Silver Creations Ltd. There were to be five plates including *Hour of Decision* and *The Big Three*. Sarah's impressionist watercolour of her Pa in a hat graced the outer presentation case. The autographed items sold for $150 apiece. For her father's centenary, a special plate portrayed him in relief in gold plate. The launch began in October with Sarah making appearances in 21 cities, often branches of the English-speaking Union. It bore a whiff of fortune hunting, just like the lecture tours of Randolph and Winston. Journalists tried to get her to comment on her disorderly conduct. 'I hate analysis,' she declared icily, stating she wasn't one for checking her temperature in a battle. Her theory was that value comes by learning in the saddle. There wouldn't be hindsight if you didn't do this. It was what her Papa would have said. He had taken the flak too.

She spent Christmas in New York piloting *Boy Who Made Magic* and saw Colin, now spending a lot of time there. He still had the studio and foundry in Rome and was riding two continents. Embracing the Big Apple was a bold choice, given the economic downturn. Much had changed since his last visit in 1953, but the city burned with energy. He took a sixth-floor apartment on 14 West 56th Street and soon met Brooklyn-born Ted Buckwald. In the hairdressing business since 1957, Ted claims his was the first salon in America to have a blow dryer. An early client hired him as stylist to a high-class brothel. By 1964 he had the means to open a Madison Avenue salon and his charm and fast talk drew the rich and famous. The sixties and seventies were a glorious time of casual parties. Looking back, Ted wonders if he was the only straight hairdresser in New York. A magnet for women, he says that at the high point, sleeping with a hundred females a month was typical. Ted's salon was two blocks from a pet shop and it was here he recalls Colin telling the girl behind the counter he didn't know where to find a good hairdresser:

> … the girl said 'look no further – he's right next to you!' I had a client's dog with me and I remember that very low voice and New Zealand accent. He had his hands full carrying a sculpture of a small bull. Colin's gallery was on the upstairs of that very same pet shop. He had many friends and patrons and he was forever recommending they have their hair done at my salon. We clicked and were great friends. Colin loved animals and he had all kinds himself. His dog was *Bayete* – the name came from the call of attack used by a tribe in Africa.

Colin started wearing his hair longer. When Sarah saw him she was stunned that he could settle into New York life so quickly. His culinary creations were sculptures in themselves. 'Red Turkey' was 1970s cuisine at its most colourful: stuffed with a chicken, stuffed with a smaller game bird then coated in cranberries. Sarah went out of her way to help her favourite Kiwi and let the British press generate publicity when *Queen of the Shells* was first shown at London's Archer Gallery. The *Daily Mail* talked about the bronze's leering expression, causing Lady Churchill great disturbance. Colin tells us she asked: 'Is that how you really see my daughter?' to which he bravely replied: 'Yes: the *beauty* and the *clown*.' Clementine closed proceedings with: 'I don't really like it. I think I shall leave now.' A joke he and Sarah apparently shared was, 'Mama can't burn the bronze like the Sutherland painting.' Sarah helped Colin get a profile and also with the practicalities of international moves:

> In my studio one day Sarah asked me to select sculptures for her to take to New York. She got them into the Environment Gallery off Madison. She knew the captain of a merchant ship and booked a passage. We decided on the pieces and that's how I got my first show in New York.

Lady Audley was in a taxi one evening with a group including journalist Jack O'Brien when the Jackie Onassis nude photo scandal came up in conversation. The paparazzi had tracked her down to a beach in Skorpios, stealing away her dignity with their telephoto lenses. Onassis allegedly tipped them off, believing she was cuckolding him and was intent on divorcing her. Sarah's sharp invective took people by surprise. She railed against the cameramen bitterly, saying they'd be poking lenses through bathroom windows next. When they pulled up at the Warwick Hotel, she stepped out, calmly turned to everyone, smiled and said: 'Never mind me. I'm just a Limey!' Press invasion was still her bête noire.

In January 1973 she went to Florida, staying with Victor and Celia Farris, king and queen of the Palm Beach social scene and foremost charity fundraisers. Victor had invented the paper milk carton. Celia was the ingénue who, back in 1941, stepped into Vic Oliver's *Get a Load of This* at the last minute. She had sat for portraits by Beauchamp and been escorted to premières by Stephen Ward before trying her luck in America in 1952. Sarah relied on Jewell Baxter's organisation, given the raft of events including silver plate events and Colin's first major American show. The Red Cross International Gala Ball on 25 January 1973 drew the uber-rich with women in priceless tiaras. The next day *Young Winston* premièred in Palm Beach, its proceeds benefitting Churchill's favourite charity, 'The March of Dimes'. Shimmering in a gold dress, Sarah greeted attendees, then Celia and Victor held a dinner for her at their home with Douglas Fairbanks Jnr, Mary Lee and Jack Hawkins among the guests. Her Churchillian eyes brooding, Sarah was overheard saying to Celia: 'I'd give everything I have for the happiness you have here with your family.'

Colin's show was at Martha Parrish's gallery and Diana's daughter Edwina, having written a light-hearted novel about coming to terms with a partner's affair, had her first US exhibition that February. Her father also painted but in an abstract style. Still involved in European matters at Strasburg, he had recently stepped down as Streatham's MP and joined the African mining group Lonrho as chairman. Sarah and Idris had plans for a hybrid of choir music, cabaret and Sarah's poems (some set to music). They called it *Words and Music* and did a show to benefit Crickhowell's Clarence Hall. Sarah called Derrick Watkins, a local tenor soloist, asking if he might form a choir and perform with them. The effect of the 48 Gwent Singers was amazing. After *Battle Hymn of the Republic* came her upbeat *I've Left Yesterday Behind Me*, set to music by Brian Rogers. Derrick remembers Sarah bursting out crying at Abergavenny's Angel Hotel bar, saying how she never expected a choir of such calibre. In New York that August, Sarah was in Frank Stanton's recording studio as he built upon past successes like *The Computer with the Hiccups* and *The Mixed Up Vending Machine* before fixing on *The Sarah Churchill Theme*. It expressed the moment 'Jan' sees through material gain and grasps that 'Happiness comes from within'. Carroll Baker's 'favorite fella' hadn't undergone such a damascene conversion, supplying the son of Saudi Arabia's King Faisal with a ten-foot bronze for a London townhouse. Sarah arranged a holiday in Sperlonga (between Rome and Naples) for Colin and friends,

Claude Eriksen recalls. Artist Cesare Orsini was there, often the butt of Colin's good-humoured jokes. Claude made fish soup especially for Sarah – probably the best she had ever tasted thanks to the ingredients of the Mer Méditerranée. In his memoir Colin writes of Sarah quite lovingly:

> She needed tranquillity. She chose to sit under a shady umbrella on the beach peacefully creating her poetry. She was happy and more precisely, content in that instant, free of her magical father and the disadvantages that her celebrity brought to her doorstep.

In their villa looking down on a fishing village, Claude's sparkling personality lightened the atmosphere, though getting a plumber to come up in the peak of summer to repair a blocked toilet was impossible. Colin got everyone improvising with plastic bags except for Lady Audley. She held her ground for three days. Following a meal in town, Colin discovered Sarah had crammed the boot with wine from a local merchant. Sick of ignoring the bloody obvious, he made a stand:

> Thus began a reign of terror. A dishevelled Sarah roared through the kitchen demanding more wine. She sat at the old wooden table and poured a drink. I tried to take it away from her. She grabbed my wrist and warned me against taking it out of her reach. I emptied all the bottles by mid afternoon. She ranted and insisted on being driven down to the piazza for more wine and to be with civilised people with decent plumbing ... She fell to the ground and passed out. Bayete stood guard until I arrived home. We carried her back to her room. Three gruelling days later she was back to being her proper English lady-self.

Having known her eleven years, he longed to draw her out: 'You are so unhappy darling,' he said. 'How can I make you happy?' She would reply, 'I'm very happy. I love you and that's all that's important.' He recalls her genuine frustration: 'I hate it when people say that I'm an alcoholic,' telling him that an alcoholic and a drunk are distinct things. She liked drink and if she had to be called something then perhaps they ought to call her a drunk. She repeated this in an interview to the American press a year later, illustrating it with a Native American proverb:

> They've damaged me with the word *alcoholic*. This (glass in hand) is my supercharge ... My father said (of drink), 'Make it your friend.' Also, remember the old Indian story: 'Never criticise a person until you've walked two miles in his moccasins.'

A deficiency turns drink into an illness. From the time Sarah Churchill was aware of her place in the wider world, being commented upon was a far more terrifying prospect than she ever let on. Drink calmed her down and enhanced her performance. One 'supercharge' she could fight for anywhere was theatre. The curator of J. M. Barrie's birthplace tried to reach her while she was in Sperlonga. Adverts were placed and contact made. Then Sarah somehow appeared on a hill in Kirriemuir on 9 September cheering on the men in white flannels. Kirriemuir CC was playing the Allahabarries (revived for the occasion). Vintage cars travelled between the hill and town hall, where that evening there were reels and a recitation by Sarah from Barrie's *Speech on Courage*. She came at her own expense, receiving no fee.

Following a meeting at the Savoy on 5 December to discuss Churchill centenary events, Baroness Spencer-Churchill presented PM Heath with fifty of her husband's books. Inspector Murray, who genuinely cared about Sarah, noticed she was overcome with emotion. He and Edwina joined forces in an operation to spirit her away via a side room, corridor and waiting car. With her eloquent self-reflections and tendency to escape danger by a hair's breadth, Sarah had a character that closely resembled the young Winston. She needed to be occupied and came alive in battles. She had some way to go to rival his literary output, but a third high-quality poetry collection was ready by Christmas, including offerings by a number of pals. Villiers's poem was about clasping what one most desires. She saw less of her *daoshi* after he had lent her his apartment and was less than enamoured with the poetess after the mess she left. He was still dealing with the mortifying reality that George Harrison had got Friars Park: 'Bought by a *Beatle*,' he said, choking on the last word.

Sarah remained in New York in January, participating in *Churchill the Man* for Statesman Films. She was still in Colin's apartment in February, commuting to Englishtown, New Jersey, for lithography classes with tutor Elizabeth Schippert. Lobo Nocho, a resident artist, had brought Sarah and Graphic House Ltd together. Lo visited her in London in 1973 proposing the idea and so she translated ten gouaches into lithographs, hoping to publish them in editions of 300 to 325. One featured Wendy Reves. *Moon Goddess* was a surrealistic Lady C. She wanted Mama to have one for her 89th birthday. While seeing her as the moon, she compared her father to the sun, his energy so badly lacking in present times. She reflected on her life – now a matter defined by choice. Previously, destiny had defined it and before that, mythology.

She flew home to vote and couldn't have been more disheartened at Wilson's victory. She had a deadline of 18 April 1974 when her lithographs would preview at the Todd Gallery in Paramus. With each priced $275, she wanted them to help finance her musical, although she got lumbered with a $1,000 payment to a Long Island gallery after lithographing one image she had given them exclusive rights to. Reported as 'plugging her watercolours in a suburban shopping centre', there were further losses to recoup following a theft from her New York apartment. Money was immaterial, however, compared to four-legged friends. Many in her circle were dog lovers. Jewell, who lived round the corner from Madison, was always walking her Pomeranians. Ted Buckwald was another dog-lover. Colin's gallery threw a party for dogs and their owners. Delphine Clues descended on them and Ted illustrates her canine affection:

> Delphine liked to party. I liked her a lot. I remember the time she was having a pedicure and the dog in her care went running off out of the salon and down the street. It was wintertime and New York was white with snow. Delphine ran through the streets barefoot after her dog, finally catching up with it.

Ted recalls a trip to Atlantic City with Colin and Sarah singing all the way there and back. They were bowled over by what a performer she was. A hairdresser learns a lot of things and Sarah told Ted that her family had always treated her like a princess. It didn't matter how old she was. Someone had to be there to dress her and take great care of her. Whether travelling, making public appearances or a theatrical engagement, support was required. Ted recalls Sarah speaking about seeing her father before she left to make *Royal Wedding*. 'Where do you think you're going?' he growled, seeing her suitcase. She told him and his response was simple yet profound: 'Do what you like – but love what you do!'

Somebody who did just that was Richard Burton – playing Winston in Colin Morris's Centenary TV drama *Walk with Destiny* and his comments about the Great Man being power-mad, barren in intellect and in some ways as savage as Hitler, caused a backlash. His agent Jack le Vien apologised to Sarah's family on the actor's behalf. Somehow, it had all been taken out of context. A centenary concert was planned and Sarah called Derrick Watkins from America. The Gwent Singers instantly re-formed and were given a Hebrew coach to help them with *Chorus of the Hebrew Slaves*. They would remain an international choir for decades. Idris was scooped from the Hilton with Ellen directing. Staged at the Royal Court on 8 December 1974, songs like Ivor Novello's *My Dearest Dear* and big Broadway numbers featured. The trust and the Bikur Cholim Hospital benefited. The Eleventh Duke of Marlborough opened the show and Sarah looked divine, her hair styled by Granville King of the Tallullah Salon whose partner was doyenne of the gay disco scene. She performed *I've Left Yesterday Behind Me, The Colour of Saying* and *The Happy Time*. She later sang *The Willows* as well as French songs that impressed Pebs and Yvonne. Stars like Burt Lancaster were in the audience. The concert made £2,000 for the joint beneficiaries.

While most people saw Colin and Sarah as 'just two beautiful friends', Colin's memoir records a jealous exchange with Mule confronting Carroll Baker: 'You don't think you're going to sleep with him do you. Because, you're not.' Carroll replied: 'It hadn't even entered my head, Sarah.' Thankfully, both ladies were reconciled over a common love of hot dogs. Sarah's favourite food, incidentally, was fondue. She recalled her father's line about Switzerland evading attack by the Nazis, owing to being a difficult morsel to chew. Sarah spent hours in the West 55th Street bistro specialising in it, immersed in the creative process. He was at Eaton Square when his mother died in March 1975. At New Zealand's High Commission (built on the site of the old Carlton Hotel) he had an exhibition. Sarah made sure people came and held a dinner for him in Soho, inviting Nemon (then in his eighties and using a studio in the grounds of Clarence House). Nemon had Colin over and they chatted with the Queen Mother, who reminded him of his own mother. Colin adds that Nemon said he wished he hadn't been tied to conventional portraiture and longed to produce works freely, 'with no blinkers on'.

At the end of the month it was Sarah's turn to exhibit art in New York but not before they had fun at the Easter Parade and Bonnet Festival. Colin let her use his gallery for three months in summer 1975. Her works had a positive reception and she gave little speeches, telling her Mama how spectacles gave her an intelligent look, deterring people from 'asking me questions I can't answer'. Colin says people queued down Madison to get in: 'She was selling! She was sober. They interviewed her for TV. She glowed.' Not everyone was kind. He and Sarah went into another gallery and he heard the owner say: 'You know that was Sarah Churchill the drunk?' His pal said, 'Oh yeah. She's big into drugs too.' Colin blew his top: 'How dare you say that! She's never touched a drug in her life and if she has a drink that's her affair. I came to talk about a show but we'll never set foot here again.'

Unfortunately, after living with her for the best part of a year, he needed space. He suggested she move into a vacant apartment at 4A 783 Madison Avenue, opposite his gallery. He could keep an eye on her. He got Ted's help in furnishing it and bought her a white Pekinese called YoYo. Unfortunately, Sarah quickly deteriorated alone. Colin came in to find poor YoYo yelping pathetically with Sarah drunk on the bed. She nevertheless proved her mettle when he hired a man to look after his pets when he left for Mexico City on business. Sarah argued with the pet-sitter who refused her entry. She pushed him aside, seeing one of Colin's dogs had died with another skin and bone.

Sarah ordered him to vacate the premises. She made sure he left, calling in vets and getting the landlord to change the locks.

Publicity can sometimes be a good thing. Jolie Gabor introduced them to media hotshots Cindy Adams and her husband Joey and Sarah's exhibition got a mention in Cindy's column next to a piece about Telly Savalas and his million-dollar English home: 'Sure he can afford it,' said Cindy. 'He saves on haircuts.' They could have used Kojak just then because break-ins were common and Delphine was smoking her joints in the loo, leaving the coast clear for thieves. This happened three times. *Queen of the Shells* took pride of place in the display until a guy grabbed it and ran down the stairs. Colin was livid with Delphine (who sent Sarah a note suggesting they offer a reward). 'You were bloody high in my gallery,' he bawled, before firing her. He must have softened because a year later Delphine was back. At Eaton Square, Clementine sent Sarah an electric blanket. Hum Hum was used to seeing Sarah sporadically and she found time for London neighbours like Coutts Chairman Sir Seymour Egerton. On 20 October she was heading back to New York.

For one whose security had long been managed on her behalf, troubling her with such trifles was an insult. As soon as she reached Heathrow, she made off to the bar: 'Torch song anyone? *My skin is Dixie satin – there's rebel in my manner and my speech.*' Some were clapping but not TWA. Could she have got into such a stink as to tug a man's beard and cosh a hostess? She lost her Pan Am seat, got barred from the TWA one, settling for an Air India jumbo to Kennedy Airport. The headlines said she'd been banned by the airlines. *Pull No Punches* would be her next book's title. 'Been naughty again, darling?' was Colin's wry remark as Sarah took her turn as gallery-minder.

18

# Dangerous You

Joey and Cindy, two of the most influential people in broadcasting, had been good to them. Joey promoted Colin's Gallery by having them on his TV show. When looking for an announcer to report the forthcoming *Miss World* (from London's Royal Albert Hall) for US TV they thought of Sarah. Colin told the couple she could do it, mentioning her concert at the Royal Court. The Adamses wanted to spend time with Sarah as a kind of interview, so a visit to Madison Square Gardens (where the Ringling Bros and Barnum & Bailey Circus was appearing) was suggested. Sarah would love it, Colin assured Cindy, given that her new musical was about circus life. Sarah promised to remain sober and yet made a short detour to the restroom to take a nip prior to meeting their guests. She was so charming and funny he was sure she would 'pass'.

They took their seats in a box looking onto the ring. It was then that the atmosphere first went to Sarah's head. She returned to the sawdust and spectacle of the Bertram Mills Circus, a cherished memory of her childhood. Fifty years earlier Papa had taken the three of them to Olympia for the 2.30 p.m. performance. The lions were a draw but many parents back then saw the circus as educational. Music halls had their animal acts but these were never places well-born children could to be taken to. Circus, by contrast, was classless. That day *June the Baby Elephant* on a tricycle with her popping eyes and inquisitive trunk was all the rage. Diana felt it was cruel. Churchill recalled a lion he had once seen on horseback. The thought was too curious to comprehend but he knew the circus's barker's reputation was one of kindness and red-cheeked Mr Bertram was frightfully nice when he was introduced. When Lord Birkenhead's youngest daughter hosted a party at Grosvenor Gardens for Pip, Squeak and Wilfred of cartoon fame, Sarah bonded with Squeak the Penguin. Endless hours throughout her childhood had been spent thinking about the circus. It wasn't just the animals but the thought of artistes travelling to distant lands, caring for each other like brothers and sisters.

Both types of clowns – the Harlequin derived from from the Italian Commedia Dell'arte and the tramp-like Auguste – were everywhere. They filled between acts, putting the rig up or playing musical instruments. Randolph asked why they had so much paint on and was horrified to learn that some of them were disfigured owing to terrible injuries. 'Circus is about horses,' Papa whispered. He was used to Lipizzaners circling the 42-foot ring and they all knew about *Mazeppa and the Wild Horse* – the story that moved him as a child. His own version surpassed those by Voltaire and Byron. Papa had always been an animal lover. He recalled the time he 'bit the tan' at Knightsbridge Barracks and one morning encountered that singular equestrienne, La Belle Titcomb, Heloise McCeney, the Parisian 'dancer on horseback', in Rotten Row. Thunderstruck, he fell off his horse. Who could blame him, given the ample proportions of that most dazzling of creatures? A vision in white, she sang operatic arias upon *Ali* the white Arab stallion, guarded by her tall, white Borzoi. Sarah's companions at Madison Square Gardens weren't aware of the imaginative world she inhabited. Only some are invested with the joy that comes from cavorting limbs and loud vocals, a spirit peculiar to the English that other nations don't quite get. Such sacraments are often derided, although some friends understood.

Sarah described her father to Claude Eriksen as having no consciousness of his body. He might walk down the hall in his vest with the lower part flapping in the wind. His stern expression could also switch unexpectedly to that of cherubic innocence. Sarah's emotions, like his, were close to the surface and child-like. With drink her '*supercharge*' ego could potentially give way to the unselfconscious id with shame and convention suspended. She was, of course, the same soul who spun a dervish, danced 'bare-hooved' in Amsterdam and received communal gratification when 'masses of children' came to her cell at Holloway Prison.

Sitting in a box slightly lower down was a lovely little girl and her father. The clown was taking the elephant round the boxes so it could put its trunk out for people to hold. When it neared, Sarah become so loud that Colin and Cindy began to wonder if she was off her rocker. The elephant stretched its trunk into the box below and suddenly the little girl got so excited she stood on her chair, bringing the trunk down so she could hold it. That did it and Sarah flipped. Desperate to sustain *her* gorgeous moment she yelled: 'What the hell do you think you're doing with that trunk? It's my fucking trunk.' She grabbed it from the girl's hands. The father was horrified. Cindy and Joey 'disappeared from the box like a shot' in Colin's story. Needless to say, the 1975 *Miss World* prospect died an instant death. Colin looked at Sarah the next day and said lugubriously: 'You really fucked up something wonderful, my darling. Such a shame.'

Can you blame Colin for standing in as publicity agent, even though it was Jewell's job? Sarah's star name sold sculptures. He adored her but never knew how 'big fish' would behave in her midst. Rex Harrison was impressed that she had pulled off an exhibition stone sober and had some work for her. Colin says Rex invited them for lunch at Twenty-One, leaving instructions that she mustn't under any circumstances be drunk. After a talk from Colin he exacted her 'as if I'd ever let you down' promise. At midday the elevator doors opened and in flew Sarah. Her words were: 'Well, if it isn't old fucking sexy Rexy. How's My Fair Lady's stud?' The actor told Colin, 'Can't do it, can't take her' and left, but it seems suspect that a comment like this would be taken so seriously. Again, there's a sense Colin's memoir repaints history in bittersweet colours. He obviously loved Sarah's bawdy side. So did Ted: 'She swore in a way that no American swore. The peculiar thing was that with her incredible voice, her cursing actually sounded good.'

Colin's incomparable memoir is perhaps a little too rich in debacle. 'He had the upper hand in the relationship,' Ted Buckwald recalls, which explains Colin's tendency to manage her. While she was formidable, 'He had the more thunderous voice.' One last story relates to a showing of Sarah's lithographs at a Jersey mall the following year. A gallery owner arranged a limo and had a red carpet ready for her personal appearance. Colin writes how he promised to join her that evening and how at lunchtime on the day called by to check on her, finding her out cold. He rushed to find Ted and asked him to stick her under the shower, do her hair, make a lot of coffee and get her ready. Ted explained what was happening to her as she came round: 'Sarah, I'm getting you ready for your show tonight. I'm your hairdresser.' She thought someone was trying to drown her and was badly sick. Troubling as this sounds, we learn that in record speed Ted made her look gorgeous and that the two of them shot off to New Jersey. Colin says she expected the focus to be on her as an exhibiting artist; but it's ridiculous to believe that Sarah believed nobody would ask her about *That Man* or that she thought she might escape the inevitable comparisons when it came to art. Her exhibition featured several images of Winston.

What seems to have happened is that she went into the event with good grace only to find it hijacked by a bunch of morons putting her centre stage in a freak-show. They didn't care a toss for her lithographs but were highly excited because a Churchill descendent was honouring New Jersey. Journalists had questions like 'Do you miss your father?' and 'Did you get your skills from him?' Colin remembers Ted told him afterwards about two women saying: 'I've always loved your father.' Without blinking she replied: 'What the fuck would you know about my father? I'm an artist. Fuck you all.' The volcano was so devastating that everyone vanished. Colin says he arrived to find only two present: Ted and the female gallery owner, hiding behind the counter, terrified Sarah was going to attack her. Lurid drama aside, it isn't really hard to comprehend why Sarah took it real bad. The question is why was it allowed to happen.

Ted is in his nineties now but shooting for 125. He offers his own account while holding back on some of the details. He admits that Colin had gone to great lengths to arrange the exhibition, creating the publicity and ensuring the presence of several notable people. He confirms the part of the story in the shower is true. Colin apparently roared: 'Make it snappy!' Time was so short, he was putting her make-up on in the car to New Jersey. Initially, she was 'the embodiment of PR'. Ted's version isn't dissimilar to Colin's. He admits Sarah was shocked, thinking it was to be 'her' night. He believes Sarah's offhand remark to the two women was unprovoked but remembers it being more like: 'Let me inform you, I'm SARAH Churchill. I'm sure the two of you know NOTHING about art.' Asked why Colin had a different account, Ted admits that Sarah might have said some of those things. The bottom line was that her behaviour emptied the gallery and she had retreated to a nearby bar fuming. They got her home by promising her that they would carry on drinking together. Colin calls it a disaster but doesn't admit to being at fault. In his defence, he was promoting her. She might have 'sold', had she gone along with it. Sarah took revenge by storming into his gallery when he was on the point of sale with a new client. He talks about silencing her 'horrific' language with: 'It's the end, my darling, between you and me. You have really pushed me too far. I want you out of my gallery right now.' Pushing her into the elevator, he pressed the button saying, 'Don't come back.'

Colin portrays Sarah on a downward slope and remembers declaring, 'I can't do this to myself,' emphasising that drink sapped his talent. His memoir, written in the 1990s, might have been different had they not fallen out. It's coloured too, by the wisdom of hindsight. Decades on, Ted says: 'One thing I learnt from Sarah was never to drink – NEVER!' But would he have said this in the 1970s? Colin obviously had his limits. 'You must understand, my art comes first,' was a phrase he used to utter that Ted remembers. But Colin's memoir also reveals that early on, he wanted to make the relationship official: 'It was sad for me, ' he writes, 'I would have married her and looked after her. I loved Sarah but our love wasn't meant to survive.' He didn't choose to marry her even though she wanted him. Colin was a huge part of her life, but her other friends knew nothing about him. Sarah still compartmentalised her private life.

Back in Britain Paul Dacre interviewed her and she spoke with candour, admitting that relationships can be dangerous if one takes a chance with the wrong person. She claimed that loneliness set in when she was just 17 and that lessening it had taken a long time. She had built up battlements around her. Nursing a Bloody Mary, she told Dacre how poetry helped but that she was aware that too much introspection is detrimental. She was in a desolate place as the Colin-Sarah era came to an end.

In the same year, 1976, *The Boy Who Made Magic* ended in frustration and pain. This was in the early spring in Virginia and pre-dates the rages at Sarah's New Jersey opening. Appalling though that episode may seem, she was incredibly vulnerable. Knowing the context helps us understand the woman who lashed out at people's crass comments and the nature of the broken-down creature who needed reviving. Sarah strived to be creative; she was such a fighter and winner. While her father fought the law once and escaped, her run-ins and near incarcerations were almost constant. A lot of herself went into Jan, the hero of her musical. He's the boy wonder whose laboured start only makes him more determined. 'You've got to turn away from your parents in order to mature,' Sarah told an interviewer early in the year, adding that it was the first survival strategy. Yet she admitted that looking back she genuinely thought that her father understood her actions better than she realised. Jan's break comes when he stumbles upon a band of gypsy entertainers. This leads to him becoming a conjurer in a circus and as luck would have it, a world success. Finding life empty, he learns from Madame Stella (Sarah's character) that happiness 'comes from within'. He then returns to the village he sprang from and, nourished by the good there, finally becomes happy with himself.

Rehearsals began on 16 February with a fortnight's run planned for 2 March at the Hayloft Theatre. An hour's drive from Manassas, Virginia, and owned by Frank Matthews, this was a professional dinner theatre with cultural and gastronomic appeal. Patrons applauded the ice sculptures. The sole income of the waiters came from tips. Kay Halle came to see Sarah preview numbers with Andy Bedale at a Hearst charity programme in Washington. The press saw it at dress rehearsal and while conceding that Act One had toe-tapping appeal, wrote off the songs in Act Two as 'advertising jingles'. Several broadsheets trashed it, saying Sarah's singing ran the gamut of three notes. *The Star* said that staging Houdini's ride over Niagara Falls was safer. None of these hacks had ever performed or sung and yet they dealt harshly with a cast that included several children. The *County Courier* described Sarah as 'graceful and beautiful to watch' and *The Carroll County Times* asked how big-name critics could think of giving such an innocent experience 'bad ink'. Kathy Conry, actress, dancer, director and one-time flatmate of Blythe Danner, began on Broadway and in touring productions. When Kathy played Mirabelle she lived in the DC area rehearsing eight hours each day:

> I still have the book written by Ms Churchill. We were all excited to be working with her and aware of her history. Many of us suspected that somehow she wrote the spirit of her Father into the story. Anyone with a Father as famous as hers can understand that the relationship was most likely very complicated. For the most part she was a delight to work with until opening night when things went awry and we eventually had to close the show. I remember her candidness and kindness as a person and her overall sweetness. Despite the difficult way the show ended I will always remember Sarah as a lovely if emotionally driven woman and I am sorry we weren't able to see what might have been happening under the surface and be better prepared to help her through.

The actions precipitating Sarah's departure have left a residue of acrimony. Her contract was terminated. Frank Matthews bought the play's rights, Kathy recalls, and had the power to remove her. Charges were cited against her via official channels involving an Equity deputy and Sarah was left in the humiliating position of having no stake in her own creation. Furious, she held the play's director responsible, making threats to end his career. Kathy feels this was unfair as he honestly did his level best to make her experience a positive one. Sarah didn't drink at work but could be the worse for wear from earlier binges. Her behaviour was her downfall but she was insensitively accommodated miles from the theatre and colleagues. Being cut off pushed her over the edge. This was the view of Claude Eriksen, living in McLean, VA. She brought Sarah to a party, took her to her home and saw the last rehearsal. The next evening Sarah called saying 'I've been sacked.' It was because of the way she performed. Driving to Sarah's chrome and plastic motel Claude recalls her receiving a visit from a black lover. It had to be Lobo. She promised to come back next morning.

When Claude arrived, she found that Sarah hadn't packed and had tripped and hurt herself. Severely depressed, she was in bed on the phone to a teacher friend (probably Lorraine Merritt). She stayed beyond her checkout time so the phone was cut off and she was too late to get to the airport. Claude booked her on the next day's TWA flight and managed to get hold of Stanton and Bedale. They came over and admitted that sticking Sarah in the middle of nowhere was a bad decision. She wouldn't have messed up if it had been better handled. They did her packing, which was far from easy. The room looked as if it had been vandalised. The men followed Claude and Sarah in their car towards DC before turning back to Manassas. Claude looked after

Sarah for another evening. It dawned on her how incapable she was of doing the little things people take for granted, like sorting out travel or choosing clothes. For years she had never carried money. 'One naturally fell into the role of helper,' Claude recalls and did so 'with great love'. Sarah panicked, saying: 'I don't want a scandal in the papers.' She begged her to buy two bottles of whisky: 'One for you, one for me.' Claude agreed and remembers her insistence on having the television blaring. Claude longed for sleep and eventually switched it off, only to hear: 'Put the TV on!' Morning came and Sarah was serene – 'fresh as a rose' to use Claude's expression. She entertained her with great stories over a long breakfast. For a while, she was 'up in arms' about the Equity business.

She didn't come clean to her Mama, referring to her 'good notices', and to the short stories *The New Yorker* was interested in. She expressed sadness on hearing that 'Old Monty' had died. Telling Clementine she would return on 19 July, she describes a dream about 'underwater Mules' with snorkels covering their noses. Meanwhile, Martin Gilbert – at work on Volume V of the Biography – wrote asking for an interview about the years leading up to the outbreak of war.

Sarah resettled in Britain with a focus on the European market for her art. Bjorn Granvolden, a magazine journalist sent to dish the dirt, chucked in his assignment and became her pal instead. He took her to Norway that September where she appeared on TV and sold work. Modestly, she admitted she wasn't motivated by any causes: 'My paintings have no message. I'm not introspective.' Detectives and staff engaged in protection still stepped in and Michael Maher, a breezy young Irishman, was part of this retinue and became more than a friend. They adopted two dogs from Battersea as siblings for her Boston bulldog and fluffy chihuahua. They had known each other some time, but Maher now shared her bed. Officially, she was single and her guardsman knew when discreetly to step aside.

Motivated by social justice, Arabella opened a restaurant in a squat in Bristol Gardens, Little Venice, embracing the challenge of how to offer a three-course meal for 80p. She paid rates, provided staff with salaries and aimed to use any profits to fund a kids' adventure playground. Nutshell, as the enterprise was called, was soon catering for two hundred good-natured hippies. The GLC's Housing Committee did its utmost to evict her, but many admired Bella's pluck including her brother (now MP for Stratford) and Aunt Sasa, who came with Mike on opening night.

Sarah's family were keen for her to make some money with the fuller autobiography she had often spoken about. Charles Hamblett had done Paul Newman's biography and Sarah appointed him co-author and literary executor. She signed with Henry Regnery in March 1975 and was paid an advance, but sadly Charles died a month later. She produced provisional material they thought 'atrocious' and reneging on the contract, she was forced to return the advance. *Keep on Dancing* was a new project that the Curtis Brown agency assigned to Paul Medlicott in 1976, knowing he had trod a thorny path in producing *All You Need Is Love: The Story of Popular Music* and survived to see it become a TV series. Visiting Sarah almost every day at Eaton Square, Paul had an immense job clarifying misty detail to achieve order and continuity. He stuck it out, despite being shockingly underpaid. One of the constant people in Sarah's life for five years, they got on well – 'OK, it was fraught sometimes,' Paul admits.

Prince Charles chatted to Sarah, Edwina and Celia on 4 May 1977 at Bond Street's Knoedler Gallery after opening the biggest exhibition of Churchills to date, which included his *Tower of Koutoubia Mosque*, his only wartime painting. An exclusive event with a few sale items, proceeds from catalogues went to the Queen's Jubilee Appeal. Sarah and Idris were next off to Jerusalem invited by the Bikur Cholim Hospital. In mid-November she was in the States focused again on graphic art. Her lithographs were at the Nationwide Art Centre near Buffalo and she was collaborating with English artist Curtis Hooper on a portrait series based on her father. Curtis had used Graphic House Ltd for artworks he produced for Peter Sellers, the subject co-signing the work. Its boss, Steven Mandarano, admired these and contacted him about an urgent vacancy.

'Would you speak to Sarah?' said Mandarano, which was how Curtis met Lady Audley. As a child living in a street not far from Hyde Park Gate, he had seen Sir Winston several times and had even spoken to him once. He would develop each idea into an individual artwork doing considerable research into events during Churchill's long life. For the Sellers and Churchill series each plate was hand-made, which made every finished item effectively an original lithograph. Early on, he came with Sarah to Chartwell where she gave him access to the family archive of photos. Many were either poor quality or battered and this initiated the idea of re-drawing elements of the photos. Curtis started on those with a wartime theme, thinking back to his childhood amidst the bomb sites. His mother had experienced the Blitz and speaking to her and others crystallised the imagery. Sarah provided her personal recollections of events associated with the photos. *Warchild,* an original lithograph, was inspired by one story. Early one morning during the Battle of Britain, Winston left the Admiralty to assess the ravages of the previous night. Not far away a bomb site was being tidied up and a small boy was sitting on a pile of rubble. Someone on the Admiralty's staff went to speak to the boy and came back telling Churchill that both his parents had been killed. Curtis listened carefully to Sarah's stories and their conversation travelled in unexpected ways. He had been a pilot and had a good knowledge of the military. According to Curtis, Sarah's experience was similar:

> She was incredibly smart. Her own work in intelligence proved this. She experienced first-hand the heavy duty of responsibility, psychological distance and difficult decision-making made by those in the military service. There was an agreement in the Churchill family that Sarah was the one who was most like Sir Winston in her private character.

Winston's sayings accompany the images. Choosing which quote to associate with a particular image fell to Curtis. The words came first, he says, creating a voice for it to stand out. At the onset Curtis and Sarah defined their roles on the project and clarified legal matters concerning the co-signing. Sarah would receive one large single payment for her part in the fine art. Aiming at 300 prints meant hard work. They didn't achieve the quantities owing to problems with scratches. Curtis confirms that Sarah didn't conceive the images or create them but added her own special mark. He noticed a book that Sarah carried around containing small pieces of tracing paper, about two by three inches. She had a habit of tracing the outline of parts of photos. They put this to good use. Along with her signature the tracings were embossed into the paper in the area below or to the side of the central image.

Organising the signing was harder than they expected. Sarah's hand would shake. When she was ill it would take time for her to sign a pile of work and she usually only managed a few at a time. She told him that Lady Churchill approved of the artworks after seeing one or two, although Curtis didn't get the chance to meet her. The family were extremely positive. Sarah introduced him to those who had a say in official affairs and liaised on his behalf. He needed permission to use the family crest and got a letter authorising this. Some in the art world believed such a modern and contemporary way of representing Churchill would offend people, but Curtis went by instinct. He's very proud of what became known as the 'Visual Philosophy' series. The Queen personally requested to view them.

New York's Hammer Galleries, London's Troll Gallery and a private exhibition at 24 Wellington Road, St John's Wood, showed Sarah's own watercolours and lithographs. The latter was the home of Henny Handler, a Holocaust survivor the newspapers referred to as Sarah's 'friend'. 'I suppose I'm an impressionist,' she told a reporter.

In March 1977 Sarah's mother had to sell the Lavery portrait painted at Hoe Farm. Clemmie could hardly see but managed to dictate typewritten letters, signing them with a shaky hand. She took an interest in her daughter's work, brooded over her poems and even wrote out stanzas of remembered verse she thought Sarah would be interested in. Among her last gifts were *Bartlett's Quotations* and the *New Oxford Book of Verse*. On 12 December Baroness Churchill died. The pain was immense and felt for years to come. Reverend Raymond Turvey officiated at Holy Trinity, Brompton, where Elgar's *Nimrod* was played.

Curtis Hooper accompanied Sarah and Michael to Chartwell at the end of the year. Clementine's paintings were distributed to family members. Sarah had had quite a bit to drink and took Curtis into a room where a stack of Sir Winston's canvasses leant against a chair. Very emotional, her trembling words were: 'You have done so much for the Churchill family. You have brought him back. I've made a decision. I'm giving them to you.' Curtis remembers:

> I pleaded with her that this was not right and that I couldn't accept such an offer. Adamant, she wrote me a note confirming her wish. Next day I smiled at her and returned the note. We both knew about the previous evening but didn't refer to it. 'Thank you darling!' She said with a giggle.

When early in 1978, newspapers brought up the burning of the Graham Sutherland painting, Sarah told *The Times* that her mother was never made aware of a clause stating that Parliament's gift should revert to it when Churchill died. Her mother was therefore perfectly at liberty to destroy it. The Archbishop of Canterbury delivered a blessing for Baroness Churchill at a Thanksgiving service stewarded by the Hussars. 1,500 gathered including Callaghan, Macmillan, Margaret Thatcher, David Steel, Princess Alexandra, 45 peers and 40 MPs. The bells of Westminster Abbey rang.

When Mrs T was voted into office on 4 May 1979 Sarah wrote a letter of congratulations. She explained that prior to Margaret's appointment, her interest in politics had waned but looked set to revive. She admired the PM's ambition to pick Britain 'out of the doldrums and apathy that has made us such an easy prey'. The future Iron Lady replied saying how much she appreciated the letter and that while she faced a difficult task, hoped her government would prove worthy of the confidence placed in it. In October, at an exhibition of works by Johnny Churchill, Sarah told Hugo Vickers about her book, explaining that it was Mary's idea and how it was better to get her version out before someone else did. The suspicious-looking man Hugo records accompanying her was Mike Maher. The book was coming on slowly, as co-author Paul Medlicott explains:

> Sarah could be spectacularly forgetful. I wanted her to be more open about the downsides of being Sir Winston's daughter, believing this might make a

> better story. I told her the 'voice' she projected was often prim and proper but Sarah refused to be swayed by such ideas.

'I didn't exist,' Paul adds, a little tartly, thinking back to *Keep on Dancing*. Because Sarah wanted to be seen as accomplishing the work alone, near farcical situations arose as she insisted on keeping Paul in the background. It was especially irksome in exchanges with the family. Sarah's pride required that whenever their help was sought, it had to seem as if *she* was making the request. It made Paul's contact with them seem odd as he chased letters and documents and did the spade work. When Lady Soames visited, the 'Emperor's Clothes' situation was even more pronounced. He made trips to New York with Sarah to meet with Coward McCann & Geoghegan. They had to turn up 'coincidentally' at their office. It later seemed ridiculous to Paul. He was on the same flight as Sarah but separate (she ensconced in First Class). He organised all aspects of Sarah's journey and because he was also doing post-production work for his previous book, got a friend, Henry, to negotiate her through the airport in a wheelchair. The stress of travel tended to induce ravings in Sarah. The extent of her illness rather shocked Henry. Despite a few hiccups, New York worked out really well. Curtis was there too. The *Visual Philosophy* series was presented for the first time in a big show on Fifth Avenue. Limos pulled up outside. Serious money was involved.

Some years later Curtis became a victim of commercial machinations and lost out hugely to Graphic House. After making $18 million on sales, Mandarano, alleged by some to be in the mafia, was found guilty of using the business as a tax shelter. Curtis was never adequately paid and never received an apology or a settlement. He valued his friendship with Sarah. Curtis later studied psychology. He accepted the fluctuations in Sarah's behaviour:

> When Sarah was sober she was fantastic. It was a matter of 'going in and out of it.' She had the sense to stay away from people until she came out of it again. My wife and I had a friend who was surmounting aspects of the illness and Sarah got on extremely well with her, which indicates that she understood her own task in hand. She stayed with us a few times.

At the Fifth Avenue show, it occurred to Curtis that at every stage of her life she had dealt with the same barrage of questions about her family. There was no swearing this time, but a little while later he noticed her make a getaway. He and Paul had to track her down. Curtis saw how the buzz related to her father made her dumb down, closing in on herself. She revealed little. Paul believes that 'being a Churchill' was both a heavy yoke and a passport that got Sarah out of trouble. Throughout her youth her father had ensured that protectors guarded the family's reputation and made any special arrangements necessary to downplay indiscretions. Many tricky situations had existed before Malibu. That time she was unluckily caught out with the world's press watching. She 'stood on her honour' declaring who she was and why they shouldn't do this to her. Paul admits that he enjoyed many hilarious times with Sarah and Mike. *Keep on Dancing* sessions ended with pub sessions. Some members of her family understood her while others seemed to make light of her career. Once they installed a telephone meter because of Sarah's costly international phone calls.

Her zygomatically striking face was familiar in Belgravia and people liked her raucous giggle and auburn hair with its floppy fringe. If friends arrived at the Goring Hotel they used word of mouth to find her. When Nigel Windridge reopened the Ebury Restaurant and Wine Bar, it was the Poetess they got. She reeled off many, toasted them with noble excess, taking no more than a nibble of her smoked salmon. At the Elizabeth Street Fair, Sarah sat with towers of books either side of her and at The Antelope or Star she would tell people she had been far too serious in her youth and how 'the sound of people's laughter' appealed to her now. She regularly went to Ronnie Scott's where Ronnie's wife Mary greeted her. Mike waited in the car outside and she always sent a bottle of Scotch out to him. At Nichols Piano Bar, celebrating Idris with Doris Hare and Hermione Gingold, she thought of Vic when the *fumed oak* wall panelling was mentioned. She had heard from Ralph Blum, now using Viking runes to make sense of a world in which too much was going on. Ralph was helping the Hogwarts generation cope with the information tsunami in 2012, working on the *Runes eBook* when he died. Songwriter Hal Shaper was another friend Sarah had known for years. He helped produce an LP of *A Matter of Choice* in early 1980 along with Harley Usill, who co-founded Argo Records (a label that specialised in spoken word and poems read by actors). Harley and his son David collected Sarah from Eaton Square and drove to Chartwell for a photo session for the cover. Her voice is deep and mature on the record, making the ideas within *Monologue for Me*, *Roses in the Dark* and *A Friend* resonate even more. The last poem – an enquiry into the value of friendship in comparison to love – she devotes to Julia Lockwood:

Friends exchange their hands.
Neither takes – yet both can give.

# 19

# Exeunt

ALICE: Would you tell me please which way I ought to go from here?
CAT: It depends on where you want to get to.
ALICE: I don't much care where.

Duty makes us go where we ought to while our minds remain our own for magical journeys. Curtis was at Eaton Square in July 1980 and there was a knock at the door. 'Hello Sweetie,' called Sarah from inside her room. Two girls hugged her. One worked at the Young England Kindergarten in St George's Square. That day two boys had been trying to see who could pee farthest and got a shock when Miss Diana caught them. They got her across the shins. It was hard not to laugh. She also worked two days at 11 Eaton Mews South as nanny to Mrs Robertson's son. Sarah introduced Diana Spencer as 'one of the family' and Curtis got the impression Sarah knew her well. Their common ancestor was Henry Bayly, Winston's great-grandfather. They were looking at the lithographs and one that grabbed Diana's eye was *Warchild* where, superimposed on Churchill's face, is a small boy staring directly at the viewer. Diana seemed moved by it. She studied the pencil marks intently and asked questions. This unsophisticated girl whose Barbara Cartland paperback lay forgotten after she left, wasn't one you would single out but a few months later, after watching Prince Charles play polo, the 18-year-old became famous. The meeting between Sarah and Diana was like Maria Verelst's study of the Dowager Duchess of Marlborough and the first Lady Diana Spencer: age and youth.

Sarah played a prominent part at a huge concert in Winnipeg, Canada. On 18 September Henry Engbrecht was at the baton as people relived the spirit of the Battle of Britain on its fortieth anniversary with music from every war film you could name. The lighting made Sarah's long triskelion-patterned gown and neat hair glow like sunset. She offered reminiscences of her Papa and the orchestra contributed to her poems. When she returned she tripped over the dogs, toppling down the stairs. With a broken hip and injured kneecap, a three-week hospital stay was required, but she was hobbling on crutches soon after. She and Paul had to finish the book and at the launch he was shockingly ignored and only received an invite at the last minute. Sarah limped across to Ireland with Mike to see his elderly father. After that there were many interviews to do.

Duncan Fallowell in *The Spectator* took a stern line with *Keep on Dancing*, questioning the author for exciting us with the prospect of a tell-all story then failing to deliver. Sir Winston's portrayal annoyed him, but not half as much as Sarah herself. Only someone who hasn't left adolescence could deny her rebellion so glaringly, he argued. (Sarah was barely in her grave when his *Odyssey*, co-written with April Ashley, was published.) In autumn 1981 Chloe Salaman brought a bright, chirpy Sarah to ITV's *The Wilderness Years*, but by New Year the original was being treated for cirrhosis and uraemia. She felt tired and bruised but corresponded with Bond Street gallery owner Wylma Wayne about selling 27 of her Dad's paintings. The Duke of Marlborough presided over the opening of the Winston Churchill Exhibition, an event that saw Sarah's legacy passing to art lovers in the US, Mexico and Japan. Heath gave a speech and Mrs Thatcher attended, writing to Lady Audley on 3 August 1982 to congratulate her, as well saying how much she liked her poems.

Sarah was no longer responding to treatment. Idris heard her say that her Papa was waiting for her. Words left her but he sat beside her, singing poems with music like *I've Left Yesterday behind Me*. She smiled and squeezed his hand. Mary, Celia and Delphine took over while Idris tinkled downstairs with the doors open so she could hear him. Sarah slipped into a coma, never again opening her eyes. In the early hours of 24 September 1982 she was pronounced dead. Six days later Christopher read the lesson from John 14, 1-6 when mourners gathered at St Michael's Chester Square. Ellen gave a moving rendition of *Forgive Me if I Do not Cry*. The very same day, Edwina joined several of Sarah's pals at the Little Church Around the Corner on East 29th Street. Alex Clark gave the reading and Colin Webster-Watson read Sarah's poems. He surprised everyone by marrying New York socialite Jane Ewing right after the service. He said he had never felt it right to marry while Sarah lived. He had apparently told his estranged friend marriage was imminent a few weeks before. Mary received a wave of condolences and Sarah was laid to rest at Bladon early in October. Julia Lockwood was stricken by sadness.

Peter: Oh, my shadow, I'll stick you on with soap. Oh, my shadow, what's the matter with you?

Wendy: Boy, why are you crying?

With her husband Ernest and daughter Lucinda she staged a short scene for the concert arranged by Celia Sandys honouring Sarah on Sunday 27 February 1983. Marlborough, Mr and Mrs Profumo, Villiers, the estate of Lord Audley, Claire Bloom, Seymour Egerton and others provided means for this concert to fund a Guildhall School scholarship. A lively first half saw poems read by Ellen and Lorraine with Idris and Vera Benenson on piano. In the second, the Guildhall String Ensemble performed Elgar, Neill McCalister sang Sarah's *Hymn* and Elizabeth Seal performed songs from *The Boy Who Made Magic*. As compère, Ellen introduced David Burke and Fenella who read from *Thread in the Tapestry*. After Julia's scene, Ulick O' Connor recited Yeats, then Ellen introduced Colin, Carroll Baker and Judy Campbell onto the stage. Ellen acted an excerpt from Shaw's *Dark Lady of the Sonnets*. Written as part of a campaign to create a Shakespeare National Theatre (Jennie Churchill's great project), Shaw's playlet has Will Shakespeare intending to meet the Dark Lady. Instead, he meets Elizabeth I taking a walk before bedtime. He becomes fascinated by her, to the fury of the Dark Lady and tries to persuade the Queen to create a National Theatre.

Sarah's old gang had come together. Edward Heath gave a speech reading messages from Mrs Thatcher and Michael Foot. Just before Julia left, Heath told her how much he had enjoyed the scene from *Peter Pan*. They thanked him and he signed his autograph for Lucinda. Meanwhile, Sarah was flying through the skies of Rome and Paris, home to her nursery, her Papa and her lost shadow.

# Bibliography

## Primary Sources


**I. National Archives:**
Hansard
Prime Minister's Papers (PREM)
Cabinet Papers (CAB)
Wiltshire & Swindon Archives 1196/52

**II. Personal papers (Churchill College, Cambridge):**
Chartwell Papers (CHAR)
Churchill Papers (CHUR)
Clementine Churchill Papers (CSCT)
Sarah Churchill Papers (SCHL)
Randolph Churchill Papers (RDCH)
Mary Churchill Papers (MCHL)
Miscellaneous Holdings (MISC)

**III. Other personal papers:**
Medmenham Collection
Robert Graves Papers, St John's Library
Charles Hamblett Papers
Franklin Delano Roosevelt Library:
  Winant Papers/Box 190
  Bernard Bellush Papers/Box 3: Mulliner Interview (MIBB) and Diary (MDBB)
NARA: OSS catalogue entry: Samek, Stefan MI U Box 673 Location 230/86/40/01

Notting Hill School Magazine Archive
New York Public Library Archive

**IV. Unpublished manuscripts:**
Colin Webster-Watson, unpublished memoir
Wing Commander Douglas Kendall, A War of Intelligence, unpublished memoir

## Secondary Sources

**Books**

Aherne, Brian, A Proper Job (Boston: Houghton Mifflin, 1969)
Alliluyeva, Svetlana, Twenty Letters to a Friend (New York: HarperCollins, 1967)
Astaire, Fred, Steps in Time (New York: Harper and Brothers, 1959)
Ashley, A and Fallowell, D, Odyssey (London: Jonathan Cape, 1982)
Barnes, Jennifer, Television Opera (Woodbridge: Boydell Press, 2002)
Bates, J.L. The Eureka Conference, Military Review (October 1986)
Beauchamp, Focus on Fame (London: Odhams Press, 1958)
Beaton, Cecil, The Years between. Diaries, 1939-44 (London: Sapere Books 2018)
Bellush, Bernard, He walked alone. A biography of John Gilbert Winant (New York: Mouton, 1968)
Benedikt, Heinrich, Damals im alten Österreich: Erinnerungen (Vienna: Amalthea Verlag, 1979)
Berezhkov, Valentin, At Stalin's Side (New York: Birch Lane Press, 1994)
Berkman, Ted, The Lady and the Law (New York: Little, Brown and Company, 1976)
Bloom, Ken, Broadway: An Encyclopedia (Abingdon-on-Thames: Routledge, 2002)
Bohlen C.E Witness to history (New York: Norton 1973)
Bullock, Alan, The Life and Times of Ernest Bevin Vol 2 (London, Heinemann, 1960)
Brett, Sylvia, Sylvia of Sarawak. An autobiography (London: Hutchinson, 1936)
Brooke, Peter, Duncan Sandys and the Informal Politics of Britain's Late Decolonisation (London: Palgrave Macmillan, 2018)
Bullock, Alan, The Life and Times of Ernest Bevin (London: William Heinemann, 1960)
Cadogan, Alexander, The Diaries of Sir Alexander Cadogan Ed. Dilks, D. (London: Cassell, 1971)

Charlton, Warwick, Stephen Ward speaks (London: Today Magazine, 1963)

Churchill, Jennie, The Reminiscences of Lady Randolph Churchill (New York: The Century Co, 1908)

Churchill, John S, Crowded Canvas (London: Odhams Press, 1961)

Churchill, Randolph S. The Rise and Fall of Sir Anthony Eden (London: MacGibbon & Kee 1959)

Churchill, Randolph S. Twenty-One Years (London: Weidenfeld and Nicolson, 1965)

Churchill, Randolph S. What I Said About the Press (London: Weidenfeld and Nicolson, 1957)

Churchill, Sarah, Thread in the Tapestry (Andre Deutsch, 1967)

Churchill, Sarah, Keep on Dancing (New York: Coward McCann & Geoghegan, 1981)

Churchill, Sarah, The Prince with Many Castles (London: Frewin, 1967)

Churchill, Sarah, Collected Poems (With Songs by Some of Her Friends) (London: Frewin, 1974)

Churchill, Sarah, The Unwanted Statue and other Poems (London: Frewin, 1969)

Churchill, Sarah, The Empty Spaces (London: Frewin, 1966)

Churchill, Winston S. The Second World War V: Closing The Ring (London: Cassell, 1952)

Churchill, Winston S. My Early Life: A Roving Commission (London: Thornton Butterworth, 1930)

Churchill, Speaking For Themselves Ed. Lady Soames (London: Black Swan, 1999)

Churchill, Winston S. His father's son (London: Weidenfeld & Nicolson, 1996)

Cochran, Charles, Cock a doodle do (London: J.M. Dent & Sons, 1941)

Cochran, Charles, Showman Looks On (London: J.M. Dent & Sons, 1945)

Colville, John, The Fringes of Power: Downing Street Diaries (London: Weidenfeld and Nicolson, 2004)

Colville, John, The Churchillians (Littlehampton Book Services Ltd, 1981)

Colville, John, Footprints in Time (London: Collins, 1976)

Coward, Noël, Future Indefinite, (New York: Doubleday, 1954)

Coward, Noël, The Letters of Noël Coward Ed. Day, B (London: Methuen, 2007)

Coward, Noël, Noel Coward Diaries Ed. Payn, G and Morley (London: Weidenfeld and Nicolson 1982)

Cowles, Virginia, Winston Churchill: The Era and The Man (London: Hamish Hamilton 1953)

David, Villiers, Self-Reflections (London: Hazlitt, 1970)
Deedes, W.F. Dear Bill (Pan Macmillan, 1997)
De Vere Cole, T and Owen, R, Beautiful and Beloved (London: Hutchinson, 1974)
Downing, Taylor, Spies In The Sky: The Secret Battle for Aerial Intelligence (London: Abacus, 2012)
Doyle, Gavin, Touring Days A Theatrical Journey (Book Guild Publishing Ltd, 1989)
Duchess of Argyll, Margaret, Forget Not (London: W.H. Allen, 1975)
Eden, The Memoirs of Anthony Eden (London: Cassell, 1960)
Eden, Clarissa, Clarissa Eden A Memoir, Ed. Cate Haste (London: Orion, 2007)
Entwistle, Vivienne, They Came to My Studio (London: Hall Publications 1956)
Eisenhower, Dwight D. Crusade in Europe (New Hampshire: William Heinemann Ltd 1948)
Fabian, Robert, Fabian of the Yard: An intimate record (The Naldrett Press, 1950)
Gaddis, J.L United States and the Origins of the Cold War (New York: Columbia University Press, 2000)
Gilbert, Martin, Winston Churchill and Emery Reves (University of Texas Press, 1997)
Gilbert, Martin, Winston S, Churchill. V. Prophet of Truth (Boston: Houghton Mifflin Company, 1977)
Gilbert, Martin, Winston S, Churchill. VI. Finest Hour (Boston: Houghton Mifflin Company, 1983)
Gilbert, Martin, Winston S, Churchill. VII. Road to Victory (London: Heinemann, 1986)
Gilbert, Martin, Winston S, Churchill. VIII. Never Despair (Boston: Houghton Mifflin Company, 1988)
Gilbert, Martin, Churchill A Life (New York: Holt, 1992)
Graves, R. P. Robert Graves The Years with Laura (Weidenfeld & Nicholson, 1990)
Green, Hughie, Opportunity Knocked (London: Frederick Muller Ltd 1965)
Hall and Holt, Perfect Gentleman (London: Blake Publishing, 1999)
Halle, Kay, The Young Unpretender: Essays by his friends (New York: Heinemann, 1971)
Halsall, Christine, Women of Intelligence (Staplehurst: Spellmount, 2012)
Hanfstaengl, Ernst, Hitler: The Missing Years (London: Eyre & Spottiswoode, 1957)

Haslam, Jonathan, Near and Distant Neighbours: A New History of Soviet Intelligence (New York Farrar, Straus and Giroux, 2015)
Ingram, Kevin, Rebel: the Short Life of Esmond Romilly (London: E P Dutton, 1986)
Jackson, Ashley, British Empire and the Second World War (London: Bloomsbury Academic, 2006)
Jacob, Alaric, A Traveller's War (London: Collins, 1944)
Jeffery, Keith, MI6: History of the Secret Intelligence Service 1909-1949 (London: Bloomsbury, 2011)
Jenkins, Roy, Churchill: A Biography (London: Macmillan, 2001)
Kendrick, Alexander, Prime Time – The Life of Edward R. Murrow (London: J.M. Dent & Sons, 1969)
Killearn, The Killearn Diaries, Ed. Evans, T.E. (London: Sedgwick & Jackson, 1972)
King, Bruce, Robert Graves: a biography London: Haus Publishing, 2008)
Kremer, R.S. Broken Threads (London: Bloomsbury, 2006)
Krickus, Richard, The Kaliningrad question (Lanham: Rowman & Littlefield, 2002)
Kyle, Keith, Suez: Britain's End of Empire in the Middle East (London: I.B.Tauris, 2011)
Larkin, Maurice, Church and State after the Dreyfus Affair (London: Palgrave Macmillan, 1974)
Leamer, Laurence, The Kennedy Men: 1901-1963 (New York: William Morrow & Company, 2001)
Lees-Milne, James, Caves of Ice (London: Chatto & Windus, 1983)
Leslie, Anita, Cousin Randolph: Life of Randolph Churchill (Hutchinson: 1985)
Lewis, Jeremy, David Astor A Life in Print (Jonathan Cape, 2016)
Lockhart, The diaries of Sir Robert Bruce Lockhart I,II Ed. Young, K. (London: Macmillan, 1973)
Lockwood, Margaret, My Life and Films (London: World Film, 1948)
Lovell, Mary, The Riviera Set, 1920-1960 (London: Abacus, 2017)
Maisky, The Maisky Diaries, Ed. Gorodetsky, G. (Yale University Press, 2015)
Major, Norma, Chequers: The Prime Minister's Country House (New York: HarperCollins, 1996)
Martin, John, Downing Street: The War Years (London, Bloomsbury Publishing, 1991)
McEvoy, Dermot, Irish Miscellany (Vermont: Skyhorse Publishing, 2015)
Mackillop and Sinyard, British Cinema in the 1950s Manchester University Press, 2003)

Macmillan, Harold, War diaries: The Mediterranean (London: Macmillan, 1984)

McDonough, Frank, Chamberlain, Appeasement and the British (Manchester University Press, 1998)

Moir, Phyllis, I was Winston Churchill's Private Secretary (New York: Wilfred Funk, Inc 1941)

Montague Browne, Anthony, Long sunset (London: Cassell, 1995)

Moran, Charles, Winston Churchill: The Struggle for Survival (New York: Constable, 1966)

Murray, Edmund, I was Churchill's bodyguard (London: W.H. Allen, 1987)

Mosley, Diana, A Life of Contrasts (London: Hamish Hamilton, 1977)

Nahum, S, Baron By Baron (London: Frederick Muller, 1957)

Nel, Elizabeth, Mr. Churchill's Secretary (New York: Hodder & Stoughton 1958)

Olson, Lynne, Citizens of London (Melbourne: Scribe Publications, 2015)

Oliver, Vic, Mr. Showbusiness (London: Harrap, 1954)

Pearson, John, The Private Lives of Winston Churchill (London: Bloomsbury Reader, 2013)

Purnell, Sonia, First Lady (London: Aurum Press, 2015)

Raczynski, Edward, In Allied London (London: Weidenfeld and Nicolson, 1962)

Rees, Laurence, World War II: Behind Closed Doors, London: BBC Books, 2012)

Roberts, Brian, Randolph: A Study of Churchill's Son (Hamish Hamilton, 1984)

Robyns, Gwen, Barbara Cartland: an authorised biography (London : Sidgwick & Jackson, 1984)

Roosevelt, Elliott, As he Saw It (New York: Duell, Sloan and Pearce, 1946)

Roosevelt, Elliott, The Conservators (New York: Arbor House, 1983)

Sandon, Henry, Living with the Past (London: Hodder and Stoughton, 1997)

Scott (Furney), Hazel, Peace and War

Sherry, Norman, The Life Of Graham Greene Volume Two (London: Penguin, 1996)

Smith, Frederick, Lady Eleanor Smith. A Memoir (London: Hutchinson, 1953)

Smyser, W.R From Yalta to Berlin (New York: St. Martin's Press, 2000)

Soames, Mary, A Daughter's Tale (Black Swan, 2012)

Soames, Mary, Clementine Churchill (London: Cassell, 1979)

Spencer-Churchill, Laura, Laughter from a cloud (London: Weidenfeld and Nicolson, 1980)

Sperber, A. M. Murrow, His Life and Times (Fordham University Press, 1998)

Stalin, Joseph, Stalin's Correspondence with Churchill, Attlee, Roosevelt & Truman, 1941-45 (London: Lawrence and Wishart Ltd. 1958)

Stone, Desmond, Alec Wilder in Spite of Himself (Oxford University Press, 1996)

Sullivan, Rosemary, Stalin's Daughter (New York: Harper, 2015)

Summers and Dorril, Honeytrap: Secret Worlds of Stephen Ward (Weidenfeld and Nicolson, 1987)

Thompson, Douglas, Stephen Ward – Scapegoat (John Blake, 2014)

Thorpe, D.R Eden, The Life and Times of Anthony Eden, first Earl of Avon, 1897-1977 (Pimlico, 2004)

Varah, Chad, Before I Die Again (London: Constable, 1992)

Veigl, Hans, Einzelgänger & Exzentriker (Vienna: Böhlau Verlag, 2008)

Waugh, The Diaries of Evelyn Waugh, Ed. Davie, M. (London: Penguin, 1984)

Williams, Allan, Operation Crossbow (London: Preface Publishing, 2013)

Willson Disher, M, Fairs Circuses and Music Halls (London: William Collins, 1942)

Winant, John G, A Letter from Grosvenor Square Hardcover (New York: Houghton Mifflin Co 1947)

Urquhart, Fred, W.S.C. A Cartoon Biography (London: Cassell, 1955)

Urwand, Ben, The Collaboration (Harvard University Press, 2015)

Zeman, Zbyněk, The Masaryks (London: I B Tauris & Co Ltd, 1990)

Ziemke, Frederick, The U.S. Army in the Occupation of Germany (Columbus: BiblioGov, 2013)

**Abstracts, Papers, Magazines**

Brenner, Marie, To War in Silk Stockings (Vanity Fair, 2011)

DeWitt, L.W. JG Winant: First chairman of the SSB (socialwelfare.library.vcu.edu 2012)

Dudzus, Olaf, Golfika (Magazine of the European Association of Golf Historians No.13, 2014)

Gilbert, Martin, The Gallipoli Memorial Lecture Transcript (26 April 1995)

Gilbert, Martin, The Beast of Bergholt Finest Hour 151, Summer 2011

Schindler & Westcott, Shocking Racial Attitudes: Black G.I.s in Europe (CESifo 6723, 2017)

Tweedie, Neil, How our Piccadilly Commandos had the G.Is surrounded (Telegraph Online, 2005)
Harriman Magazine, Winter 2015 issue, published The Harriman Institute
Dennis Sherwin Blog 2018
Ancestry UK

**Oral Histories**

Johnson, Lamont, televisionacademy.com
Mulliner, Maurine, 1965 ssa.gov
Colville, Sir John, Radio210 1985, BL C1000/170/85/1
Wick, Charles Z. millercenter.org
Blaisdell, Thomas, Truman Library
Roberts, Frank, 1986 WGBH Openvault
Murden, Myra, Imperial War Museum 80022274

**Film, TV, Radio**

*The Churchills* TV Mini-Series – 1996 Directed by Greg Lanning (Brook Associates, WGBH)
*The Vic Oliver Story* – 26.09.1960 (British Library Sound Server C1343/54)
*24 Hours* – 12.06.1967 (British Library Sound Server C1398/0264)
*Below Stairs* – Georgina Landemare speaks to Joan Bakewell (BBC 1973)

**Newspapers**

Austrian National Library
British Newspaper Library
newspaperarchive.com

# Text Permissions

*The author gratefully acknowledges permission to reprint copyright material as follows:*

Extracts from The Years Between 1939-44, Cecil Beaton Diaries © Cecil Beaton (Sapere Books) published by arrangement with literary executor of the late Cecil Beaton and Rupert Crew Ltd.

Extract from Kathleen Harriman letter by permission of the Mortimer Family Archives.

Extract from Wing Commander Douglas Kendall, A War of Intelligence, unpublished memoir © The Medmenham Collection (Archive Reference MHP 16)

Extract from Eden: the life and times of Anthony Eden, first Earl of Avon, 1897-1977 D.R. Thorpe published Vintage. Reproduced by permission of The Random House Group Ltd. ©1997

Extracts from Behind Closed Doors by Laurence Rees, 2008 by arrangement with Andrew Nurnberg Associates, Robin Straus Agency, Penguin Random House.

Extracts from The Noël Coward Diaries by Graham Payn and Sheridan Morley and Winston S Churchill, The Second World War V: Closing The Ring, by arrangement with Orion Publishing Group.

Extracts from Caves of Ice, James Lees-Milne used with the permission of David Higham Associates.

Extracts from The Fringes of Power, Sir John Colville used with the permission of Hodder & Stoughton.

Extract from Lockhart Diaries p535, extract by permission of Dugald Bruce The Marsh Agency Ltd., on behalf of the Estate of Robert Bruce Lockhart.

Extracts from Women's Weekly Kay Keavney (TI Media Content and Brand Licensing)

Extracts from Colin Webster-Watson, unpublished memoir © Colin Webster-Watson by arrangement with Anne Manchester.

Extracts from Sarah Churchill, The Collected Poems of Sarah Churchill – OWLS000198

# Source Notes

*The following are used in the Source Notes. See Bibliography for books.*

**People**

| | |
|---|---|
| AB | Antony Beauchamp |
| CH | Charles Hamblett |
| CSC | Clementine S. Churchill |
| CWW | Colin Webster-Watson |
| ESE | Eleanor Sotheran-Estcourt |
| JGW | John Gilbert Winant |
| RSC | Randolph Spencer Churchill |
| SC | Sarah Churchill |
| WSC | Winston Spencer Churchill |

**Interviews**

| | |
|---|---|
| FF | Fenella Fielding 11.03.2018 |
| DB | David Burke 23.05.2018 |
| ND | Nicola Dantine, 07.06.2018 |
| TB | Ted Buckwald, 12.07.2018 |
| SSH | Susan Seaforth Hayes 05.08.2018 |
| HS | Henry Sandon, 06.08.2018 |
| CH | Curtis Hooper 11.08.2018 |
| JLC | Julia Lockwood-Clark 18.01.2019, 23.01.2019 |

**Books**

| | |
|---|---|
| EMAE | Memoirs of Antony Eden |
| LD | The Diaries of Sir Robert Bruce Lockhart |
| NCD | Noël Coward Diaries |
| TLAE | Eden: the Life and Times of Anthony Eden |

**Diaries**

| | |
|---|---|
| CFP | The Fringes of Power |
| COI | Caves of Ice |
| CPSC | Collected Poems of Sarah Churchill |
| IWWC | I Was Winston Churchill's Private Secretary |
| MSFS | The Struggle for Survival |
| RBCD | Behind Closed Doors |
| TTT | Thread in the Tapestry |
| TYB | The Years Between |
| UPM | Unpublished Memoir |
| WI | Women of Intelligence |

**Newspapers**

| | |
|---|---|
| ABEE | Aberdeen Evening Express |
| ABPJ | Aberdeen Press and Journal |
| BDG | Birmingham Daily Gazette |
| BDP | Birmingham Daily Post |
| DH | Daily Herald |
| DT | Daily Telegraph |
| DunC | Dundee Courier |
| DunET | Dundee Evening |
| ES | Evening Standard |
| ILN | Illustrated London News |
| JC | Jewish Chronicle |
| MG | Manchester Guardian |
| Nmer | Northampton Mercury |
| NotEP | Nottingham Evening Post |
| NotJ | Nottingham Journal |
| NTD | Northampton Times and Directory |
| WLEG | West Lancashire Evening Gazette |
| YorkEP | Yorkshire Evening Post |
| YorkEPr | Yorkshire Evening Press |
| YorkP | Yorkshire Post |
| YPLI | Yorkshire Post Leeds Intelligencer |

**Archives**

| | |
|---|---|
| BMHS | British Music Hall Society |
| CAC | Churchill Archives Centre |
| FDRL | Franklin D Roosevelt Library |
| HP | Hallmark Playhouse |
| IWM | Imperial War Museum |

| | |
|---|---|
| MDBB | Mulliner Diary |
| MedmC | Medmenham Collection |
| MIBB | Mulliner Interview |
| NA | National Archives UK |
| NHEHS | Notting Hill School Magazine |
| PMED | Sarah's papers (P. Medlicott) |
| SJL | St John's Library |
| TA | Television Academy |
| TBTRU | Thomas Blaisdell Interview Truman Library |

*Page number, keyword and source is given below:*

**Chapter 1: Waves and Tussles**

11 more ill' 01.1958 CHUR 1/56 p82-106, 'in his past' SCHL 1/8/5, 'were here' ND, 'soap' 07.03.1958 Belfast Telegraph

12 'Terraqueous' 03.05.1951 CBS HP, 'Breath of Air' 'history of music' Television Opera

13 'distinguished show' SSH, 'better occasion' SSH

14 hamburger 30.10.1953 ABEE, 'high school teacher' SCHL 1/8/2, 'break, insult or criticise ' SCHL 4/2, 'manner in which ' SCHL 4/2, 'better ambassador' 17.12.1953 JCHall-WSC CHUR 1/50 p144-168, almost lost 10.08.1954 DunC

16 'unspoken' For R.B CPSC, 'medical' 25.07.1955 SC-WSC CHUR 1/56 p57, 'seven picture' 24.08.1955 Portland Press Herald, 'questing' 'pushing too hard' 17.09.1955 SCHL 2/2/2

17 'monumental' 'raised a hand' 17.09.1955 SCHL 2/2/2, 'Was He there' 'pray do anything' 22.09.1955 SCHL 2/2/2, efforts, TA Lamont Johnson

18 'nebulous' 21.06.1948 SC-Villiers SCHL 1/4/9, 'salad' 15.10.1957 CSC-SC SCHL 1/2/4

**Chapter 2: Why Am I alone?**

20 'convenient' 23.03.1961 DH, 'born happy' 29.03.1961 Southern Evening Echo, HMS Diana 19.09.1922 YorkEP

21 'be long' Iain Kerr and Ann Rachlin 10.05.2019, 'hullabaloo' 'howling' Crowded Canvas, bunks 09.10.1936 Mirror, NY

22 'Bible' Barbara Cartland, 'do that' Twenty-One Years, 'adventurer' Diana Mosley 'The Churchills' Mercy 09.11.1940 Australian Women's Weekly (Mary St Claire)

23 Roehampton 04.06.1920 Diana-Jennie CHAR 28/131/6061, 'ask' Miss Constance Irons, NHEHS SCHOOL MAGAZINE 1983.

24 'cowed' 13.02.1921 CSCT 3/21, 'bounty ' Irish Miscellany

25 'little' 04.08.1922 CHAR 1/158 4243, 'goose' 04.08.1922 CHAR 1/158 4243, 'flame' 13.09.1922 DunET, 'be kind' 08.11.1922 DunC

26 Asthall – 14.08.1923 Diana-CSC MCHL 5/8/31, Duke of Yorks – 31.12.1958 DT, 'whipping boy' JLC, 'imaginative' 02.12.1958 Star (Roy Nash), 'Facts' 07.1948 SC-Villiers SCHL 1/4/9, 'Austerlitz' COI p418-9

27 barred – NHEHS 1983 (Miss Irons memory), 'Mussolini' 20.01.1927 Western Morning News, 'pros' NHEHS no.41 March 1926, 'deficit' 01.11.1927 Sheffield Daily Independent, 'get me changed' SCHL 1/1/2

28 'concertina' SCHL 1/1/2, 'exhilaration' 26.05.1928 Tmitford-RSC RDCH 1/2/40

29 'rushing' 18.01.1930 SCHL 2/2/1, presented – 08.05.1928 08.05.1928 Sheffield DT, 'her age' 08.05.1928 SCHL 2/2/1, 'Any fool' TTT

30 sharing – 29.12.1933 LD p281, 'REPRODUCTIONS' 1932 DianaG-RSC RDCH 1/2/39, Victorian lady 03.07.1929 Sketch, trusted – David Lloyd George, accident 24.05.1929 Chelmsford Chronicle, 'fools' 06.03.1930 SCHL 2/2/1

31 'annoying air' 'temper' 21.01.1930 SCHL 2/2/1, less attention – Colville Radio210, husky – Twenty-One Years

32 'lighthouse bright' 1931 MISC 108/4, 'conventions' 08.1931 SCHL 2/2/1, 'best friend' 06.03.1932 SCHL 2/2/1, 'miss her very much' 06.1931 SCHL 2/1/1, 'shaking' 'egg' 04.03.1932 SC-ESE MISC 108/1

33 'clown' 'scars' 04.03.1932 SC-ESE MISC 108/1, 'good-looking' 02.04.1932 SC-ESE MISC 108/1 employment -21.04.1932 SC-CSC SCHL 1/1/4, 'lugged' 20.07.1932 SC-ESE MISC 108/2 'lunch' 07.1932 SC-ESE MISC 108/2

34 'giggle' 08.1932 SC-ESE MISC 108/4, 'like a tree' 06.08.1932 SC-ESE MISC 108/3, 'manipulator' 28.10.1920 Stage, p15, 'Dreams' 19.02.1933 SC-ESE MISC 108/4

35 red shoes 10.03.1933 Bournemouth Graphic, 'old-fashioned' 22.04.1933 Belfast Newsletter, her Season – 08.04.1932 SC-ESE, MISC 108/1

36 in Kurgan – NA 1196/52 Wiltshire & Swindon Archives

37 'big house' 01.01.1934 SC-CSC SCHL 1/1/4, of Empire 28.04.1934 Wiltshire Times & Trowbridge Advertiser

**Chapter 3: We Went to the Arts**

38 'Robin Pool' 18.02.1952 SC-CSC SCHL 1/1/14, well aware – 1969 ST PMED , Devon 17.12.1914 Stage p22

39 Decorations 03.06.1930 SC-CSC SCHL 1/1/2, 'arts' 30.04.1975 Levittown Bucks Courier Times, Napoleon lm Kevin Brownlow 24.02.2018 , 'set against' SCHL 1/1/2

40 'funny' 30.12.1929 SCHL 2/2/1, 'philosophy' CH ,'good speech' 23.11.1977 Akron Beacon

41 nursing 05.09.1930 Chelmsford Chron, Surprise 14.10.1930 TomM to RSC RDCH 1/2/40, 'pyjamas' Gemma Jones 29.01.2019, objection – 24.01.1931 SCHL 2/2/1

42 'trees' 05.11.1930 Lady R to RSC RDCH 1/2/40, 'Mata Halle' Dennis Sherwin Blog 2018, 'plighted' 29.11.1930 T Mitford-RSC RDCH 1/2/40, 'older' Young Unpretender, 'cane' 'English money' 05.03.1931 Stage, p6, 'drawn by' 09.1931 SCHL 2/2/1

43 'Charlie to his left' TB, 'actress' 19.11.1931 SC-CSC SCHL 1/1/4, 'being vain' 02.10.1931 SCHL 2/2/1, 'mystic' 16.01.1932 SCHL 2/2/1 ,'aware of' 09.06.1932 SC-ESE, MISC 108/2

44 'spoil' 19.11.1931 SC-CSC SCHL 1/1/4 ,'coarse' 'greasy' 09.01.1932 SCHL 2/2/1, 'his beauty' 'list' 21.11.1931 SC-CSC, SCHL 1/1/4 , 'another term' 22.11.1931 SC-CSC, SCHL 1/1/4 'gangster' 'excused himself' 14.01.1932 Oakland Tribune

45 her choice IWWC, 'interference' 01.02.1932 Kingston Daily Gleaner, 'appeasing Nazis' The Collaboration, 'proper' 13.02.1932 HarryWarner-CSC, CHAR 1/398A/6

46 for fun 07.03.1932 DT, 'hectic' 06.03.1932 SCHL 2/2/1, 'slavery' 27.02.1932 Bowen Independent (Qld), 'diplomatic stuff' 23.02.1932 Urbana Daily Courier, tripped 16.02.1932 Gettysburg Times , Murat 17.02.1932 Tipton Tribune, monopoly 09.03.1932 Washington E. Journal

47 'great dream' 'living' 06.03.1932 SCHL 2/2/1, 'I love Pebin' 15.03.1932 SCHL 2/2/1, 'in vain' 05.1932 SC-ESE MISC 108/2, 'fooling' 19.01.1932 SCHL 2/2/1 'natural' 19.01.1932 SCHL 2/2/1, 'rest cure' 20.07.1932 SC-ESE MISC 108/2, 'act' 06.1932 SC-ESE MISC108/4

48 'thrilling' 12.11.1932 SC-ESE, MISC 108/4, 'new era' 12.11.1932 SC-ESE, MISC 108/4

49 'unromantic' 'trundle' 'stopped' 28.08.1932 SC-ESE MISC 108/3, 'Herr Hitler' Churchill: A Life, 'film acting' 17.12.1932 Advertiser, Adelaide p9, Australian 11.02.1932 LD, p203

50 'useful brother-in-law' 11.1932 SC-ESE MISC 108/4 , 'Boring' Life of Contrasts, 'patience' 14.11.1932 JBailey-WSC, CHAR 1/231/48, study dance 20.11.1935 Sheffield Independent

51 Patchwork Players William Graves Collection, 'photo of Jenny' Lucia Graves 24.01.2020

52 . 52 'standoffish' 01.01.1934 SC-CSC, SCHL 1/1/4 'horrid, facetious', 01.01.1934 SC-CSC, SCHL 1/1/4, 'father and mother' 03.12.1958

Star (Roy Nash), 'men have to be alone' TTT, 'erratic' Robert Graves: a biography

53 'madly' Barbara Cartland, Highfields NotJ 17.11.1934, 'not so fast! 22.01.1935 SC-CSC SCHL 1/1/4, Sidney 'meet someone' 17.02.1935 SC-CSC, SCHL 1/1/4

54 'married again' Dear Bill p23, 'worshipped' 17.02.1935 SC-CSC, SCHL 1/1/4, 'conceited' 17.02.1935 SC-CSC, SCHL 1/1/4, 'Unionist' 23.02.1935 ABPJ, 'never offered' 07.1953 MSFS p420

55 'Baby' 24.08.1935 NotJ

56 16 Ackers lodgings directories BMHS, 'shy' 05.12.1958 Star (Roy Nash)

57 'thermometers' 21.11.1935 Performer

**Chapter 4: He Who Divided Us**

59 'will come' 03.01.1936 SC-CSC CHAR 1/288

60 'stomachs' 19.02.1936 Tatler, 'so much dancing' 14.02.1936 ILN, 'guardian' Peter Flax 15.08.2018, Winston came – 03.12.1958 Star, 'wonderful hair' 15.03.1934 Stage, p11 'future' 03.12.1958 Star (Roy Nash), 'sequins' 04.12.1958 Star (Roy Nash)

61 religious 24.05.1968 DT (Ian Ball), 'benefitted' CH/SC dialogue c.1965 PMED

62 'distract' Eileen Broster 09.12.2018, 'If you can' Vic Oliver story

63 'Robb' 'nuisance' Edward Thomas 01.02.2019, 'twin-sets' Touring Days

64 'Moravian' My thanks to Tomáš Zapletal, Dr Bohumír Smutný & Kateřina Tučková, half Germany's textile firms Broken Threads , Saville Row NARA: OSS: Samek, 'ventures' 22.06.1913 Neue Freie Presse

65 'Germanic traits' Stefanie Samek 03/2018, stolen – 15.11.1902 Reichspost, 'Mark this,' 17.10.1900 Neuigkelts Welt Blatt, 'Paul Grüssner' My thanks to Olaf Dudzus, 'Christian Women' 08.12.1907 Grazer Volksblatt, world-class Golfika, 'likeable' 28.09.1912 Illustriertes Sportblatt

66 'army comics' 25.12.1915 Illustrierte Kronen Zeitung, 'good-for' Damals im alten Österreich p304-305

67 silver-fox – Mr Showbusiness, p44, 'Fugitive' 23.03.1919 Neues Wiener Tagblatt

68 originality' 08.07.1924 Bridgeport Telegram, 'Harding' 01.06.1925 Tipton Daily Tribune, 'musical ability' 24.10.1925 Olean Times , 'eloping' 'Bessie' 08.07.1936 CSL-WSC CHAR 1/288/32-33, 'bad luck' 18.09.1926 Terre Haute Spectator

69 'servants' 'beautiful' 25.01.1932 Wiener Sonn & Montags Z, 'stockings' 1932 Die Bühne: Heft 325, Frankfurters Einzelgänger & Exzentriker, 25.01.1932

70 400 miles 06.11.1936 Radio Pictorial (Evelyn Dall), 'Dear Friend' 07.05.1927 Vaudeville News, Proctors – Vaudeville News, 23.04.1927, 'pure vaudeville' 22.01.1925 Hutchinson News

71 'Cooking' 26.04.1931 San Antonio Express, 'Helen Kane' 06.08.1931 Performer 'debut' 19.08.1931 Performer, 'Adrian' NARA: OSS: Samek, 'relation' Tony Orsten 19.09.2018, 'gumbo' 11.01.1934 Murphysboro Daily Independent

72 '£7000' 07.02.1936 JC p35

73 'Beula' My thanks to Richard Sell (Crangle relative), 'filled' Wyn Calvin 29.03.2018

74 'moral' 05.06.1936 CSL-WSC CHAR 1/288/7-10, 'phoned Laura' 14.09.1936 Robert Graves's Diary, telegrams – William Graves Archive

76 'hollow' 15.09.1936 SC-CSC SCHL 1/1/5, 'foot right' 28.04.1971 Australian Women's Weekly (Kay Keavney)

**Chapter 5: Life with the Magician**

78 'engaged' 02.10.1936 American, 'job-hunting' 21.09.1936 Daily Times Chicago, 'Blotz' 22.09.1936 NY Evening Journal, Winchell 'telegrams' – 09.10.1936 NY Mirror

79 'kindest' 22.09.1936 NY Mirror, 'Colony' 21.09.1 23.09.1936 World Telegram

80 'found speech' 45th Street New York City CPSC

81 'mugs' 26.09.1936 Baltimore Sun, Mayfair - 27.10.1936 D. Express, 'electrify' 02.10.1936 Boston Post

82 'stalwart' 12.10.1936 SC-CSC SCHL 1/1/5, 'notions' 16.10.1936 Cumberland Evening Times

83 heartbreak – CSC-SC MCHL 5/7/5, 'strategic' – Churchill A Life p934 Attlee speech, 'Blind Mice' 23.09.1915 Stage, p14 carry the can - Gallipoli Memorial Lecture, awful dream 05.06.1914 CSC-WSC, 'pain' 28.11.1936 CSC-M.Ozanne

84 'syrup' 16.10.1936 Star, Kansas City, 'front page' 31.12.1936 Daily Herald, 'out of love' SC-WSC 12.1936 CHAR 1/288 p71-72

85 'milk' 'trouper' 06.01.1937, Holborn Book, BMHS

86 'springy' 20.01.1937 WSC-CSC CHAR 1/298/20, 'Ages' Stage 11.03.1937 p11

87 stopped Reed My Life and Films, 'luxurious' CFP p167, 25.07.1940

88 'cheque-forger' 21.07.1937 Gloucester Citizen, 'forced' ESE 1983 MISC 108/5, tug – 11.08.1937 Variety, 'knocking' 29.08.1937 SC-M. Ozanne SCHL 1/1/4, conference 09.07.1938 Gloucestershire Echo

89 'blame' 29.08.1937 SC-M.Ozanne, SCHL 1/1/4, succumbs – 11.10.1937 ES CBF – 22.03.1935 JC, p15

90 'pro-Semite' 01.03.1935 JC p12 , 'Maccabi' 30.11.1940 Innsbrucker Nachrichten, censors – 07.10.1937 ES, 'ambitions' 17.12.37 Portsmouth E. News

91 'clean' – 13.05.1938 Nmer, 'curtain' 19.05.1938 Stage, p8-9

92 Last word – Prophet of Truth p908-12, longing Unity-WSC 05.03.1938 Churchill Vol 5. Companion

93 'talked about'14.09.1938 Portsmouth Evening News

94 hoops 18.06.1938 WSC-A.Maxwell CHAR 1/326/2, Nazi camps 05.06.1937 Nation, Anti-Chamberlain, Appeasement p124–133, contract – 15.09.1938 D. Express

95 'talk to' 'Maria' Tony Orsten 19.09.2018, 'cross talk' 09.02.1939 Era

96 'Alington' 18.11.1938 ES, 'students' 24.05.1947 Wiener Zeitung

97 'Whatever' 'old Sarah' Victory' TYB loathed – Riviera Set p188 '5000 children' 19.04.1939 YorkEP, 'fiddling' Brian O'Gorman 23.04.2017, 'interest' 'nails' 06.10.1939 Bournemouth Times attentiveness – IWWC

98 'Baltic' 19.05.1939 WSC-Commons 'sits down' 15.02.1937 Der Morgen 'sire' 10.1939 Der Stürmer, No. 43, cruellest – 09.1939 Der Stürmer, No. 36 'Minister und Jüdin' 10.1939 Der Stürmer, No. 43 senile – Wiener Stadt und Landesarchiv, Krankheitsgeschichte I, 1052/40 Am Steinhof , 'laying on' 15.08.1939 Star

99 'gleaming' 17.10.1939 Star 'box' 13.10.1939 Epsom Herald, 'downtime' 19.04.1939 East Kent Times

100 'prised' P. Churchill 1965, RDCH 10/21

101 'adolescent' Damals im alten Österreich, 'takeover' 06.10.1939 Hampstead and Highgate Express , '18%' Ref. M-OA: FR 523 B in Jews in British Society Ch.5 ARJ Kushner (1986), 'enough' 23.08.1940 Tribune, Redesdale's 09.1940 Birmingham Mail, 'bored' 09.03.1940 Christian Science Monitor, 'modern' 23.12.1939 New Statesman

102 'unpopular' 06.02.1940 YorkEN, 'side' 10.02.1940, 14.02.1940 YorkEN, 'Malvolio' 11.01.1940 Times, 'Good old' 23.03.1940 Norwich Mercury, 'emotional' 29.03.1940 Wiltshire News

103 'faith' 02.06.1940 Sandys-WSC CHAR 1/355/37-38, ran around MSFS p321-3 07.12.1945, 'completely' 11.05.1940 Vic-WSC,

CHAR 1/355/28, 'soaringly' 09.05.1940 Western Morning N, 'Not to me' 01.05.1975 Defiance Crescent News p14

104 'spirits' 19.06.1940 Sussex Daily News

105 'busk' Vic Oliver story, 'unblushing'13.11.1940 Tatler

106 France 11.06.1940 CFP p123

107 'lovelier' 25.07.1940 CFP p167, champagne 25.07.1940 CFP p167, free 03.08.1940 DT

108 'daughter' 13.08.1940 Western Mail, baptism 21.08.1940 Sunday Pictorial, 'life and love' 05.09.1940 Stage, 'honour' 03.1941 Woman's Journal, 'serious' 08.1940 Vogue, Gen. Marshall - Churchill would later call Marshall 'the greatest soldier of them all' despite differences over war strategy.

109 'exchange' 30.08.1940 JC p18-19, 'Red-Head' 29.09.1940 Sunday Dispatch, Dale Cottage – 01.10.1940 E.Bagnold-Beaton SJL Beaton A1/25/2, 'River Room' 09.10.1940 ES

**Chapter 6: Re-claimed and Re-educated**

111 'First Rate ' 06.11.1940 Sketch, 'story-teller' 29.10.1940 Leicester Mercury, 'asset' 29.10.1940 Leicester Evening Mail, 'served' 08.08.1943 LD p248, 'kitchen' Glandemare-J.Bakewell BBC, 'kills Hitler' 09.11.1940 Southport Guardian, auction -12.11.1940 Oxford Mail

112 'brought tears' CH, 'joined Vic' 17.11.1940 Sunday Dispatch 'Dowdy' TYB, 'worth' 29.11.1940 Huddersfield Daily Examiner, 'Lord' Era and The Man, p327

113 'patient' 07.12.1940 J.Martin-SC CHAR 20/7/44, etherealised 11.12.1940 MG, 'devil character' Fay Lenore 15.01.2019

114 'don't laugh' 01.1942 Lynx MedmC, Future Europe -13.12.1940, CFP p265-267 waltzes Finest Hour

115 Vice-President– 28.12.1940 American Science Monitor, 'Nabobs' 'FDR is tied' 02.01.1941 WLEG

116 'elocutionist' 22.01.1941YorkEPr

117 'funniest' 04.02.1941 Evening Citizen, 'swollen' 04.02.1941 Evening Times, 'gallantry' 04.02.1941 Glasgow D. Express, welcomed – Fay Lenore 15.01.2019

118 sexual – Perfect Gentleman

119 'emotion' 07.12.1938 Queenslander p14, 'cry' 19.02.1941 Diana Cooper to JJ Norwich, 'Armageddon' Kennedy Men, 'my belief' 04.03.1941 DH

120 'gallant dead' 11.11.1941 Liverpool Echo, 'lover of peace' 06.12.1947 Age (Melbourne), 'bomber' 15.03.1941 Liverp. Echo

121 'folly' 08.03.1941 CFP p312, 'Utopian' S.Shurtleff 24.12.2019, 'agreeably' 'ordeal' 'inventions' 20.03.1941 NotEP, 'secrets' 19.03.1941 Newcastle Sun (NSW), 'first rate' 28.03.1941 Illustrated Sporting and Dramatic News

122 'Hepburn' 12.03.1941 Telegraph and Argus, 'not only' 14.03.1941 Berkshire Chronicle, 'luxurious' 29.03.1941 CFP p318, 'swell' Visitors book SCHL 2/1/3

123 'Treasury' 03.04.1941 Performer

124 brooding' Murrow, His Life and Times

125 'detached' The Roof – CPSC, 'shadowless' SC-unknown SCHL 1/8/5, 'so ends' SC-unknown SCHL 1/8/5, 'someone'12.11.1932 SC-ESE MISC 108/4

126 'combination' 05.12.1958 Star (Roy Nash), 'peace plan' 09.06.1941 DT

127 'Ireland' 25.05.1941 CFP p338, 'ways'10.08.1948 MDBB

128 'sheep' 07.02.1941 ABPJ, 'Arab' 15.04.1941 DT, 'rations' 16.01.1942 Jedburgh Gazette

129 Monitor, spoof 02.01.1941 Evening News, Oi! 08.05.1941, Performer, 'humming' 17.11.1940 Sunday Dispatch, 'laughing' 19.05.1941 Daily Mail

130 Appassionata Mr Showbusiness, p143, 'feared' 07.06.1941 Oxford Mail, Frenchmen 21.09.1940 CFP p206

131 'greatest living' Evening Citizen 03.06.1941, 'final' Evening Citizen 03.06.1941, 'tradition' Evening Citizen 03.06.1941

132 able Letter from Grosvenor Square, accede TLAE, 'produce' 01.12.1941 DT (Sydney)

133 'husband' 07.07.1941 K.Harriman-Mary Fisk, 'unsupervised' War in Silk Stockings

134 angry 06.05.1941 Killearn Diaries, 'fascinating' 06.1941 RSC-WSC CHAR 1/362/41, 'call' 25.03.1946 LD p535 , 'conspiracy' Das judische Komplott – Holocaust Museum

135 Savings 29.08.1941 WSC-Winant CHAR 20/22A/82, 'civilisation' 30.08.1941 CFP p378, 'passport' 20.08.1941 Morecambe & Heysham Visitor, Statecraft, spectacles – 11.10.1941 Picture Post, 'darkness' 27.09.1941 ABPJ

136 'governesses' 01.08.1941 Radio Times, RAF boys – 25.09.1941 MG, 'Dirsztay' Visitors Book SCHL 2/1/3, 'cruel – and just bolt' COI p232, 'never grew' 'greatest' 'witnessed' 09?10.1941 Vic-SC SCHL 1/8/5

137 'nothing' 17.10.1941 Rollo-WSC, CHAR 1/362/109 pile – 10.04.1981 Daily Mail
138 'meant' 05.11.1941 SC-CSC, SCHL 1/1/6

**Chapter 7: Like Father I Fight Alone**

139 'restyled' WI 'school' SC-Paddy Carstairs, WCHL 1/21
140 'swarmed' A War of Intelligence MedmC 'blinking' 'top-line' 'smasher' ACW2 To Pilot Officer – CPSC 'index' 01.1942 Lynx MedmC
141 'Sarah nor' 01.1942 Lynx MedmC, 'shameful' Peace and War MedmC 'bespoke' Peace and War MedmC
142 'harem' 22.02.1942 Banater Deutsche Zeitung, determination 27.02.1942 DT, 'good stuff' 29.07.1941 Killearn Diaries
143 'cocksure' 'missed him' Travellers War, 'planes' CH/SC dialogue c.1965 PMED, 'unusual' Tim Fryer MedmC, 'lighting up' Constantine Normanby 15.08.2018, 'interrogations' Operation Crossbow, 'violent' Self reflections
144 whizzed past WI, 'NOT your friend' Peace and War MedmC, 'ten times' 11.05.1943 Star
145 'time-sensitive' A War of Intelligence 'Polet Roti' Menu 31.10.1942 MedmC, The Bombers CPSC, shock – Peace and War MedmC, Screwtape 26.11.1942 Portal-SC SCHL 1/8/1
146 'two of' Spies In The Sky, 'trying' Notes C. Bonham Carter MedmC, 'nobody' WI, 'manners' 24.03.1943 Völkischer Beobachter, 'rocket' NA DEFE 40/12
147 pencils Operation Crossbow, 'raised £755' Ted Wood Collection, MedmC, 'bitterness' SC-CSC SCHL 1/1/7 , OSS 03.01.1959 Irish Times
148 'ancient' Lord Willoughby de Broke, 'Progressive' 10.04.1943 Officer-SC SCHL 1/8/1, 'blotting' Myra Collyer IWM

**Chapter 8: Our Secret Place**

149 'scorched' 14.11.1941 DH, 'ground the enemy elects' 11.11.1941 DT 'unsure' Forget Not
150 'ethereally' Churchill, A Biography, 'opportunities' 04.10.1941 Newcastle Sun (NSW) p5 'justice' 01.01.1942 Northern Whig, 'chew' TBTRU , 'Ramblers' 10.08.1948 MDBB, 'flash' 09.07.1942 Edinburgh Evening News
151 'paternal towards Gil' SSA Mulliner

152 'highway' 29.01.1942 BDG 'Idleness' 29.01.1942 NotJ, inkling - 07.07.1942 Mary-SC SCHL 1/3/1, 100,000 – Shocking Racial Attitudes

153 'rest' 06.07.1942 YPLI, 'gates' 23.07.1942 Devon Journal, 'facial' 24.09.1942 Southern Reporter, Leslie Howard 03.10.1942 DT, coastal Road to Victory p282, fl at back – 27.10.1942 LH Buck to SC SCHL 1/8/1, backstage – Peace and War MedmC, stepping-stone – British Empire & the Second WW.

154 gift CHAR 20/54C/255-256, 'Gettysburg' TBTRU , attract– Churchill, A Biography p651, GYMNAST – EMAE - 24.07.1942, 'FDR's ear' TBTRU

155 best off 18.09.1942 SC-WSC, CHAR 1/369/68-70, bursitis - He Walked Alone, 'adventure' – 03.01.1943 CSC-JGW FDRL/Winant Papers/Box 190

156 seriously – As he Saw It, 'way of life' 14.02.1943 Stars and Stripes, Cope 06.02.1943 DT, 'restitution' NA T160/1280/1

157 recipes - 1965 SSA Mulliner, ill – 05.09.1943 JSChurchill-CSC CHAR 1/374/69, 'deplorable' 08.07.1943 SC-Balfour SCHL 1/8/1, 'especially' Georgina Landemare 1973, prostitutes – How Piccadilly Commandos . . .

158 'manners' 03.12.194 Tribune 'As I Please' George Orwell, rejected – Citizens of London, shot WI , Karl Hulten D. Mirror 05.03.1945, send word 22.12.1943 SC-JGW SCHL 1/8/1, 'failed me' 22.12.1943 SC-JGW SCHL 1/8/1, 'left for' Christmas 1943 CPSC, valued – 22.02.1944 CSC-JGW FDRL/Winant Papers/Box 190 bibelots - 01.03.1945 CSC-JGW FDRL/Winant Papers/Box 190

159 'thingimmybob' 10.04.1944/28.02.1944 SC-Jack SCHL 1/8/1, 'bothered' 28.02.1944 SC-Jack SCHL 1/8/1, birth control 13.07.1939 Catholic Press (NSW) p12, 'Gerry' 19.10.1944 Pam-Gil FDRL/Winant Papers/Box 190

160 big hand 13.09.1944 Bystander, trusted – 14.07.1945 MDBB, Eden marriage 16.05.1951 MIBB, special friend – 06.10.1948 MDBB, Winant a divorce – 08.10.1948 MDBB detested 16.05.1951 MIBB, teetotal - Steve Shurtleff 14.04.2018

161 affection 17.12.1944 JGW to M. Mulliner FDRL/Bernard Bellush Papers/Box 3, divorcing 16.05.1951 MIBB, 'light' He Walked Alone, 'aunt' 16.05.1951 MIBB, 'madly' 04.01.1956 SCHL 2/2/2

162 'the best' 13.02.1945 SC-JGW FDRL/Winant Papers/Box 190, 'Ambass!!' 15.02.1945 SC-CSC SCHL 1/1/8, confronted 17.02.1945 CSC-Mary MCHL 5/1/117 (1)

**Chapter 9: I Shake Hands with Uncle Joe**

163 no idea 06.04.1981 ES p7 , swan – 02.05.1942 WSC-RSC CHAR 1/369/5-8 , reaching 18.09.1939 Boothby-LG, Lloyd George P. G/3/13 H.Lords Record Office, 'new tank' 16.09.1941 DH, special football matches Road to Victory, £5,000,000,000 HC Deb 01 October 1941 vol 374 cc613-68 , 60,000 Conservators, 'enemies' 22.09.1955 – SCHL 2/2/2

164 gun – Prime Minister's Country House, 'frightfully' – EMAE, formation RBCD, '25LB' 30.09.1941 Evening Despatch, patronized – At Stalin's Side p267

165 'he said' Patrick Kinna 'The Churchills', 'your spirit' 12.08.1942 Cadogan Diary, subaltern 07.1953 MSFS p420, 'Look at me' – Twenty Letters to a Friend p171, 'assured' – Travellers War , 'defence of' 15.08.1942 Cadogan Diary, 'refreshed' 25.08.1942 BDP

166 constitutional US and Origins of the Cold, protocol – 07.01.1942 NA F0 371/ 32 864, abandoned 28.03.1943 D. Mirror, How could it be RBCD, abominable – 07.05.1943 NCD p20

167 stopped short – In Allied London p141, 'speak to Sarah'-Myra Collyer IWM, 'hitch' – 08.05.1932 SC-ESE MISC 108/2, 'limitations' Annotations Yalta PMED

168 'champagne' Colville, Radio210, 'OBE' 09.07.1969 W.Donald-SC SCHL 1/8/3, 'books' 16.11.1943 MSFS p126-7, 'got on well' CH/SC dialogue c.1965, 'beat us up' TTT

169 'repairs' 11.12.1972 Boston Evening Globe, 'exotic' 24.11.1943 SC-CSC SCHL 1/1/7, black-clad Mr. Churchill's Secretary

170 'relic' 26.11.1943 SC-CSC SCHL 1/1/7, 'fun' 23.11.1943 SC-CSC SCHL 1/1/7, 'gaudy' 'Lysol' 24.11.1943 SC-CSC SCHL 1/1/7, 'opportunist' As he Saw It, 'your Simon' TLAE

171 'conduct' 16.10.1952 RSC-WSC CHUR 1/51, 'family affair' Closing The Ring p300, 'pro' 26.11.1943 SC-CSC SCHL 1/1/7

172 whisked Mr Churchill's Secretary, 'bitten' 04.12.1943 SC-CSC SCHL 1/1/7, 'bag' Downing Street: The War Years, reluctant As he Saw It, promised Winant MIBB

173 'creatures' 04.12.1943 SC-CSC SCHL 1/1/7, 'vulgarity' – 04.12.1943 SC-CSC SCHL 1/1/7, 'doomed' 27.02.1945 WSC-Commons

174 'wisdom' 1954 SC-WSC CHUR 1/50 p194-218, 'silence' – Annotations Yalta PMED, 'smiling' 24 Hours

175 'previews' Downing Street: The War Years, fall – RBCD, total Churchill: A Biography, as if he – Kaliningrad Question, 'take the US' Witness to history

176 'sick' President at Home, Lt. Miles, F.O. 371/38516, 'Zohak' FDRL/ John G Winant Papers , salute 07.12.1943 Daily Record 'What do I do?' 'Missed' RBCD, 'delicious stuff' Laughter from a cloud, 'great man' 04.12.1943 SC-CSC SCHL 1/1/7

177 'trying' 04.12.1943 SC-CSC SCHL 1/1/7, boisterously – 01.12.1943 MSFS p143, sedan – Eureka Conference, 'bloody' 02.12.1943 MSFS p144

178 'bull' War diaries Macmillan, worn at – 13.01.1944 CFP, 'speak a word' (30.01.1944 WSC-Eden) NA PRO PREM 3/353

179 oranges WI, 'twice' – 04.12.1943 SC-CSC SCHL 1/1/7, 'strike'- 23.03.1944 Evening News, 'position' 14.05.1944 RSC-WSC, CHAR 1/381/35-37, 'suited' CH/SC dialogue c.1965 PMED, expertly – Crusade in Europe

180 'R.C' Church and State, 'flowers' CH/SC dialogue c.1965 PMED.

181 cabled – Stalin's Correspondence, 200,000 members AIR FORCE 09.2012, struck – 08.09.1944 LD p352, 'two lions' 'tear at' CH/SC dialogue c.1965

182 'hope' 14.09.1944 Diana-WSC, CHAR 1/381/2 'peculiar' – CFP p499-503

183 'Old Bear' 07.10.1944 SC-CSC, SCHL 1/1/7 'share' 'women-minded' 07.10.1944 SC-CSC, SCHL 1/1/7, bowed – At Stalin's Side p267

184 their hands Road to Victory, 'regards' 17.10.1944 PM-WarCabinet CHAR 20/181, 'brooch' 23.10.1944 Colville-Lawford CHAR 1/381/63, 'horseman' 17.10.1944 PM-WarCabinet CHAR 20/181, 'given up' WGBH Frank Roberts, 'gas bill' 29.10.1944 SC-WSC CHAR 1/381/64-65, blackmail CFP p503, slaves – Operation Crossbow

185 'saved' 31.01.1945 SC-CSC SCHL 1/1/8, 'puce' 'filthy' 'flirting' 01.02.1945 SC-CSC SCHL 1/1/8, socialist realist 01.02.1945 MSFS p217

186 'bleak' 04.02.1945 SC-CSC SCHL 1/1/8, 'ineffective' EMAE 04.02.1945, lemon tree – Cutting PMED, Chekhov's Villa – Cutting PMED, missing – Harriman Magazine, Winter 2015

187 'goes down' 06.02.1945 SC-CSC SCHL 1/1/8, 'not well' – Annotations Yalta PMED, 'dancing' – Cutting PMED, 'touch' 09.02.1945 SC-CSC SCHL 1/1/8, Danubian – WGBH Frank Roberts, lettuce 11.02.1945 MSFS p230-233 , 'no need' 12.02.1945 SC-CSC SCHL 1/1/8

188 'Melba' 13.02.1945 Cadogan Diary , switched 13.02.1945 MSFS p234, 'bridal' 'shaggy' 'care' 'red kitten' 12.02.1945 SC-CSC SCHL 1/1/8, optimistic 13.02.1945 SC-JGW FDRL/Winant Papers/Box

190, 'owed' Laughter from a cloud, vengeance –Etiquette of the Thick Ear Tatler, 20.03.1940

189 'outnumbered' 'demands' – Annotations Yalta PMED, 'thugs' 01.05.1975 Defiance Crescent News p14, 'shielded' 22.09.1955 SCHL 2/2/2, 'daughter' 'wear' 12.02.1945 SC-CSC SCHL 1/1/8

**Chapter 10: The Bell Tolls**

190 tears 17.04.1945 Lincolnshire Echo, 'FDR man' TBTRU, bedrooms Westminster Archives

191 Arlingford Road 24.06.1945 Sunday Mirror, Hopewell Road 15.08.1945 Hull Daily Mail

192 'shattered' – 1945 SC-WSC SCHL 1/8/1, 'flat' Joy Hunter, IBTimes UK, caring – 26.07.1945 CFP p576, 'effortlessly' JLC, 'the cost' 27.07.1945 SC-CSC SCHL 1/1/8, Paintings Neville Conder BL SS, 'good influence' – 20.07.1945 MDBB, troubled – 08.08.1945 MSFS p289

193 hoped-for 14.07.1945 MDBB, 'spare life' 23.11.1944 WSC-RSC, CHAR 1/381/45,'snafu' 02.08.1945 MDBB, rings - 06.09.1945 MDBB, rescuing- 09.09.1945 MDBB, no surprise – 01.09.1945 MSFS p291, 'business' – 05.10.1945 MDBB, discuss – 31.10.1945 MDBB

194 'vile' – 31.12.1945 Mulliner MDBB , let down – 02.01.1946 MDBB, Clemmie 21.01.1946 CSC-JGW FDRL/Winant Papers/Box 190, ebb – 31.01.1946 MDBB, remote – 18.09.1946 LD p568-9

195 former ADC 01.04.1946 S SC-WSC CHUR 1/42 p61, meddling 18.03.1946 Sydney Morning Herald p3, rage – 25.04.1946 MDBB, 'dared' Congress Honors FDR 01.07.1946 politico.com

196 'tear up' 'old age' 06.09.1946 SC-CSC SCHL 1/1/10, trapped 06.03.1947 SC-WSC CHUR 1/45 15-39, seriously –10.08.1948 MDBB, $750,000 – He Walked Alone , arguments 10.08.1948 MDBB

197 checks – 06.09.1946 SC-CSC SCHL 1/1/10

198 'never bad' 18-19.10.1946 SC-CSC SCHL 1/1/10, 'five minutes' 21.10.1946 SC-CSC SCHL 1/1/10, 'leave me' Footprints in Time p156

199 'secrets' 11.11.1947 SC-CSC&WSC CHUR 1/47 p47 'hopes' 07.02.1947 RSC-WSC CHUR 1/47, 'spirit' 12.02.1947 SC-Villiers SCHL 1/4/6

200 'indifferent' 12.02.1947 SC-Villiers SCHL 1/4/6, 'hurt' 14.02.1947 SC-Villiers SCHL 1/4/6, 'expense' 06.03.1947 SC-WSC CHUR 1/45 p15, 'goose' 06.03.1947 SC-WSC CHUR 1/45 p15-39

201 'worst of all' 10.03.1947 SC-Villiers SCHL 1/4/6, 'prettier' 10.04.1947 COI, p126, Ilchester 20.04.1947 COI, p129, enlist 18.06.1947 NCD p86 , Engraved 21.03.1947 WSC-Vic CHUR 1/42 p104, cottage 12.6.1947 Scottish D. Express, jumping – 15.05.1947 P.Moore-SC SCHL 1/8/1, 'dignified' – 23.06.1947 Vic-WSC CHUR 1/42 p107, Brussels – 25.06.1947 Salzburger Tagblatt, 'un-commercial' 17.07.1948 Leader

202 'gin' 15.03.1949 SC-Villiers SCHL 1/4/10, 'best role' 31.10.1946 Townsville Daily Bulletin p6, 'Bonnie' 01.07.1947 WSC-SC CHUR 1/42 p107 platinum -14.02.1947 MDBB , Soldati – 16.08.1947 Diaries Evelyn Waugh p685, problem 14.09.1947 MDBB

203 'throat' 10.08.1948 MDBB, awful 28.11.1947 MDBB, 'translucent' COI p183, 'breasting' COI p199 speakeasy – 10.08.1948 MDBB

204 savings Winant: First chairman of the SSB, 'no money' Steve Shurtleff , viable – 10.08.1948 MDBB, discharge – 06.11.1947 New England General Advertiser p1, unshakeable New York Times, 06.11.1947

205 'goodness' 11.1947 SC-CSC&WSC CHUR 1/45 p47, 'stopped' 11.11.1947 SC-CSC, CHUR 1/45 p47, 'mingle' 17.11.1947 SC-WSC CHUR 1/45 p47-71, 'played' 11.11.1947 SC-CSC&WSC CHUR 1/45 p47, 'chill' 11.1947 CSC-WSC CHUR 1/41 p62, 'soldier's business' CH/SC dialogue c.1965 PMED, 'fruitless' – Reappraisal – CPSC

206 'destroy' 09.01.1948 SC-WSC CHUR 1/45 p47, 'every embassy' Story Walter Graebner

207 'change for them' 22.01.1948 News Review, London letters – 16.05.1951 MIBB, 'celestial' Of Love and War – CPSC

**Chapter 11: He Took Me for Life**

208 burglar – 21.10.1947 D. Mirror, 'anaesthesia'- 09.04.1948 SC-CSC SCHL 1/1/12, 'bettered' 07.1948 SC-Villiers SCHL 1/4/9, 'to hell ' 11.10.1950 SC-Villiers SCHL 1/4/10 'concrete' 14.01.1950 SC-Villiers SCHL 1/4/10

210 'vital' 03.10.1953 SC-CSC SCHL 1/1/15, weird - Focus on Fame, 'truth' 14.06.48 SC-Villiers SCHL 1/4/9, 'liberation' 21.06.48 SC-Villiers SCHL 1/4/9

211 'future' 07.48 SC-Villiers SCHL 1/4/9, 'landed' 'ire' 30.06.48 SC-AB SCHL 1/6/1, 'Nippy' 19.07.1948 CSC-SC SCHL 1/2/2, 'harbour'

21.06.48 SC-Villiers SCHL 1/4/9, 'Come off' 'TREATMENT' SCHL 3/1/1

212 reception 03.11.1948 Times, Streatham 26.11.1948 Norwood News, 'gigolo' 'dirt' COI p333, 'rudeness' 'dignity' 'hoofs' 12.1948 SC-WSC CHUR 1/46 p69-93

213 stack - Focus on Fame, 'knows' 12.1948 SC-WSC CHUR 1/46 p69-93, 'patted' 15.04.1949 Belfast Newsletter, 'courier' 05.05.1949 CHUR 1/46 p28-52

214 future 11.09.1949 AB-CSC MCHL 5/1/149, debts -13.10.1949 CSC-RSC RDCH 1/3/9

215 'quality' HS, Leonard - Princeton Alumni Vol 50, 'unbearable' 'fat' ??.49 SC-AB SCHL 1/6/1, 'ability' 'hogging' 25.08.1949 Westport Herald, 'work' Pat Crowley, 04.04.2019

216 'serenity' 29.08.1949 SC-CCS SCHL 1/1/12, 'harness' 14.10.1949 SC-CSC WSC SCHL 1/1/12, telegram CHUR 1/46 p69-93

217 mistaken - 20.12.1949 CSC-AB SCHL 1/2/2

218 'photogenically' AFI Catalog USC Library, 'celluloid' 04.02.1950 SC-Villiers SCHL 1/4/10, 'smile?'12.09.1970 Reveille

219 'Sarf' HS, dogs - Living with the Past , outstanding -18.10.1938 Gloucester Echo, designed 15.09.1971 Australian Woman's Weekly, citing - 29.07.1942 DunET, '10 most' Beautiful and Beloved

220 dash 10.03.1943 ABPJ, 'means' Alison Moore, 2019, 'miniature' 21.12.1949 CSC-SC SCHL 1/2/2

221 'gnome' 19.05.1950 SC-CSC SCHL 1/1/13

222 'ghastly' 20.05.1950 SC-CSC SCHL 1/1/13, 'diamante' 20.05.1950 SC-CSC SCHL 1/1/13, 'Socrates' 02.06.1950 Northern Whig, 'unreliable' 30.06.1950 SC-CSC SCHL 1/1/13, 'crisis' 30.06.1950 SC-CSC SCHL 1/1/13, 'taller' 30.06.1950 SC-CSC SCHL 1/1/13

223 Miss Kerr 18.09.1950 D. Mirror, 'incompetent' SC-CSC SCHL 1/1/12, 'Crystal Room' Olivia de Havilland 2019, 'Soldiers' 08.10.1950 People

224 'wouldn't' 25.02.1951 SC-CSC SCHL 1/1/14

225 'foreign' Transcript Richard Wesp PMED

**Chapter 12: Cold War, Warm Heart**

226 'old man' 21.10.1951 Sunday Chronicle

227 jig - Touring Days, 'taut' 18.02.1952 Sunday SC-CSC SCHL 1/1/14

228 'half-bearded' 06.1952 SC-CSC SCHL 1/1/14, 'lookalikes' 28.05.1952 CSC-SC SCHL 1/2/3, 'first rate' 16.06.1952 RSC-SC SCHL 1/3/2

229 'human' 16.06.1952 SC-WSC CHUR 1/50 p94, 'shoulders' 'fog' 29.06.1952 AB-WSC CHUR 1/50 p94-118, luncheon - 09.07.1952 ES

230 'psychological' 16.10.1952 RSC-WSC CHUR 1/51 p768, 'ties' 09.10.1952 SC-CSC SCHL 1/1/14, 'Pimlico' 19.10.1952 Sunday Graphic , tricks 14.10.1952 AB-WSC CHUR 1/50 p94, Windsors 07.01.1953 CFP p619

231 'hinge on it?' CH , chances - 11.03.1953 Daily Mail, 16,000,000 27.04.1953 Evening News

232 'dread' 03.10.1953 SC-CSC SCHL 1/1/15, 'Roll em!' 09.05.1953 D. Express, 'birdie' Henry Sandon, 30.09.2018

233 'snapped' Baron by Baron

234 'barriers' Honeytrap p23

236 flings JLC, party - YPLI 08.06.1953, 'complimented' 17.06.1953 CSC-SC SCHL 1/2/3, worrying 09.07.1953 SC-WSC CHUR 1/50 p119

237 'pornographic' What I Said About the Press, reproached -ITN's In the News 28.03.1955, 'died' 19.10.1953 SC-WSC CHUR 1/50 p119-143, 'sure' 03.10.1953 SC-CSC SCHL 1/1/15 , 'truce' 19.10.1953 SC-WSC CHUR 1/50 p119, 'vulgar' 30.10.1953 AB-WSC CHUR 1/50

238 helicopter 25.04.1953 Lanc. Evening Post, tucked - I was Churchill's bodyguard, 'tension' 09.01.1954 SC-WSC SCHL 1/1/15

239 face value 06.04.1954 MSFS p538 , Baron 05.1954 SC-CSC SCHL 1/1/15, 'much better' 10.05.1954 SC-CSC SCHL 1/1/15, 'life' 10.05.1954 SC-CSC SCHL 1/1/15, 'distressed' SC-CSC SCHL 1/1/15, decay - 30.05.1955 MSFS p659-660, 'good life' 13.11.1954 AB-WSC CHUR 1/50 p169-193

240 'overwhelming' 'suffer' 13.11.1954 AB-WSC CHUR 1/50 p169-193, life story Lady and the Law, 'tried' 03.12.1954 Bedfordshire Times and Independent

241 distribution 18.06.1955 Billboard, 'introduced' Miller Center: Charles Z. Wick

242 'painful' 02.03.1955 CSC-SC SCHL 1/2/4, 'sort of' 02.07.1955 SC-CSC SCHL 1/1/15, 'sturdy' Hansard, 5th Series Vol 537, tests 16.05.1955 Life, 'sentimental' - 03.05.1955 SC-CSC SCHL 1/1/15

243 'planted' 06.1955 SC-CSC SCHL 1/1/15, 'one-sided' 22.09.1955 - SCHL 2/2/2

244 'tadpoles' 'brain' 17.10.1955 - SCHL 2/2/2, 'cause' 09.11.1955 SC-CSC SCHL 1/1/15, 'abandoned' 04.01.56 - SCHL 2/2/2

245 notice Alec Wilder in Spite of Himself , 'independent' 28.04.1971 Australian Women's Weekly (Kay Keavney)

**Chapter 13: The Unwanted Illusionist**

246 farewell -15.02.1956 Shields Daily News, Selwyn - Suez: Britain's End of Empire

247 'cunning' 14.08.1956 Sacramento Union, reservists -16.10.1956 Liverpool Echo

248 'sober' Lamont Johnson, 'blessings' 15.11.1956 WSC&CSC-SC CHUR 1/56 p82-106, 'experiment' 16.11.1956 Kingsport News, 'fire-power' Cutting, LA Examiner

249 'first friends' ND, 'succeed' 24.01.57 SCHL 2/2/2

250 'freezing' 06.05.1957 MG, repressed 09.06.1956 NCD p322, stature Blog Mark Scholz 24.05.2016, 'in love' Lady Rayne 27.06.2018

251 Milwaukee 24.10.1956 Broadcasting, £6000 - 22.08.1957 Daily Mail , owed 27.10.1957 SC-Vivienne SCHL 1/8/2

252 'sophisticated' Diana Melly 07.07.2018, 'common' 22.08.1957 D. Mirror

254 'victory' 27.10.1957 SC-Vivienne SCHL 1/8/2, nil 29.03.1959 DT, 'pride' 27.10.1957 SC-Vivienne SCHL 1/8/2

**Chapter 14: Neverland and After**

256 'set-back''carrot tops' 21.03.1958 SC-WSC CHUR 1/55 p396-420, 'Wendy' 26.03.1958 Wendy-SC SCHL 1/8/2

257 'demands' 16.06.1958 Meerwein-Leichti SCHL 4/2, 'remarkable' Interview ND , prostitutes 13.02.1959 CSC-SC SCHL 1/8/2, 'longhair' 10.07.1958 SC-CSC SCHL 1/1/17

258 thermals 24.02.1997 Daily Mail, 'rehearse' 'spinning' 05.11.1958 SC-WSC CHUR 1/55 p396-420, 'fairies' British Cinema in the 1950s

259 'rufescence' 'find myself" 01.12.1958 Star

260 'soul' JLC

262 'unique' 'didn't like' JLC

263 excess - S. Hobart (at Sarah's car insurance firm) 08.2019, 'troupe' 25.07.1959 AD-SC SCHL 1/8/2

264 'Peter, Pam' Peter Flax, 15.08.2018, 'great deal' 19.01.1959 BDP

265 'carefully' 'Now my Baby' JLC, 'Miss Russell' Geoffrey Chater 18.05.2018

266 'alone' 23.03.1960 Newcastle E. Chronicle, 'Geisha' 15.03.1960 SC-WSC CHUR 1/153/48, unannounced -Forget Not

267 consoled - 08.05.1960 NCD p437, 'Coward' 06.05.1960
CSC-SC SCHL 1/2/4, Festival - 11.05.1960 ABEE

268 'natural' 'mature' 'forest' Interview, DB
269 'charm'"nervous' FF
270 'thunderous' Christine Ozanne 15.06.2018
271 Dolphin 07.07.1961 Times, 'dreary walls' 'adopted' 'butch' SC-AD SCHL 1/8/3
272 verdict' 'hug' 27.07.1961 SC-AD SCHL 1/8/3

**Chapter 15: My Darling**

273 'gang' JLC
274 Fortinbras 10.07.1937 Times, Barons - Directory National Biography Vol XIX
275 guilty 22.03.1962 SC-CSC SCHL 1/1/17, 'beauty' 03.04.1962 Henry-WSC SCHL 1/1/17, inspired - 07.05.1962 SC-CSC SCHL 1/1/17, 'got on best with' JLC, transformational - 25.10.1963 BDP, 'creaky' 'fraught 25.08.1962 SC-Yvonne SCHL 1/3/2
276 'Bore' 30.03.1963 ABEE
277 socialism' 17.07.1963 Tribune (NSW) p7, 'iron broom' 17.07.1963 Tribune (NSW) p7
278 outlive - 26.11.1962 SCHL 4/2, 'arms of God' 18.07.1963 SC-CSC SCHL 1/1/18
279 'trust' 03.11.1963 Surrey Advertiser (Maud Lindsay) CHUR 1/139 p80-81, happier - 25.10.1963 BDP , capsules - 25.10.1963 BDP
280 'young men' - 16.11.1963 Wicklow People, 'Amber' - 11.1963 SCHL 2/2/4
281 'skill' 'Jane Spencer' Christine Ozanne 15.06.2018 whispered - Edina Ronay 26.05.2019, 'water' Christine Ozanne 15.06.2018
282 'seen him' Christine Ozanne 15.06.2018, 'lovely' 'whipped' UPM CWW p74
283 blacks - 28.01.1965 Jet
284 'sound' Annie Ross 09.08.2018, Mocking - 27.12.1964 SC-
CSC SCHL 1/1/18
285 'great love' JLC, 'imaginary' CH 'turned round' DB
286 'do that' JLC

**Chapter 16: One's Own Way**

287 'abstract' 05.07.1965 NCD p602, 'trade' DB
288 Vidor 01.10.1964 SC-CSC SCHL 1/1/18
289 'pulse' 'repartee' Carey Hamblett 01.06.2019, 'bellhop' 'disregard' 02.07.1966 London Life
290 'Jordan' DB, 'fifteen' Norman Coburn 13.08.2018
291 'uppers' 'gold lamé' 03.12.1966 SC-Lobo SCHL 1/8/3

292 'domestic' 'disfigurement' 1967 SC-Pete SCHL 1/8/3, 'knocks' 'Private Lives' 'resources' Michael Gaunt, 27.04.2018

294 'Barbara' 'square one' 'entangled' 03.12.1966 SC-Lobo SCHL 1/8/3, Claridges - 24 Hours, fire-fighting – NA INF 6/169

295 detract 27.10.1967 SC-RSC SCHL 1/3/2, Olivier planned -25.10.1967 Variety, 'blow' 06.11.1967 Guy Bolton 12.02.1968 RSC-SC SCHL 1/3/2, debate - SCHL 1/3/2

296 'heroic' Unwanted Statue CPSC, 'glass eye' Cutting CAC, 'settings' 'relax in' 23.01.1969 Star Johannesburg Cutting CAC

297 Tussauds 26.10.1969 DT, 'slap-happy' 01.1969Miscellaneous Cutting CAC, 'winning over' 04.02.1969 Cape Times, 'palter' 10.02.1969 Evening Post Port Elizabeth Cutting CAC

298 Poseidon 02.1969 Evening Post Port Elizabeth, paintings 29.04.1969 Sun , Maserati 1969 Parade cutting PMED, alone 09.09.1969 People

299 'Niger' Kathy Conry 11.02.2019, balloons - 07.1961 Popular Science, 'Lo' 12.11.1970 Jewell-SC SCHL 1/8/4, 'steadily' 'binge' UPM CWW p92-94, writers - 15.04.1970 Daily American

300 'alive' 28.04.1971 Australian Women's Weekly (Kay Keavney)

**Chapter 17: Smile of La Gioconda**

301 shopping list CH Archive 'staggeringly' JLC 'private' ND

302 'lunch with Mama' UPM CWW p77

304 'neat' O. Temple 20.05.2018, 'Ezra' R.Temple 18.03.2018 Holland - 20.10.1971 Variety, 'overwhelmed' 26.04.1972 SC-CSC SCHL 1/1/18, 'crowd' O. Temple 19.03.2018

305 'met her' 'don't think' Claude Eriksen 03.08.2018, 'Virgin' UPM CWW p80

306 'uniting' Elizabeth Seal 18.07.2018, 'Goody' UPM CWW p95, 'temperature' 05.12.1972 Miami Herald

307 'dog' 'Red Turkey' TB , disturbance - 27.10.1972 Daily Mail, 'daughter' 'bronze' 'UPM CWW p73

308 'Limey' 01.12.1972 Star-Ledger, 'everything' 27.01.1973 Palm Beach Post-Times, 'crying' Derrick Watkins 17.09.2019

309 'soup' Claude Eriksen 03.08.2018, 'tranquillity' 'unhappy' UPM CWW p95, 'fella' 23.01.1975 Chronicle Telegram 'emptied' 'ranted' 'hate it' UPM CWW p95, 'damaged' 30.04.1975 Levittown Bucks County Courier Times

310 Courage 06.09.1973 Kirriemuir Herald , spirit her – Churchill's Bodyguard p224, compared 15.02.1974 Red Bank Register

311 exclusive 05.02.1975 Kittanning Simpson Leader Times, plugging 26.06.1974 Colorado Springs Gazette , theft - 29.05.1974 Defiance Crescent N, 'party' 'what you do' TB
312 'beautiful friends' TB, 'sleep with' 'pen' UPM CWW p101, 'intelligent' 04.1975 SC-CSC SCHL 1/1/18, 'selling'
313 'high' UPM CWW p102 p112, 'banned' 07.12.1975 Santa Ana Register

**Chapter 18: Dangerous You**

315 Titcomb – Fairs, Circuses & Music Halls, 'vocals' 'trunk' 'Rexy' UPM CWW p112-15
316 'swore''upperhand' TB
317 'Fuck' UPM CWW p116, 'NOTHING' TB, 'the end' UPM CWW p116, 'never to drink' TB, 'loved' UPM CWW p95
318 'turn away' 03.03.1976 Glasgow Herald, Houdini's 03.03.1976 Washington Star, 'graceful' 17.03.1976 Carroll County Times
319 'book' Kathy Conry 11.02.2019 , 'sacked' 'scandal' Claude Eriksen 03.08.2018
320 'Monty' 04.1976 S to CSC SCHL 1/1/18, 'underwater' 20.06.1976 SC-CSC SCHL 1/1/18, 'introspective' 23.11.1977 Akron Beacon Journal, 'co-author' 12.12.1974 Observer (local paper)
321 'atrocious' 08.12.1976 Salina Journal, 'small boy''smart' CH
323 'so much' CH, 'impressionist' 08.12.1977 Cutting, Sutherland - 19.01.1978 Times, 'doldrums' May 1979 SC-Thatcher SCHL 1/8/4, 'forgetful' Paul Medlicott 24.07.2018
324 tax shelter - law.justia.com/cases/federal/appellate-courts/F2/864/569/239804, 'sober' 'closing in' CH
325 'comfortable' Mary Scott 10.08.2018, 'hands' A Friend CPSC

**Chapter 19: Exeunt**

326 'Sweetie' CH, stern - 11.04.1981 Spectator p20
327 read Sarah's poems 04.12.1982 Daily News, 'while Sarah lived' UPM CWW p132

# Acknowledgements

This book owes everything to the Churchill Archives Centre, where each visit is a new gold rush. May I thank in particular: Allen Packwood, Andrew Riley, Sarah Lewery, Sophie Bridges and Heidi Egginton for their enthusiasm as well as their dedication and professionalism. They allowed me to bring to light something of the unknown early life of Sarah Churchill and her siblings.

In researching Sarah's theatrical career, film career and so much more I would like to express my thanks to these fine people who shone like stars: Pietro Basso, David Burke, Anna Calder-Marshall, Geoffrey Chater, Norman Coburn, Sharman Collins, Kathleen Conry, Pat Crowley, Niki Dantine, Evelyn Ellis (Shaw Society), Dr Henry Engbrecht, Fenella Fielding, Peter Flax, Neil French, Michael Friend, Michael Gaunt, Lucia Graves, William Graves, Peter Hourahine, Iain Kerr, Ann Rachlin, Julia Lockwood-Clark, Justin Martin, Simon McKay, Christine Ozanne, Cliff Richard, Edina Ronay, Ellie Samuels (Spotlight), Roger Sansom, Mary Scott, Susan Seaforth Hayes, Elizabeth Seal, David Smallwood, Chiara Soldati, Derrick Watkins, Dr Anne Wright and the incomparable Olivia de Havilland.

For Sarah's career in the Services and life during the years of the Second World War, I give special thanks to: Aileen and Jonah, MOD Chicksands, Barbara Cronin (Reigate History Museum), Taylor Downing, Katharine Eustace, Tim Fryer, Christine Halsall, Professor Richard Hesse, Virginia Lewick (Franklin D. Roosevelt Presidential Library), The RAF Medmenham Collection, Ronald John Meyer, Mike Mockford, David Mortimer, National Archives (UK), National Archives at College Park, MD, Lord Normanby, Ruth Pooley, the School of Slavonic and East European Studies Library, Steve Shurtleff, Masha Udensiva-Brenner and Allan Williams.

In craving all things Vic Oliver, I stress the invaluable help of: Brad Ashton, Bob Bain, Geoff Bowden (BMHS), Eileen Broster, Wyn Calvin, Olaf Dudzus,

Julian Glover, Michaela Hejlová (Knihovna Pražské konzervatoře), Ellen Higgs (Waddesdon Archives), Tessa LeBars, Fay Lenore, Central St Martin's Library, Natalie Martin, Severin Matiasovits (Universität für Musik und Kunst Wien), Dr Lenka Matušíková, Vera Morley, Brian O'Gorman, Tony Orsten, Tony Pickett, Christa Prokisch (Jüdisches Museum Wien), David Read, Royal School Association, Stefanie Samek, Richard Sell, Dr Bohumír Smutný, Edward Thomas, Kateřina Tučková, Universität Wien Archiv, Universität für Musik Wien, Wiener Library, Wiener Stadt und Landesarchiv, Alexandra Wieser, Lord Willoughby de Broke, Barbara Wilson, Paul van Yperen and Tomáš Zapletal.

I extend my wholehearted gratitude to the following for memories and help on the trail of the elusive Antony Beauchamp: Lord Aberdeen, Jonathan Dimbleby, Richard Clarke, Bob Edwards, Annie Eglington, Toby Hadoke, Phillip Haycock, Diana Melly, Jean-Claude Michel, Bryony Millan, Alison Moore, Abby and Andy, Dr Anthony Morton (Royal Military Academy Sandhurst), David Oswald (Aberdeen Local Studies), Terence Pepper, Stephen Pound, Lady Rayne, Liz and Graeme Roberts, Dr Alison Rosie (National Records of Scotland), Ian Whitaker, Surrey History Centre, Jane Turner and the wonderful Henry Sandon.

To these gracious ladies I offer thanks: Susan Scott (Savoy Archives), Elizabeth Broekmann (NHEHS), Esther Gilbert, Gemma Jones, Sonia Melchett, Lady Rosemary Muir, Lady Young, Alice Nemon-Stuart, Penny Charteris, Katherine Carter (Chartwell), Minnie Churchill, Lady Eresby, Elizabeth L Garver (University of Texas at Austin Harry Ransom Center) and Emma Soames.

I bear a debt of gratitude to The BFI Reuben Library, The British Library and Listening Service, The Television Academy Foundation (USA), Theatre Collections at the V&A and the Universities of Bristol and Glasgow. My thanks also to Tom Plant (Wiltshire and Swindon Archives), Gillian Butler (Westminster Archives) and staff at Kent History Centre. As I madly pursued initiatives, chased a few rainbows and barked up some wrong trees, I was struck by the helpfulness of staff at Blind Veterans UK and Alleyn's School Archives.

I would not have got to grips with Sarah's literary career and life within the art world without the kindness and trust of: Claude Eriksen, Ted Buckwald, Carey Hamblett, Curtis Hooper, The Makaro Press, Anne Manchester, Paul Medlicott, Staff at New York Public Library Archives, Richard and Olivia Temple, David Usill and the legendary Annie Ross. Finally, I thank Dolly, Brian, Paddy, Simon, Suzanne, Malcolm and Michael for their unwavering support.

# Index